Liberation and Change

Liberation and Change

Gustavo Gutiérrez

and

Richard Shaull

Edited and Introduced by Ronald H. Stone

JOHN KNOX PRESS • Atlanta

Copyright © 1977 John Knox Press
Atlanta, Georgia
Printed in the U.S.A.

Library of Congress Cataloging in Publication Data

Gutiérrez, Gustavo, 1928–
  Liberation and change.

  Includes bibliographical references.
  1. Liberation theology—Addresses, essays, lectures.   2. Christianity and politics—Addresses, essays, lectures.   3. United States—Civilization—Addresses, essays, lectures.   I. Shaull, Millard Richard, joint author.   II. Title
BT83.G87   261.8'097   76–44970
ISBN 0–8042–0661–9

Contents

Introduction

The theological dialogue contained in these pages originated in the question: "What is the meaning of the North American revolution for contemporary, third-world revolutions?" Exploration of the question revealed that there were many answers to the question and that the answer depended in part on the respondent. Pittsburgh Theological Seminary decided to ask a Latin American and a North American theologian to prepare its Schaff lectures for 1976 on the theme, broadly conceived, of theology and revolution. The North American, Richard Shaull, had experience in Latin America and the Latin American, Gustavo Gutiérrez, was coming into theological prominence in North America.

Revolutionary change which remakes the consciousness of the humanity that undergoes the revolution has always been a matter of religious concern. Since the advent of Christianity in the Western world, revolution has been a movement of theological significance for the Church and, sometimes, theological changes in the Church have unleashed revolutionary change in society.

Christianity's message of salvation is one of liberation from sin and the consequences of sin that enslave humanity. It proclaims a transformation of alienated humanity into a reconciled humanity living happily with one another in the presence of the divine. These motifs of liberation and transformation have not always had social revolutionary impact. However, the concepts themselves and the divine-human power they symbolize have broken forth again and again in ways which forced humanity to reorganize its communal life.

Therefore, when Pittsburgh Theological Seminary chose to address the question of the meaning of revolution, it undertook a properly theological task. As an institution standing in the Calvinist tradition, it remembers the revolutionary consequences of Calvinism throughout the Europe it influenced. As an American institution, it reflects on the heritage of the American revolutionary tradition. It asks how these heritages are to be appropriated today. The two lecturers use contrasting theological approaches. Gutiérrez works on changing the perspective of theology by recasting its arguments from within the tradition. Shaull, protesting against the failure of theology to realize its transforming potential, takes the tradition seriously while utilizing resources outside of the tradition for its correction. Both are within the theological circle by reason of their theological commitments and radical seriousness of their theological concerns.

The question of revolution in the 1970s is, of course, a question concerning the meaning of the contemporary turmoil. It is this question: what is God doing with the present confusion? Both Gutiérrez and Shaull believe God is troubling the present and that aspects of the present social-economic situation will be changed or destroyed. The suffering of God's poor people in his world combines with the meaninglessness of the lives of many of the rich in his world to point to the need for change. Gutiérrez addresses the question of liberation primarily from the perspective of the suffering of the poor. Shaull's perspective reflects the cries of the poor, but even more fundamental is his conviction of the meaninglessness that haunts the contemporary North American situation.

The United States is locked into a struggle with the poor of the world. Our education and experience have not equipped us to appreciate the needs or perspectives of the poor. Our economic interests prevent us from responding to their cries. The struggle is made even more horrendous by the schizophrenic ideological competition which divides the world. Both the U.S.S.R. and the U.S.A. act as if the most important issue is the prevalence of Russian state capitalism or American multi-national capitalism. Economic-ideological competition is reinforced by rampant nationalisms and the poor become the battleground over which foreign ideologies contest. Neither Russian totalitarianism or American liberalism are native to the experience of the poor, nor is either very helpful. Vietnam is the extreme case of United States' unwillingness to allow a national revolution against the French colonialists to reach its inevitable conclusions. For nearly a quarter of a century, we supported the French or their local allies to hang on in Vietnam. The reasons for American folly and defeat in Vietnam are many, but one concerns our subject here. The American refusal to allow a war of liberation to succeed was central to American motivation in the struggle. We could not defeat the war of liberation and in the attempt we disrupted our domestic peace and our economy. Hundreds of thousands of casualties in Vietnam and thousands of casualties in the United States testify to the horrible costs of the American prolongation of that struggle.

The struggle with the poor and their efforts to revolutionize their situation corrodes North American life. The tactics used abroad, and even personnel used abroad, return home to corrupt democracy. Watergate and the attendant political scandals revealed CIA-trained personnel carrying out directives of a political committee committed to maintaining a government in power which was heavily engaged in counter-revolutionary struggle around the world. U.S. corporations, exposed in corrupting officials abroad, were found guilty of the same tactics at home. It is probably too much to expect corporate policy of political corruption abroad to stop at the United States border. If ITT is involved in a struggle jointly with the U.S. to oppose a Chilean elected government, why should it hesitate to provide help for its political friends in the United States? Some corporations violate the law whether it is Chilean law or American law. The U.S., in its automatic counterrevolutionary stance and policy, has gotten itself committed to a position from which it cannot sort out progressive revolutionary tendencies from reactionary tendencies. The fate of the poor and of the United States are inextricably interwoven in the struggle in the developing world.

The United States' position in the world requires tremendous energy and organization. Challenges to the dominance of the U.S. like Vietnam, Dominican Republic, Cuba, or the oil embargo, send shocks through the country. Vietnam, in its cost of human suffering and economic dislocation, revealed the cost of maintaining that dominance. The rebellion of youth, particularly, focused on the draft boards, was indicative of the protest against organized conformity with national policy. War, energy policy, food policy, economic policy, all require decisions effectively implemented through masses of people. Such cooperation requires communication, bureaucracy, and shared assumptions about the meaning of it all. Corporations and government have refined communication and bureaucracy to a level of sophistication never before achieved. Ideological consensus as to the system's meaning has not yet been enforced in the U.S.A., but the voluntary internalization of values of the system has been complete enough to maintain it. Dissent, other than verbal, has been pushed to the margins of the society.

Shaull has listened carefully to that dissent on the margins. He recognizes in it voices of integrity which call for a transformation of the system itself. Many of us within the system hear the dissent from the margins reflect values we also want to realize. Also, many within the system find it meaningless and search for meaning within themselves and within the dissenting movements.

The hope within us for self and social transformation is reinforced by the hope of those of the third world who find in our society the oppressor. We hope for a nation that will put its emphasis on the export of food and agricultural knowledge, not arms and military technology. We hope for a society that will reduce its violence. We hope for a society that will consume less and nurture the earth more. All of these hopes can resonate to hopes from the undeveloped world. The world is a unity finally, and the tendencies that oppress people abroad also repress North Americans at home. The prophets of the Old Testament prophesied against foreign alliances which encouraged idolatry and oppression at home. The issue is similar today; by alliances with oppression and totalitarian values abroad, we reinforce oppression and totalitarian values at home.

Our hopes for a better country, then, are reinforced by Third World hopes for less American control. In their refusal of American dominance, they are encouraging us to refuse to go along with aspects of the system which destroy meaningful life. Their refusal of American dominance can reinforce our refusal to accept the dominance of the CIA, FBI, and military in our domestic life.

The issues are subtle, for nothing in this introduction should be taken to mean the abandonment of a realistic awareness of the need to resist totalitarian forces abroad. Rather, it is the realistic recognition that destructive tendencies in North American life become intermixed with, and dependent upon, creative thrusts of American energy. The assumption is that we must resist attempts to further militarize this society even while we maintain military strength. The alliance of nationalism, capitalism, and militarism is a heady brew and must be challenged to protect human freedom, welfare, and democracy. The alliance of nationalism, capitalism, and militarism reaches a climax in the counterrevolutionary policies of American society.

Counterrevolutionary trends can be countered. In that affirmation the hope of democracy and the Third World resides. In the awareness of thorough systematic changes needed to stop counterrevolutionary tendencies the realism that should always grace Christian hope is found. The Christian forces supporting change in the United States can no longer afford to alternate between spurts of optimism and seasons of pessimism. Hopeful realism is normative for a Christian perspective on society.

Gutiérrez's argument starts from his own commitments to revolutionary change on behalf of the poor. The starting point of the theology of liberation is the theme of chapter three. Christ is found in the poor oppressed Indians of the Andes. Gutiérrez attempts to make clear to the Church the message of Christ to his Church from the suffering of the exploited. This starting point distinguishes his theology from the political theologies of Europe or from the progressive or conservative theologies of North America. The difference is political-social before it is theological.

Gutiérrez's second chapter answers the question of the relevance of the North American revolution to South American revolutions in the negative. The South American revolutions of liberation theology are social revolutions on behalf of the poor. The North American revolution was a political revolution on behalf of the middle class. The relevance of the North American revolutionary experience for the liberation theologian is parallel to the importance of that revolution to the North American Indian or the Black slave. Political liberalism, republican forms of government, and laissez-faire capitalism were tools for the ascendancy of the middle class. In South America, the middle class is the oppressor and those virtues of European and North American middle class life are not first priorities for the poor engaged in revolutionary change.

Gutiérrez's first chapter, which the non-specialist is urged to read after chapter three, is his argument that freedom has always been understood in the Church in relationship to salvation on the one hand, and political power on the other. Because salvation, freedom, and political power are tied together in history and in understanding, theology has political consequences. Christian theology has Christian political consequences. The argument of the first chapter supports the conclusions of the third chapter that to love God requires love of the brother and sister. To believe in God means to practice God's love. The union of belief and practice in Gutiérrez's thought drives him to oppose the present order on behalf of the Indians as radically as did the sixteenth century Bartolomé de Las Casas.

This work of Gutiérrez is an advance beyond his earlier *Theology of Liberation* in several ways. First, the meaning of *freedom* in its historical complexities is made clearer. Gutiérrez means nothing less than the freedom *from* all that prevents the fulfillment of humanity and as much as the capacity *to* express love. To be truly free is to live in God's love and this includes the struggle against all that hinders love. Secondly, the theology of liberation's claim to be an indigenous theology is established. It does not mean that it ignores world experience or neglects classical theology. It means that it is rooted frankly and openly in the struggle of the Latin American poor to find freedom. It is a matter of social location and commitment by the rendering of theological understanding adequate to the situation. Third, the work and the dialogue at Pittsburgh established in the minds of those who participated that Gustavo Gutiérrez is a hopeful realist. He is decidedly not utopian in any pejorative meaning of that term and is openly political in the best meaning of that term. Fourth, the demonic implications of North American privileges and liberties for life in Latin America were demonstrated in the volume and in the dialogue. The argument of his chapters, rich in scholarship and addressed to the theme of "Freedom and Salvation," meets the challenge of the responsible critics of liberation theology and, consequently, moves the conversation on to a deeper level.

Gustavo Gutiérrez's theology says no to North American counterrevolutionary thrusts in South America. Richard Shaull says no to the demonic in North American society from the inside. Shaull argues that the "American" dream has turned into a nightmare for many within the country, as well as for the Third World. His experience in Brazil and at home informs him that the American story, on which he built his life, has come to a deadend. If present trends persist, the future promises increasing disasters as an affluent, but meaningless America defends itself against the poor of the world. Only a revolution of human consciousness which can revolutionize the society will save the country. So he calls for an experience of the judgment of American society, affirms alienation as appropriate, urges a transformation of values, hopes for a new society, and questions all the foundations of industrial society.

Shaull's second chapter provides suggestions as to how a new passionate subjectivity can find space in an adminstered society. Social transformation requires a new humanity, not just the old humanity seeking power. In small groups, new patterns of intimate relationships can be found and new meanings of vocation put to the test. Shaull refuses to work within the assumptions of the American system and he strives to affirm and build small communities in which those assumptions can be challenged. With a few friends, he is urging us to begin living a future worth living now.

For Shaull, the question of politics has become a religious question. In the third chapter, the apocalyptic expectations of his previous two chapters are made clearer. His view is that of the apocalypticist. Judgment on America is present and is coming and the only proper responses are those that accept the apocalypse and the death of the America of the past.

Those who accept its death can begin to live the future in communities which support each other and new possibilities of life. His hope rests in *koinonia* and in his writing, he outlines its meaning. From the *koinonia* can come new political strategies and new visions of patterns of ministry.

In the concluding part of his work, Shaull calls for a radical transformation of classical theology. In the spirit of the reformation he pleads for Christians to begin with their faith and include in their thinking the crisis of values, the social and psychological sciences, their autobiographies, and the resources of Christian history. So he has come full circle from the death of the American dream and the failure of theological thought to calling for a transformation of theology and the liberation of America. In his contribution, Shaull has boldly laid out his theses, and his call for others to join him is clear.

The theological and political consciousness of the Pittsburgh Theological Seminary was raised by the Schaff Lecture Convocation. Both speakers found supporters and critics among students, faculty, and guests. As one who stands comfortably in the classical theological tradition of Paul Tillich and Reinhold Niebuhr, the appeals to apocalyptic were unconvincing. Revolution throughout most of Latin America will be a regretful necessity when the conditions for successful revolutions have been laid. At present, the rightist military juntas, generally speaking, are secure. Our task from a perspective of an ethic of Christian love is to combat the counterrevolutionary tendencies in America and to secure a society of a little more justice and a little less oppression.

Among many at the Seminary who willingly exhausted themselves to prepare for the Schaff Lecture Convocation, I am particularly thankful to the President William Kadel, The Dean David Shannon, Professor Gordon Chamberlin, Professor Samuel Roberts, Mr. David McCreery and Miss Deborah Ann Davis for their many contributions which made the convocation a success.

The lectures in the volume will illumine the relationship of politics, freedom, and salvation. The question of the meaning of contemporary American experience is addressed both from without and from within. If the meaning of the no to American dominance abroad and the no from within to oppression is heard, the American experiment may go on. It will not be transformed into the kingdom of God in this history, but it may become a republic which will be a sign of hope to the world.

PART ONE

Freedom and Salvation: A Political Problem

Gustavo Gutiérrez
Translated by Rev. Alvin Gutterriez

Introduction

The Christian conscience is always being challenged by the question of human freedom. In the first centuries, this challenge was expressed in the request for freedom in religious matters. For Tertullian, Lactantius and other Christian writers of those times, religious freedom is a human and natural right and, therefore, the necessary condition for an authentic encounter with God. After the fourth century, the situation of the Christian community changed, and these first insights became dim, but the community maintained the idea that the freedom of the act of faith cannot be imposed. That is a minimal demand which was not always observed, giving way later to what was called religious tolerance and its byproduct: the thesis and hypothesis doctrine. Recently, this question has moved outside the ecclesiocentric framework of Christendom and can now be taken up in order to recapture the true meaning of freedom in religious matter, including the social and political implications of the matter. In all of these positions on religious freedom, there exist different ways of considering the meaning of God's salvific work in history.

On the other hand, God's love that we receive in faith was considered from the beginning to be the fullness of human freedom. According to Augustine of Hippo, to be authentically free is to live in God's love. The idea is profound and remained valid in spite of the persistence of many Christians in the course of history trying to impose this fullness of human freedom. Medieval theology helps us understand precisely Augustine's intuition, and following St. Paul, it distinguishes between a *freedom from* all that impedes the person from being fully free and a *freedom to* love; this is the human fullness. As St. Paul says, "For freedom Christ has set us free," but it is a freedom to "let love make you serve one another." (Gal. 5:1 [R.S.V.] and 13 [T.E.V.])

At present, we are more and more sensitive to the social and political implications of freedom and salvation. Large sectors of humanity live in situations of misery and exploitation. The struggles for the *freedom from*

3

become more urgent every day. A broad and deep aspiration for liberation inflames the history of humanity in our day. That is the case of Latin America. This aspiration is lived with distinctive characteristics by exploited classes, oppressed cultures and discriminated races in Latin America. The peculiarity does not limit the question only to the political field. On the contrary, it permits us to see from a concrete viewpoint all the human dimensions which are involved in the relation between freedom and salvation, that is to say, in the process of liberation. In a word: all the exigencies of *freedom to love*.

In this work, we will try to take up these questions in a reading of the *practice* of the Church in reference to the questions. (In general, we will refer to the Catholic Church, and this is one of the limitations of the work.) That is the reason for the historical perspective. We are aware that some of the presentations are still very schematic, and perhaps it will be possible to take up again and broaden this perspective.

One

Freedom and Truth

The best way to study the scope and limitations of the freedom of religion is to follow its historical development and to be attentive to the modifications of the social conditions in which the Christians are living. Our study, in section A, shows that from the very beginning, the question of freedom and religious truth is marked by the way salvific work in history is understood. Section B articulates the permanence of this relation; but in addition, it underlines something which, although present already in the previous stage, will become the decisive factor in the Christian community's life and reflection: the role of political power. The theology of tolerance, examined in section C, systematizes the experience of a Church in a society where Christianity is dominant. With this theology the Church confronted the challenges of modern liberties which the ascending bourgeoisie asserted.

A. FREEDOM: THE CONDITION OF ACCESS TO RELIGIOUS TRUTH

When faced with the hostility of the Roman state, the Christians of the first centuries assumed an attitude affirming the rights of their faith which they considered inalienable. They found the ultimate grounds for this in sacred Scripture, but, due to their historical situation, they developed a keen and growing consciousness of these rights.

In reality, Christianity originally developed in the lower strata of society: city workers, slaves, freedmen and women. In the New Testament there are many testimonies of this social composition of the Christian communities (cf. for example, 1 Cor. 1:26-27). This explains the attitude towards the rich (Luke, James) and the insistence on economic aid among the communities (Acts, the Epistles of Paul). Only at the end of the second century was there any indication that some persons from the

5

privileged social strata had converted to Christianity. This indicated the newness of this rare happening. Some pagan writers directed criticism against this religion of the common people thus giving witness to the Christian social composition.[1] These people were under a hostile political authority and without power in society.

There are two clear positions taken by the first Christians: the person's freedom in religious matter and the political power's incompetence in this field. It is as if two complementary schools of thought are defended simultaneously; these schools can be distinguished according to the arguments in which they are grounded. It is also important to point out that in the last analysis both claims have their roots in the consciousness that there is a relation between salvific *truth* and human *freedom*. Or, more precisely, these claims are grounded in the conviction that freedom is the underlying condition of access to truth.

1. *Freedom in religious matters*

The repression which Roman power imposed on the Christian community led the first Christian thinkers to look for arguments with which they could defend the free exercise of religious life. In doing this they frequently turned to a general principle of Roman legality: the right of every citizen to have his own religion. "Each province, each city has its god . . . We are the only ones who are denied the right to have a religion," said Tertullian.[2]

Actually the situation of Christianity was different from the other existing religions in the empire. Christianity claimed a distinctiveness as the holder of religious truth. Judaism also did this, but it remained within racial and national limits. Christianity, however, presented itself as having religious truth for all people. It would have been possible to come to agreement over the right to have a particular religion, but the claim for truth created difficulties. Christians refused to associate themselves with the official cult in the empire, for Christianity claimed to be universal and exclusive.

As a result of this conviction, early Christians realized that it was not enough to claim in the name of positive law the right to practice one's religion. The apologists perceived this and sought to ground themselves in something more profound than Roman legislation.[3]

There are two exceptional witnesses in this period whose thought reflects the struggle of the early Christians for freedom. These are Tertullian and Lactantius. Separated by more than a century, both of them have left texts which reflect the vitality of the Christian communities when faced with the absolutism of political power.

Tertullian. For Tertullian the terms of the question are clear. Christ has come to bring all human beings to knowledge of truth,[4] but the road which leads to this knowledge has its starting point with freedom in religious matters. Tertullian directed his apology, the *Apologeticum*, to the Roman magistrates to vindicate this freedom.

> It is a crime of impiety [*irreligiositatis*] to take away man's religious freedom [*libertatem religionis*] and to forbid him to choose a divinity. That is to say, not to permit me to honor whom I want to honor. Nobody wants forced homage, not even a man.[5]

Step by step, and thanks to this recognition of free opinion in religious matter, Tertullian proved that the human being was capable of arriving at monotheism, and at Christian faith. The defense of freedom in religious matters was not an occasional thing; it was the centerpiece of Tertullian's argument in his apology of Christianity. In order to arrive at the *truth* of Christian faith it was necessary to begin with legal recognition on the part of political authorities of the *freedom* of religious activity.

Therefore, it was not simply a matter of freedom for the Christians. Tertullian broadened and deepened the question. We are faced with a "human and natural right." God cannot be worshiped authentically except by persons free from coercion.[6]

This way of posing the problem introduces a question which we will find repeatedly as we look into the relationship of faith to culture: how are we to understand the nature and breadth of salvific work in history? In effect, the Fathers who were confronted with the pagan world were particularly attentive to religious values which were found outside Christianity.

Justin was one of the most affirmative in this respect. For him there were aspects of truth in pagan philosophies and religions. His theology of the Word permitted him to give this opinion: "Christ is the first-born, the Word in which all men participate . . . Those who have lived according to the Word are Christians even though they have been considered atheists as Socrates, Heraclitus and others."[7]

Tertullian himself, though emphasizing the differences between Christian and pagan philosophies in a famous text, clearly claimed that through creation and the witnessing of their own spirits human beings are capable of arriving at God. When the soul is left to itself and "is in a normal state of health, it names God with this only name because it is the proper name of the true God . . . the witness of the naturally Christian soul (*animae christianae*)."[8] Even more, in its best and most responsible aspects, the soul is inspired by sacred Scripture. These considerations permitted him to see the possibility of salvation for those who have not arrived at Christian faith and, as a consequence, he lays the foundation for dialogue with the pagan world.

Lactantius.   A century later we find that Lactantius expressed these ideas in the same perspective and with the same vigor. He is not as original as Tertullian, but he knew how to find the incisive formulas for treating religious freedom.

Lactantius wrote a few years before the Edict of Milan. His concern was that shared by all early Christians: hostility and persecution by the political power. Lactantius reaffirmed that Christians should aspire to reconciliation with the pagans and work for religious peace.[9] However, it was not a matter of obtaining peace by the sacrifice of what was proper and original in the Christian faith. For him Christianity was the true religion and can only be known through divine revelation.[10] As in the case of Tertullian, the non-intervention of civil power was based upon the rights of all persons to practice the religion of their choice.

"True sacrifice," he wrote, "cannot be offered under external pressure. If it is not offered spontaneously and in good faith it is a curse. This is what occurs when it is obtained through torture, violence, prison."[11] In another work, in an even more energetic manner, he affirmed the value of freedom: "Religion is the only thing in which freedom has chosen its home. Religion depends above all on the will. No one can be forced to adore what he does not want to adore."[12] Truth and violence cannot be united: access to that truth must be free, not forced.

However, like Tertullian, Lactantius had a very broad position on the reality of saving grace for persons outside of Christianity. For him, philosophers and pagan religious personalities had, by the grace of God, partially discovered many Christian truths. This did not keep him from strongly asserting that the Church "is the only one which integrally maintains the cult of the true God, is the source of truth, the home of faith and the temple of God."[13] But few authors underlined with more insistence the possibilities of salvation in the heart of paganism. He also emphasized the means used by God to provide all persons with revelation independent of that which is found in fullness in the Church.[14]

Tertullian and Lactantius faithfully reflected the Christian consciousness in the first centuries.[15] However, they also expressed the permanent values of the Christian spirit, and therefore they were quoted throughout all of the years of the unfolding tradition.[16] In this historical situation, these authors held that the defense of liberty was a condition for access to and practice of religious truth. They made this defense with a pureness and firmness which the following centuries diminished or forgot.

2. *Incompetence of political power in religious questions*

Confronted by the intolerance and totalitarianism of the pagan state, the first Christians claimed freedom in the individual religious act. Political power, they argued, should not intervene in this area. Ecclesiastical writers of the first centuries thus worked out a defense of freedom of the Church as a religious community, to practice its cult and to preach the gospel.

The Christian community, faced with the threat of a requirement to offer sacrifices to pagan gods, arrived at an understanding of its faith which allowed the community not only to affirm the free and personal character of religious conduct but also to mark the limits of civil power. Civil power should not intrude in the relation between God and the person. In the year 204, Hippolytus wrote:

> Whoever believes in God cannot be a hypocrite, however, neither does this person have to fear the orders of civil power when it imposes something prohibited. Indeed, on account of faith in God, if this power obliges the person to do something against good conscience it will be sweet to go to death and resist the command.[17]

The fields of political power and religion were seen by these Christians as distinct. Therefore political authority was incompetent in religious matters. The responsibility of the Church was to preach and to be the mediator of salvation. To fulfill its mission it used only spiritual means and the persuasive power of truth. As this view became more precise[18] the political authority was required not to hinder the Church's task.

From many texts of this period[19] we draw the same conclusion. Faced with a political authority which treated religion as its own affair, the Church perceived its distinction from civil power. It was aware that through revelation it possessed a religious truth which transcended the forces of this world. Actually it is the realization of what this truth implied that led Christians to deny sacrifices to pagan gods and to deny the competence of political authority to legislate in the area of the relation between God and persons.

This does not mean a contempt or underestimation of the civil power's function. Christian writers were happy to cite Paul saying that the emperor's authority comes from God and therefore should be respected.

However, this view presupposes that the emperor accept his place and not usurp that of God.[20] That is to say, it requires that he remained in his own field: that of conserving and promoting a just order and social peace[21] without entering into the intimacy of religious conscience.

The first Christian writers did not soften the demands of religious truth in claiming religious freedom as a human right and in declaring the incompetence of political power in this matter. They considered that this truth was the ultimate ground of these claims. Indeed, because there was a truth, the human being should have arrived at it and freely put it into practice.

So these are the terms of the question, but a new element appeared and played the role of "mediation" in this relation between the human person and God: civil power which up until then had been a stranger to Christian influence.

B. THE MEDIATION OF THE CHRISTIAN STATE

The situation of the Christian community in the empire changed beginning with the fourth century. Much has been written on the importance of this period. In fact for some this period, or more correctly the persistence of the mentality which began in this period, was responsible for all the evils which troubled and continue to trouble the Church today. In reaction to this some have been led to idealize the pre-Constantine period. Some maintain, a bit too quickly, that everything was going well until Constantine unfortunately appears and things begin to go bad.

Without judging for the moment what might be valid in this outlook, we will try to recall as objectively as possible what this period means for the Church's doctrinal reflection. In the fourth century, civil authority appeared at the service of the Christian religion. As a result the church no longer experienced persecution. However, a very subtle question remains. In these new circumstances, what happened to personal freedom and to the freedom of the Church which was claimed by the apologists when they had faced a hostile power? The situation which was created and the two aspects of our investigation indicate the three points of this section.

1. From tolerance to the confessional state

The events moved in rapid succession in the fourth century. In the beginning, the Christian religion was tolerated and given the same footing as other religions. However, the civil power quickly became

inclined to favor Christianity and changed it into the religion of the
Roman State.   313 A.D

Christianity as "tolerated." The "Edict of Milan" partially responded
to the demands for more tolerance towards Christianity, and it established the freedom of cults in the empire. Naturally this is a text of capital
importance for the history of the Church, but it is also important for the
study which we have undertaken.[22] Some points need emphasis:

a) The freedom to practice the religion of one's choice was "regulated,"
"granted," "not denied" by the emperors. The idea that religion was a
state matter remained strong, and in a certain way we can say that it
dominated the text. Therefore, it would be more appropriate to speak of
the Edict of Milan as a decree of *tolerance* rather than as a recognition of
freedom in religious matters.

b) The assumption that religion was a political matter appeared in the
reasons given for the promulgation of the edict; in this way the divinity
will be "propitious and favorable both to ourselves and to those who live
under our rule"; "it is convenient for the tranquility which the Empire
enjoys." Religious tolerance was really seen as a necessity for social
peace.

c) This regime of freedom of cult was considered "a very good and very
reasonable system." It was a matter of good government and convenience. This implied that in other circumstances this right could be
denied.

d) A vague natural theology appeared to be the religious doctrinal
context of this compromise text.[23] "The divinity" can be adored in
different ways.

In brief, we are dealing with a text that grants freedom to practice the
religion of one's choice in order to preserve the peace in the empire. The
text is based upon the recognition of a supreme divinity which can be
adored by Christians as well as by pagans.[24] The affirmation of a religious truth is absent. On the other hand, the idea that religion is a matter
of state is the *dominant notion.*

The confessional state. After the Edict of Milan things began to change
rapidly. The events themselves resolved the alternative which Christians
seemed to be facing; either to renounce the world and lose interest in the
temporal city or Christianize it by domination. The Christian cult ceased
being simply accepted alongside the other religions. Constantine took a
series of measures which protected the Church in an exclusive manner
against heretics and schismatics.[25]

As we know, except for the period of Julian the Apostate, the official support for the Church continued to grow until in 380 the Edict of Thessalonica instituted Christianity as the state religion.[26] In the Edict of Thessalonica, we find a clear defense of specific religious beliefs. Here, we are far from the more ambiguous natural theology which underlies the Milan text. However, the defense of the *true* religion was made at the expense of religious *freedom*. Those who rejected Christianity would be punished by the civil power. Force established religious unity in the empire.

The defense of the true religion became one of the major concerns of the emperors, consistent with pagan tradition, they saw the prosperity of the empire to be dependent upon this defense.[27] In this way Christianity passed quickly from the state of being "tolerated" (Edict of Milan) to that of being the state religion (Edict of Thessalonica).

And so the ideal of a Christian state was born, and this has had a tremendous influence on the history of the Church up until our days.[28] God's and the state's causes appeared to be increasingly united. St. Ambrose, a contemporary and friend of Theodosius, maintained that treason against God is treason against the Emperor Gratian.[29]

What was the Church's attitude in its new situation? In this context what happened to the principles of freedom in religious matters and to the conviction that civil power was incompetent in this field, principles which were so arduously defended in the first centuries?

The tone of the demands was lowered. It was not the same to make demands of an authority which was hostile to religion as it was to make them of a state which wanted to be at the service of religion. However, there did remain an echo of the principles defended in the preceding period.

2. *Freedom of the act of faith*

The energetic defense of personal freedom in religious matters during the first centuries had only an echo in the period after the Edict of Milan. However there were nuances which are important to point out and which have not always been considered.

From freedom in religious matters to freedom of the act of faith. Beginning with Constantine, civil power placed itself at the service of the Church's mission. This new situation gradually brought about a shift from the defense of *freedom in religious matters* to the affirmation of *freedom of the act of faith*. From then on, the freedom claimed appeared to be "focalized" by the act of faith, and it practically did not exist in a positive form outside of this act. Freedom in religious matters will be synonymous with the *right not to be pressured by the forced imposition of the faith*.[30] This shift in meaning reveals a fundamental mentality which the circumstances brought to the surface and which is of capital importance.

A text of St. Athanasius (his struggle against Arianism and against the support which Arianism found in the public authorities made him attentive to aspects of the question which escaped other Fathers) marked the transition. He wrote, "The truth is not announced with swords, lances and soldiers. It is proper to religion not to impose but to persuade."[31] The truth of the Christian faith is not to be imposed. This seems to be based upon a more general affirmation: no religion can impose faith.

However, from then on it always, or almost always, was a matter of protests against the imposition *of the faith*. St. Augustine consecrated this idea in a strong formula which has carried through the centuries: "Credere non potest nisi volens."[32] His statement that the faith could not be imposed upon people can be conceived as only a minimal response to the most elemental demands of the gospel, but nevertheless, his putting the matter this way was a clear indication that the situation had changed. The fact that this problem arose suggests that for some at least there was a genuine *possibility* that faith could be imposed by force. In fact this possibility did exist for the first time from the moment that Christianity was converted into the official religion. This was not the case in the first centuries, for during that time people spoke about the *freedom of the human person* (including as "a natural and human right" that each one adored what had been freely chosen) rather than about the need for free acceptance of the Christian faith itself.

However, this view that personal freedom was an integral and undeniable part of the act of Christian faith, rather than a general condition of all religious life, led in time to three very specific consequences:

a) As spiritual freedom came to be seen as a unique dimension and characteristic of the Christian faith, the Church eventually came to hold that only Christians had a full claim to religious liberty. This view was developed step by step over a period of time. It was based primarily on the right not to be forced or pressured by violence to accept the truth and secondarily on the ensuing simple right not to be coerced into adopting the *Christian faith*. The key to this series of developments is that religious freedom was thought of as a function of the act of faith. Outside of this relation to the act of faith religious freedom did not exist. Above all, it did not exist as a right to live personally and socially according to one's own religious convictions. This perspective led little by little to the claim that only those who profess the true faith have full rights in religious matters. Those in error were "tolerated" at the most.

b) This explains the famous distinction between, on the one hand, *pagans and Jews* who had no access to the faith, and on the other, *heretics* who abandoned the faith after having accepted it. When dealing with the first group the necessity of freely accepting the faith was considered. This dictated an attitude of tolerance. The second group, on the contrary, were considered guilty of having separated themselves from the truth after having received the gift of faith. Therefore they merited severe treatment.

c) Thirdly, faith was considered an inestimable gift for persons, and freedom was seen exclusively in function of the faith. This led to a series of measures, not to *impose* the faith, but simply to *favor* it. The repression of evil and the fear of punishment, for example, helped persons to behave well.[33] Here an opening for the use of force was justified by saying that force was not destined to impose the faith (the principle will always be saved) but to eliminate obstacles which actually hindered the free embrace of the faith.[34]

Religious freedom and salvation. This shift in meaning and the consequences which we have just recalled found support in the new ways of conceiving the salvific work. Christianity advanced rapidly in the ancient world, and the religious context changed. Within the Church people began to think that there were only two classes of persons: those who accepted the faith of Christ and those who culpably rejected it.

The Fathers continued to teach the doctrine of the universal will for salvation: all human beings were saved in principle through Christ, but salvation only worked with the free acceptance on the part of the person. The situation was such that there was no excuse for ignorance of the Savior, because thanks to the Church's ministry, the voice of the gospel had reached all persons in one way or another: "Where a preacher's presence has been lacking, the sound and fame of the Gospel's voice has always been present, as in the past the noise of the miracles fulfilled in Egypt reached all nations as Rahab, the courtesan, testifies."[35] Jews and Gentiles, therefore, had no excuse.[36] As the possibilities for hearing the good news changed to give greater opportunities for those outside the Church to respond, the attitudes of the Church Fathers thus changed in the matter of religious freedom.

The case of Augustine is typical in this respect. In spite of what some of his apologists might say, there is a great distance between what he claims in the matter of religious freedom and salvation at the beginning of his work and his later works. Augustine began with a respect for the personal process of each individual in the search for truth. This respect came from his own experience.[37] Little by little he came to harden his position and ended by accepting and proposing forced conversions of heretics. He explains his position in an audacious exegesis of the evangelical *compelle intrare*.

This evolution, which Augustine himself recognized[38] ran parallel to his evolution in the other question which interests us. In *De libero arbitrio* and in *Ad simplicianum*[39] we find an appreciation of pagan virtues and an ample solution to the problem of salvation for those who are outside the Church while in *De dono perseverantiae* and *De predistinatione* we move on to the known affirmation concerning the *massa damnata*. The truth is that, just as in the case of religious freedom, the polemics—this time with the Pelagians—hardened Augustine's position. However, it is no less certain that the parallelism of these two doctrinal evolutions is particularly instructive. Religious freedom and access to salvific truth are connected questions which mutually influence one another as we pointed out in discussing Tertullian and Lactantius.

These ideas which were presented in a vacillating and even anguished manner in the fourth and fifth centuries were slowly strengthened. In the Middle Ages, for example, with the Church co-extensive and strongly intermixed with the known world, it became relatively easy to hold that "outside the Church there is no salvation." Further, being for or against Christ was fully identified with being for or against the Church. Therefore, at this time, it is not strange at all that no one speaks of partial truths which could be found beyond the boundaries of the Church. Spiritual truth was located in the Church. The Church was seen as the only holder of religious truth. Spontaneously and by force of events, a Church-centered perspective was adopted which determines Church life and reflection even today.

This evolution in the conception of salvation had necessary consequences in the question of religious liberty. More attention was given to the point of view of religious truth and less to the subjective conditions of access to the truth, as for example, God's action outside the Church. This led gradually to the claim that only those who professed the true faith had full rights in religious matters.

Tolerance became the attitude observed by those in the Church towards those who were outside the Church, those who were in error. This was tolerance, then, within certain limits. It was not recognition of a "natural and human right" that each one could worship privately and publicly as religious conviction indicated. This right no longer seemed to have meaning in a world which was almost unanimously Christian and in which access to salvific truth was confined to the Church.

The move from the defense to the affirmation of religious liberty led to expressing the problem in terms of tolerance. However, as we have said, this presupposed that civil authority served religious truth.

A testimony against the current. An exceptional testimony against the official tide of the Constantinian settlement was provided by Salvian, monk of Lerins. In 1440 in an attempt to defend Divine Providence, he wrote "On the Government of God." The barbarian invasions had weakened Christian morale, and the question had been raised: "If everything which happens in the world is by divine permission, why is the barbarian situation superior to ours?"

Salvian answered the question by praising the barbarians, pagans as well as heretics: "Among the barbarians there are two classes in each nation: the heretics and the pagans. We are incomparably superior to all of these in what concerns divine law, but as far as conduct and customs are concerned, I say this with vivid pain, they are worth more than we."

This open attitude, however, went even further. Salvian advocated patient and magnanimous conduct towards the heretics basing his argument on their good faith:

> They are heretics, that is true, but they do not know it. For us they are heretics, but they do not believe they are. They consider themselves Catholics and give us the infamous name of heretic. What they are for us we are for them. The truth is with us, but they are convinced that it is with them . . . They are in error, but their mistake is one of good faith, not out of hate, but out of love of God . . . even though they do not have orthodox faith, they think they are in perfect love of God.

Salvian, in a tone which is not common in his times, claimed with fidelity to sacred Scripture that the punishment can only be God's work:

> How will they be punished on the day of judgment for their mistaken opinions? No one can know, but only the Judge. Until that time in my opinion, God recommends patience with them. Indeed, he sees that they do not have an orthodox faith and that their error is of good faith. They believe that their opinion is in accord with true piety. God does this even more so when He knows that they do what they are ignorant of, while we do not bother about what we believe.[40]

These texts show a surprising sense of the value of the personal process in gaining access to the truth, without falling into doctrinal relativism.

This testimony keeps certain claims alive which the Christian community will only rediscover much later.[41]

3. *Temporal power at the service of religious truth*

The acknowledged incompetence of political power in religious matters in the first centuries left room for a remarkable degree of personal religious freedom. This freedom was officially recognized by the Edict of Milan which asserted that political authority should not interfere in ecclesiastical questions. One result of this was that Church freedom came to be vigorously defended against civil power.

With Constantine however, the official recognition of the Church's status left it vulnerable to increasing measures of political interference. The Church, therefore, began a constant struggle to defend its own originality. Its privileged position, which reached a high point with the decree of Theodosius, was in reality a "poisoned gift." While this position favored the propagation of religious truth, it also held many dangers that made the Church energetically claim its distinction from civil authority, and it limited state authority in religious questions.

Every time political power sought to interfere in religious questions, there were persons of the Church to protest, mark out distances, and to claim Church autonomy from the state. There are many texts along this line, but it is not just a matter of writings. These claims were corroborated by vigorous personal attitudes which more than once resulted in ill treatment and deportation.

However, even if the line of distinction between the two powers seemed to continue what was defended in the first centuries, in reality, the Church's perspective on the civil authority's function in religion had changed.

Many texts argued that the temporal power should serve the cause of God as represented by the Church. Ambrose of Milan claimed that political power should be at the direct service of the true faith.[42] It is true that Ambrose supported the idea of the independence of the Church, [43] but he presupposed the primacy of the spiritual power which had civil power at its service. The emperor had no right over the Church. He was within it as a son and should serve it not only as a private person, but also and above all in his function of governor. The distinction between the two powers was valid in that the state had become subservient to the Church.

However, from the moment that civil power's service to the Church was demanded, was there not a claim that the religious element was within the competence of civil authority, even if the situation were one of subordination to the Church? This remained a permanent factor from Constantine on, and it occasioned a truly political pendulum: according to the circumstances and personalities involved, sometimes there was more insistence on "service to the Church" and other times more on "the religious element as part of the competence of the State."

In this perspective it was normal that the theme of *tolerance* appeared. Evil is tolerated, and in this case the evil was religious error. As a matter of principle, this evil should have been eliminated, but the means used had to take into consideration "Christian charity."

Church persons often went to civil power in order to avoid violent repression or to moderate the action taken against those who were in error. But all these demands only confirmed the principle that political power had the right to intervene in religious questions.[44] The spirit of the gospel, however, demanded that this intervention be carried out gently and with moderation.

The Popes assumed the responsibility of compelling temporal power to serve religious truth. In a well known text, sent to Emporor Leo I of Byzantium, Pope Leo I said: "without any hesitation you should realize that you have been given real power not only for temporal matters but above all for the defense of the Church."[45] The "above all" clearly expressed the ministerial function of political power which the Middle Ages simply reaffirmed and deepened.

We are certainly far from the assumption in the first centuries that political authority was incompetent in religious matters. However, the Church's freedom from civil power continued to be maintained, even though it involved an emphasis on the distinction of the functions of the two powers, a distinction which never has been lost.

The survival of these ideas, in spite of lacunas and eclipses which would make us think they had been forgotten, explains texts such as the famous one of Pope Gelasius I who clearly and firmly defined what the relations between Church and state should be. The clarity and firmness of the document's doctrine are surprising in the context of the times.[46]

The text points out that the newness which Christ brings to the relation between the two powers has its origin in the reason for his coming to the world; the salvation of all people. "In this way, Christ separated the functions of *both powers* . . . desiring that his people find *salvation* in a healing humility and that they not be lost again in human pride."

Therefore, the question of salvation was closely bound to the Church-State relationship and to the question of religious freedom.

The document does not limit itself to demanding the Church's freedom, but rather, it indicates that "temporal matters" are the domain of the state. Can we deduce from this that the document formally denies civil power all direct intervention in religious questions? This would necessitate ignoring the historical context of Pope Gelasius, but it would have avoided many future errors.[47]

In spite of this great text, the unity of Church and civil society increased in the following centuries. The Church conformed to the privileged situation because it facilitated its task of bringing persons to the faith and maintaining them in it. The idea of religious unity as the basis of social unity was affirmed. Without doubt this had been Constantine's intention, above all a political one, but Church people also greatly worked in its favor.

Then a shift took place which should be noted. From the idea that everyone had been saved in principle by *Christ* and was indefectibly tied to him we passed to the claim that it was absolutely necessary for all persons to have ties with the Church. This was fundamentally due to two things: the polemic against the heresies which led to claiming the ecclesial unity and the idea which we have already alluded to that there is no one who had not heard, in one way or another, the Church's preaching.

We thus moved from the unity and involvement of all persons with Christ to a unity which was understood as unity *in the Church*. This unity, it was then held, was harmoniously expressed by the unity of civil society. In this way and at the same time, civil society found in religion its most solid armature and reinforcement. Medieval theology did not question this political-religious unity, and for some people even today it remains the Christian answer to the problem.

C. THE THOMISTIC DOCTRINE OF TOLERANCE

This change which occurred in the Christian social situation in the fourth century was increasingly affirmed. The Church took an active part in the birth of feudal society and profoundly gave itself over to this society in its different levels: economic, social, political, juridical, and ideological.

Christendom was presented as the only society with two views of persons: ecclesiastical and civil. Many of the problems debated at this time involved controversies over the way in which the relationship between these two powers was understood.

In Thomas Aquinas we find for the first time the doctrinal scheme of tolerance presented in a clear and systematic form. In the basic essentials of his scheme, Thomas reflects the mentality of his times. But in his own distinctive contributions, however, he signifies a moment of matureness in the reflection on this question.[48] His influence became decisive in the centuries which followed.

Thomas Aquinas explicitly faced the problem of the attitude which should be adopted towards infidels and heretics. We find his thought synthesized in two questions of the "Summa Theologiae": "De infidelitate" and "De haeresi" (II,II, q.10 and q.11). For Thomas Aquinas tolerations means the attitude which can be taken towards evil in certain circumstances.[49] More specifically, it is a matter of "human government's" tolerance towards infidels and heretics, that is to say, the attitude of political power towards religious error. This focus on the problem takes as given the principle that civil authority is closely bound to spiritual power, for it was considered to be evil for any area of life to be outside of religious truth. The problem of infidels and heretics is therefore within the realm of civil authority and justifies its intervention.

1. Civil tolerance of Jews and Pagans

Thomas Aquinas came out favorably for tolerance towards Jews and pagans. His argument was fundamentally based on two considerations:

The principle of the good to be obtained and the evil to be avoided. The attitude of civil power towards Jews and pagans should have been directed by this principle. Thomas applied it to this case[50] by beginning with a comparison between God's government and human government. The latter had received its authority from the former and therefore should have imitated it in the exercise of authority. Christian revelation has proved to us that God is tolerant with persons who are in error. Civil power should also be tolerant with the infidels.[51] The right of civil power to govern was recognized as a fundamental principle, a heritage of past centuries. For this reason, St. Thomas tended to suggest the practice of political prudence which was inspired by the Christian spirit.

It should be noted that this principle rejects the idea that tolerance of error is an immoral act. God himself proceeds in this manner. However, this does not mean the rights of religious truth should be renounced, but rather these rights should not be made "absolute and unconditioned."[52]

In addition, we should also note that St. Thomas sought to justify this tolerance further by turning to the issue of the good to be achieved and the evil to be avoided. To this point St. Thomas establishes a distinction between Jewish and pagan people. In the religious rites of Jews there is a kind of prefiguration of our Christian truth and in that way a testimony for our faith. Thus we practice a genuine good when we tolerate them. On the contrary, a pagan cult does not bring any truth and it can only be tolerated to avoid evil. Thomas thus indicates his concern to avoid a situation which could be an impediment to the eventual conversion of pagans to the Christian life. In this way, the particular good to be obtained and the evil to be avoided by the attitude of tolerance are explicitly based in the distinctive demands of Christian faith.

Freedom of the act of faith. In the last analysis, the explanation of this principle, in effect, is based on the free character of the act of faith. The idea of obtaining good and avoiding evil depends on concrete circumstances, but it is ultimately directed towards impeding "coactio ad fidem."

Thomas repeatedly claims that infidels cannot be forced to accept the faith, and he bases his claims on Augustine's famous: "to believe is a matter of the will." This concern even appears in Thomas' justification of the crusade against the infidels. It is not a matter of forcing them to the faith but of compelling them not to impede the profession of the true faith.[53] Another clear example is the question of baptizing the children of infidels against their parents' will. Thomas Aquinas maintains that this goes against natural law. Baptism should only take place when such persons have the use of reason and therefore can be brought to the faith "not by compulsion but by persuasion."[54]

2. *Repression of heresy*

Thomas Aquinas' position is different when he treats heresy. Heresy is compared to other transgressions and considered susceptible to the death penalty.[55] Our author slightly mitigates his stance pointing out that the Church's mercy leads it not to abandon a heretic to secular power except in the case where obstinance in position is present after having been admonished.[56]

How can this severity be reconciled with the defense of freedom in what concerns the act of faith? Thomas has already faced this difficulty and resolves it by distinguishing between access to the faith and its conservation once received: "Accepting faith is a matter of will, once accepted conserving faith is a matter of necessity."[57] The principle of freedom of faith is applied only in the cases of Jews and pagans. The heretic's situation is different, and here there are two aspects which should be distinguished. By rejecting the integrity of the faith the heretic loses the right to demand respect for religious convictions, and further-more this rejection is a sin which places the heretic at the margin of Christian society.

† For Thomas Aquinas it is impossible to abandon the faith without being culpable. This explains his strictness towards heresy. Religious truth, once accepted, imposes itself on the conscience, and if its integrity is rejected, respect cannot be demanded from others.

In addition, the abandonment of the faith breaks social unity. Heresy is an "infectuous vice"[58] and can be punished by civil power, even with death. If faith guarantees social unity, religious nonconformity means a break which attacks society itself. Therefore, heresy should not be toler-ated by civil power.

3. Perspectives

Even if Thomas Aquinas' doctrine is clear when treating heresy directly, other parts of his work contain principles which open the door to other perspectives. These perspectives are found in the two aspects discussed below.

*False conscience.** The first aspect concerns an old theme of medieval theology. We are referring to the question of "false conscience." The expression itself contains the terms of the problem we are treating: "false" presupposes the affirmation of religious truth; "conscience" pre-supposes the access to that truth.

Medieval theologians asked what should be the norm of conduct for those who did not know religious truth. This led to underlining the role played by conscience in moral conduct. Abelard went so far as to affirm that the persecutors of Christ and of his disciples "would have sinned even more seriously if, against their conscience, they had pardoned them."[59] Compared to these audacious theses we find the Franciscan school which presented itself as defender of the objective order. Bonaventure represents this school, but he reflects very well the difficul-ties which are encountered. False conscience puts the person in an

---

*The Spanish *conciencia* and Latin *conscientia* have the meanings of both *conscience* and *consciousness* in English translation.

impasse: the person sins mortally if false conscience is followed because he or she goes against God's law. However, the person also sins if the false conscience is not followed because he or she goes against what is believed to be God's law.[60]

For his part, Thomas Aquinas underscores the subjective aspects of moral conduct. He says, for example:

> To believe in Christ is in itself good and necessary for salvation, but the will only moves to this belief under the aspect in which reason presents it. Therefore, if reason proposes that act as evil, then the will, in tending toward it, does evil, not because the act is evil in itself but because of the reason's accidental apprehensions.

The article ends with this affirmation: "As a consequence, it must be affirmed that any will in disaccord with reason, be it false or correct, is always evil."[61] The will has to conform itself to what reason proposes as good, even if it is in error.

But the following article asks if it is a good act to follow false conscience. The answer reveals an uneasiness. To follow false conscience is not an offense; since it was a sin not to follow false conscience, it can be deduced that false consciences put people under obligations, but they do not make the acts good. And so, for our author there are only good acts and bad acts. Therefore, what is the norm of conduct in conformtiy with false conscience? This is a difficulty which Thomas does not seem to have resolved.[62] Be this as it may, in spite of the fact that Thomas Aquinas does not grant the heretic the benefit of good faith, this problem introduces a factor of evolution in the position held on the rights of the person who dissents from the faith.

The autonomy of the temporal sphere.   Something similar happens with a theme Thomas Aquinas develops, and this development greatly influences the theology of the sixteenth century: the autonomy of the temporal sphere.

The context of Thomistic thought is that of the social and religious order of Christendom, and therefore it deals with the doctrine of harmony between religious and civil powers, implying the submission of civil to religious power. However, Thomas introduces the concept of the natural order's consistency. This will permit him to use other grounds for distinguishing the function of political power and that of the Church.

Precisely in one of the questions of the "Summa Theologiae" which we previously studied, in treating political authority which pagans had over Christians, Thomas claims that "the dominion and authority have been introduced by human law; however, the distinction between the faithful and the infidels belongs to divine law. But divine law, which proceeds from grace, does not eliminate human law but rather is grounded in natural reason."[63] Grace does not extinguish human law which comes from natural reason. The distinction between faithful and infidel, however, is made in reference to the faith. That is to say, this distinction between those who have faith and those who do not is a divine perspective. The public order subsists since it is based on natural law, and it embraces both the faithful and the infidel.

Thomas Aquinas did not draw out all the consequences of these distinctions. They introduce corrections to the theme of the social unity based on faith. The theologians of the sixteenth century called on these scarcely sketched ideas when they faced the problems which arise out of Christendom's coming into contact with other peoples.

4. Civil tolerance and heresy

Feudal society began to break up. New systems of production appeared and were centered in commercial activity. Along with these new systems, forms of absolute political power rose up in conflict with old privileges. In this context the break up of religious unity in the West during the century of the Reformation had consequences of major importance for our concern.

Up until this time, heresy appeared as a localized and episodic phenomenon. However, from the sixteenth century on, Christendom was divided within itself. The question of religious freedom turned into something very acute and personal, and the historical manifestations and the ardor of the polemic harden positions. Many saw only the most rigorous and severe aspects of the doctrine which was elaborated in the Middle Ages. They were convinced that religion was a matter of civil power and stood against all tolerance towards dissidents with the faith. They called upon civil power to combat them with force. We find this attitude among Catholics as well as Protestants.[64] This was the time of diffusion of the famous principle: "Cujus regio, ejus religio"; the prince is the master of religion.

But another line of thought timidly began to make its appearance. Some theologians sought other ways out of the difficult political-religious situations which Europe experienced. They applied the Thomistic doctrine of tolerance towards heretics. Thomas Aquinas would have explicitly rejected this application. However, the principle which he proclaimed concerning the Jews and Gentiles "in order to achieve the greater good or avoid the greater evil," seemed to theologians like John de Lens (1541-1593), John von Meulen (1538-1585) and Martin Becanus (1563-1624) to be applicable to the situation created by the Reformation.

This attempt did not come to dominate theological thought on the question. Further, in spite of trying to resolve the most acute and difficult aspects of the religious struggles of the times, these theologians clearly remained within the limits of tolerance, the tolerance of political power towards religious error. This presupposed the general acceptance of the power's directive task in the process which leads one to reach the saving truth. As a consequence, as paradoxical as it seems, this theme signified simultaneously that in the last instance, everything is found to be subject to spiritual authority. We are still far from any real effort to rethink the very basis of the relationship between truth and liberty.

CONCLUSION

The process which we have traced in broad lines leading to the elaboration of the Church's classical doctrine concerning the relation between human freedom and salvific truth has much to teach us.

The decisive fact was the rise of political power as the mediating element in that relation. Up until the fourth century the Church did not recognize, at this level of force and organization, human mediation at the service of the Gospel message. When this human mediation did occur as the result of the historical events described above and when Christianity tied itself to civil power, the Christians' situation changed radically. Although in the previous stage we were not faced with a neutral absence of this mediation, the Christian communities made up of the empire's poor and helpless valiantly and explicitly denied that political power had a role to play in a person's access to religious truth. Actually, from this beginning, the relation of freedom and salvation was situated in a political context.

The Christian state which began at the end of the fourth century had as a corollary the rise of Christianity as a new type of "political religion."[65] From that moment on, the dominant theological point of view was that of power.[66] From there the shifts began as we have noted: from freedom in religious matters to freedom of the act of faith, from political power's incompetence in spiritual matters to political power at the service of

religious truth. Really both shifts presupposed that Christianity's relation with civil authority had changed.

For the same reason the political perspective's point of departure was
different. The great interlocutor of Christian thought in the first centuries was the pagan, the master of political power and of the culture of
the times. Christian writers directed their arguments to him in their
efforts to show the presence of God's salvific action before Christ's
coming and beyond the visible Church boundaries. According to those
Christians who were the privileged bearers and heirs of the biblical
message, the best of pagan culture came from that message. Therefore
they demanded the freedom to live and preach this good news. Later, in
the Middle Ages, theology was done in a Christian world for Christians,
but now the interlocutor was the infidel who was part of a social minority. Religious truth was only to be reached in the Church. The infidel was
in error and at best, could be tolerated; the former Christian, the heretic
could not even be tolerated. The very problem of tolerance indicated the
existence of a new relationship with power: the problem of tolerating
error was something that the Christians of the first centuries could not
even bring up.

All this implies that theological reflection on the relation between
freedom and salvation was done from an ecclesiocentric point of view. To
be for or against Christ became synonymous with being for or against the
Church. Outside the Church there was no salvation. The problem was
within Christendom, and there was no consistent world outside. Or as
some said, "Extra ecclesiam nulla jus."

In this context, a model was elaborated for the relation of the Church
with the political world whose coherence and harmony was lacking in
the centuries that followed. This was the model which was normally
taken up, although not without struggles and difficulties, by the Christians of this time. In modern days, however, the defense of this model
justified an intransigent position. At this moment, and because of popular movement pressure, it appeared as an outstanding part of the dominant classes' ideology.

Two

Freedom and Critical Reason

The eighteenth century marks the beginning of revolution in different fields of human activity. In this period, humanity acquired a clear awareness of its capacity to know and transform nature and society; that is to say, to transform history by taking it into hand. This exercise of human reason appeared to be radically free in the measure that persons recognized themselves as able to change the conditions of their lives and to situate themselves differently within social relations. It is in this context that bourgeois society sprang up. The Christian faith faced new challenges, and the Church and theology reacted at first with categories which were elaborated and lived in the earlier centuries. Afterwards, the questions opened up by the bourgeois revolution and by the movement of ideas which accompanied that revolution left their mark on contemporary theology up to and including Vatican Council II. Post-conciliar theology, especially the new political theology, responded to these questions in a creative and direct manner which deserves to be mentioned.

A. MODERN TIMES

What is called the modern spirit is the result of a historical process which abruptly and radically changed the old mentality. In this way, a new revolutionary stage began which set a new rhythm in the history of humanity, especially in the western world.

1. *A global view*

Reason and freedom. In the eighteenth century people began to experience that they were increasingly capable of transforming the world in which they lived through individual initiative. The industrial revolution signified the beginning of a stage of rapid production and distribution of goods for consumption. This production was based on the ability to transform nature, an ability which was previously unknown. The productive forces expanding beyond foreseeable limits radically changed the economic activity of society. The industrial revolution was above all a productive revolution. It gave individuals of the modern era the consciousness that they were capable of profoundly modifying the conditions of life and their relationship vis-à-vis nature.[1]

A different historical process accounted for these events and had its origins in the same period. We are referring to the social movement which demanded modern liberties and which took form in a very speical way in the French Revolution.[2] What was demanded were the individual liberties within the core of society,[3] and this was the origin of the famous distinction between the citizen and the person, that is to say, between the public and private worlds.[4] Henceforth, religious freedom was bound to the other freedoms and rights of persons.

These historical events were not only contemporary, they were mutually interdependent and came to consciousness in the group of intellectual currents known as the Enlightenment. Diderot's *Encyclopaedia* clearly represented the Enlightenment in France, but the Enlightenment was also present in Germany and England. One of Kant's famous statements characterized it in this way:

> The Enlightenment consists in the event for which man leaves his minority of age. The minority of age lies in the inability to use one's own understanding without the direction of another. One is to be blamed for this minority of age when its cause does not lie in a lack of understanding, but rather in the lack of decision and spirit to independently use understanding without another leading. "Sapere aude!" Have the courage to use your own understanding. This is the slogan of the enlightenment . . . However, this Enlightenment only demands freedom, and certainly it is the most inoffensive of all freedoms which bear the name, that is, the freedom to make public use of one's own reason in any field.

The Enlightenment meant that, thanks to the free use of reason, humanity was coming of age. Reason and freedom enabled humanity to free itself from all bondage, and this was especially valid in religious questions where, as Kant says, the minority of ages is "the most dishonorable."[5] This critical position towards religion influenced contemporary theology.

The culmination of a process. What we have just recalled is the result of the fermentation of events and ideas which began in the latter part of the Middle Ages. Between the sixteenth and eighteenth centuries a new bourgeois society was born.

Experimental society began in the sixteenth century with the physics of Galileo, and with it began a new type of knowledge which differed significantly from philosophy. Science was "methodologically atheist," that is, the "hypothesis of God" was not needed for an adequate explanation of natural phenomena or for further advances into natural science. From this a consciousness slowly developed which made science an important factor in secularization. From very early, science's significance for the transformation of the concrete conditions of human life guided the spirits in the search for "practical philosophy."[6] At the same time, important changes took place in the field of politics. As Christendom broke up, reflection on political matters was renewed, and the Modern Age began to appear. Machiavelli tried to introduce a distinct rationality into these questions, conceiving the state as autonomous from religious bondage and analyzing political decisions with purely political criteria. This effort culminated in the lay state which the French Revolution promoted.

Without modern science and politics we cannot understand the philosophy of this time. The birth of science posed serious epistemological questions which occasioned Kant's lucid and critical theory of knowledge. Scientific and political reason, as an interlocutor, led to a reflection by Kant on new openings for ethical questions and to the elaboration of Hegel's philosophy of history. All these efforts were marked by that search for a practical philosophy.

Another important fact was the process of the Reformation. This was the beginning of a weighty current of religious individualism in harmony with the mentality of the age. As Hegel said:

> This is the Reformation's essential content: man remains self determined to be free . . . It is of greatest importance that the Bible has now become the basis of the Christian Church: in the future each individual, beginning with the Bible, should enlighten himself and should be able to determine his conscience according to the same source. This is the enormous modification that the principle has undergone; all the tradition and edifice of the Church become problematical, the principle of its authority is tumbled.[7]

In Germany, the Reformation initiated a criticism of the ecclesiastical institutions and occasioned religious forms in which the subjective aspects of religious experience were prized. The ideas of the Reformation took root, even though very moderately, in England where other forms of liberalization were already known on the political level.[8] Somewhat different, France of the eighteenth century had not lived through any of these experiences. Therefore, in this country, which was Catholic and subject to centralized power, the anti-clerical and libertarian explosion was the greatest. What happened in France conditioned the life of the Church throughout the nineteenth century.

Present situation and perspectives. In his study and critique of the Enlightenment, Hegel spoke of the "unsatisfied Enlightenment." In fact, for many reasons, including among others its own inner contradictions,[9] the great aspirations and illusions of the Enlightenment were not fulfilled. For many, this Hegelian statement is still characteristic in the present situation,[10] for new perspectives have appeared which have led commentators to speak of our time as a "Neo-Enlightenment."[11] As we will see, this is the immediate context of the most alert wing of European theology today, attentive to the situation of the faith and of the Church faced with contemporary rationalism and with the ever increasing impact of the social history of freedom.

2. *The ideology of the modern times*

The ideology of the modern times is a bourgeois ideology. The bourgeoisie is a social class which sprang up in the cities of the feudal world and little by little achieved dominance. The geographical and scientific discoveries, as well as the economic crises of the sixteenth century accelerated the rise of this new social class. The former serfs were emancipated, but, at the same time, they lost their direct access to the means of production. Thus, the growing capitalist economy found in them the needed workers, the proletariat. This economy was based on commerce, and the new avenues of communication favored capital investment in commercial activities. This merchant capitalism became more and more complex due to the rise of manufacturing; work was no longer done at home but began to create worker-entrepreneur relationships. The bourgeois class, which from now on significantly stimulated the growth of economic activity, reached its greatest strength with the industrial revolution. It was this development which produced what has been called "machine-facture." From this moment the economy, centered in private enterprises and in the most cruel exploitation of workers, was in bourgeois hands.[12] This social class, which represented the modern spirit, was forged as the economic and political power fell into its hands.

Individualism and the modern freedoms. Individualism is the most important aspect of bourgeois ideology. It is expressed, for the modern mentality, in the conception of the individual as an absolute beginning, an autonomous center of decisions. Individual initiative and interest are the starting point and motor of economic activity. As is said in the declaration of the rights of man of the French Revolution, "every man is free to employ his arms, his industry and his capital as he sees fit and useful for himself. He can produce what pleases him as he likes." This freedom, however, does not lead to chaos. The different individual interests find a regulation in the market: the law of supply and demand. This law makes the free play of individual interests coincide with the general interest. This coincidence thus results in a natural order. It is not something forced by an authority which arbitrarily imposes and decides what is to be done. Rather, it occurs naturally. This is the origin of the idea that capitalism is the economic regime natural to the human person. [13]

The absolute principle that the economic activities of persons should be free led to the corresponding notion that freedom should also be absolute in the organization of the society to which they belong. Individual freedom is the first exigency. Social order cannot be imposed from without by means of authority, as it was in the Old Regime; it is the result of the person's free action. Society presupposes a free association, a "contract society," which will give rise to a general will in addition to individual wills. [14] During the French Revolution it was said that individual rights end where the exercise of other individuals' rights begin. However, this contract can only be made among equals, and from this we have the affirmation of social equality.

The demands for individual freedom and social equality are thus related to the new economic forms. Similarly, the right to private property is fundamental for bourgeois society, for above all, this right concerns the matter of ownership of the means of production. "The freedom of industry," wrote G. de Ruggiero, "is the daughter of modern individualism; even more it is its favorite daughter." [15] Social equality also has a clear economic reference: persons are equal in the moment of buying and selling. Furthermore, the formal equality is a condition of mercantile activity. [16]

Rationalism and empiricism. This individualism was also reflected in the conceptions of knowledge. According to rationalism, each individual's reason is the starting point of all knowledge. Truth does not come to us from revelation or from human authority. Everything should be submitted to the judgment of the individual's critical reason. This means that the person begins to be master of the world and of him or herself. Hegel saw in the individual's free use of reason what is proper to the Enlightenment:

> Against a faith in authority the subject's authority for him or herself was claimed, and the natural laws were the only thing which could connect the exterior with the interior. Arguments were made against all miracles, because now nature is a system of known and accepted laws; within these laws, man finds himself in his own field, and only what is proper to him has any value. The knowledge of nature makes him free. Afterwards, thought was also directed to the spiritual aspect: it was considered that law and objective morality are based in the present ground of man's will, while before these things only existed as commandments from God, imposed from outside . . . The name "reason" has been given to these universal determinations founded in the present consciousness, to the laws of nature, to the content of that which is good and just. The name "Enlightenment" has been given to the practical effectiveness of these laws. The Enlightenment moved from France to Germany, and there a new world of ideas arose. [17]

As L. Goldmann[18] points out, empiricism is also an expression of individualism. It is the affirmation that the individual conscience is the absolute beginning of knowledge and action, beginning first with innate ideas and secondly with experience. In both cases, the knowledge of nature seems to have no limits, and in this ample horizon, the person knows and affirms him or herself as individuality. The rational capacity leads to the elimination of the mysterious and to a great confidence in knowledge and in the progress of humanity.

3. *The critique of religion*

Rationalistic and optimistic bourgeois ideology will severely criticize the religious traditions.

The social function of religion. From the perspective of the modern spirit, the peoples and periods marked by religion have lived in obscurantism and superstition. Religion is the enemy of human progress, dogma is the enemy of science. Machiavelli and Montaigne had already sketched the critique of the social function of religion.[19] This became more incisive in the century of light. For the Enlightenment, religion did not give a solid base for a true ethic or a just society. Rather it was based on immorality and on unjust society. Traditional religion stands against freedom and autonomy. Both the deists and atheists of the period agreed that an individual could have one or the other but not both; the alternative was religious belief or science.

This critique of the social function of traditional religion was interestingly enough, carried out from the perspective of a natural and rational religion. However, it was not entirely new. Renaissance humanism had provided an antecedent to this activity. In the fifteenth and sixteenth centuries a universal religion was sought which would appreciate the natural world that was just being discovered and which would, as a result, place the person before God in a different way. This new religious consciousness was not presented as hostile to Christianity. Rather it was thought that Christianity, if well understood, would respond to the desired religious form.

Contrary to this, the eighteenth century sought to replace the revealed and authoritarian Christian religion with a rational and universal religion. The universality of reason was, in fact, one of the characteristic traits of the modern spirit. A freely accepted religion, without bondage or dogma, was desired, one which would permit full human development. As a result, the Christian doctrine of original sin seemed to persons of this period to be an aberration. The individualistic principle could not accept that one person could be responsible for the sin of another. In the same way the democratic spirit could not accept that God arbitrarily gave the grace of salvation to some and not to others. Such a God appeared to be a tyrant. This led to the postulation of universal salvation which did succeed in maintaining the theological focus on salvation which had been affirmed in the Church since the fourth century.[20]

Rational religion was seen as the religion of philosophers, of the enlightened, who have come of age and have dared to use reason. This was an elitist perspective which has as a corollary the affirmation that the popular masses are sunk in superstition and ignorance.[21]

Tolerance. Along the same line the ideal of tolerance in religous matters became an important postulate. This was not the negative sense of a toleration of evil. It was, rather, the tolerance that a figure such as Bayle demanded out of respect for the religious opinions of others. Each person was free to believe or not to believe, to assume this or that religion. Thus in religion as in economics and politics, the person was the absolute beginning. It was held that the superstition which denies scientific rationality and the ignorance which denies human freedom must be combated. The tolerant attitude towards religious convictions was without doubt accompanied with a note of skepticism towards the possibility of arriving at truth in these questions. This was reinforced by the new economic order of society, for this order was not based on religious doctrine. Indeed, in the economic activity centered in commerce, religious convictions had no intervention. One exchanged not with someone who believed but with someone who had something. In spite of certain initial ties with religion, there is in economic capitalism a factor of desacralization, which Max Weber has pointed out. [22]

From this time on, the respect of religious freedom was closely bound to the defense of the other modern freedoms. In bourgeois society religion was, as a consequence, increasingly relegated to the private sector. In turn, this later led to the opposite view. Political theology, in both its older and contemporary forms, rose up, although from opposite perspectives, against this dislodging of Christian faith from the public terrain of society.

B. CHURCH REACTION IN THE NINETEENTH CENTURY

The Catholic Church, shaken by the French Revolution, became suddenly attentive to the modern mentality. The majority of Church people read into these events and ideas a denial of God and of the concrete conditions of faith in him. As a result, the cultural divorce begun in the sixteenth century was accentuated. However, movements simultaneously sprang up in the heart of the Church which assumed another attitude towards the defense of modern freedoms. Time worked in favor of these movements.

1. *The papal attitude*

Rejection on principle. The Popes' doctrinal rejection of modern liberties was clear and complete and they were repeatedly judged as being "absurd liberties." Here, we will enumerate synthetically the reasons cited for this repulsion.

There is a central preoccupation in the pontifical texts which is expressed in diverse forms: the liberties endanger the salvation of persons, and salvation is the primary task of the Church. The elimination of Catholicism as the state religion and the proclamation of civil equality of cult are, according to the Popes, the fruit of indifferentism which puts truth and error on the same level.[23] This implies that God "has given humanity freedom so that each one can choose the sect and opinion which fits one's private judgment without losing salvation."[24]

From this point of view, the affirmation of liberty in religious matters and the subsequent recognition of this liberty by political powers would ✗ actually sustain the idea that it is possible to be saved outside the Church.[25] That is to say, if truth is found only in the Church and correspondingly, if one is free to look beyond the Church, the conclusion is that persons can be saved in spite of being in error. From this we can see that these affirmations were looked upon from the point of view of heresies.[26] Consequently, the concern for the eternal destiny of persons is indicated as the ultimate reason for the rejection of modern liberties. Once again we find the close ties between salvation theology and the problem of liberty.

A second reason for the rejection of modern liberties lies in the political expression of that relationship. Actually, the documents from this period maintain that the means for leading and keeping persons in truth is part of a seriously determined social order, for without this social framework, the persons would fall into error. It is precisely the liberty of conscience, ✗ and its translation into civil life, which tends to "remove the restraints which are capable of keeping people on the paths of truth. This is so because people are already being led to perdition by a natural inclination towards evil."[27] It is this line of thought which directly leads to the necessary "concordance between priesthood and empire." Princes care for the religious life of the subjects. Leo XII, on the occasion of the 1825 Jubilee encouraged the rulers "to care for the faithful and the servants which are subject to them, out of the obligation of their own dignity and office especially in those things which concern the faith and the health of souls."[28] The Popes supported this idea repeating with insistence the famous text of Pope Leo I: "power has been given to the kings not only to rule the world, but especially to support and defend the Church."[29]

Within the same order of ideas, the Popes recalled that religion is the strongest pillar of social unity. This is an added reason for rulers to defend the Popes' rights: Pius VII wrote, "there can be no sturdier foundation for the empires, no more sure and solid manner of affirming public prosperity than religion, and its defense and propagation should be the primary concern of princes and rulers."[30] There was more. Leo XII affirmed: "that just as reason and experience prove, they (rulers) defend their own cause when they defend the authority of the Church."[31] The Popes responded because they sensed that modern liberties undermined at the same time "the foundations of religious and social order."[32] The interests of the Church were intimately bound with those of the old regime because society rested on the premises of the faith, and this basis was denied by the propagators of modern liberties. In this fashion, they felt that political power should be used to repress religious errors, for these errors were seen as threatening both church and society. All this brought the Church to take great pains to restore the old political order in alliance with, first, the aristocracy, and, later on, with the conservative bourgeoisie. With both the Church tried to guarantee a type of society in which its essential claims were recognized.

There was a third motive for rejecting the current ideas born in the French Revolution. This was the question of defending the liberties of the Church against state absolutism. This concern is expressed by Pius VI, a contemporary of the first years of the revolution, but it decreased with his successors.[33] Pius VI based this defense on the claim that the Church must be free in its task of working for salvation.

He rejected, consequently, the revolutionary claim of an absolute liberty on the basis that it contended with God and asserted a radical individualism against the social responsibilities of the creature.[34] The presuppositions of the bourgeois claim for liberty were explicitly rejected.

Practical acceptance of the new situation. The doctrinal rejection of modern liberties was accompanied by a practical acceptance of the liberal governments.

A constant attitude was already present in Pius VI and little by little was confirmed in his successors throughout the nineteenth century as liberal ideas gained ground in Europe. The Popes gave a resigned and reluctant acceptance which they tried to limit to particular cases which they pretended to consider as exceptional and transitory. The hope of a return to more favorable situations remained firm and was even actively promoted.[35]

There are multiple examples of that acceptance and they indicate the behavior of Rome throughout the nineteenth century. In spite of the opinion of a Cardinals' Commission, Pius VI abstained from condemning the taking of oath which was imposed by the French National Assembly in 1792.[36] Pius VII approved the Concordate of 1801 in spite of the fact that the new Constitution did not recognize Catholicism as the state religion. He took the same attitude towards the constitutional Charter of 1814 which proclaimed the freedom of cult,[37] and Pius VIII quickly recognized the new, particularly liberal, French government of 1830. Gregory XVI, even though he condemned liberalism (including Catholic liberalism) in his encyclical "Mirari Vos," accepted the alliance of liberals and Catholics in Belgium along with the constitution of the new kingdom.[38] All of this was done out of consideration of the concrete circumstances and without thinking of the principles which were affected by these concessions. Even Pius IX, in spite of the Syllabus, acted similarly at the level of concrete politics.

But no doctrinal argument was given to justify this attitude. It was simply a matter of political prudence and was motivated by the desire of avoiding greater evils for the Catholic peoples. There is not even so much as a trace that the Thomistic schema of tolerance was applied to the new situation.

But how can you persist in the rejection of the liberal thesis and at the same time accept its concrete political results without creating a certain confusion? Concessions in the practical field demand a doctrinal justification, but for some time the Holy See "voluntarily maintained an ambiguous position."[39] Perhaps the rapid succession of events did not permit the necessary distance. As time passed, however, the need for doctrinal elaboration imposed itself in order to give coherence to this complex activity and to permit the foreseeing of new issues. A first effort in this area came from the sector called "liberal Catholics," especially in France where the confrontation with liberal ideas was sharpest.

2. *Doctrinal elaboration*

The complex conjunction of ideas which were stirred up during the French Revolution began to be developed in the following years. The defense of individual liberties was recognized as a vital issue, and it became distinguished from the totalitarian concept of state and the background of religious indifferentism, both of which were initially quite influential factors.

The Catholic circles then began to see the true significance of the fact of revolution and of the stream of ideas which flowed from this fact. They even began to perceive the possibilities which all this had for the faith. Therefore, the difficult process to reconcile the revolution with traditional theology and with the interest of the Church in modern times was begun. In this search new paths opened for the presence of the Christian community in history and for reflection on the faith.

A precursor: Lamennais.   Among the first of these efforts we find that
of Felicite de La Mennais[40] who initiated the so-called school of Catholic
liberalism.[41]

By 1820, Lamennais had become an outstanding defender of Church
liberty and the Papacy against the intrusions of civil power. In his eyes,
the Concordate of 1801 made the Church submit to the state while the
true social order presupposes the spiritual primacy of the Church as
incarnated in Papal dominion.

But around 1828, even while continuing his vigorous defense of Papal
rights, Lamennais showed himself to be more open to liberal ideas.[42] A
key distinction permitted him to systematize that opening: on the one
hand there is a dogmatic liberalism, that is to say, a *philosophic theory*,
and on the other hand there is liberalism as the *sentiment of liberty*. The
first destroys spiritual society, and therefore destroys civil society as
well. The second, however, is perfectly compatible with Christianity,
and even more, if it would only become the Church's ally it could be a
success.[43]

Lamennais passionately took up the battle. In October of 1830, the first
issue of "L'Avenir" appeared in which the rights of "God and Liberty"
were defended. "United all the internal and permanent needs of human
nature are satisfied . . . Divided, the difficulties begin and grow until
their unity is once again achieved."[44] We can distinguish two lines in his
thought which will not converge in him and which will remain throughout all the variations of Catholic liberalism. The first is represented in the
famous distinction between thesis and hypothesis and in the thought of
Leo XIII; the second after many siftings will lead into Vatican II and the
fuller statements on religious liberty.

Lamennais says that theoretically, there are three possible social systems: the first is based on God, the source of authority and order who
guides the reason and will of creatures to unity by means of their
obedience. In this society, persons are perfectly free because they obey
only supreme reason. The second is based on human reason alone
without relation to God. It is characterized by the affirmation of individual freedom because it excludes all dependencies: the freedom of each
individual ends only where the freedom of others begins. In the third
system, the will of one individual, independent of God's will, is imposed
upon all as a supreme law. This is the violation of all rights.

Then Lamennais says:

> . . . of these three types of society, the first unites order and freedom
> and therefore has the perfection of both the other two systems. How-

ever, in the present disposition of the people this system is clearly impossible since it presupposes what does not exist: the belief in the same law which is universally recognized as divine and belief in an authority which infallibly interprets and promulgates that law.[45]

The first system is ideal, but concrete circumstances do not permit its realization. The presupposition of unity of belief and respect for an authority which interprets infallibly God's law is not "in the present disposition of the peoples." It is, therefore, necessary to direct ourselves towards another social system. "We must understand that between the unity of the divine system and the unity of a brutal system which is founded on obedience which is forced upon man . . . there is no middle term other than an individual freedom which is equal for all and complete for all."[46] A regime based upon "equal freedom for all" is obviously the one which is derived from the principles contained in the declaration of human rights; circumstances lead us to desire and to work for such a system.

As he breaks with his old convictions, Lamennais is inclined more and more to consider that modern liberties represent real progress for humanity.[47] He will find in this progress a new way of maintaining the claim which is very dear to him: the necessity of the freedom of the Church in relation to political power.[48] Actually, the freedom of the Church appears to him to be tied to political liberties:

> For Catholicism, servitude is death, and there is no religious liberty without the other liberties which we claim. . . . They are closely tied to religious liberty and are derived from it as consequences. Their destiny is indivisible. Whoever attacks the liberty of Catholicism at the same time attacks all liberties.[49]

Lamennais came to look with sympathy and optimism on the democratic regime which was slowly taking its place in the world. "From here on, he says "there can only be life in liberty, in equal liberty for all."[50]

The declaration that political liberties are intimately united to the liberty of the Church does not diminish for Lamennais his conviction that the Church is the holder of religious truth. What he demands is a "civil tolerance" of cults; this should be carefully distinguished from dogmatic tolerance which would only be religious indifferentism: "On the one hand it (equal liberty for all) leaves each person the right to believe all that seems to him to be true and to act according to his beliefs insofar as public order is not disturbed. Consequently, on the other hand, by establishing the most complete civil tolerance, it in no way implies dogmatic tolerance which is only the absence of all belief including the absence of all opinion."[51]

But even if Lamennais distinguishes, as we noted in the preceding paragraph, between an ideal order of harmony between Church and state and the particular historical situation which makes us content with another social system; when we look more closely at what he understands by this ideal order and when we examine his enthusiasm for the historical situation to which he seems to be resigned, things take on a different aspect.[52]

It cannot be denied that Lamennais looked with optimism on history which was in his view moving towards a democratic regime in which the Church would be freer and would be able to complete more fully her mission. If Lamennais had limited himself to making a distinction between an ideal order (whose model was found in the past) and a concession to the concrete situations, he would perhaps not have suffered the attacks and condemnations which fell upon him. But this distinction was not the essence of his thought. Consequently, his ideas received clear reprobation from Pope Gregory XVI.

The confidence in individual liberty is not an isolated element in Lamennais' thought. His political position can be seen clearly when certain unfortunate, time-bound expressions are removed. Though following very different routes, Lamennais arrived at conclusions closely related to the contemporary theological situation. This is particularly the case in regard to his perception of the relationship of the person to the truth which is of central importance in questions of religious liberty.[53]

He appeared to his contemporaries to be a Christian apologist, as he published between 1817 and 1823 the four volumes of his *Essai sur l'indifference en matière de religion*.

This work, whose first volume had notable success is a refutation of the indifferentism of Rousseau and others whose works dealt with the destruction of religion and of society. Lamennais opposes the authority of reason which claims to be the judge of truth and falsehood. In order to know what is true we should not consult individual reason but rather human tradition which will give us what we have always believed to be true. This is what has been called Lamennais' theological traditionalism.[54]

According to Lamennais, by consulting the universal tradition we can prove that persons always have believed in the great religious truths: knowledge of the one God, father of all that exists, the existence of divine law, the immortality of the soul, the need for expiation.[55] Tradition has preserved all these truths.[56] This permits him to affirm that "Christians believe all that the human species believed before Jesus Christ, and the human species believed all that Christians believe."[57] The consequence of this is that persons have always found around them what is necessary to keep them from "leaving the path which leads to the eternal goods."

But this is not valid only for humanity before Christ. It continues to be valid even after his coming: "All true faith is part of the Christian faith. The nations which have not been reached by Christian preaching have their own duties; and if they fulfill those duties they are acting as Christians."[58]

In a polemic with Rousseau who stated in *Emile* that according to Christianity persons who had not heard evangelical preaching were condemned, Lamennais answered:

> Who told this sophist that a person will be condemned for not believing in mysteries which he could not know? . . . A good person . . . who searches for truth will not be condemned . . . and will be saved in Christianity. This is so because whoever has not heard evangelical preaching and believes in the dogmas of universal tradition, believes implicitly everything that we believe. It is not faith which is lacking, rather a developed teaching. The person is Christian.[59]

Although it was not often that someone affirmed the possibility of salvation outside the Church, it was not new in the nineteenth century. But what is important is that for Lamennais, persons can have access to *salvific truth* through universal tradition. Religious truths are scattered in humanity. This makes him look on the movement of history with great optimism and confide finally in liberty as a means of discovering truth.

It would not come within the scope of our work to go further into the study of this aspect of Lamennais' work. It will suffice to point out that contact with the non-Christian world, both in Lamennais' case and in the first centuries, gave an awareness to God's action in the world beyond the Church boundaries. There is no doubt that Lamennais expressed himself with ambiguity on these points, for his ties with traditionalist thinking weigh upon his outlook. However, it is not our place to judge, and it suffices to show the relationship which exists between his philosophical and theological concepts and his political doctrine; that is, between his ideas on the presence of elements of salvific truth in the history of humanity and his affirmations concerning the goodness of a regime based on modern liberties. This relationship confirms and explains why along with a position which will soon be considered "traditional" and which distinguishes between an ideal social order inspired by Christianity, more or less bound to historical models and an acceptance of the present situation, we find in Lamennais the project of a new political order based on liberty desired for itself and considered as something good and not a lesser evil.[60] The unity of theological and political aspects in his works gave Lamennais a tremendous influence on Catholic thought in the nineteenth century.

The liberal Catholic.   The attempts simply to restore the old regime failed in Europe. The old monarchies were forced to reconciliation with the new bourgeois class and with their ideological doctrine. There are many reasons for this, but especially important is the pressure of the popular socialist movements. This pressure leads to alliances among social classes which, in spite of their mutual contradictions, form the dominant sector of society.

Liberal Catholicism recruits its members from the most advanced sectors of the aristocracy and from bourgeois society. Their openness to a democratic regime does not prohibit many of them from holding clearly conservative positions as regards the social movements of the nineteenth century.[61] However, their conflict with the most reactionary sections of the Church led them to be considered a progressive group. In spite of their past difficulties, this group continued looking for a reconciliation of the Church with the regime of modern liberties. The members of the group were encouraged by the concessions which the bourgeois governments were prepared to make to religion in the wake of the popular and revolutionary movements of 1848 in France, Germany, and Italy. The period which extends from "Mirari Vos" (1832) to the "Syllabus" (1864) brought to light the urgency of formulating a doctrine taking into account the different aspects of the question: pontifical teaching, the politics of the Holy See, the persistence of liberal ideas in Catholic circles, the intransigency of certain groups which are strongly bound to "traditional" principles, and the necessity of dialogue with modern society. Gregory XVI harshly condemned Lammenais' ideas. His collaborators and sympathizers were obliged to use more prudent language and to make careful distinctions, but the two lines which we recognized in Lamennais emerge once again.

Bishop Parisis, bishop of Laggres and one of the dominant figures of the French episcopacy in the middle of the nineteenth century wrote his famous "Cases of Conscience" (Paris, 1847). "In the present circumstances, when all has been considered, our modern liberal institutions are the best for the State and for the Church, the best for morality and the best for the faith, for public order and for the liberty of each one."[62] This concession to "present circumstances" is based upon a series of considerations which seek to eliminate or soften the resistance in Christian circles to liberal ideas.

Lacordaire expresses a similar line of thought. In recalling the condemnation of "L'Avenir" he wrote to a friend that this was due to the defense therein of modern liberties which Rome took in an *absolute sense*, and not in the *relative sense* which, in spite of imprudence in language, the authors always wanted to defend.[63] This justification of the thesis, defended by "L'Avenir," does not reflect completely what the review was proposing, but without doubt it does express Lacondaire's ideas. As a matter of fact, similar types of distinctions can be found in many of his writings. In spite of this, there are texts in which the regime of liberties is seen with greater sympathy and more positively. However, this point of view is not so elaborated and is found more often at the level of what Lamennais called "the sentiment of liberty" than at the level of a coherent doctrine.

Charles de Montalembert had been one of the closest disciples of Lamennais, and he strongly regretted his departure from the Church. In 1852, he published "Catholic interest in the nineteenth century." His thesis is that the situation of Catholicism is very favorable and that this is due in large part to the regime of liberty which is beginning to reign in the world. However, he clarifies this by noting that by the defense of modern liberties he does not intend to profess *"an absolute theory"* which would be universally applicable to all centuries and to all peoples. "I only intend," he added, "that in the greater part of Christian peoples, given the present state of the world, liberty is a good, a relative, not absolute good."[64] This distinction is similar to the one Parisis made, which makes some of the ideas acceptable.

But this distinction does not express all of Montalembert's thought. For him, liberty is human progress and its installation is favorable to the life of the Church. This distinguished politician of the Second Empire writes that where absolute power reigns, the Church loses force, but on the other hand, "by some marvelous secret of divine mercy," where liberty rules, "it has always been fruitful for truth, that is to say for the Church."[65] Liberty and truth appear as united and favorable to each other.

The famous speeches in the Catholic Congress of Malinas in 1863 were Montalembert's occasion to reaffirm brilliantly his faith in freedom, and to leave what he called "my political testimony." Montalembert considered the State "which is completely incompetent in matters of religious doctrine, to be obliged to protect me in the practice of the truth which I have chosen." It is, therefore, obliged to establish the freedom of cult, to guarantee religious liberty "for groups, associations, and the churches." However, the incompetence of civil power is not due only to passing circumstances. It is a question of principle: "The State, generally incompetent to judge cults and religious opinions, is the competent judge in what concerns public peace and public customs." Under those conditions the old regime in addition to having "a defect is dead, and this is of capital importance. Nowhere will it be resurrected." It is a type of society which must be rejected because "it did not admit civil equality, nor political freedom, nor freedom of conscience"; that is to say, the same values which Montalembert set out to defend in his speeches. A second line of thought, which we find since Lamennais, inspires these speeches. A faulty sketch is made of the distinction between "absolute theory and the present state of affairs." A paragraph almost at the end of the speech sums up clearly his position:

> It is before all else equally important to me that I not be suspected of any complicity with any of those who only accept the new freedom as a passing evil and whose ideal would be to return to a world that has disappeared, under the wings of an orthodox Caesar to whom all would be permitted.[66]

Rome's reaction to these speeches was, as we might expect, unfavorable.[67] It is interesting for us to underline one of the basic reasons of this attitude. In a letter to Montalembert, Werner de Merode tells him of an audience that he had with Pius IX on November 28, 1863. "Not all that he said can be accepted," the Pope was supposed to have confided in talking about the speeches. Merode then defended his friend and relative saying that he only wanted to speak "about civil liberty, political tolerance, and in no way about dogmatic indifference." The Pope responded by accepting that the speaker might have made such a distinction, but he also pointed out the true motive for his reproach: "Oh, on this matter there is nothing to say, but my dear friend, it is a sin not to believe that outside the Church there is no salvation."[68]

For the Pope this was the heart of the question, and this is important for us. The accusation surprised Montalembert and he tried in vain to defend himself saying that "I have not said one word which could be interpreted as a negation of that dogma." The perspectives were different. The Catholic liberals, politicians rather than theologians, did not see clearly the doctrinal consequences which the theology of the times would find in their defense of modern society. We have already seen that for the Popes and Roman theologians, what was fundamental was that the Catholic Church possessed salvific truth and that civil power, which directly supported the Church's mission, aided persons in fulfilling their eternal vocation. Otherwise, by permitting the propagation of error, persons would be led to their perdition. It was not enough to have explicitly rejected religious indifferentism. The Pope did not deny Montalembert's good faith, but to want to change a social order which was in conformity with religious truth was "to believe that persons can be saved outside the Church." This "sin" was deduced from the whole of Montalembert's affirmations. It was implicitly contained in them.

The repercussions of the Malinas speeches hastened events. The Pope believed himself obliged to make a solemn condemnation in the style of Gregory XVI. But the times had changed. The encyclical, "Quanta Cura," and the added "Syllabus" provoked even more violent reactions than the Malinas speeches, but in the opposite camp. The hour had rung for the half solutions which try to reconcile both extremes and to calm the unrest on both sides. The distinction between thesis and hypothesis presented in systematic form between the Malinas speeches and the "Syllabus" seems to have been intended for this purpose.

Thesis and hypothesis. The discrediting of the once famous distinction between thesis and hypothesis can make us forget that it expressed a good part of the Church's practice in confronting liberalism. And it can also make us forget that for many years it was presented as the traditional doctrine on the question. Indeed, this distinction is simply a prolongation of the old scheme of tolerance which later was backed by the pontifical Magistry: Leo XIII and his immediate successors.

The distinction between thesis and hypothesis was first presented in an article published in the Roman review, *La Civiltá Cattolica.* The author[69] beginning with Montalembert's speeches sets out to find a formula to overcome the division of Catholics into "integrists" and "liberals." Actually, his deepest concern is to return Catholic liberals to a greater fidelity to Rome at a time when political conditions make it urgent to unite all Catholics.

The thesis is that civil power should serve religious truth, reflecting the union of nature and grace. "This is the thesis, the universal doctrine which responds to the intrinsic nature of things and consequently to the sovereign ordinance of the Creator." However, it is not simply a question of an ideal. This type of society existed. It was society's own state, the true state as God made it and as Christ remade it. Really, the thesis is not only a universal doctrine. It is also a past historical era inspired by Christian principles, the old regime. On account of all this, "the reasons for the existence of the so-called liberties should be considered highly lamentable."

We go from the thesis to the hypothesis when instead of considering things in themselves as they should be in the divine ordering, we take into account, "how things are presented due to the intervention of fortuitous circumstances which are often culpable and always lamentable, particularly in certain peoples and in a few countries." If they have fallen into this situation, "it is indubitable that Catholics consider it a distinct advantage for them that the government concede equal liberty for all without distinction of good or evil, truth or error." In order to justify this the author, without quoting Thomas Aquinas, calls upon the classic principle of the higher good to be obtained and the greater evil to be avoided. It is, therefore, a question of civil tolerance. This situation makes a regime of liberties legitimate but not legal. This last adjective is merited only by governments which conform to the thesis.

The author ends by summing up his position. Speaking on the level of truth, he affirms the value of the Christian system, he accepts wholly the sovereign Pontiff's teaching on this matter, he respects the Christian past, and he repeats what in principle should be the role of civil power in the defense of the true religion and in the repression of error. But at the same time, on the practical level, the author takes into account the "system of modern liberties," the new society, the adverse circumstances which impede the realization of the Christian ideal, and he accepts that political authority should tolerate error as the lesser evil.

There are basically three assertions which constitute the tripod which supports this distinction: only the religious truth which the Church holds has any rights in society. Civil power has the function of protecting truth and repressing error. Error can be tolerated by political authority in view of obtaining a greater good or avoiding evil.

Therefore, even though the hypothesis is extended throughout much of the world, the principles will never change. The thesis justifies itself because it is derived from the ultimate reason of things, and its validity is not subject to the aberrations of the times. It is all a matter of not making the hypothesis into the thesis, of not making what is useful into truth as liberal Catholics have a tendency to do. As a consequence, the author ends his article expressing again his conciliating soul:

These simple and loyal considerations can be taken into account and considered just by some of the strayed Catholics from beyond the hills which we hold in highest esteem. For these persons, we only want to give praise for the great services they have given the Church and to encourage them to give her even greater services. [70]

Classical doctrine.   The repercussions of the encyclical "Quanta Cura" and of the "Syllabus of Modern Errors" are well known. There were energetic reactions from different European governments. And in intellectual spheres this was a confirmation that the Church was an institution of the past. As a result there was suffering on the part of many Catholics who faced this break with the modern world. In Rome itself, these reactions caused concern. The interpretation, however, given to the acts of Pius IX by the Bishop of Orleans, Mons. Dupaulop, alleviated the situation. [71] This interpretation fell back on the distinction between principles and concrete situations.

Leo XIII assumed this distinction explicitly. He never uses the terms thesis and hypothesis, but the idea is clearly present.

If it is certain that the Church judges it to be illicit for the diverse forms of divine cult to enjoy the same right as the true religion, nonetheless, she does not condemn for this reason those governments which in order to reach some good or to avoid an important evil tolerate by use and habit that these different forms take place in the State. [72]

The Thomist schema of tolerance was certainly used and extended to different cults, including those which are dissident to Christian faith. For Leo XIII, the ideal continued to be state religion. Civil power should be at the service of religious truth, and its action favored the Church's salvific task. Modern liberties, the basis of what the Pope calls "the new right," put this in danger.

As regards the so-called *liberties* invented in these very new times, it is necessary to hold to the judgments of the Apostolic See, and what it feels everyone else should feel. Take care that honest appearances do not deceive, and rather think what principles (these liberties) have and with what intentions they are correctly sustained and fomented. [73]

They can only be accepted in situations in which it is impossible to achieve the ideal.

Therefore, Leo XIII adopted, even though reluctantly, one of the liberal Catholic lines of thought, the one that considers the regime of liberties as the lesser evil. Leo XIII's teaching partially achieved what the author of the article in *La Civiltá Cattolica* proposed: a certain understanding between Catholic groups which up until that moment had been harshly confronting each other. In addition, the Holy See had other concerns: the political unity of Italy, the temporal power of the Popes, and the socialist movement. Leo XIII changes politics, a change which was seen in his effort, within very traditional molds, to make more precise the sense of "true liberty."[74] This change involves attempts to distinguish the sphere of civil society from religious society, to take into account the social problems of the nineteenth century, and to reaffirm the principle of authority on the civil and religious levels. These interests and efforts make his political doctrine an organic body inspired by neothomism which is imposed as the particular Church philosophy. In spite of an enthusiastic response to this political doctrine from those of an authoritarian and conservative bent, it was a realistic position strongly supported on solid doctrinal grounds.[75]

Since Leo XIII, the distinction between thesis and hypothesis has been converted into a "classical doctrine," as regards the theme of religious liberty. Theologians and canonists dissertate on account of it. Popes, such as Pius X, support it from more conservative positions. It inspired concordates which the Holy See celebrated during the first half of the twentieth century. However, the lack of confidence and the hostility of the modern world persisted even though moderately expressed. Many Christians continued to struggle for a more open position. Especially where the Protestants were minorities, the rigidity of this position in matters of religious liberty became a motive for hard and passionate confrontations.

C. THE CHURCH: DEFENDER OF MODERN FREEDOMS

The reasons which brought Leo XIII to this pragmatic position became even more urgent in the first decades of this century. Capitalism and liberalism, as political ideology, were check-mated by the increasing popular movement which, thanks to socialism, achieved a greater awareness of its force and historical possibilities. The war of 1914-1918 expressed a serious crisis for the dominant bourgeoisie in the warring countries. The war put an end to the "belle epoque" of the European bourgeois democracies. Those same years marked the birth of the first socialist experience in Russia, a country of complex social composition. And shortly after this, fascism began to materialize and threaten the liberties which the bourgeois ideology proclaimed.

The dominant bourgeoisie became increasingly ambiguous towards religion. Religion, and the aristocratic class which found its protection in religion, was no longer an important adversary. In principle, the liberal governments and parties maintained their demands: social individualism, the secular state, etc., but, in practice, they conceded much ground. Even though the difficulties with religion continued and at times became sharper, it was clear that there was a new enemy.

In addition, as time passed, certain distinctions, for example, between religious indifferentism and civil tolerance in religious matters, slowly began to gain a foothold. The social changes mentioned above influenced this process and strengthened the importance of that sector of the Church which was most alert and open to the ideas of the modern world.

1. Up to Vatican II

The "renovation of theology." It is a common practice to speak of "the renovation of theology" in the first half of the twentieth century.[76] The beginnings were not easy as the modernist crisis and the subsequent condemnations prove. In spite of this and other conflicts, such as those with the "new theology" around 1950, there was a real renovation. Actually, it was a matter of a moderate and partial assimilation of certain aspects of the modern spirit: a critical attitude, a sense of history, a scientific mentality, the value of subjectivity, a democratic spirit, appreciation of human progress, openness to contemporary philosophic currents, etc. All of this brought about biblical, patristic, liturgical, moral, dogmatic, and apologetic renovations, which sought to use modern language. However, for this very reason these attempts at renovation remained on the margin of the official teaching and were often rejected by it. Nonetheless, this renovated theology dominated Vatican II, and this is the cause of the progressive character which marked this great event of the Church.

Religious freedom. Progressive theology is very critical of the Church's official doctrine in the twentieth century regarding the theory of thesis and hypothesis, this by-product of the old doctrine of tolerance. One of the most significant criticisms concerns the so-called "rights of truth" which according to contemporary theologians reflects a mentality centered in *objectivity*.[77] In this context, it is held that faith is reasonable because the truths it believes in are objects of divine intelligence, and therefore must be the most reasonable truths that can be imagined. This same line of thinking even becomes the basis for respect for authority and tradition. The modern world, as we have already recalled, is marked by the discovery of *subjectivity*. This perspective creates a greater awareness of the concrete conditions of persons in their access to truth. It seems to be misleading to speak of the "rights of truth." Truth, as well as error, is an abstraction and can have no rights. Only the person is the subject of rights, and therefore, what is correct is to speak of a person's duty to respect and seek truth and of the right to risk making a mistake. From this point of view the old themes of freedom of the act of faith and false conscience will be reworked. The new mentality grounds itself on these themes in order to go further in the defense of personal freedom in religious matters.

Criticism of the confessional state opens up new paths of reflection. The confessional state is the product of the historical events of the fourth century, more the work of Theodosius than of Constantine. The modern state, which affirms itself as lay, attacks the confessional state which the doctrine of tolerance defended. Progressive theology joins the attack. M.D. Chenu and Y. Congar offer a subtle criticism of the mentality of Christendom, and in well known writings they proclaim the end of this mentality. Jacques Maritain incorporates certain of the ideas which we called the second current of Catholic liberalism into a political philosophy which is based on the renovation of Thomism which was called for by Leo XIII. From this point, Maritain champions the creation of a "profane Christendom" which will take into account some aspects of the contemporary democratic situation. John C. Murray, familiar with the United States' experience, distinguishes between cult and service of God. The cult presupposes an act of faith which is impossible for the "complex of institutions" which make up the state. The service of God, if interpreted as respect for the law of God and for the Church's rights, is a duty for the state which it will fulfill to the extent that it is faithful to its own mission.[78] These efforts to elaborate a new doctrine in religious matters is in accordance with the great demands of the bourgeois revolution in the latter part of the eighteenth century. It will be insisted that it is not enough to speak of a distinction between two powers within the same society as was the case in the Middle Ages. It will be said that it is necessary to go further and to distinguish two *societies*: civil and religious.[79] The task of political power is reduced to the goals of civil society, and religious truth does not enter the field of politics.

The "sacrament of the neighbor."   The awareness that it was necessary to rethink the great theological themes from the perspective of modern mentality influenced the old question of the so-called "salvation of the infidels." After the pat doctrine that "outside the Church there is no salvation," new questions were raised as a result of the internal breakup of Christendom and the discovery of new peoples in the sixteenth century. From that time on, one theological theory followed another, trying to explain these new situations. This was a painful effort to take into account the salvific status of religious persons who do not belong to the Church, broadening and making more flexible the old theological schema without breaking it.

Some of the theologians attentive to the theme of religious liberty also take up the problem of the salvation of infidels. This is the case, for example of Y. Congar who takes a decisive step in asking the question about the salvation of atheists. Within the modern mentality it is really the non-believer who poses the most radical problems.[80] The path which Congar indicates signifies a break with the doctrine which began with the concept that "outside the Church there is no salvation." All who generously love their neighbors are saved. The "sacrament of the neighbor" is as valid for the non-Christian as for the Christian.[81] Although Congar himself does not explicitly link his position in this matter with his defense of religious liberty, the mutual influence is clear—as we have found on various occasions.[82]

The pontifical teaching.   The modern world and its democratic and liberal demands are felt in a more moderate form in the pontifical teaching than in the theology of the period.

Beginning with Pius XI and Pius XII we have a more constructive language concerning some of the conflictive points debated in the nineteenth century. Rather than complaints and condemnations it is a question of positive expositions concerning the Christian doctrine of society and freedom. However, the Popes take up again the condemning language in reference to totalitarian doctrines among which communism is considered in a special manner.

Pius XI made an important distinction in recognizing a difference between a legitimate "freedom of conscience" and a less acceptable "freedom of conscience," displayed by "an absolute independence of conscience, something absurd in souls which were created and redeemed by God."[83] Even though at times the emphasis of the defense of the "freedom of consciences" seems to be on religious freedom for Catholics alone, at other times the argument goes further and is demanded as a right of the human person.[84]

Both Popes clearly affirm the distinction between Church and state. The latter has its own mission which "certainly is not limited to the corporal and material but is limited to the boundaries of the natural, earthly and temporal."[85] Political power cannot force anyone in matters of faith. "Conscience escapes the power of the State."[86] Both Popes insist more on the penetration of Christian principles in temporal society than on the duty of civil authorities to render public homage to God.[87] This is the origin of the role given to the Christian laity in the construction of a social order impregnated with Christian values.[88]

These positions express a greater openness to the modern spirit. However, in the last analysis, the schema of tolerance is not abandoned. On the contrary, in a famous speech Pius XII took up the schema again and placed it in an international context which led to greater flexibility. In this the Pope recalled that only the truth and the moral law "objectively have the right to existence, to propaganda and to action," but he maintained that the duty to suppress religious and moral deviations "should be subordinated to the highest and most general norms which in certain situations permit that error not be prevented in order to promote a greater good."[89]

With John XXIII a new language began which culminated in Vatican II. The encyclical "Pacem in Terris" spoke of the human person's rights as springing "immediately and simultaneously from the same nature," and consequently, they are "universal, inviolable, inalienable." The distant echoes of the declaration of the Rights of Man in the French Revolution, and the recent influence of the declaration of human rights in the United Nations are easily perceived. Among the proclaimed rights is that which concerns religious questions. The encyclical claims "that cult can be given to God according to the correct norm of one's own conscience and that religion can be privately and publicly professed." The distinction which the Pope established between "historical movements" and the "ideologies" that accompanied them greatly influenced the debates of that period in Vatican Council II.[90]

2. Vatican Council II and the modern world

Openness to dialogue.   John XIII's great intuition in calling the Council was that which he described with an image: to shake off the imperial dust. The hostility toward the modern world which began in the sixteenth century and which reached a high point in the eighteenth century had kept the Church in the sphere of the empire, in the world of Christendom. The challenges of the modern spirit were more an occasion for pulling back rather than one for finding new ways of preaching the gospel. Vatican II tried to respond to the great questions of the moment brought about by the modern liberties and the Enlightenment which we pointed out at the beginning of this chapter. These changes seemed to be an urgent necessity for those Christians in countries ruled by the old revolutionary social class, the bourgeoisie, which brought about the ideology of the modern times (Central Europe, the United States). They regarded them as merely making up for lost time. It is not surprising that these same changes seemed to be a dangerous novelty for those who did not have the same historical experience (Spain, Italy, the Roman Curia). This also explains the presence of what was called a majority and a minority. The latter dominated in the preparation of the schemas before the Council began, but it lost ground during the conciliar debates. Its force was in the coherence of a theology built up throughout the centuries and accustomed to defending itself against the "modern ideas." Its weakness rested in its being out of phase with contemporary society.

The constitution of the Church in the world (originally not foreseen) presents a new perspective on the Church's action. This is an optimistic vision of the world, its progress, its science and technology, and its freedom. This vision is accompanied by the affirmation that these values, however good they might be, do not reach fullness unless they are related to the Christian message. The constitution recognizes the presence of atheism in the world today, but it points out the Christians' responsibility in this matter, and it calls for the collaboration of believers and non-believers in the "just construction of this world in which they live in common." In this world which is distinct from the Church but not necessarily hostile to it, the Lord of history is present and active, and from this world he also calls the Christian community to a greater fidelity to the gospel. In this world the Church should fulfill its mission as the "universal sacrament of salvation."

The great demands of modern times are taken up with moderation: the rights of the human person, the values of subjectivity, freedoms, social equality, and the sense of human progress. On the other hand social conflicts are only treated in the general terms of the presence of misery and injustice in the world. Even though the individualistic root of bourgeois society is maintained at a distance, there is no serious criticism of the importance in our days of the domination monopolistic capitalism exercises over the popular classes, especially those of poor peoples. The Council's concern was different; we are in the hour of dialogue with the modern world. The fact that society is not a united whole but is full of conflicts among social classes is something that is out of the field of vision.

Freedom and universal salvation. The declaration concerning religious freedom provided an atmosphere for dialogue with the modern world. It was the most controversial and most arduously debated document in the Council. In the preparatory stages it had two sections dealing with the subject. One represents unchanged, as if nothing had occurred in history, the doctrine of tolerance and marks a continuity with the position of the Popes in the nineteenth century, including a careful elaboration of Leo XIII. One text validates the rights of religious truth.[91] The other responds, not without ambivalences, to the contemporary mentality within the perspective of religious liberty. It underlines the values of human subjectivity.[92] The second text was the true point of departure for the document we now have. It sprang up in the interior of ecumenism, marked by the history of the old religious conflicts and the struggle for liberty on the part of Christian minorities. However, little by little, this text opens up to a more ample problem: the right of every person to freedom in religious matters.[93] Those opposed to the schema champion the right of religious truth. For them the affirmation of freedom in these questions seems to deny Christian revelation and to endanger the salvation of persons. The defenders of the text sought to avoid these objections by remaining on a merely juridical level.[94] This helped to calm the passions in the irritating debate inasmuch as it was easy to distinguish the essential issue from the accessories. However, the conciliar "minority" was very lucid in perceiving that its theological vision of salvation did not coincide with the underlying matter of the schema on freedom in religious matter.[95]

Indeed, it would have been difficult to approve the declaration, if at the same time, changes had not been made in the way of understanding the salvific work of Christ in history. The doctrine of tolerance is based on a theology of salvation which the Council abandoned. The advances of progressive theology just before the Council are expressed directly in the constitution on the Church. In this constitution the possibility of salvation, and access to religious truth, outside the visible Church are affirmed in an argument developed in graded steps which recalls the concentric circles of the encyclical "Ecclesiam Suam." In addition, the same attempt to answer the questions of the modern spirit is found in different ways in other conciliar documents and affirmations.

What has been said up until now will permit us to understand easily that the Council denies political power all intervention in religious matters. The affirmation of its incompetency joins the best of Christian tradition before the time of Constantine. In the declaration on freedom in religious matters, there is no mention of duties towards religious truth, rather the document speaks of respect for the right of all citizens to religious freedom (notes 3 & 6). The confessional state is seen as an exception, a product of definite historical circumstances, and even in this case a respect for religious freedom is imposed. In addition, this doctrine on the incompetence of political power in this matter[96] is situated within an important change of perspective. Traditionally, these questions were treated at the level of the relation between political and ecclesiastical powers, between Church and state. This is what one of the preparatory schemas did. The Council had another view of things, and this was evident in the declaration. For the Council, it was more a matter of considering the relation between two societies: civil and ecclesiastical. It spoke more of temporal, civil, political societies, etc., than of power. This manner of considering things is not strange to the modern distinction between society and state just as it is not strange either to the fact that the Christian community maintains a presence in society, even where it has lost its presence on the level of political power.[97]

D. THE CHALLENGES OF MODERN TIMES

The adherents of the type of theology which was prevalent at the time of Vatican II tried, with partial and moderate success, to respond to the big questions which had sprung from the Enlightenment and from the movement for human liberties. Post-conciliar theology seeks to take up the questions which were left unanswered. Or, more exactly, it tries to take into account the radicalness of the Enlightenment's questioning and of the social history of liberty. It also tries to take into account the present situation because we are faced with an on-going process.[98] This theology wants to go to the very roots of the matter and to accept directly the challenge of modern thought, something which the Council did not and could not do.[99]

1. *How to speak of God in an adult world*

Few perceived and expressed better this challenge than that great Lutheran theologian, Dietrich Bonhoeffer. For this reason, he is situated in a tradition historically linked to the birth of the modern spirit, and he is attentive to the questioning of the society which springs up with the scientific advances, the bourgeois economy and politics. Also his thinking is done within classic German philosophy. Bonhoeffer formulates his incisive question: how does one speak about God in an adult world? This is the question of a Christian who wants to communicate his faith, and therefore, it is a radically theological question which has brought about the most important theology in the last years.

For Bonhoeffer, that adult world is the stage of the majority of age to which humanity has arrived through a long process. He writes:

> The movement towards human autonomy (that is to say, the discovery of the laws according to which the world lives and is self-sufficient in the domains of science, of social and political life, of art, of ethics and of religion) which begins in the thirteenth century . . . has reached a certain maturity in our days. The human being has learned to confront all the important questions without relying on the hypothesis of God. [100]

The Enlightenment, according to the famous definition of Kant, had already placed us in this adult world. Bonhoeffer explicitly refers to this moment and thinks that for the believer the leaving of the minority of ages is a necessary condition for "finding God in what we know and not in which we are ignorant. God wants to be understood not in questions without answer but rather in those which have been resolved."[101] Bonhoeffer says that it is necessary to preach God, not in moments of weakness for the human being, but rather in moments of strength, where the human being's critical reason and creative liberty are affirmed.

This leads Bonhoeffer to champion an "irreligious Christianity." The criticism which Barth had made of religion seems to Bonhoeffer to be insufficient because in Barth's theology, religion has been replaced by the "positivism of revelation" and has left the world to itself. Bultmann has not gone far enough. He has questioned the "mythological" notions, but it is also necessary to question the "religious notions." Beyond the question of salvation which has ceased to be important ("not the thing but the question" as Bonhoeffer will precisely point out) it is a matter of "this world: how was it created, maintained, ruled by laws, reconciled and renovated?" Bonhoeffer goes even further and asks, "Aren't justice and the Kingdom of God the center of everything?"[102] In these conditions, to live in a world without God means for the Christian to "participate in God's suffering."[103] In coming of age, we perceive our true situation before God: "before God and with God we live without God." Without the all-powerful God of religion and with the weak and suffering God of the biblical message:

> God lets himself be thrown from the world and crucified on the cross. God is powerless and weak in the world, and only in this way he is with us and helps us. Matthew 8:17 clearly indicated that Christ does not help us with his power but rather through his weakness and sufferings. [104]

This is what differentiates Christianity from other religions.

Bonhoeffer puts forward positions which are hardly even outlined, full of intuitions and which cannot be reduced to the theology of secularization. In spite of some initial confusion, the differences appear to be clear. Robinson's famous book *Honest to God* placed the interpretation of Bonhoeffer on a path which today is more and more abandoned. [105] Without doubt, this is one of the greatest efforts to assume the challenges of the adult world in the modern period, to ask oneself what it means to be a Christian in these conditions. "To ask oneself," indeed, because Bonhoeffer's reflections are almost reduced to this. But few let themselves be questioned by a world without God, and, therefore, few were able to formulate the questions with such sharpness or profundity.

2. *The new political theology*

There is an attempt being made to answer the questions raised by the world which has come of age. This attempt is on the part of Johannes B. Metz in the "new political theology" and the "political theology of hope" as Jürgen Moltmann likes to call it. [106] The problem of the Enlightenment and especially its critique of religion and society are the explicit point of departure for this valuable theological effort. [107] In a recent article Metz writes:

> The occasion for a new political theology grew out of the question concerning the possibility of a theology of the world in relation with the world of modern times, with its processes of Enlightenment, of secularization, and of emancipation. This question is definitely identical to the question concerning the very possibility of a theology and of the constitution of theological reason in connection with the world of modern times in general. This is the fundamental theological and theoretical place of the new political theology. [108]

The political theology is, indeed, a theology of the world. If theology is to take into account the modern mentality, and especially if it wants to be understood by this mentality, it must assume the form of political theology. Political theology restores the public meaning of Christian faith over against the privitization of the faith by the Church in its defense against the Enlightenment. However, this public character is not a rehabilitation of the old "political Catholicism,"[109] the theological expression of what Moltmann calls "political religion." The new political theology is presented more as a criticism of these positions, and perhaps it is the only effective and radical criticism. In order to be effective and radical, it seeks to situate itself, even if with independence, in the same process of the modern Enlightenment and modern emancipation.

Metz distinguishes three contemporary theologies of the world. The first is represented by the theology of secularization. In this perspective, theology, in confrontation with modern times, is possible because theology is perceived in its radical otherness in relation to the world. In this point of view, faith is bound to this world only through the fact of having contributed historically to the world's becoming conscious of its own reality. For Metz, such theology makes the faith private, and initiates the dissolution of theological reason. For Metz, this theology has a predilection for the "doctrine of two kingdoms."[110] The second theology of the world represents the new version of "liberal theology." This theology is marked with an uncritical conformism to today's world. It considers as Christian what the modern spirit considers rational. This identification, which is purely apologetical, leads just as well to the "autodissolution of theological reason into the emancipatory and abstract reason of the modern times." Here, faith has no critical function vis-à-vis the anthropological model which considers the human being as "the dominating subject of nature." Human realities such as suffering, play, joy are left aside.

Between these two theologies of the world, political theology is presented as "an attempt to express Christianity's eschatological message in relation to the modern times as a figure of critical-practical reason." Therefore, it interprets Christianity as a dangerous reminder of freedom within the processes of modern times. Just like the theology of secularization, and the new liberal theology, Metz affirms his intentions to assimilate and take into account the advances and questions of the modern spirit, but he tries to do this critically. He does this for two reasons: (1) because the process itself of emancipation, Enlightenment and secularization has an internal dialectic which must be kept in mind, and (2) because the Christian message is critical and freeing and can only be proclaimed publicly. In this way, theology will help critical reason become practical reason. And this is the fundamental step in the process of Enlightenment. Metz, therefore, comes to say that political theology seeks to express the Christian-theological version of practical reason in relation to modern times.

To recuperate this dangerous critical-freeing reminder fulfills "the old and always new task of the Christian message: to speak of God." And this must be done as Bonhoeffer demanded, in a way that is intelligible to persons today. As Bonhoeffer also insinuated with his theme of God's weakness, it is a matter of the reminder of the message of salvation, pardon and reconciliation in Jesus Christ, "a message made public in the death on the cross."[111] However, the cross expresses here Jesus' mortal conflict with the political powers of his times. The crucified is the foundation of the liberation of persons through faith and hope. The cross unmasks all political idolatry, and it takes from those who hold power their justification from "on high." Beginning from this point, Metz has exploited a very rich vein for theology. According to him, death and resurrection are accessible through narration.[112] Narrative language should also be that which brings to memory the suffering of persons, of the poor of this world. Theology and theologians have been far from that suffering of the people and they should "allow themselves to be interrupted by the mute suffering of a people."[113]

In this way, political theology seeks to confront the questions of the modern history of freedom, of the Enlightenment, of the critique of religion in Marxism. It is a new type of fundamental theology. Placing itself critically within the modern spirit it demands a public presence of the Christian message. The public character had only been known in the form of the precritical "political Catholicism," which, therefore, was unable not only to speak to today's world but also to rethink its own Christian faith and concept of the Church.[114] This inability is what led to making the faith private (liberal theology, theology of secularization, etc.). Beginning with greater attention to the claims of bourgeois society, those theologies had accepted the confines of this society: the sphere of the private. This meant renouncing the dimensions of faith which political theology takes up in a new mentality giving full value to the critical dimension of the gospel message. In this way, the message is made to play a part in the process of modern liberties.

Likewise, the new political theology is situated in an original and fruitful way in the path opened up by what was called "humanity's majority of age." However, this theological perspective begins to be sensitive to the perspectives of liberation theology even though it still does so with a certain uneasiness.[115] Perhaps this initial theological effort comes from another perspective and not only from another perspective, but also from a contradiction of the dominating elements of the process described in this chapter.

Three

Freedom and Liberation

For the incipient bourgeois society which came to life in the cities of the feudal world the discovery of new worlds in the fifteenth and sixteenth centuries constituted a decisive factor in the development of the mercantile capitalist mode of production of the following centuries. The participation of the first representatives of this capitalism in the conquest and colonization of the West Indies is well known.

For western Christendom, the encounter with the American Indian posed a series of new problems in which the religious and political spheres were strongly intertwined. The old categories of Christendom were questioned by the impact of the "other" of the western world, the Indian. This disturbing discovery of the "other" has continued. Today we clearly perceive that what represented a movement for freedom for Europeans and North Americans was a new and more refined form of exploiting the poor, "the condemned of the earth." For them, freedom will come when liberation from despoilment and oppression is carried out in the name of "modern freedoms and democracy." In this process of liberation the faith lives among the poor of this world; and from there a theological reflection expresses itself—a reflection that does not want to be a slave to those sufferings. This theology refuses to give itself over to the dominating ideology, and increasingly breaks with the dominant, conservative, or progressive theologies.

A. GOSPEL PREACHING AND THE INDIAN

The conquest and colonization of the continent which Columbus discovered quickly came to be considered missionary work.[1] The famous and disputed bulls of Alexander VI granted the new territories, just

60

months after their discovery, to the kings of Spain making them "Lords of these Lands with free, full and absolute power, authority and jurisdiction." This was done in order that the peoples that live there "receive the Christian religion."[2] The salvation of these infidels through their incorporation into the Church was the recognized motive for Spain's work in America. The religious motivation not only justified, but also judged, the colonial enterprise. This double function was at the center of what is called "The Controversy of the Indies." Two groups were visible: those who defended the work of colonization and those who denounced it as an injustice to the Indians. Between these two groups there were many middle positions. Bartolomé de Las Casas (1474-1566) was the most well known name of those who, from the point of view of the gospel and of the poor denounced the conquest and the colonization of the Indias.

1. "On the only way to bring all peoples to the true religion"

This is the title of one of Bartolomé de Las Casas' important works in which he presents a thesis which he himself summarizes as follows:

> Divine Providence established for the whole world and for all times the one, same and only way to teach people the true religion, that is, the persuasion of the understanding through reasoning and through inviting them and the gentle moving of the will. Undoubtedly this concerns a manner which should be common to all peoples of the world, without distinction of sects, errors, corrupt customs.[3]

The perspective in which de Las Casas situated the task of evangelizing is clear in this text. Throughout his life he insisted upon the persuasive methods as a demand of the faith. However, this was only a vague and general statement without consideration of the concrete conditions of evangelization in the Americas.

Salvation and justice. The Spain which came to America in the sixteenth century was the Spain of medieval Christendom. Therefore, the new missionary event was approached with the salvation theology of the times. According to this theology the infidels could only be assured of their eternal destiny by incorporating themselves into the Church. Otherwise, they were destined to perdition. This theology explains a good part of the missionary zeal of the sixteenth century, both in America and elsewhere.

Bartolomé de Las Casas, like many other missionaries who defended the Indians, does not escape this mentality. Without knowledge of divine things, he wrote, "it is impossible to be saved."[4] This was one of his motives in bringing accusations against the colonizers for their despicable conduct in driving the Indians away from the Christian faith. The salvation of the Indians in America, conceived in basically traditional terms, was the great concern of his life, the motive for his missionary effort. Even though at times de Las Casas seemed to question the orthodox position on the salvation of the infidels[5] it was not his main contribution.

Yet Bartolomé de Las Casas followed a new and fruitful path when he insisted that social justice was one of the demands of the gospel. Justice for de Las Casas was closely bound to salvation. The covetousness and thirst for gold of the conquerors and colonizers led them to exploit the Indians iniquitously. This behavior condemned to failure any attempt at evangelizing. Throughout his life, Farther Bartolomé denounced the unheard of injustice of which the Indians were victims. In one of his last works he considered this situation to be "much more unjust and more cruel than that which the Jews suffered when oppressed by the Pharaoh."[6] Gospel preaching was in vain without the testimony of a life committed to justice. It was a matter of the Christian message's credibility.

There was a second reason for linking salvation to justice. The Spaniards' own salvation depended upon their behavior towards the Indian. If they did not stop robbing, plundering, and exploiting the Indians, without doubt they wre condemned "because no one can be saved without observing justice."[7] Father Bartolomé did not confront the problem of the salvation of the infidels theoretically; he did so from his experience, "the mother of all things."[8] His questioning came from what he saw and heard in America. This allowed him to put his finger in the wound: the infidels' salvation depended upon the "salvation" of the faithful, of those who claim to be Christians. And not only did they claim to be Christians, but they also justified their crimes and injustices by pretending to evangelize and save the Indians. Bartolomé de Las Casas energetically denounced this lie. He wrote to the emperor:

> It is not true that they want to save and convert the Indians, rather they want to protect themselves in this in order to rob, despoil, oppress and enslave their neighbors. They do not want to save the Indians, nor preach the faith, nor do any other good.[9]

To do justice is a necessary condition for salvation and for preaching salvation. Bartolomé, a man of his times, accepted the traditional theological doctrine concerning salvation. What is particular to his thought in this matter is the strength of the link he establishes between salvation and justice. This came to him from having lived a long time in a continent where Christians were submitted to a systematic violation of the most elemental human rights. What happens is that even if de Las Casas sees the Indian as an *infidel*, a non-Christian, by preference he sees him as the *poor* of the gospel. This perspective was not present in the traditional theology, and it led him to make audacious statements like the one in the text sent to the emperor. De Las Casas denounced the ideological use made of the necessity to evangelize in order to cover up the injustices towards the Indians, and he said that it is not permitted "that they do evil in order to bring about good." He concludes by asserting that if death and destruction of the Indians were the condition for their becoming Christians it would be better that "they never be Christian."[10] In other words, he says that "a live Indian, even though infidel" is better than "a dead Indian even though Christian." Supernatural salvation cannot overlook social justice.

Tolerance and liberation. The traditional theological doctrine which we have referred to brings along with it an attitude of tolerating evil towards the non-Christian. In our first chapter we saw how this attitude of tolerance was susceptible to a rigid interpretation leading to the use of force to further the preaching of the faith.

The use of war in order to subdue and then evangelize the Indians was legitimated by many theologians of the conquest, and it became a permanent practice of the Europeans who arrived in the Indes. A curious text called *Requerimiento* (Demand), is one of the first attempts to justify theologically the use of force to preach the faith. It is concerned with a proclamation which should be read to the Indians. The text asserts the rights which the Pope granted to the Kings of Spain over the Indians, threatened the inhabitants of these lands with war if they would not accept the true faith and recognize the Spanish authorities. Whatever the scope of this document might be,[11] it expresses well the conquerors' practice.

Many of the missionaries claimed to be opposed to the use of force under the pretext of evangelizing. In the theological discussion, Thomas Aquinas' texts on infidelity played an important role. Bartolomé accepts the distinction between the two classes of infidelity, that of those who receive and later reject the faith, the heretics, and that of those who never received the faith, such as the Gentiles and the Jews. Bartolomé de Las Casas does not question the medieval intolerance towards heretics. He

accepts the traditional doctrine. He is concerned with the attitude towards the second type of infidel because this is the case of the Indians.
However, he does not limit himself to asking for the tolerance which
Thomas Aquinas recognized. More clearly than Thomas he demands the
use of persuasive method and pacifistic methods of evangelization. The
Indians should be seen not only as Christians but also as the poor of
the gospel.

In order to support his thesis on the use of pacifistic means of evangelization, de Las Casas tries to grasp the true sense of the kingdom of
Christ. The poor, humble, and pacifistic life which Christ chose gives
the key.

> The saints, and especially St. Thomas, indicate some of the foundations
> of this behavior. The first of these reasons is the following: to make
> known the difference which exists between Christ's dominion or prin-
> cipality and that of the earthly princes.

The kingdom of Christ is spiritual, of service. It leaves its subjects in the
greatest freedom and is orientated towards the salvation of souls. The
kingdom of the earthly princes is temporal, of power. It often seeks to
submit its subjects and is orientated towards transitory goods.[12] As Ruiz
Maldonado points out, this presentation of a poor Christ contrasts with
that which recognizes him as Lord of the universe and King of kings. It
puts in question the grounds for the temporal power of the papacy.[13]

Secondly, de Las Casas supports the rejection of war against the
Indians and revindicates the pacifistic methods of evangelization in
what he will call the "pristine freedom" of the inhabitants of the Indies.
In accordance with an old tradition, our author repeatedly insisted that
no one can be coerced into accepting the Christian faith. The gospel can
only be received freely.[14] However, according to de Las Casas, the
freedom of faith should be placed within the broader framework of the
freedom of every human being. Every human being is born free and with
the right to have his or her freedom respected. The peoples of the Indies
have the social organization which they have chosen, their political
leaders are legitimate and no one can question their authority. Bartolomé
argues untiringly along this line. In his testimony he asserts that the
Indians suffer slavery, oppression and tyranny "against all reason and
justice," and that it is necessary to give them back "their pristine freedom which has been unjustly taken from them and to free them from the
violent death which they still suffer."[15] The bishops of the Indies are
obliged by divine precept to insist before the Spanish authorities that

"they order the Indians who are held as slaves freed from the oppression and tyranny which they suffer and that they be returned to their pristine liberty. This should be done, if necessary, at the risk of lives."[16] Freedom in religious matter plants its roots in the free nature of the human being. In the condition of slavery and oppression in which the Indian lives there is no religious freedom possible, and therefore no authentic evangelization.

Salvation demands social justice. Evangelization presupposes the recognition of political freedom. This leads de Las Casas to a bitter criticism of the economic and social regime which Spain imposes on the Indians.

2. "Encomienda" and tyranny

Bartolomé de Las Casas did not limit himself to establishing the relation between salvation and justice or to supporting persuasive methods for evangelizing the Indians. He also energetically fought the social-economic system implanted in the Indies. His great life-long enemy was the *encomienda* (estates granted by the Spanish kings in America), a key piece to this system.[17] In the end, the *encomienda* defeated him. The ultimate reason for this struggle in the political field is already known to us: his concern for the preaching of the gospel and the salvation of the Indians.

Father Bartolomé rejects the very fact of the conquest.

> This term or name "conquest" used for all the lands and kingdoms of the Indies, discovered or to be discovered, is a terminology and vocabulary which is tyrannical, abusive, improper and infernal. The wars against the Indians are unjust because they have full right to live free and in peace on their lands. One should not speak of conquest but rather of preaching the faith, conversion and salvation.[18]

De Las Casas' objective is to suppress the *encomienda*. On one occasion he suggests to the emperor different "solutions" to the situation of the Indies. His eighth solution is the suppression of the *encomienda* which our author considers "the fundamental and most substantial solution because without this all the others would come to nothing since they are all ordered and directed toward this one as means to an end." The *encomienda* is contrary to all natural and divine law. "Indeed, the Indians should not be given to the Spaniards in estate . . . because they are free and have a natural freedom."[19] Bartolomé will repeat this in many different tones. He will take measures before different civil and religious authorities. He proposed manners of combating the *encomenderos*, polemicized against the theological justifications, carried out experiences of pacifistic evangelization, and wrote a treatise on the sacrament of confession in which he proposes that absolution only be given to the *encomenderos* if they return all they have robbed from the Indians. Until the end of his life he continued to insist that the *encomendero* is nothing but a thief and a tyrant.[20]

That tyranny of the *encomenderos* should be denounced and called by its name: "Will it be a lie, father, or a great sin to call these *encomenderos* by their proper name, tyrants?" This need to denounce became more urgent as the *encomenderos* looked for the religious who would preach the gospel without questioning the social-economic system which assured them their privileges. Bartolomé attacked them very strongly:

> And since the Indians know that their only protection is the friars, they confide in them. The friars cry out for justice or they write, and with all this some solutions are found and implemented although without advantage. All is a mockery . . . And the tyrants fight to keep the friars away from their peoples . . . And trying to fulfill the obligation to evangelize them without creating difficulties for himself, the tyrant takes a stupid clergyman and gives him 100 or 150 *castellanos*. And the clergyman, with the name and position of Father, commits a thousand abominations such as publicly selling the sacraments or giving them to him who most cruelly robs, afflicts, tyrannizes and threatens the Indians.[21]

We have already had a chance to see how the relation of salvation and freedom could not be considered outside a political context. The situation in the Indies of the sixteenth century confirms this conviction, but it is helpful to underline the fact that here the political perspective enters by a different door, that of the *poor* and *exploited*. This will bring about a different theological reflection.

3. *Theology of oppression and theology of liberation*

From the very beginning there was an effort to justify the conquest theologically. The *Requerimiento* marked the first formulation. In the debates which preceded the Burgos Laws of 1512, theological theses were considered concerning the rights of the Spanish kings over the Indies, the war previous to colonization and evangelization, and the human nature of the Indians.

Juan Ginez de Sepúlveda is the best representative in the mid-sixteenth century of the theology of conquest and colonization.[22] Bartolomé de Las Casas debated with him in an assembly invoked by Charles V in Valladolid in 1550. The central question of the debate was the following: was it legitimate for the Spanish king to conquer the Indians so that it would be easier to instruct them later in the faith? This polemic had been very much studied,[23] and our only interest is to bring out two points.

Sepúlveda's justifying argument has as its main point that the Indians are naturally servants, inferior to the Europeans who are their natural masters. This distinction into two classes of human beings is based on one of Aristotle's famous texts and on some texts of Thomas Aquinas concerning slavery which are not very clear. The submission of the Indians to the Spaniards is therefore according to human nature, and the wars to achieve this submission are fully justified. In addition, they are necessary in order to evangelize these crude peoples, barbarians with unnatural customs. All this is proposed with brilliant and abundant quotes and is presented as the traditional doctrine. It is theological justification for oppression carried out by the class of *encomenderos*, who quite naturally applauded this determined defender of their privileges. We have had many other Sepúlvedas since in America, advocates for the exploitation and slavery of the majority in the name of "western and Christian civilization"; but perhaps only in the last years do we find some so frank and clear as he to justify the oppression and massacre of the poor and exploited of the continent who fight for their liberation.

We already know Bartolomé de Las Casas' position. The central ideas have been presented. Although I will not follow his argument in detail, it is worth the trouble to make a few remarks; this will allow us to be aware of the theological perspective of which he was the precursor.

In beginning his argument with an abundance of quotes and subtle distinctions against the theses of Sepúlveda, Father Bartolomé makes an observation which disqualifies his adversary's position. Sepúlveda had defended theses which were the cause

> of the Spaniards using new and cruel methods of inhumanity which had depopulated the Indies over an area of more than two thousand leagues of land in their conquests and establishment of their estates.[24]

The greatest refutation of a theology lies in its practical consequences and not in intellectual arguments. This is not an isolated text. Father Bartolomé often reproaches Sepúlveda for his intellectualism, his lack of knowledge of the Indies, and for the concrete implications of what his theology maintains. Bartolomé de Las Casas was a man of action, and his theological work is just one moment of that action, of his commitment to the Indians.

This way of doing theology differentiates de Las Casas from the more classical and academic theologians—for example, Francisco de Vitoria, the most famous of his time. It seems to us to be an error to reduce de Las Casas' argument in the controversy on the Indies to de Vitoria's positions.[25] De Vitoria, it is true, was a man of solid Thomistic influence, and he had been alerted to the situation by the Dominican religious missionaries in the Indies. This allowed him to advance the theological-juridical reflection towards what will be called the Rights of the Peoples and the International Rights. It is also true that there are many points of comparison between these two great Dominicans. However, in the concerns raised by the conquest of the Indies, de Vitoria ends up in the middle of the road. He vigorously refutes the adduced reasons for making war and conquering the Indians. Yet, he reintroduces this possibility by pointing out as hypotheses the motives that would justify those wars in determined circumstances. These were abstract hypotheses which anyone familiar with the situation of the Indies knew were false. Francisco de Vitoria is a centrist theologian, and as Perez de Tudela says, he represents "the rights of a progressive humanity in the process of extending its dominion over the planet." This is the most advanced wing of the dominating sectors. Bartolomé de Las Casas' point of view is different. His point of departure is the Indian, that "of a historically backward humanity"[26] (we would say exploited humanity). For this reason, Father Bartolomé quotes de Vitoria very little. This theological centrism opened the doors to a warlike action, even if moderate, against the Indians.[27]

With this we come to a third consideration. Is it true that a theology which is not so close to a practice, to commitment, to the calculation of effective action is more serious and more scientific? We do not think this is true. Often de Vitoria and de Las Casas are set off against each other in these terms. Direct participation in the historical process, in the struggles of the poor, in the construction of a Church by the poor allows the perception of aspects of the Christian message which escape other perspectives. This we have seen in presenting de Las Casas' ideas on salvation and liberation. We insinuated that this richer perception resulted from the fact that the Indian is seen not only as an infidel to be evangelized, but rather as the poor of the gospel, as the "other" who questions western Christianity. Bartolomé de Las Casas deepens this perspective with one of his greatest concepts: Christ speaks to us from the Indians. This appears in the account which he himself gives of his conversion,[28] and he will often repeat it. He writes: "I leave Jesus Christ in the Indies with our God, beating him, afflicting him, insulting and slapping him, and crucifying him, not once but thousands of times."[29] This is inconceivable in Sepúlveda's theology. The Indian who was born to be a servant cannot be identified with Christ, but without a doubt the lords can. Nor is this seen in de Vitoria's theology. In Bartolomé de Las Casas' theology we touch this base: Christ questions from the oppressed, he denounces a regime of exploitation imposed by those who call themselves Christians; he calls for a greater fidelity to his gospel.

Bartolomé de Las Casas, and those who took the part of the Indian, are witnesses to the confrontation of medieval Christendom with the "other" of the then known world. Bound to the traditional theology, persons of his time, nonetheless, found new ways to try to interpret the gospel from the perspective of "the beaten Christs of the Indies."

B. BOURGEOIS LIBERALISM AND A NEW DOMINATION

The nineteenth century opened a new stage in the history of the American peoples, a stage in which the great industrial countries, in complicity with local sectors of society, dominated Latin America. During this period we do not find a theological reflection which springs from the situation of the continent as was the case in the sixteenth century. With the exception of one or another original spark, we find only repetitions of the dominant European theology. Theology follows the path of life, and those Christians capable of expressing themselves theologically at this time were far from the life and sufferings of the poor classes of the continent.

1. Capitalism and liberal theology

The wars of emancipation were marked with the ideal of freedom. The people fought and died for it against the Spanish metropolis. The movement demanded modern freedoms which culminated in the French Revolution and also developed in the republic which sprang from the union of the thirteen colonies in North America. The demand for those freedoms was accompanied by the Enlightenment's liberal ideology and thought. Avoiding the watchfulness of the Inquisition, French books had diffused those ideas in the intellectual strata of the American creoles. This diffusion of ideas was helped by the momentous inclination of important sectors in Spain toward a moderate liberalism. Another force which favored this diffusion was the economic influence of the new imperialist power, England, who was called to play a decisive role in the emancipation of Latin America.[30]

Latin America was born dependent. The changes in Europe determined the modifications in its situation. Throughout the eighteenth century, the Spanish power entered into political and economic crisis. England had asserted itself against Spain and Holland as a commercial and sea power. The beginning industrial revolution reinforced the European bourgeois class, and little by little this development asserted the bourgeois domination in the international field. By the end of the eighteenth century this class had been able to penetrate the markets of the Spanish colonies under the limits imposed by the Spanish crown. The colonial independence favored England's domination. In this setting, the so-called "Neocolonial pact" was constituted: the New World countries furnished raw materials and the industrial countries sold them manufactured goods. This meant the frank entrance of the old colonies into the capitalistic system.[31]

The transformation of the economic relationship of the Spanish colonies with the capitalist powers took place in the second half of the eighteenth century, but this called for new political forms. The wars of independence were waged to bring about these needed forms. The bourgeoisie of the capitalist countries supported these wars and collaborated with some of the local dominating sectors of colonial society, which were bound to the bourgeoisie through commercial ties, to install a new political regime. The liberal utopia promised the new countries a political organization based on freedom and modernity. A more or less ambiguous liberal ideology influenced the political constitutions. The break with Spanish domination and the entrance into a new situation of oppression in relation with the great capitalistic countries was the work of a white creole elite and of a few other sectors won over to the ideal of freedom. The poorer sectors, Indians, Blacks and Mestizos, either had no participation or they had a passive participation, in many cases only sporadically. The freedom which the new political constitutions guaranteed did not reach the whole of society and was limited to favoring the privileges of the dominant groups at the service of the rising international bourgeoisie.

For several decades, those dominating groups were divided into liberals and conservatives. The first represented an intellectual and progressive sector which was sensitive to the ideas coming from Europe and the

United States. They expressed the interests of the merchants and financiers tied to European capitals. Culturally, their objectives were those of the Enlightenment, and they sought to overcome the backwardness and barbarism of the poor people of the continent.[32] The second group, the conservatives, tried to prolong the economic model of the colony within the new political forms. They sought support in the big property and land holders as well as in the bureaucracy built up during the colony. This group was also tied to the Catholic Church which maintained an important presence in the majority of the population. This opposition between liberals and conservatives was a pale reflection of what took place in Europe in the same years, and as in Europe, it became less important as the grass-roots (or "popular") movements began to threaten the privileges which both sectors enjoyed. At this same time, the center of economic and political decisions was shifting from England to a new capitalistic power: the United States of North America whose "manifest destiny" was to occupy the West of North America and to dominate the South of the continent.[33]

The liberal stage in Latin America was only an imitation of what took place in the central countries. Actually, the social and economic structure was hardly modified, but it was put to the service of the rising international capitalism. Helped by the complicity of the local dominating sectors of society, the bourgeois interests installed a refined exploitation of the poor classes of Latin America. Many of these sections saw their situation worsen in relation to the colonial period. Everything was adorned and dissimulated by using a vocabulary of modern terms for political freedoms to fool some factions of the population, but little by little all the adornments were revealed to be lies. The movement for modern freedoms, democracy, and the universal and rational thought in Europe and the United States, meant for Latin America a new type of oppression and more cruel forms of despoilment of the poor classes. The exploitation carried out by the modern countries, champions of freedom, constituted a traumatic experience which cannot be forgotten when one speaks of freedom and democracy in the continent.[34]

2. Church and state

Many priests participated in the struggles for emancipation. Some led subversive movements against the Spanish authorities (Hidalgo and Morelos in Mexico), others played important roles in the assemblies which decided the political organization of the new nations. All of them were more or less influenced by moderate liberal ideas, and especially they were influenced by the libertarian emotion which was alive in those days. The episcopacy, on the contrary, with a few exceptions remained faithful to the Spanish crown. The bishops, Spanish by birth, followed in this way the indications sent from Rome, for the latter was worried about the breakup of the Old Regime in Europe and was tightly bound to the work of restoration of the Holy Alliance.

The new political constitutions assumed the form of a relationship between Church and state which had existed during the colony, known by the name Patronate. Both liberals and conservatives were interested in dominating the Church. However, under pressure of the more belligerent liberal groups there were some flareups of anticlericalism and some battles against the religious intolerance opposed to the modernization of society. In some countries the doors were opened to Protestant churches, in general maintained by the Anglo-Saxon countries, and they played an important role in the modernization of those countries.[35] This occasioned some disputes on religious freedom, lay teaching, and the separation of Church and state. The arguments were more juridical than theological, a poor echo of those used in Europe during the same years.

The Church sought to maintain its old privileges and supported the conservative groups. Its economic interests bound it to the conservatives. The Church began to lose its political power in the second half of the nineteenth century, and in spite of its opposition some separations were made between Church and state.[36] This was a period of withdrawal, defensive attitude, and theological poverty. However, some social concerns did open up in the first years of the twentieth century. And, little by little, concern was expressed regarding the Christians' participation in politics.

3. Christians and politics

Christian-social thought sprang up, and it was backed by Thomistic philosophy. This took place under the influence of the moderate wing of Catholic liberalism, some ideas of French social Catholicism, and Church social doctrine conceived by Leo XIII. Jacques Maritain was the principal representative of this current. It was an attempt to eliminate the mentality of Christendom and to open up moderately the Church to the values of the modern world and to the ideals of freedom and democracy.

Around 1930, the political and economic structures of some Latin American countries underwent important changes due to the interna-

tional crisis. In the more economically solid countries the first steps were
taken towards the change of industrialization through the substitution of
imports. New questions confronted Catholic circles in the southern
countries of Latin America (Argentina, Southern Brazil, Chile, Uruguay)
which are racially and culturally closer to Europe and more open to its
influence.[37] This favored the transference to Latin America of the
Christian-social movement, which played a role in awakening the social
consciousness of certain Christian groups. The people of Latin America
who lived in poverty and misery were no longer viewed as mere objects
of charity. Social injustice was recognized as the basic cause of that
misery. How can anyone be Christian without a commitment to rem-
edy that state? Everyone felt summoned by this hard reality, but it
was less clearly seen that the whole of society and its system of values was
being questioned at the roots. So, too, was every Christian being questioned, but in a more global and demanding way. In that perspective, to
create a more just and Christian society was to transform that same
society into something better, to integrate the marginated and take care
of the most blatant injustices. Sometimes the project went further, but
the socio-economic analysis, for lack of scientific method, did not give
place in the final instance, despite intentions, to anything more than a
vague general defense of the dignity of the human person. All this was
surrounded by the "concrete historical ideal" (the expression is Maritain's) of society inspired by Christian values, perceived as compatible
with the modern vindication of democratic freedoms and social justice.

With the appearance of a more scientific understanding of the situation language became more aggressive and action somewhat more
efficient, but the point of departure stayed the same: statements of
principles were doctrinal and ahistorical. These positions which the
establishment initially accused of being subversive, maintained a certain ambiguity and thereby the capacity to be reabsorbed by the social
order which they were trying to modify. And in some countries, these
positions were carried to the extreme of being converted into political
allies and ideological supporters of the most conservative and reactionary sectors.[38] In this context, theological reflection was tinged with
social concern but continued as before.

The Christian-social perspective did not have the same weight in all
Latin American countries. In many of them, in circles closely related to
lay apostolic groups, the insufficiencies and ambiguities of Christian
ethics in the political arena quickly became clear. Insertion of them into
party politics was then made through several organizations in which

Christians and people of other spiritual families openly participated. Christians got together, as such, on another level, that of a frank profession of faith, forming communities in which they shared the experiences of their Christian life starting from different political commitments. Although viewed with suspicion by those who preferred to make the Christians into a religious-political bloc, those Christians gradually grew stronger in some Latin American countries. They, thus, made battle to hinder the obligatory channeling of Christian sectors into only one political perspective. They were open to other points of view and more than a decade ago began a struggle against certain ideological uses of the Christian faith, both by the conservative sectors and by the Christian social groups.

This mental hygiene endeavor was accompanied by a theology which accentuated the sphere of faith and distinguished it from the plane of worldly action. This contribution was of capital importance and led to a step forward, but its context continues to be very much within the Church.[39] The "worldly," the historical, the political, seemed to raise no real questions about how to live the faith and be intelligent about it. Even so, this effort had its consequences later when the process of political radicalization was initiated. This occurred earlier in countries in which this distinction of planes was lived with some intensity. However, the entrance into a new political posture was at first made in a polemic with the immediate past of worldly institutions of Christian inspiration. That indeed left a mark on other processes.[40]

Social Christianity sought a third way between capitalism and socialism; it implied a social reformism open to the modern world and, not without some reservations, also open to the liberal ideology whose genesis and characteristics were discussed in the preceding chapter. This permitted a greater presence of Christians in the political processes of some American countries. Later on, the outlook of the distinction of levels bound certain Latin American elites to the progressive theology which immediately preceded Vatican II. The central themes of this theology took into account the historical repercussions of the salvific message, a change of attitude towards religious freedom (a question not resolved in most Latin American countries), a full acceptance of the democratic regime, and a concern for social justice. All this received a great impulse from the Council which, as we have already pointed out, sought to respond to the questions of modern times and to reconcile itself with the economic, social, political, and cultural world formed by the bourgeois class of the wealthy countries.

In 1968, the Latin American bishops met in Medellin in order to take a look at the political and ecclesial reality "in the light of Vatican II." The demand of those situations threw a different light on reality. The results were somewhat complex, but in a certain way the poor of the continent made their voice heard.

C. LIBERATION AND FREEDOM

To live and think the faith from the situation of the "absent of history" questions the manner of understanding the salvific message of the gospel as well as its free acceptance by the believer. We have already seen that the political implication of these Christian notions is a historical constant. To situate oneself fully in the world of oppression, to participate in the struggles of the poor and oppressed for liberation leads to reinterpreting the gospel, but this reinterpretation presupposes a location in history which is different from that of the dominant sections of society. The break of traditional theologies and progressive theology with the theology of liberation is not simply a theological break. There is a political break without which it is impossible to understand the effort of the theology of liberation to rethink and express again the faith of the poor and oppressed of this world.

1. *The absent of history*

From the beginning of the conquest, the indigenous peoples of America revolted against their oppressors. The written history speaks very little of this. However, gradually, we have recuperated the memory of the struggles for liberation in the continent. As time has passed, Christian motives have become present in these rebellions. The Indians who received the gospel found in it reasons for rejecting the oppression to which they were being submitted. They interpreted the gospel from their own situation and from their own culture. This opened up points of view which did not correspond to traditional orthodoxy and which included more influence from the biblical sense of justice.[41] The ideological foundation often took the path of a political-religious messianism. It was an ambiguous but rich vein for following the route of liberation of the poor in history.[42]

Certain poor and oppressed groups took part in the war of emancipation, but without leaving a trace of their aspirations. In the second half of the nineteenth century the grass-roots movement began to be channeled by the currents of a socialism called utopian. Later on, the union organizations were challenged by anarchism. Scientific socialism came on the scene at the end of the century and gradually became solid in the first decades of the twentieth century, in labor and intellectual spheres, without yet reaching wide sectors of the grass-roots or "popular" classes. With very few exceptions,[43] Christians remained alien to these beginnings of "popular" movements.

The recent history of Latin America is distinguished by the disturbing discovery of the world of the other—the poor, the exploited class. Heretofore, a few have created economically, politically, and ideologically a social order for their own benefit; now the "others" of that society—the lower classes who have always been marginated and oppressed are beginning to make their voice heard. As they find their own voice they are speaking less and less through intermediaries. As they rediscover themselves they are making the system feel their throbbing presence. As they change from objects of demagogical manipulation or of more or less disguised social welfare they are gradually becoming subjects of their own history and are forging a radically different society.

That discovery, however, is only made in a revolutionary struggle which radically questions the existing social order and postulates the need for power for the common people in order to construct a truly equalitarian and free society. From this society private ownership of the means of production will be eliminated. Because private ownership has permitted the few to capture the fruits of the labor of the many, it has generated class divisions and the exploitation of one class by another. In this new society, to the social appropriation of the means of production will be added the social appropriation of political control, and, quite definitely, new dimensions of freedom. This will lead to a new social consciousness.

Today in Latin America, we are above all, face to face with a radical questioning of the reigning social order. The kind of poverty and injustice that are lived in the continent is too deep to think only of stop-gap measures. Hence, some speak of social revolution rather than reforms, liberation rather than development, and socialism rather than modernization of the ruling system. To the "realists" these assertions seem as romantic and utopian. And this is understandable. The assertions are part and parcel of a rationality which is alien to them—the rationality of a historical project that announces a different society, a built-in function of the poor and the oppressed, and one that denounces a society built for the benefit of a few. It is a project in the process of being elaborated, based on rigid and rigorous scientific studies. It starts from the exploitation of the great majority of the masses. Latin America is a dependent continent—economically, socially, politically, and culturally—controlled by the centers of power outside of Latin America: the rich countries. External dependence and internal domination characterize the social structure of Latin America. This is why only a class analysis will permit us to see what is really at play in the opposition of oppressed countries and dominating countries. To see only the confrontation between countries waters down the true situation. The theory of dependence would be deceitful if it did not situate its analyses in the frame of class struggle that is taking place all around the world. All this will lead us to understand the social formation of Latin America as a dependent capitalism and to foresee the necessary strategy to get out of that situation.

Only the transcending of a society divided into classes, a political power at the service of the great popular majorities, and the elimination of private appropriation of wealth produced by human work can give us the foundations of a society that would be more just. It is for this reason that the elaboration in a historical project of a new society in Latin America takes more and more frequently the path of socialism.

For years a growing number of Christians have shared in the revolutionary process in Latin America and thereby in the discovery of the world of the exploited people of the continent. This commitment is the major event in the life of the Latin American Christian community. It leads to a new way of being a person and a believer, to a new way of living and thinking the faith, to a new way of being gathered into the "ecclesia." This commitment creates a dividing line between two experiences, two epochs, two worlds, two languages in Latin America and thus in the Church.

The participation of Christians in the liberation process has varying degrees of radicalism with shadings peculiar to different Latin American countries. The participation expresses itself in searching languages which advance by "trial and error." Sometimes it is obstructed by turns in the road; at other times, due to different events, it moves faster.

At the present time, Latin America is not only a continent of oppression, it is also a place of ferocious repression in order to detain the aspirations which the grass-roots classes have for liberation. However, the "popular" movement continues to assert itself at the grass-roots level. The political consciousness of the deprived majorities grows, and their autonomous organizations grow. Their achievements and failures are learning experiences. The blood spilt by those who rose up against secular injustice quickly gives unexpected property titles to a land which is ever more alien and at the same time, increasingly demanded by those whom the Bible calls "the poor of the country." The grass-roots movement experiences setbacks and ambiguities, common to every historical process. However, this "popular" movement also experiences the firmness, the hope, and the political realism which the defenders of the established order understand with difficulty.

The theology of liberation grew out of this context. It could not spring up without there first being a certain development in the "popular" movement and a certain maturity in the movement's historical praxis. These struggles are the place for a new way of being man and woman in Latin America, a new way of living the faith and encountering the Father and brothers and sisters. This spiritual experience, in St. Paul's sense, "to live according to the Spirit," in the very heart of social conflict is the beginning of this theological effort.[44]

2. Theology from the world of oppression

Theology and a new cultural world.   Theology always uses some rationality, even though, theology and rationality are not identified. This rationality belongs to the cultural world of the believer. All theology asks the question about the meaning of the Word of God for us in the today of history, and the attempts to answer are made from the point of view of our culture, of the problems that men and women of our time are asking themselves. It is from this cultural world that we formulate the gospel and Church message to our contemporaries and to ourselves.

This is precisely what Thomistic theology, for example, attempted to do, making brave use of Aristotelian philosophy and of the vision of the world to which it was tied. Thus, we entered into a new understanding of the meaning of faith. Today, we are witnessing a crisis of the rational categories traditionally used in theology. The question has been studied in detail and its causes have been clearly identified; that is why it is not important here to enter into the minutiae. This has given rise to a certain philosophical eclecticism, which is one of the characteristics of a certain contemporary theology. We make use of different rational categories in the discourse of faith. This has also given rise to research which tries to find new ways of reformulating the Word.[45] In a more radical sense, perhaps, this has provoked some question in reference to knowledge.[46] While this problem may not be explicit in theological thought, it has become an urgent personal concern. What are the suppositions in the theological approach to historical reality? What weight does the situation

of the ecclesiastical institution in our society bear on our theological
reflection? Or, to say it another way, from where does the theologian
speak? why does he speak? to whom? These questions have led to an
important question which is always asked when an era is closed to let a
new one come in: why do we theologize?

In this questioning, the rise of scientific knowledge plays a very
important role, especially when it enters the field of the historical and of
the psychological. Sciences are the expressions of human reason that
uncover us to aspects of nature and of the human person which escape
other forms of approach to these realities, and which, consequently,
cannot be left out by theology. Philosophical reflections keep all their
validity.

In a continent like Latin America, the challenge does not come to us
primarily from the non-believer, but from the *non-person*, that is to say,
from the individual who is not recognized as such by the existing social
order: the poor, the exploited, who are systematically deprived of being
persons, they who scarcely know that they are persons. The non-person
questions before anything else, not our religious world, but our
economic, social, political, and cultural world; and thus, a call is made for
the revolutionary transformation of the very bases of a dehumanizing
society. Our question, therefore, is not how to announce God in an adult
world; but rather, how to announce him as *Father* in a non-human world.
What are the implications when we tell a non-person that he or she is a
child of God? These were already the questions that were asked in the
seventeenth century of Antonio de Montesinos, of Bartolomé de Las
Casas and of many others, after having encountered the indigenous
Americans. The discovery of the other, of the exploited, has led to a
reflection on the exigencies of faith, in contrast to the reflection that had
taken place on the side of the dominator, as for example, Ginez de
Sepúlveda.

Today, the historical frame is different, social analysis is different, but
we are witnessing a rediscovery of the poor in Latin America. To come
into solidarity with them is to enter consciously the historical conflict,
the clash between countries, and social classes. It is also to enter it on the
side of the dominated, the oppressed. But one cannot really question the
social system that creates and justifies this situation unless one participates in the efforts to transform it radically and to forge a different
society. To enter into the praxis of liberation means to embrace what we
earlier called the complex and pluridimensional character of human
knowledge; it means, in the last analysis, to enter into a different cultural
world.

Liberating praxis and understanding faith.   The commitment to the process of liberation introduces the Christian to a world which is not very familiar, and challenges one with a qualitative change: radical questioning of a social order and its ideology, a break with the old form of knowing things. This contributes to the fact that any other theological reflection which starts from a different cultural context will have little personal meaning. Other theological reflections will give a view of how other Christian generations understood their faith, and the ways that faith was/is expressed can serve as general points of reference, but they will still leave the individual theologically an orphan, because they do not speak with the strong, clear, and pressing language which is demanded by the human and Christian experience in which the person lives.

Theory and praxis.   Nevertheless, simultaneously, the roots of a new type of understanding of the faith are being grounded on those same experiences. People learn to link in them, in a different manner, theory and practice. Today, we see something which appears as a fundamental trait of contemporary consciousness: knowledge is linked to transformation. History—which according to Marx indissolubly includes nature and society—is seen as the object of change and transformation as well as an agent for self-transformation. Vicus used to say that people know well only the things they do. The modern human person likes to verify the truth, to give it a consistent reality. A knowledge of a reality which does not lead to changing that reality is an unverified interpretation, does not have the consistency demanded by truth. This way, historical reality contrasts with the abstract truths and idealist interpretations of life, and it becomes the privileged ground from which one starts and to which one returns in the process of knowledge. The transforming praxis of history is not the moment in which a clear and well-conceived theory takes on a lowly and degraded form, but rather, it becomes the matrix and generating force of an authentic knowledge and decisively proves its real value. It is the ground in which we create again our world, build ourselves up, know the reality around us, and know and find ourselves. In this perspective Karl Marx places his contribution to a scientific knowledge of history.

The Word of the Lord is accepted in faith, understood, and lived today by people who are accustomed to thinking in other cultural categories; this can be seen as a parallel to what happened in the past with people who had been conditioned by Greek philosophy. Conflicts and misunderstandings thus easily arise when a system of reasoning is used in understanding and responding to the Word which is far different from the one which lies at the root of current theology. It has always happened. We could here remember the hostility and the accusations of distortion (and of "humanization") which greeted the adaptation of Aristotelian philosophy to theological thought. In our present case, the attempt—like others in the past—is evidently a modest one, but the virulence of the reactions it has provoked has reached a very high level. This is, possibly, best understood if seen outside the theological perspective: it is part of an attempt to defend a type of social order which does not accept questioning and criticism, and much less, elimination, from the person whom it oppresses, isolates, and ruins. As in the past, in spite of their success in provoking groundless alarm and occasional condemnations, these attitudes have no future. The future is in the hands of a faith which does not fear the progress of human learning nor the challenges of social practices, but which lets itself be questioned by them and questions them in return, enriching itself. It is a very complex task which takes into account many lines of specialization, philosophical and scientific, without which it is impossible, today, to elaborate a theological process. It takes into account, among others, those sciences which provide us with instruments enabling us to know the natural world of which we are a part, and particularly of those which allow us to discover our psychological, economic, and social dimensions which militate against justice and fraternity. It also takes into account philosophical thought which embraces the totality of human life and which maintains a constant dialogue with scientific knowledge. The task of understanding the faith can only be undertaken from the viewpoint of the historical praxis in which people struggle to live as persons and are inspired by the hope in him who, revealing himself, reveals to humanity all his fullness. It is inspired by a hope in the Lord of history in whom everything was made and salvation obtained.

The biblical truth. It becomes necessary to read again the gospel. This way persons will rediscover something traditional, authentically traditional, which was forgotten by more recent "traditions": the truth of the gospel is acted and enacted. We must act in truth, as St. John tells us, and that truth is love. A life of love is a true affirmation of our existence, and it carries with itself a commitment of one's life to God and to all people. To have faith is to go out of oneself to give oneself to God and to others. Faith operates through charity, as St. Paul points out.

To reflect on one's faith is to rethink that faith which is given a real consistency through actions and which transcends a simple affirmation or confession. It makes a start with a promise which is fulfilled along the course of history and which at the same time is open to something beyond. Truth, in the Bible, includes fidelity, justice, and firmness. To believe is to have confidence, to give oneself to God, to be faithful. God is worthy of faith because he is truthful, for, as the prophets often repeat in the Old Testament, his word is firm and he always fulfills what he promises. The fulfillment takes place in history, and thus, God appears truthful through history.

Christ is the fulfillment of the Father's promise which makes us his children in him. This is according to the acts and words of Jesus. The Father fulfills his promise in the death and resurrection of Jesus. To be a Christian is to accept that the promise begins to be fulfilled and realized in a historical context. To be a Christian is to work to verify and make true that promise of the Father in history revealing the love of the Father in the love for our neighbors ("we know that we have passed from death to life because we love for our brothers [and sisters]) and to hope and to expect the fulfillment of the promise.

In the Bible, the act of knowing is not relegated to a purely intellectual level. To know is to love. The prophetic word (*dabar*) is always an event, a happening; the word pronounced in the name of Yahweh becomes history. True orthodoxy is an orthopraxis.

Theology from and on the praxis.   We are not trying to adopt here the contemporary yearn for a mechanical correspondence in the relationship between knowing and transforming and living a truth which verifies itself in history. Nevertheless, the cultural world in which we live allows us to discover a starting point and a horizon in which we can delineate a theological reflection which must appeal to its own sources.[47]

Theology, in this context, will be a critical reflection on the historical praxis when confronted with the Word of the Lord lived and accepted in faith; this faith comes to us through multiple, and at times ambiguous, historical mediations which we make and discover everyday. Theology will be a reflection in and on faith as a liberating praxis. The understanding of the faith will proceed from an option and a commitment.[48] This understanding will start with a real and effective solidarity with discriminated races, despised cultures and exploited classes and from their very world and atmosphere. This reflection starts from a commitment to create a just fraternal society, and must contribute to make it more meaningful, radical, and universal. This theological process becomes truth when it is embodied into the process of liberation. Theology, thus, will be liberated from a socio-cultural context which prevents it from establishing its presence where the oppressed and the discriminated in the world are struggling to be accepted as human persons. Theology becomes a liberating and prophetic force which tends to contribute to the total understanding of the Word which takes place in the actions of real life. This fact, and not simple affirmations or "models of analysis," will free theology from all forms of idealism.

The theology of liberation differs from such theologies as those of development, revolution, and violence not only in a different analysis of reality based on more universal and radical political options, but above all, in the very concept of the task of theology. The theology of liberation does not intend to provide Christian justification for positions already taken and does not aim to be a revolutionary Christian ideology. It is a reflection which makes a start with the historical praxis of people. It seeks to rethink the faith from the perspective of that historical praxis, and it is based on the experience of the faith derived from the liberating commitment. For this reason, this theology comes only after that involvement, the theology is always a *second act*.[49] Its themes are, therefore, the great themes of all true theology, but the perspective and the way of giving them life is different. Its relation to historical praxis is of a different kind.

Jesus Christ: principal hermeneutic of the faith. To be Christian is to believe that one man of history loved us by loving his contemporaries enough to give his life for them. He loved the poor by preference and for them confronted the great and powerful of his times, and he was put to death as subversive: he is God.

The great principal hermeneutic of the faith and, therefore, the foundation of all theological discourse is Jesus Christ. In Jesus we meet God; in the human word we read the word of the Lord, in historical events we recognize the fulfillment and the promise. And this because Jesus is the Christ, the One sent by the Father, the Son ("God loved the world so much that he gave his only Son."); because Jesus is the intrusion into history of the Son in whom all things were made and in whom all things were saved.

That is then the fundamental hermeneutic circle: from people to God and from God to people; from history to faith and from faith to history; from the human word to the word of the Lord and from the word of the Lord to the human word; from fraternal love to the love of the Father and from the love of the Father to fraternal love; from human justice to the holiness of God and from the holiness of God to human justice; from poor to God and from God to poor.

Theology, intelligence of the faith, is strengthened by the will of helping to live according to the Spirit.

3. *Salvation of history*

Historical liberating praxis and salvation. To state that the theology of liberation does not pretend to be a revolutionary Christian ideology does not imply that it disregards the revolutionary process. On the contrary, it states, precisely, that it attempts to make Christianity more self-critical, and, therefore, more radical and global. This will be achieved for the theology by placing the political commitment to liberation in the perspective of the free gift of the total liberation brought by Christ.

Faith, being an acceptance of, and the answer to the Father's love, penetrate to the last root of social injustice: sin, the break in our friendship with God and humanity. This is not obtained by leaving aside historical mediations or avoiding socio-political analyses of historical realities. Sin is found in the refusal to accept any person as a neighbor, in oppressive structures built up for the benefit of a few, in the despoilation of peoples, races, cultures, and social classes. Sin is basically an alienation, and as such, it cannot be found floating in the air, but is found in concrete historical situations, in individual and specific alienations. It is impossible to understand one without the other. Sin demands a radical liberation, but this, necessarily, includes a liberation in the political order and in the different dimensions of person. It is only by a fighting and efficacious participation in the historical process of liberation that it will be possible to pinpoint the basic fundamental alienation present in all partial alienations. That radical liberation is a gift brought by Christ. Christ, by his death and resurrection, redeems us from sin and all its consequences. Medellin says:

> The same God is the one who in the fullness of time sends his Son, so that becoming incarnated, He will come to liberate all men from *all* forms of slavery to which sin has subdued them; namely, ignorance, hunger, misery, and oppression or in other words, the injustice and hatred which are rooted in human egoism.[50]

The transformation of history will necessarily suppose the simultaneous transformation of nature and society. It is this that we call a *historical* praxis. In this historical praxis there is more than a new consciousness of the meaning of economic activity and political action; there is also a new way of being man and woman in history. But to speak of transformation of history from the perspective of dominated and exploited peoples, from the perspective of the poor of this world brings us to see it as a *liberating* praxis, that is to say, to see in that transformation something that escapes us when we consider it from the point of view of the

minority of humanity that owns the majority of scientific and te_____
means as well as the political power in today's world. This is why this
liberating praxis acquires a *subversive* perspective. It is subversive of a
social order in which the poor person, the "other" of this society, scarcely
begins to be heard.

What is really at work is not just a greater rationality of economic
activity or a better social organization, but, rather justice and love
working through these. The terms are classical and perhaps seldom
employed in a strictly political language, but they remind us of all the
human density rooted in the affair. They remind us that we talk about
people, of entire nations that suffer misery and exploitation, who cannot
enjoy the most elementary rights of humanity, who scarcely know that
they are human. That is why the liberating praxis, in the measure that it
starts from an authentic solidarity with the poor and the oppressed, will
be, in short, *a praxis of love*. It will be real love, efficacious and historical,
towards concrete individuals. It will be a praxis of love of neighbor and
therein, of love of Christ who identifies himself with the least of
humanity. Any attempt to separate the love of God from love of neighbor
gives birth to impoverished attitudes in one sense or the other. It would
be easy to oppose a "praxis of Heaven" to a "praxis of the earth" or vice
versa. It is easy, but it is not faithful to the gospel of God. It is for this
reason that it seems to us more authentic and more profound to speak of a
praxis of love that takes root in the gratuitous and free love of the Father
who established himself historically in solidarity with the poor and
dispossessed and through them with all people.

As we repeatedly said, political action has its demands and specific
laws. To recall the deep meaning it has for a Christian makes it necessary
to look back and reflect upon times when people were in no position to
know the internal mechanisms of an oppressive society and in which
political action had not reached its adulthood. To receive the gift of
Sonship, making all persons our brothers and sisters, will be little less
than a self-gratifying thought, unless we make it alive daily in a conflictive history; also, unless it leads to a real identification with the persons
suffering oppression from other persons, with the struggles of the
exploited classes. It must enrich creatively and scientifically, from
within, the political processes which have a tendency to get closed in
themselves and mutilate authentic human dimensions. It must use the
instruments provided for by human sciences and philosophy so as to
make its action more efficacious.

The liberation of Christ cannot be equated with political liberation but it takes place in historical and political liberating acts. It is not possible to avoid those mediations. On the other hand, political liberation is not a political and religious messianism, for it has its autonomy and laws, and presupposes well determined social analyses and political opinions; but, looking at human history as a history in which the liberation of Christ is operative, widens the perspective and gives to what is at stake in the political commitment all its depth and true meaning. We are not creating easy and impoverishing equations or simplistic and distorted reductions of one to the other,[51] but we are bringing to light the mutual and fruitful demands of both.

The theology of liberation is a theology of salvation incarnated in the concrete historical and political conditions of today. Those historical and political mediations of today, valued in themselves, change the life experience and pattern, as well as, the reflection on the mystery hidden from of old and revealed now, the love of the Father and human fraternity, and the operating salvation in time, all of which give a deep unity to human history. We do not have two histories, one by which we become children of God and the other by which we become each other's brothers. This is what the term liberation wants to make present and underline.

Maskings and perspectives. A theological reflection in the context of liberation, takes its point of departure from the perception that the context obliges us to rethink radically our Christian being and our being as Church. This reflection upon the Word accepted in faith will appeal to the different expressions of contemporary human reasoning, of human sciences and also of philosophy. But above all, it will have reference to the historical praxis in a new way. This new way distinguishes it from attempts to cover old Church practiceu with issues and social concern or the vocabulary of "liberation theology." Easy attitudes and a certain preoccupation with contemporary styles have in effect led some to speak of the same old things while simply adding the adjective "liberating" and, thereby, selling old merchandise which was beginning to pile up. Another attempt along the same lines is to interpret in a "spiritualistic" (not spiritual) way everything which has to do with the liberation of Christ. In this way, all the human and historical impact is taken away and it can be accepted by the political and ecclesiastical system to the degree that it questions nothing, to the degree in which the "other" of such a system is not made present, and one remains "within the family."[52] But, as we have said already, what we understand by theology of liberation supposes a direct and precise relation with the historical praxis. And this historical praxis is a liberating and subversive praxis. It is an identifica-

Prayer of Love

tion with persons, with races, with the social classes which suffer misery and exploitation, identification with its concerns and its battles. It is an insertion into the revolutionary political process.[53] We do this so that from within this process we can live and proclaim the gratuitous and liberating love of Christ. This love goes to the very root of all exploitation and injustice: the rupture of the friendship with God and with humankind. This love permits persons to recognize themselves as children of the Father and brothers and sisters with each other.

The theological sketch of which we dispose ourselves today in this line of thought is but the point of departure keeping in mind the importance of the theory of knowledge. This knowledge should be applied to the construction of a society which functions for the poor. The theology of liberation poses certain fundamental questions in the field of theological method; it demands continual questioning of biblical hermeneutic, conditioned by a greater clarification of its Old and New Testament foundations; it introduces a distinct perspective in order to think of the articulation between faith and politics; it underscores the importance of a Christology for a committed Christian in the revolutionary process; it leads to radical questions in ecclesiological matters. But, all this is but the initial planning. Furthermore, the experience of the insertion into the liberating praxis is fundamental for this theological perspective, and hence, a greater communication is necessary between the attempts which are made from diverse realities by those who are already committed to a revolutionary method. To this day, there have been few attempts to relate the theological perspectives which have risen in the committed Christian communities in Asia, Africa, and the racial and cultural minorities of the developed countries.[54] The sketch which we have today of theology of liberation would gain much from such a confrontation. Faith comes to us through historical mediations. The theological task supposes the critical examination of the forms in which the living of the faith has been translated throughout history and is translated today into the political practice of Christians. To do otherwise, is to remain in an abstract and ahistorical level and, thus, betray the fundamental intuition from which the theology of liberation stems. If we evaded this critical examination, we would once again fall easily into new ideological utilizations of Christianity. This last aspect is not avoided by simply using "magically" the term *liberation*.

Speaking definitively, we will not have an authentic theology of liberation until the oppressed are able to express themselves freely and creatively in society and as the People of God. In effect, this begins to hap-

pen when critical reflection takes place on the part of important and growing sectors who are in true solidarity with the interests and struggles of
exploited social groups. In these sectors many people belong to popular
classes, but if we consider all the continent, in particular the most dispossessed people, one must say that the popular classes do not yet have a decisive and massive presence in the process of liberation. We have made
one step in this theological perspective. Gradual perfection is possible,
necessary, and even urgent, but they are only improvements of the first
intuitions. For this reason, it is necessary to understand that there will
not be a real qualitative jump into another theological perspective, until
the marginal and exploited become more and more the artisans of their
own proper liberation, when their voice will make itself heard directly
and without mediation. This will come about when they testify to their
own experience of the Lord in their effort to liberate themselves, and give
hope for the total liberation in Christ of *all* persons. There will not be a
distinct theological perspective until it comes from the social practice of
the true Latin American people, of the people which has its earthly roots
within the geography, the history, the indigenous race, and the culture
of a profound and today silent people. From this point, a new interpretation of the evangelical message will take place along with the expression
of the experiences it has brought about throughout history.

All this implies a historical process of vast proportions. If what we
have today as the theology of liberation can contribute to it and raise the
possibility for new understanding of the faith, it will have accomplished
its task of transition. It is nothing more than a Christian generation
declaring its consciousness in ecclesial communion at a given moment of
history. And this generation begins just now to break with the dominating system and to discover the "other" of the world in which it still lives.
In recent times I have begun to discover the presence of the Lord in the
very heart of the Latin American people.

4. *Evangelization and subversion of history*

To believe in the God who reveals himself in history and puts his tent
there means to live in that tent, that is to say, in Jesus Christ, and to
preach from there the liberating love of the Father.

Gesture and word.   The God who liberates in history, the Christ made
poor, can only be preached with works, with gestures in a practice of
solidarity with the poor. That was the fundamental demand of the
covenant. The fact of Jesus Christ makes this demand even more urgent.

Faith without works is dead, says St. James in a text which is worth quoting.

> What good is it, my brothers, if someone says, "I have faith" if he does not have works? Will the faith save him? If a brother or sister is naked and lacks their daily provisions, and one of you says, "Go in peace" and becomes angry and fed up yet does not give what is necessary for the body, what is the faith worth? And so, faith without works is dead.

Without "what is necessary for the body," the supposed reception is just an empty attitude. Faith shows itself in works: "Do you have faith? Well, I have works. Prove your faith without works and I will prove my faith with works." Faith in God does not consist in asserting his existence but rather in acting for him.

> Do you think there is only one God? That is correct. The devils also believe this and tremble. Would you like to know, foolish person, that faith without works is sterile? Did not our father, Abraham arrive at justice through works when he offered his son Isaac on the altar? Don't you see that the faith cooperated with his works, and that through works, the faith reached its perfection? And so the Scripture was completely fulfilled which says, "Abraham believed in God and he was known as 'justice' and was 'God's friend.' " (James 2: 14-25)

Justice and fidelity to God are expressed in works. That is the practice of sanctity.

Practice is the place for verifying our faith in the God who liberates by establishing justice and law in favor of the poor. It is the verification of our faith in Christ who gave his life to preach the kingdom of God, fighting for justice. The paschal life is the life of practice. "We know that we have gone from death to life because we love our brothers." (1 John 3:14) There is no life of faith without what the Scripture calls "testimony," and this is given in works. To believe is to practice.

Only from the level of practice, from action can the preaching by word be understood. In the act of doing, our faith is made truth, not only for others, but for ourselves as well. The gesture is consistent in itself, however the world expresses and completes it. Without action the word is susceptible to many interpretations. Moreover, saying what one lives and does leads to a more conscious and profound living and doing of what one expresses.

However, the relation between act and word is asymmetrical: the act is what fundamentally counts. In addition, this distinction should not become hardened. It only serves to express better the complexity of reality. In fact, Jesus Christ, the heart of the gospel message, is the Word made flesh, the word made gesture. Only from this profound unity is there meaning in the distinctions which we can make in the task of preaching liberation in Jesus Christ.

From the poor. Evangelization announces Christ's liberation, a liberation which goes to the roots of all injustice and exploitation: the break with friendship and with love. However, this is not a liberation which is susceptible to a "spiritualist" interpretation which is still so tenaciously present in certain Christian spheres. Love and sin (that is, the negation of love) are historical realities. They live in concrete conditions. It is for this reason that the Bible speaks of justice and liberation as opposed to slavery and the humiliation of the poor.

The gift of being a child of God is lived in history. In making sisters and brothers of all others we receive this gift, not of word but of work. This is to live the Father's love and to give witness of him. The preaching of a God who loves all persons equally should become flesh in history. In a society marked by injustice and the exploitation of one social class by another, the proclamation of this liberating love will convert this "making self-history" into something questioning and conflictual. God becomes truth in the heart of a society when the social classes question themselves and take the part of the poor of the grass-roots classes, of the despised races, of the marginated cultures. From there we try to live and preach the Gospel. This preaching to the exploited, workers, and farmers of our continent will make them perceive that their situation is contrary to God's will which is made known in liberating events. This will help them to become aware of the profound injustice of their situation.

We cannot forget that in reality, the Bible was read and communicated from the dominating sectors and classes. This is what happens to a great deal of the exegesis considered to be scientific. Christianity has been forced to play a role within the reigning ideology which affirms and knits together a society which in reality is divided into classes. The "popular" or grass-roots classes will not arrive at an authentic political consciousness without direct participation in the popular struggles for liberation. However, in the globality and complexity of the social process which must breakup an oppressive system and lead to a society without classes, the ideological struggle has an important role. For this reason, the communication of the message with an understanding of the poor and the oppressed and their struggles will have a function of demasking every attempt to use the gospel to justify a situation contrary to "justice and right," as the Bible says.

This is what we mean by liberating evangelization. Only from the poor do we understand the radicalness of Christ's liberation. As the Peruvian writer, José María Arguedas, said, "The lords' God is not the same," not the God of the poor, not the God of the Bible. The God of the Bible is one who announces the Good News to the poor, and this had concrete implications:

> The Spirit of the Lord Yahweh is upon me, in that Yahweh has anointed me. He sent me to announce the good news to the poor, to bind the broken hearts, to preach liberation to the captive and freedom to the prisoner, to preach Yahweh's year of grace the day of our God's vengeance. (Isaiah 61: 1-2)

It is God who has taken the part of the poor and who considers the rich to be like a blasphemer because he or she speaks of God in order to oppress better the poor:

> Listen my dear brothers. Didn't God choose the poor of the world to make them rich in faith and heirs of the Kingdom of God which he promised to those who love him? You, on the other hand, have downgraded the poor. Aren't the rich those who oppress them and drag them to court? Aren't they the ones who blaspheme the beautiful name which has been called down upon you? (St. James 2:5-17)

Faith in God. The God who reveals himself in history cannot be reduced to our way of understanding him, our theology, or our own faith. It is impossible to take possession of that God who makes himself present in events, that God who makes himself history. God is a love which always surpasses us and surrounds us. "Indeed, we live, move, and exist in him." (Acts 17:28) He is the completely other, the Holy: "I am God, not a man, for you I am Holy." (Hosea 11: 9; cf. also Isaiah 6:3)

God manifests himself in the fire and smoke as a powerful God (Exodus 19:18), or he makes himself heard discreetly in the breeze (1 Kings 19:12), but in the last analysis, he is a God who dwells in the heart of the contrite (Isaiah 57:15), in the midst of the people. From there he demands an attitude of confidence in him, of reception of his Word, his Son. To those who receive, he gives the power to be "sons of God." (John 1:12) Faith is an attitude of giving, of confidence in the others. It supposes a going out of oneself, a collective project. It supposes a contemplative attitude, one of ex-tasis (going out of oneself). Faith implies break. This is what was demanded of him who Paul calls the father of the faith: "Yahweh said to Abraham, 'Leave your land and your nation, the house of your father and go to the land I will show you.' "

(Genesis 12:1) This means entering a new world, to a certain extent unforeseeable. It means to walk without knowing beforehand the route we will follow (John 21:18).

It is a matter of faith in the Father who loves us first and who fills our lives with love and gratuity. Love is the very source of our existence, and therefore, only by loving can we realize ourselves. It is a matter of believing that God loves us in establishing justice and right in our conflictual history. To believe is to love God, to be united with the poor and exploited of this world from within the very heart of the social confrontations and "popular" struggles for liberation. To believe is to preach, as Christ did, the kingdom from within the struggle for justice which led him to his death. To evangelize is to communicate this faith in an irreducible God who demands an attitude of confidence and whom we recognize in his liberating works, in his Son.

Subversion of history.   When we encounter human beings we encounter the Father of Jesus Christ, and in Jesus Christ we preach the love of the Father for all persons. We have recalled that this history is conflictual, but it is not enough to say this. It is necessary to insist that history (where God reveals himself and where we preach him) must be interpreted from the viewpoint of the poor, "the condemned of the earth." Human history has been written "by a white hand"[55] from the dominating sectors. A clear example of this is the history of our continent and of our country, Peru. The perspective of the "defeated" of history is different. Efforts have been made to wipe from their own minds the memory of their struggles. This is to deprive them of a source of energy, of historical will, of rebellion.

Christianity as it has been historically lived has been, and is, closely tied to a culture: Western; to a race: the white race; to a class: the dominant class. Its history has also been written by a white, western, and bourgeois hand. We must regain the memory of the "beaten Christs of the Indies" as Bartolomé de Las Casas called the Indians of the American continent. This memory lives in cultural, religious expressions, in their resistance to accept the impositions of an ecclesiastical apparatus. It is a memory of Christ present in every person who is humbled, thirsty, hungry, in prison, present in the despised races, in the exploited classes (cf. Matthew 25:31-45). It is the memory of Christ who "freed us to make us free." (Galatians 5:1)

However, to reread history means to *remake history*. It means making history from below, and therefore, it will be a subversive history. History must be changed around, not from above but from below. There is no evil in being a subversive, struggling against the capitalist system, rather what is evil today is to be a "superversive," a support to the existing domination. This subversive society is the place for a new experience of the faith, a new spirituality, a new preaching of the gospel.[56]

A "popular" Church.   The gospel read from the perspective of the poor and exploited classes and with an understanding of the militancy which has been evident in their struggles for liberation calls for a "popular" Church, a grass-roots Church. A Church which is born from the people, from a people who rip the Gospel from the hands of the powerful of this world, who impede its use as a justifying element for a situation which is contrary to the will of the liberating God.[57] Arguedas, from his own experience, called that liberating God "He who rejoins." He rejoins the "popular" struggles for liberation and the hope of the exploited.

That reintegration of God in history takes place when the poor of the land produce a social appropriation of the gospel, when they expropriate the gospel from those who consider themselves its privileged owners. The gospel tells us that the sign that the kingdom has come is that the poor are evangelized. The poor are those who believe and hope in Christ; they are the Christians. Strictly speaking, the Christians are, or should be, the poor who accept the gospel. They are those who are united with the interests, aspirations, and struggles of the oppressed and repressed today. Rather than trying to make the Church poor, it is a matter of the poor of this world becoming the Church.

Evangelization will be really liberating when the poor themselves are the bearers of the gospel message. Then, to preach the gospel will be a rock of scandal, it will be a gospel "unpresentable in society." It will be expressed in an unrefined manner, it will smell bad. The Lord, who hardly has the figure of a person (cf. the Canticles of the Servant of Yahweh in Isaiah) will speak to us in the voices of the poor. Only in listening to that voice will we recognize him as our liberator. This voice will convoke "an ecclesia" in a distinct manner. For a long time the Church has been built from within to function for Christianity and its extension and conservation in the world. This is what gave us the so-called ecclesiocentrism. A more recent perspective has led us to think of the Church from without, from the world, a non-believing world, frequently hostile. In this world the Church should be a sign of salvation, as Vatican II asserted. Today we understand better that we are called to build the Church from below, from the poor, from the exploited classes, from the marginated races and despised cultures. This is what we call the project of a "popular" Church.

"How do you sing to God in a strange land?" the Psalmist asked in exile. Without "songs" to God, without celebration of his liberating love there is no Christian life. But, how do you sing to God in a land alien to his love, in a continent of oppression and repression? This is a serious questioning of the faith which leads us to something like a New Alliance "with us who are here today all alive" (Deuteronomy 5:3), breaking the historical alliance with the classes, culture, races which up until now are dominating. This leads us to an alliance with the world's poor, towards a new type of universality. In some this creates real dread, and in others, uneasiness, the loss of old securities. It is a path where to once again use Arguedas' words, what we know is much less than the great hope which we feel.

PART TWO

The Death and Resurrection of the American Dream

Richard Shaull

Introduction

> The word *story* . . . refers to the way in which one generation tells another how the future shapes the present out of the past; how destiny draws heritage into the human reality and meaning of experience, which is always a compound of happenings, hope and remembrance; how promise and disillusionment, celebration and suffering, joy and pain, forgiveness and guilt, renewal and failure, transfigure the human condition and are transfigured in it.[1]

We have lived and flourished as a nation, and our personal lives have been rich and purposeful, to the extent that we have been able to pull together and live out a story: a story which interprets present and past and holds together events which overtake us and those which we create around a vision of who we are as a people; a story in the light of which we, as individual men and women, get a sense of what we want to do with our lives.

America[2] is, of course, many stories, just as each of our personal stories is, in some sense, unique. I am here interested in the fact that, from the beginning of our national history until only a few decades ago, our American story had a special vitality and power because it centered around and was held together by *the American dream.*

Innumerable books and essays have been written about that dream: where it came from and what it meant. Here I am more interested in one simple fact: that dream, whatever its specific shape, has until recently been alive for most of us, the central focus of the story by which we put our lives together.

That certainly has been the case with me. As I grew up on a small farm in Pennsylvania during the Great Depression, I was captivated by that dream. As I worked long hours in the fields so that our family could keep body and soul together, I knew that someday I would have a chance to go away to school, to choose a profession, and make a life for myself. I was confident that, living that way, I would also contribute my bit to making

97

the world a better place in which to live. My parents sacrificed everything they had to give me an education. In doing this, they were motivated not only by their belief that I would have a better life than they did,
but also by their trust that my life would count for something in service to
others. I saw America as a land of opportunity. The chance it would give
to me would be available to others. I saw America as a land with a future.
The old geographical frontiers had disappeared, to be sure, and I was not
especially attracted by the promise of continued expansion of a powerful
industrial society. But I was convinced that new frontiers lay before us;
that, as we conquered them, we would create structures and institutions
offering a better life not only to our own people but to the rest of the
world as well. During the Depression, I had seen and experienced a great
deal of poverty, suffering, and injustice. But I believed that all this could
and would be gradually faced and overcome. I knew this called for a
constant struggle, but it was precisely such a struggle that lay ahead of
me, a struggle worthy of my time and energies as long as I lived.

In my late teens, Christian faith, which had had an important place in
my upbringing since birth, came to provide the compelling vision for my
life. It affirmed and strengthened my faith in the American dream, at the
same time that it transformed it. I was grasped by a perspective on life
and the world in which human existence was seen in the light of its
redemptive potential. To be a Christian meant to be impelled toward the
future by a messianic hope. In the context of that hope, my own life had a
clear direction as I saw myself participating in a divine process of human
transformation—individually and socially.

My earlier vision of America and my place in it was confirmed at the
same time that it was broadened and deepened. Two visions, though not
identical, converged to produce a passionate commitment to the struggle
to create a better world and a desire to communicate that vision and
passion to others of my generation. Years later, I found, in the writings of
Eugen Rosenstock-Huessy, words which expressed that stance of faith in
a striking way. In *Out of Revolution,* he wrote:

> "The history of our era . . . is . . . one ineluctable order of alternating
> passions of the human heart. . . .
> When a nation, or individual, declines the experiences that present
> themselves to passionate hearts only, they are automatically turned out
> from the realm of history. The heart of man either falls in love with
> somebody or something, or it falls ill."[3]

My decision to become a minister, and later to go to South America as a
missionary, seemed a natural consequence of this experience.

More than two decades later, that dream began to erode. It happened first in Brazil. There I was living and working with an extraordinary group of young men and women who had become aware, as I had, of the incredible burden of poverty and exploitation under which the masses of their people suffered. They soon realized that such a state of affairs called for radical changes in the economic and political structures of their society, and they took this task upon themselves. They chose their professions and their political commitments with the expectation that their lives could and would make a difference in shaping the Brazil of the future.

I rather naively hoped to have some small part in that same struggle in which they were engaged. They did not exclude me from it, *but* they soon convinced me that one of the major reasons for the injustice and exploitation around them was the fact that they were dominated, economically and politically, by the United States. We had allied ourselves with a very small elite who profited by a system forcing Brazil to sell coffee and raw materials to us at low prices while allowing our major corporations to enter their country, produce cars and a wide variety of luxury items for a small percentage of the population—and make high profits while doing so. These elites welcomed our interference in their national life, for only in that way could they remain in power and reap the benefits of such exploitation of the masses. Eventually, this meant our complicity in the military coup of 1964 and our support of a repressive regime that imprisoned or forced into exile many of those whose dream I shared; it also destroyed all hopes they had of using their lives to change their society.

One pillar sustaining the American dream for me fell. I had believed that our existence and power as a nation offered new opportunities for economic development and social transformation of the nations of the Third World. Now I realized that the American dream was built, at least in part, on the suffering and exploitation of those peoples, and required the persistent destruction of those movements working for a more just social order. And I, as an American, was inescapably involved in the whole thing.

Shaken by that experience, I arrived in the United States in the mid-Sixties. I very soon realized that the American dream had never been an option for large segments of our population. It was reserved primarily for those of us who were white and middle class. Black Americans had no place in it. They never had the chance to become somebody or to participate significantly in the creation of a more human society. The same thing was true for many members of other ethnic minorities; for vast numbers of poor and dispossessed in the slums of our cities and in poverty stricken rural areas. Eventually I realized that an increasing number of women were becoming aware that there was little place for them in that dream.

With this, another pillar fell. My acceptance of the American dream was due, in large part, to my belief that it offered *everyone*—or almost everyone—a chance for a better life. Now I knew that was not the case. I also knew that the fact that I had a chance was somehow related to the fact that others did not.

Gradually, I began to see what was happening to so many of my own generation: men and women who trusted the basic institutions of our society and believed it was possible to reform them. They chose their professions and worked hard at them over the years, convinced that their efforts would count for something. They took on social and political responsibilities in the expectation that they were doing their part to create a more human world for their children. At some point in late middle age, they realized that their trust had been betrayed. They began to admit to themselves that they had not been offered an opportunity to do good but only to observe and often to perpetuate evil, against their wills. Defeated and victims of their own frustrations, many of them have sought some way to numb their awareness. Others have kept stoically at their posts without asking questions—in order to avoid the pain.

With this, the dream collapsed. As I saw and felt their pain, I could no longer believe that our present structures and institutions offered us the possibility to work for gradual progress toward a more just society. More than this, I had to admit to myself that their story was my story; their failure, mine as well.

In the midst of the turmoil of the Sixties, I was forced to face the fact that, for many of the most sensitive of a younger generation, *the American dream had become a nightmare.* Institutions which had offered me and my generation the hope of a better future, were now experienced as structures of death. I shall never forget the day my daughter said to me: "Remember one thing: Our generation has known only death from the time we were born. We have no reason to believe we will even be alive twenty years from now, much less to hope for a better future. And we can't count on the adults around us to inspire us with a new vision of a world transformed."

This was the final blow. As I came to share their experience, I also shared their perception of what was going on. The American dream had died, not only for many others *but for myself as well.* And with the death of each piece of it, something more died in me.

My experience is by no means unique. The year of the Bicentennial, which was originally planned as a time of celebration, became a time when a variety of voices were speaking out about the death of the American dream. Some expressed regret or bitterness because it had happened; others urged us to mourn its loss. I see no reason to repeat their cries of pain or their laments.

If I dare to speak out at this moment, it is because something radically different has happened to me. As I have experienced more and more deeply the crisis of our life as a nation, I have come to realize that this crisis offers us an opportunity to begin again. In the midst of the collapse of the old order, I see signs of a new world taking shape; I begin to perceive and work for a *new* future. The loss of those values by which we have lived until now is not primarily something to be grieved but to be *willed*. You and I can bring death into the center of our lives—individually and collectively—and overcome it.

To overcome death is to experience resurrection; to discover that we are, in some sense, new human beings, beginning to live new relationships and to create beachheads of new life in dead institutions. It means that, as we risk letting go of those things which sustained life for us in the past, we discover not only that we continue to live but to be surprised again and again by possibilities of meaning and fulfillment we did not know of before. To the extent that we die *to* the old order, we need not die *with* it.

I can speak of resurrection because I have experienced it. Out of the failures of three decades of hard work as a missionary, minister, and teacher, I have discovered a new task for the rest of my life. Awareness of the breakdown of my relationship with people of the Third World, as a missionary and as a participant in the Ecumenical Movement, has opened the way for a new and exciting experience of international solidarity. The collapse of my middle class way of life and the values that went with it has meant that I am coming alive in a way I had not known before. As I have faced the barrenness of primary relationships formerly taken for granted, I have come to know a growing convergence of my life journey with that of others, by which I am being enriched and challenged day by day.

It is because of this unexpected experience at the center of my life that I am grasped by a new vision of the future of America. Out of this personal experience of resurrection, I am compelled to speak of the possibility of a resurrected people, a resurrected America. I use the word *resurrection*, knowing that it may sound strange to many of you. I use it because it is the only word I know that describes a unique interpretation of our present experience as Americans. It emphasizes radical discontinuity with the structures of death around us. These structures are destroying us; they are also destroying themselves. When we once realize this, we know that they have no power to create a future for us. We are thus no longer locked into the mystifications that keep them going; we can thus expect to be presented with opportunities to create a more human life precisely as they collapse around us. Consequently, we are freed to reconnect with and appropriate elements out of our past that can empower us, and to develop new patterns of human relationships; to be, in some small way, agents of transformation. If we cannot pass on to our children a social order in which they will feel more at home, we can at least pass on to them *the legacy of a struggle for a new order,* and expect new life to emerge from the ruins around us.

With this new starting point, we can look more closely at the original vision out of which America—and the American dream—was born, the vision which shaped our emergence as a nation. In his fascinating history of the American Revolution, *A New Age Now Begins: A People's History of the American Revolution,* Page Smith declares:

> In the long struggle that resulted from the effort of Americans to be masters of their own destinies, a new understanding of the relations between the governors and the governed developed, a new sense of the potentialities that lay in ordinary men and women, a new appreciation of possibilities of a better life for people in every continent and nation.[4]

One particular historical expression of that vision is dying and must die. The essential elements in it make us who we are and what we are as Americans. These elements can now burst forth again, taking forms appropriate to our time, and giving shape to our historical experience as a people. These elements, linked with the aspirations they *now* produce, can set the terms for the creation of a new people with a new sense of destiny.

This defines the task before us. It is a task I for one take up as an act of faith, and these pages are precisely an affirmation of faith. In the last few years, I have discovered that I belong to an underground community of faith that has survived across the centuries and, in times like this, has provided vision and power for individual men and women, groups and movements, that have sprung up expectedly and set about turning the world upside down; men and women who see the world around them in the light of what *could be,* who dare to live by a vision of a social order which transcends the limits and the dead ends of the present, trusting in a power not their own.

I see no need to justify such an act of faith: it makes more sense than any other response to the present situation. At the same time, I recognized the limitations I face in trying to speak of it or work out its implications.

It forces me to abandon conceptual frameworks in which I have felt secure for many years, in order to concentrate on and immerse myself in a growing but limited experience of social transformation. And for the sake of these lectures, I must try to articulate and reflect on that experience, knowing that I have no adequate language with which to do it. I choose to speak theologically but to do so in historical terms. This means that, as far as possible, I must speak in everyday language rather than relying on traditional theological concepts. I will also draw on and use language and insights from the social sciences and from philosophy, as well as from current ideologies. But I will make no effort to preserve the "integrity" of my own discipline or any other, or to work out some sort of integration or synthesis of theology with any particular ideology, philosophy or social analysis.

I have gradually lost faith in all such approaches. If we are to contribute to putting together a new story, we will have to move out of the security of our separate disciplines. We will have to discover once again how to think creatively and symbolically about the human condition as we work together on common problems, share our insights, make use of any tools we find that prove helpful, and develop processes of interaction which push us beyond the categories and perspectives we now have. In this situation, I am convinced that the theologian needs to become more aware both of how little he or she has to say and of how important the questions are that one is compelled to raise. For the theologian can insist again and again that our intellectual efforts are to be tested by their capacity to clarify our struggle for a more human future, more than by their conceptual integrity or epistemological soundness. The central issue is not how to *control* a world that is falling apart but how to *transform* human nature and the value systems into which we are locked. Hope for the future is not so much a matter of salvaging the present order as it is of discovering how to live for and participate in an order of human life beyond the collapse of present structures. Especially in a time of transition, what we need are not only new models for the future but also resources for a process of living and experimenting without answers.

We theologians are slowly becoming aware of our poverty in the face of questions such as these. Those who dare to face them from other disciplines are hardly likely to fare much better. Therein lies our hope. Our mutual recognition of the breakdown of our western cultural tradition and the bankruptcy of so much of our intellectual work could open the way for a renewal of thought that is desperately needed at this time.

I have no illusions that what I am here trying to get at will meet a ready welcome within the religious community. For a long time, the religious establishment in America has been closely tied to the very perspectives and values that are now being called into question. At this moment, its growth seems to be most evident among those who, consciously or unconsciously, want to use God to shore up all that is most threatened. Religion thus ends up helping such people avoid the experience that their world is falling apart when it could stand with them as they face the loss of what they most cherish and provide them with resources for new life on the other side. Many of our theological and ethical discussions are far removed from contemporary struggles for transformation. They are often so determined by concepts and language that has little meaning or power precisely for those who are most sensitive to what is happening around them.

At the same time, I am convinced that there is a scattered community of men and women who are wrestling with the same problems I am dealing with in these pages. Many of them are searching for new perceptions and power to keep them going and are attempting to give expression to an emerging experience of grace. For them, this is an invitation to dialogue and hopefully a tool to facilitate it.

One

The Failure of Our Success:

An Interpretation of the

American Experience

If we look closely at the power of the American dream over the centuries; if we are convinced that this dream is now dying and are not willing to stand idly by and watch it happen—then we are compelled to take a new look at ourselves and ask a number of questions: Where did we go so wrong? What was so compelling about the dream of our Founding Fathers? What happened when that dream began to be transformed into reality on American soil? What does it mean for us, in light of our history as Americans, to respond to the crisis before us?

These and other questions call for a re-interpretation of the American experience, a formidable task for historians as well as many others of us. A magnificent example of what I am getting at has just been presented by Page Smith in his recently published two volume study, to which I have referred, *A New Age Now Begins: A People's History of the American Revolution*.[1] I would hope that, in the years ahead, many others will offer us similar studies of our historical development as a people, as well as analyses from the perspective of other disciplines. What follows in these pages is my own limited attempt to suggest some lines for further exploration.

"Planting a New Heaven and a New Earth"

If we are still haunted by such a vision, we have come by it honestly. Our Puritan ancestors were possessed of a tremendous drive for histori-

cal transformation. This drive was an important factor in the development of seventeenth century England and in the founding of America.
Something of its power has been passed on from one generation to
another, shaping people's experience of what it means to be an American. And those who, in recent years, protested against the most destructive forces in our society out of a concern for a better life for its victims,
were reaffirming that original stance of our Puritan forefathers.

By isolating this one aspect of the Puritan experience, I do not intend to
deny the importance of other elements in the complex historical reality
we know as Puritanism. Nor am I trying to overlook the negative
elements in the Puritan way of life which some of us would like to forget
and for which we are still paying a price, individually and collectively.
What is important to me is the early Puritan experience of breakthrough,
which released tremendous energies in our Anglo-Saxon world and
produced the first revolution of modernization. This breakthrough occurred as a result of the impact of Calvinism on the "masterless men" of
that time, men alienated from the culture and institutions around them.
It led to a new self-understanding centering in the vocation to create a
new society. As Stephen Matshall put it, in a sermon preached in 1641,
"you have great works to do, the planting of a new heaven and a new
earth among us. . . ." It produced men and women who dared to break
with the most sacred myths from their past, to live in discontinuity and
risk a new beginning. As Jared Eliot put it:

> It may be said, That in a Sort
> They began the World a New.

We are well aware of what this meant for England. Around the year
1580, a group of Puritan ministers drafted a parliamentary bill which
would have thrown down all existing laws, customs, statutes, ordi-
nances, and constitutions. Sixty years later, the Puritan minister Thomas
Case preached a sermon before the House of Commons in which he
declared:

> "Reformation must be universal . . . reform all places, all persons and
> callings; reform the benches of judgement, the inferior magistrates . . .
> Reform the universities, reform the cities, reform the countries, reform
> inferior schools of learning, reform the Sabbath, reform the ordinances,
> the worship of God . . . you have more work to do than I can speak . . .
> Every plant which my heavenly father hath not planted shall be rooted
> up."[2]

Considering that here the word *reformation* really means *revolution*, we can understand Michael Walzer's comment that "it is hard even to conceive of a politics of such destructive sweep in the Middle Ages."[3] It is also not surprising that the words and actions of these men and their colleagues led directly to the Revolution of 1648.

Others among the Puritans felt so alienated from and disloyal to their nation that they decided to leave. Their calling was to embark on an Exodus, to dare to face the terrors of the ocean, to cross the seas to America in order to build "a New Zion" in an inhospitable wilderness. They did this with a strong messianic sense, convinced that they were raising up a beacon for misguided mankind. John Winthrop expressed their sentiments in a sermon he preached on the ship Arbella, as it made its way to Massachusetts Bay in 1630: "We shall be as a city upon a hill, the eyes of all people are upon us."

This vision evolved in the colonial period as it blended with ideas and ideals from other sources and eventually led to the struggle for independence. It motivated the move to the frontier, the creation of a nation, and the struggle to give shape to economic, social, and political institutions which could offer a new hope to the world. If today we tend to minimize the radicality of their efforts, we would do well to remember a remark by Leslie Fiedler: "There is, indeed, something blasphemous in the very act by which America was established, a gesture of defiance," a drive to break all limits set by God and men.[4]

We hardly need to remind ourselves of the other side of the story, the negative consequences of this same messianism as it has worked itself out in our history. It gave us a sense of manifest destiny. It led us to assume that the rest of the world would want the institutions we had created—and to be tempted repeatedly to impose them by force on other nations. It left us so enamored with our own creations that we could not see how they were destroying the very same human aspirations to which they first gave expression.

All this cannot negate the fact that our Puritan heritage has left an imprint on us which I, for one, want to affirm. To the extent that we are faithful to our origins, we are a peculiar people who understand ourselves in terms of the future toward which we are moving. At its best this heritage has operated to breed dissatisfaction with our past, to keep us open to novelty, and to prepare us for discontinuity. Hans Morgenthau stressed this in an article he wrote during the Watergate crisis, in which he declared:

> The great majority of Americans . . . have never known a status quo to
> whose preservation they could have been committed. For America has
> been committed to a purpose in the eyes of which each status quo has
> been but a stepping-stone to a new achievement . . . .
>   American politics does not defend the past and present against the
> future; rather it defends one kind of future against another kind of
> future.[5]

Because of this heritage, we are a people who, with all the vigor of our
striving for self-interest, find it hard to suppress a desire to make our
lives serve the common good and to contribute to a better world for our
children. We have always been surrounded by many who ignored
this. We have known others whose unique blending of the two has
tended to justify and intensify the struggle for power and wealth for
themselves. At the same time, a significant number of men and women
of each generation—many of them unknown except in narrow circles—
have lived out a creative tension between the goals of self-interest and
commitment to social transformation. I could quickly name a number of
such men and women I have known over the years who have touched
and changed my life decisively. You could do the same. Because of them,
our culture has been made and kept more human and a certain degree of
justice has been achieved in one sphere after another of our common life.

When I was young, this sense of what made life worth living was still
strong in myself and in many of my friends. We were out to have our
careers but what we struggled with was our vocation—the way in which
our lives might count for something as we followed one profession or
another. We had certain ideals and we expected the structures of our
society to give us a chance to live them out. For many of us, this
expectation has not been fulfilled. As a result, we may well be the last
generation to live by such a naive assumption.

What is now clear is that this story could hold together only as long as
we had confidence in the direction in which our nation was moving:
confidence in the potential for economic justice to be achieved through
the use of countervailing power, as we perceived it in the time of the New
Deal; confidence in the overall aims of our foreign policy up to and
immediately following World War II; confidence in the role our various
institutions and professions played in our society, and in our belief in
their openness to constant renewal.

Looking back from where we now stand, we find it hard to understand
the superficiality of our analysis of a few decades ago as well as our
failure to grasp the nature of the destructive forces at work around us. We

can now realize the price we have paid and will continue to pay for the lack of an authentic and continuous radical tradition. Because of it, our social criticism has rarely gone deep enough; dissent has been too easily co-opted, and those who are now committed to struggle for systematic change have no points of reference in our history.

We may regret this failure. Because of it our struggle today is much more difficult. But for me, this is not sufficient reason to turn away from our Puritan sense of vocation. As I have lived in other cultures and come to realize what happens when that drive is not an integral part of a nation's heritage, and as I have witnessed the power of Marxism to provide motivation for a life of service where none existed before: I have come to a new appreciation of this part of my own history. I cannot settle for any story of America that fails to give a central place to this vision; I doubt if there can be a rebirth of national purpose without it.

Prisoners of Our Trends

We can expect no rebirth of passion for social transformation as long as we remain in the situation in which we are now trapped. The sorry spectacle·of the naive ambitions of the young men in the Nixon White House, the deep alienation among the most concerned of a new generation, the growing cynicism and stoicism among middle-aged intellectuals, professionals, and public servants[6] say to us: we have reached the end of the road.

The reason for this is not some loss of moral fiber, the supposed corruption of our youth, or our departure from the values and ideals that "have made America great." To find the cause, we must take a much more critical look at our historical evolution as a nation. A subtle change occurred early in our American sense of destiny. As Daniel J. Boorstin sees it, our successes in carving a new society out of the wilderness and developing as a nation with an ever expanding frontier meant that very soon the IS became our guide for the OUGHT. Or, as I would prefer to put it, what *we were becoming* as our nation evolved was identified with what *we could be.* Success as mastery over a new land overcame our earlier sense of mystery. The common good, toward which our institutions were hopefully moving, was identified with the self-interest of those in power. The future we wanted was soon envisioned as the continuation and expansion of the present order of things. We settled for the slow evolution of our institutions along a line of uninterrupted continuity. As a result, *we became victims of the trends we ourselves had developed.* We saw ourselves as a people free to experiment and respond pragmatically to new problems, without realizing that all the time we were limiting our options more and more to the trends already set.

Consequently, a nation which affirms that it lives in the light of the future has become a victim of its past. Faced by a profound crisis in our economic system and the exhaustion of natural resources, we still function in terms of unlimited expansion and new frontiers. In our educational institutions as well as others, we continue to go about our business as usual in spite of the signs everywhere of our failures. Our foreign policy still functions basically on the lines set by the Cold War. A people who pride themselves in their capacity to create institutions that serve the common good allow themselves to drift into situations in which human aspirations are thwarted and human lives destroyed in ways that stagger our imagination: in the ghettos of our dying cities, in our massive destruction of Third World peoples, our wanton waste of natural resources, etc. And worst of all, when we begin to see what has happened to us, *we are incapable of imagining, much less of struggling for, radically new alternatives.*

The *New York Times* provides two small examples—among the hundreds we could find—of what this means. In an article entitled, "When Everyone's a Loser," Robert L. Rothstein (June 5, 1975, p. 37), a fellow of the Woodrow Wilson International Center for Scholars, examines the present conflict between the rich and the poor countries. He admits that the poor countries have good reason to protest. The cards are stacked against them by the present structures, and as these structures continue, their situation will probably get worse in comparison to ours. But this does not lead Rothstein to stress the need for new patterns of relationship or propose new strategies to bring this about. He can only conclude: "I would venture that there is no way the underdeveloped countries . . . can win the long-term struggle to overturn the existing order." Thus the weight of his argument is to urge them not to protest too much (that would force us, in self-defense, to take an even more negative attitude toward their struggle), as they "are going to need all the external support they can get."

On June 6, 1975 the *Times* reports on the way in which our educational ideals and system have pushed young people for decades to pay any price to get a liberal arts education, expecting it to unlock the doors to the executive suite. This no longer works and increasing numbers of young people are beginning to question our values of success, status, and affluence as well as the competitive struggle to achieve them. But the writer gives no hint that this might call for a radical change in our system of values or of our sense of what is important in life, with consequent implications for fundamental changes in our educational system. Rather, he concludes with these words:

> "The choice we face is really a serious social issue," said Frank Newman, president of the University of Rhode Island, who, while at Stanford University, pioneered important studies on the effects of modern higher education policies.
>
> "You have to ask, is it a good thing for people to have to compete to get the jobs, or would you rather have them compete to get into college? . . .
>
> "And what we've ended up with, is that society is better served, in many important ways, by letting the competition occur at the job level."
> ("Job Problems Stir Doubts About College," Iver Peterson, p. 12)

If we are stuck today with such limited options, it is only because we are willing to settle for intellectual and moral bankruptcy, helpless prisoners in structures we ourselves have created. If we persist in staying there, we should recognize that our imprisonment is the result of our complete abandonment of a central element in the vision of our Founding Fathers. The Puritan drive to create a new world was intimately tied up with the conviction that God transcended and stood in judgment of even their greatest achievements, those of which they were most proud. He also had no hesitation in bringing down those structures which blocked his will in order to clear the way toward a more human future.

We cannot blame previous generations for their failure to sustain a vigorous faith in Calvin's God. I have no desire or expectation to see it re-emerge as a powerful force in contemporary society. But we can recognize the fact that, if we had taken the implications of that heritage seriously, we could have chosen a quite different route. We could have maintained in the past—and we would be prepared to maintain today—a vital critical stance over against trends in the evolution of all aspects of our national life. For in that context, we know that every element in our system—our patterns of relationship to other nations, our economic system, our political structures, and all our institutions—as well as our system as an integrated whole, has no divine or absolute authority. They are human creations, forged to serve human ends. Their validity depends upon their capacity to serve such ends in particular historical situations. They deserve our support only as long as they are open to transformation in response to new historical challenges and changing human aspirations. If and when they become sclerotic and imprison us, in faithfulness to our historical vision we must assume all the risks of exposing their demonic character, breaking their power, and creating space in which to imagine and shape new alternatives.

This is what we have failed to do. This is what we are now incapable of perceiving, much less carrying out. The failure is as evident in the economic realm as in public life, in the church as in the halls of academe. As a result, we have no compelling story. We have no picture of our future as a nation capable of capturing our imagination and providing us with a goal for our individual lives. The story we thought we had—the story we still try hard to convince ourselves is the one by which we are living—has lost its power to sustain us. We may of course stick with it because everything we now think important is tied up with it, or because we have no other story ready to take its place. If we do that, let us be clear that that is *our choice*, not our fate. Let us also admit to ourselves that we are *choosing* to live without passion and without hope, to shore up and defend values and trends which will leave us more and more deprived as time goes on.

Negate, Break Loose and Die—To Live

Let me suggest another scenario. We begin by admitting to ourselves that one era in our national history has played itself out, that along the road we are now going we can expect only one catastrophe after another. We do everything possible to identify those trends that are leading us toward this death and to bring to visibility the contradictions built into our present structures. We recognize our own bondage to the present order and seek ways to free ourselves from its control over us. As we do this, we discover that we are slowly creating a space within which we can gain new perspectives on present problems and see a new future opening up for us in a quite different direction. We may even experience, in a limited way, new possibilities of being alive. The more this happens to us, the more we realize that until now we have been locked into a slow process of death. By risking the loss of what we formerly held on to, we break this power; we experience a resurrected passion and hope. From this vantage point, we see the approaching apocalypse, in one area after another of our national life, not so much as our doom but as an occasion for unexpected and more radical transformation than would otherwise be possible. We admit that we do not have, and cannot have at the present time, political solutions or strategies to propose. But we know that something much more fundamental is happening. We are going through a change in our outlook and way of life that may allow us to enter a new historical era. As that happens, we will find forms of political action capable of breaking the power of the old order and of laying the foundation for a new future.

Let me try to indicate what this might mean in several areas of our common life.

Having lived for several decades in Latin America, I see no future for our country in our relations with the Third World along the lines we are now following. We assume that the American way of life will be the choice of other people around the world. We continue to use our power to impose our will on them. We do everything we can to destroy those alternatives that are different from ours and are seen as a threat to us.

Meanwhile, in one country after another, the conviction grows that each nation must invent and develop its own institutions and structures. It alone can respond authentically to its own culture and history, to its particular social and material conditions which are very different from ours. Our intervention in Indo-China and our continuing support of brutal and reactionary dictatorships around the world have convinced millions of people in the Third World that our talk about freedom, democracy, and economic well-being are myths we use to serve our own interests. As we continue our present policy, what we have come to symbolize is radically repudiated. Our present patterns of economic relationships with Third World peoples serve our interests and work to their detriment. By continuing them, we tend to become richer every year while the poor become poorer. This, combined with our support of those small groups in the developing countries who are concerned about their own profits rather than about overcoming the millennial poverty of the masses, makes us accomplices in maintaining a situation in which millions are now near starvation and are likely to die of hunger within the next few years.

For those who have eyes to see, it is not hard to discern the shape of the coming apocalypse. Continuing along the present path, we will soon be an island of relative affluence surrounded by hundreds of millions of starving people. We will be hated and despised by nations who, in desperation, will resort to every weapon possible—blackmail, terrorism, and the like—in their struggle for survival. And we will become Fortress America, trying to police a starving world in order to maintain our privileged position. We are horrified by what we did in Vietnam, by the attempts of the CIA to assassinate Fidel Castro and others, and by our part in training those who control the torture chambers in Brazil and elsewhere. But we cannot abandon these tactics if we try to exist as

Fortress America. We may in fact find ourselves involved in even more horrendous acts. And if something essential to our humanity was destroyed by what we did in Vietnam, we are headed for a much more devastating experience of dehumanization in the years ahead.

There is probably very little we can do right now to avoid this apocalypse. As we approach it, we can engage in a process of self-examination which puts us in touch with human values buried deep within us and within our tradition. We can get a new sense of what is really important for us and gradually be captured by a new vision of our place in the world that is coming into being. If we are willing to go through such fires or purgation, we may discover that a worthwhile future for us means interdependence for the sake of survival, with the commitment of our wealth and technical know-how to that end.

If we dare to pursue that goal, a new historical era may open up for our nation as well as for the rest of the world. To encourage other peoples to go their own way and develop their own authentic institutions is only to support what we achieved by our Revolutionary War. If we risk supporting other nations in that search, they will be less inclined to adopt one or another brand of Communism; they will be free to invent other, and perhaps still unknown, solutions. And if we are free to recognize the increasing bankruptcy of our own institutions, we can join others in a common quest in which we will all be able to learn from and contribute to each other.

United with others in the struggle for human survival on this planet, we will come to realize that interaction with other races and cultures, economic systems and forms of social organization, offers an exciting and enriching experience for all of us, in the midst of tension and conflict. Even more important, we will be enabled to undergo a revolution in our present values in relation to material goods. As we face, with other peoples of the world, the threat to survival implied in the gradual exhaustion of natural resources, food shortages, and the present inequality in the distribution of goods, something may happen to us that has never happened before. We may begin to question our obsession with material things, our consumer society, and the mentality that goes with it, and our desire for personal affluence when surrounded by spreading poverty. If that should happen to us, we might become aware of how small our lives have become and find other sources of satisfaction, other roads to self-realization. This would prepare us to accept and work for a more equitable distribution of the world's resources, recognizing that it would mean a lower material standard of living for us.

I admit that this sounds, at present, like a wild utopian dream. Speaking quite realistically, it could eventually become the price we will have to pay for survival as a nation and as human beings.

I have gone into some detail to give just one example of what will be involved in reworking our story of who we are as a people. If we hope to move beyond our present impasse, we will have to do something similar in a number of other spheres as well. One of these is our present economic system. Over the last 150 years we have achieved remarkable success in our capacity to produce, in our development of technology, in our ability to meet basic material needs. We have demonstrated that it is possible to overcome the age-old burden of toil, misery, and deprivation. We have also allowed this productive process to develop according to trends that are rapidly exhausting our natural resources, depriving men and women of the opportunity for meaningful and creative work, creating gross inequalities in the distribution of goods, destroying our major cities and depriving us of many of the services we badly need.

Here too we are faced with a fundamental choice. We can decide to allow present trends to continue indefinitely. But now we know that this means inevitable disaster, as stated sharply by a team of British scientists and philosophers:

> The principal defect of the industrial way of life with its ethos of expansion is that it is not sustainable. Its termination within the lifetime of someone born today is inevitable—unless it continues to be sustained for a while longer by an entrenched minority at the cost of imposing great suffering on the rest of mankind. We can be certain, however, that sooner or later it will end (only the precise time and circumstances are in doubt), and that it will do so in one of two ways: either against our will, in a succession of famines, epidemics, social crises and wars or in the way we want it to—because we wish to create a society which will not impose hardship and cruelty upon our children—in a succession of thoughtful, humane and measured changes.[7]

Or, we can question these trends, as we recognize that this economic process is our creation and can be changed by human decisions made in the light of new goals. Here also, such a decision could open a new historical era. A new era in which the economic order was harnessed to serve human ends and in which we could concentrate our major energies around the creation of conditions for a richer and fuller human life. Such a change in direction is possible. It will occur only if those who see what is happening redefine what is important for them. Only then can they challenge the present order and make room for creative minds to imagine and experiment with alternatives to what has until now been taken for granted.

The task before us, just in the two areas we have mentioned, is staggering! But the crisis we experience in America today is an even wider one. It has to do with modern bureaucracy and present patterns of administration, with the nuclear family and other primary communities. We have no overall analysis which can give us a neat picture of what has gone wrong or easy clues as to what is involved in bringing about change. What we do know is that all these spheres are interrelated, that what happens in one affects the others, and that to have a *human* future requires an overall process of transformation of consciousness and of the social order.

The Challenge of the Bicentennial—To Repeat the Act of Our Founders

The task we have outlined is indeed an overwhelming one. It is not impossible. The question is whether we can get in touch with aspirations, social vision, and sources of individual and social power capable of taking it on. This is the problem that will engage our attention in the next two lectures. I want to conclude this one by reminding you that, when faced by such a task, we Americans have one very important historical point of reference. *Our existence as a nation is evidence that a historical transformation of these dimensions can occur, and that we as a people once found the power to do it.*

If our commitment to this vocation means that we are considered to be wild anarchists or mad subversives, we are doing no more than repeat, for our time, the act of our founders. In fact, we will have to work hard to be as radical in our understanding of what we are doing as they were.

To experience our society today as standing under judgment and headed for an apocalypse;

To feel thoroughly alienated from it and to intensify that sense of alienation in the light of an alternative vision of the future;

To embark on an Exodus, not by leaving this country but by breaking free from our present value systems and the terms they set for us within the established order;

To hope to enter a new time and contribute our part to laying the foundations for a new historical era, even as they sought a New Land with the will to build a New Zion;

> To question the very foundations of our industrial, capitalist society, and the institutions and values it has produced, as they denounced the "false foundations of the centuries since Jesus."

All this is part of the re-invention of their act of founding. It is also our opportunity, as Americans, to begin to live and tell a new story in which heritage and destiny meet and promise the possibility of life to the next generation. We have arrived at a point in our history where the test of our faithfulness to our founders and generations that came after them is our freedom to break with and transform the values and institutions they created.

Marxism and a New Historical Era

Any radical critique of our present order leads us directly to a consideration of socialism as the alternative future for this country as well as for the Third World. Thus far, most of us have responded to this problem in terms of irrational fears: the fear that socialism must inevitably mean Stalinist Communism; the fear that whenever any nation goes socialist, it inevitably joins our enemies and is out to destroy us.

If we can begin to admit to ourselves the absurdity of this logic, we will realize that some type of socialism has and will continue to have a powerful appeal in the Third World as the form of the revolution of modernization that makes sense at the present time. Marxism offers a compelling vision of a new society capable of motivating the struggle for social transformation. It provides patterns of economic, social, and political organization that promise rapid national development, *and* the possibility of overcoming the poverty and exploitation of the masses in the process of modernization.

As for this country, we can see how much we have lost as a consequence of blocking out an ongoing debate with Marx and Marxism in the course of our national history; we can also begin to break the taboo against socialism as a response to our present crisis. In fact, whether we like it or not, in the years immediately ahead, we are probably going to move toward national economic planning and increasing involvement of the state in the ordering of our economic life. The question will be whether we will allow that process of socialization to continue in the direction it is now moving, toward increasing domination by our major corporations and their servants. Or will we decide that the time has come to use our economic resources to meet the most basic and urgent needs of our society: rebuilding our cities, overcoming poverty, providing employment for all, etc?

Such a shift now seems completely impossible; it will make more sense to an increasing number of people as our economic and political situation becomes more catastrophic. But the question we are trying to pose here goes beyond this: how do we understand the basic contradictions in our society as they *now* confront us and overcome them so as to move into a new historical era? At this point, in my judgment, Marxism cannot help us very much, especially if we take it too seriously. Marx himself may help us to find the reasons why.

Marx was strong in his critique of those who built systems, who tried to construct "a science of society" that was not based on an adequate understanding of social reality. He was convinced that true knowledge of the shape of things to come depended upon a thorough analysis of existing reality. I have long been impressed by the thoroughness of Marx's analysis of *his* society and his capacity to identify the fundamental contradictions in nineteenth century capitalism. I am equally impressed by the incapacity of most Marxists I know to do anything comparable in identifying the nature of the contradictions in our post-industrial society and thus helping us to grasp the shape of the future.

I am not a sociologist or an economist. One does not have to be an expert in these fields to recognize that certain fundamental changes are occurring in the nature of the issues confronting us. The question is no longer primarily who owns the means of production, but the assumptions underlying the productive process itself. We now begin with limited natural resources and the consequent limits to production, and work out from there. As a consequence of present developments in technology, the issue is no longer principally that of who controls it. More important is the question regarding the nature of tools. Do they serve to extend human power and creativity or do they enslave us? Recognizing the cultural history of people in non-Western countries, how can they develop the tools which, *in their situation,* will enhance the power of men and women, contribute to creative work and to a new and richer relationship between human beings and the world of nature? As modern bureaucracy has developed, in industrialized socialist societies as well as in our own, it has extended one dominant pattern of human relationships to the exclusion of others. That pattern is hierarchical; it emphasizes limited tasks and roles, and is increasingly ineffective in responding to human needs. Precisely in the serving professions, it has deprived women and men of control over their own lives in one area after another, at the same time that it has trained a specialized elite, many of whom are becoming aware of the limits of their "service." At a time when limited production and highly developed technology free us to choose a rich variety of life styles and goals, Marxism seems to have little to offer. In modern socialist societies, the sense of self-worth defined by one's position in the productive process and in the acceleration of technological advances—and the competition for such positions as well as for the education that opens the door to them—is as strong as in capitalist countries. .

To find one or another text in Marx which shows some awareness of any of the issues I am getting at is really beside the point. It is not essentially different from our attempt, as Christians, to find some verse in the Bible to relate to any new problem arising in our history. Nor is it of much help to insist that in China or in Cuba one or another of these problems is being worked on. One thing, and one thing only matters: where do we get the insight and power to identify the contradictions now determining *our* society, and to experiment in finding new directions to overcome them?

Ultimately, Marx was concerned to overcome the fundamental dichotomies in our Western cultural tradition; to solve the traditional problems of Western philosophy which Hegel attempted to solve but failed to do: the dichotomies between subject and object, human being and nature, existence and essence; between labor as "mere means of life" and labor as "life's primary want"; between "the all-around development of the individual" and the increase of "all the springs of the cooperative level."[8] Much has happened in the last hundred years, especially in the last two decades, to expose the failure of Hegel—and Marx—at this point and the reasons for it. To take these discoveries into account raises serious questions about "objective" social analysis, and about attempts at macro-social analyses which do not start with human experience and work out from critical reflection on it. The "new consciousness" widely evident among young people, women, and others sensitive to the accelerating crisis of a post-industrial society presents interesting possibilities for connecting with and developing further Marx's reflection on the human condition. Thus far, few Marxists have given serious attention to this issue. Marxism may have an important contribution to make in these various areas; it will be able to make it only as those who turn to it for help admit its limitations and poverty and are thus free to *re-create* the Marxist vision and perspective for a new time.

Two

A Future Worth Living Now

"The morning comes, the night decays, the watchmen leave their
  stations;
"The grave is burst, the spices shed, the linen wrapped up;
"The bones of death, the cov'ring clay, the sinews shrunk & dry'd
"Reviving shake, inspiring move, breathing, awakening,
"Spring like redeemed captives when their bonds & bars are burst."

> William Blake's prophecy of America as a res-
> urrected passion. In *America—A Prophecy.*

For those who dare to consider the task I have just outlined, one thing is
absolutely essential: the rebirth of passion. The disillusioned, the
frightened, the cynical—be they conservatives, liberals or radicals—do
not lead the way to the future, no matter how profound their insights
may be regarding the nature of the present crisis. That journey is reserved for women and men of passion.

We may not know exactly what it is that produces a passionate response in one or another historical situation. We do have some idea of
what does and does not destroy it. It is not as likely to be destroyed by a
"hopeless" situation as by the loss of hope that comes when those who
reject the given order of things are still bound by its perspectives and
assumptions. The established order encourages us to confuse a particular
way of looking at the world with reality itself. As long as we do this, we
are imprisoned by it. Passion is not necessarily strangled when we are
deprived of conditions for a satisfying life; it dies with the loss of a sense
of the worthwhileness of life when lived according to the dominant
values.

When old perspectives fail and the promise of life is not fulfilled,
passion can re-emerge only as a *resurrected* passion. When we realize that
our perspectives on society are rational constructs which no longer help

120

us to be in touch with and understand the dynamics of society nor empower us to shape it to serve human ends, we may experience loss and chaos. Our eyes may also be opened to see the destructiveness and impotence of the established order and to perceive new ways of working for change. Likewise, we can question the values by which we have lived until now, more through a crisis of self-identity—and find something more important and satisfying to live for than increasing production, competing for position, or exercising power over other people and things.

The Question of Perspective

If we accept Daniel J. Boorstin's interpretation of the American experience,[1] one perspective on our society has completely dominated our self-understanding as a people. We as North Americans *assume the GIVENNESS of our basic institutions.* We take for granted the terms set by the evolutionary development of our society. In this, we are supported by our pragmatic approach to things. This makes it unnecessary for us to ask basic questions about goals or about the functioning of the system as a whole. It is sufficient to work on and solve specific problems, in one field after another, as they come along. Such an approach served us well as long as we could drift comfortably in the direction in which we were going. Now that we are forced to face fundamental questions about our goals and the direction in which our evolutionary development is taking us, this same approach breaks down. In fact, it has now become a major cause of the bankruptcy of our social thought.

Consequently, our political struggle in the coming decades is going to become increasingly a battle about assumptions and perspectives. It will be a matter more and more of how we make sense out of what is happening around us. What frame of reference do we have for deciding about the goals we want to pursue and how to work for them?

What amazes me about the perspective to which Boorstin calls our attention is the fact that we have bought it for so long without questioning it. I don't start out any longer accepting the givenness of our institutions or assuming their adequacy. I begin by questioning their capacity to respond to the needs we now have. This is a much more rational approach, if I take into account how historically conditioned all our responses are. At the best, they are far from perfect; given the speed of change, their answers may be out of date before we know it. Those institutions most successful in meeting particular human needs often create new aspirations and tasks with which they are unprepared to cope. When nations and societies respond most creatively to challenges before them, they tend to become bound by their own success, to be enamored by their responses. Often, that happens just when they have helped to create a new situation calling for a radically different response, which they are incapable of offering.

When such a moment comes, a nation can move ahead only as it is free to look critically at its institutions, structures, and the values underlying them, and if necessary, to give them up and replace them by others. If and when this task becomes the order of the day, politics is turned upside down. The important thing is not to come up with pragmatic solutions, within the terms already set, but to get hold of new approaches which makes such solutions impossible in the short tun. To act responsibly in the political sphere is a matter of identifying and pressing the contradictions that have appeared, and of encouraging those aspirations and dreams for a new life which do not fit into the dominant system.

This approach makes sense out of what I see happening in this country today. The American system and its corresponding way of life is awakening new aspirations within us, without the satisfaction of which we cannot live; yet it cannot meet those aspirations. Our technological, industrial society has eroded the authority of the past and of all structures of domination; it has thrust us into a world of change in which we can order our lives only as we respond to new challenges and orient ourselves around the future we want to create. And having done that, this same system is now bound by the trends it set in motion in the past. The development of technology in relation to the production of goods has been so successful that many of the major obstacles to a full human life can be removed: the burden of toil, subjection to the vagaries of nature, the persistent threat of poverty and starvation, the necessity to spend long hours working to produce the bare essentials of life. All this has begun to free men and women from obsession with the struggle to produce—and consume. It has created a longing for a richness and meaning in life that can no longer be provided by a society oriented primarily around economic growth. We have arrived at a point where the whole productive process can be seen for what it is: one—and only one—of a number of tasks we must perform to make and keep human life human. In other words, *the very success of our industrial society has now made a society and a way of life centered on its continued expansion obsolete.*

To face that shift, and to contribute to the transformation of human values it calls for, is, in my judgment, the most rational response possible. In reality, it is the one thing the present order and those locked into it are incapable of perceiving, much less carrying out. This becomes especially clear if we look at the current political scene:

1. Many liberals are aware that things are not going well and long to see basic changes in the present order of things. A few of them are quite radical in their perception of what is wrong and provide us with a critical analysis of the crisis of our society. But when it comes to responding to the problems they have so clearly enunciated, a curious thing happens. They quickly fall back into the old categories and perspectives that have already been tried out and have failed. The solutions they offer are part of the problem; the reality they are trying to deal with no longer fits into their frame of reference. Thus far, the liberal approach has been the main source of our political illusions, illusions that we are being forced to abandon one by one.

2. A new conservatism will probably have a much greater appeal, at least for a number of years. However critical it may be of specific aspects of our recent system, it is incapable of grasping the perspective of which we are speaking. It can increase people's dissatisfaction with the present order; what it cannot do is offer them a vision of a new future for America or help them move toward it. Because it exploits the frustrations and fears of those who are most threatened, it tends toward a vicious type of cynicism. Those who mouth its slogans have a hard time really believing them. As one of the leaders of the presidential campaign of Governor George Wallace put it recently:

> "You can think all day long how you would like to change human nature, but you can't: People are more strongly motivated by negative issues than positive ones. When there are no negative issues, the appeal isn't too strong."[2]

Conservative movements may eventually arise which will represent honest attempts to solve our present problems. But however sincere they are , they fail at two points: at their best they are determined more by the past than by the future; and they have a low view of human nature. They fail to perceive the potential in men and women for facing reality and opening their lives to change. As a result, they cannot motivate people for such transformation or provide them with resources for it.

3. In the last few years, a number of our most concerned and capable intellectual leaders have attempted to move beyond conservatism and liberalism and provide us with new insights into the nature of our present crisis. In the next few years, we will almost certainly have a

greater number speaking to us in this vein. When I read their writings, I respect their hard assessment of what is happening and what lies ahead of us; their honesty in facing these prospects, and the seriousness of their struggle to find a way out. But somehow most of them fall short of offering us the one thing we need: a New Starting Point, a new perspective from which to analyze our society and respond to the challenge it presents.

Let me try to show what I mean by taking a brief look at Robert Heilbroner's *An Inquiry into the Human Prospect*.[3] I find most of his analysis of the problem congenial. I agree with his conclusion that "the long era of industrial expansion is now entering its final stages, and we must anticipate the commencement of a new era of stationary output and . . . declining material output per head in the advanced nations."[4] I also share his evaluation of the failure of both capitalist and socialist societies in the West to meet the deepest needs of the human person, as well as his expectation of cataclysmic events ahead.

I too expect the apocalypse; I know it will bring incredible suffering and destruction. But I also live by the hope that the apocalypse can open the way for a type of social transformation we cannot now envision, and thus be the beginning of a new historical era. Heilbroner cannot contemplate that possibility. As a result, he settles for a picture of the future we have already transcended historically; his vision is too limited to inspire or sustain the struggle for survival at this time.

> Individual achievement, especially for material ends, is likely to give way to the acceptance of communally organized and ordained roles. . . . the public must take precedence over the private. . . . In our discovery of "primitive" cultures, living out their timeless histories, we may have found the single most important object lesson for future man. . . . The spirit of conquest and aspiration will not provide the inspiration [humanity] needs . . . . It is the example of Atlas, resolutely bearing his burden, that provides the strength we seek.[5]

4. Karl Marx stands almost alone among political philosophers in his concern to look at the world in the light of its future transformation. Because of this fact and the thoroughness of his analysis of early industrial society, he and his followers have made an immense contribution to social and political thought and action over the past hundred years. In the development of his messianic and utopian perspective, Marx drew on resources which originally came from the symbolic language of religion. When he expressed this vision in conceptual language and formu-

lated an integrated rational system centering in a philosophy of history, he greatly limited the power of Marxism to follow his lead, to continue to look at society in terms of its future transformation. The results of this are especially evident in the Communist societies of Eastern Europe. In our own country, it has meant that thus far Marxism has not given us much help in our efforts to grasp and overcome the contradictions in a *post-industrial society*. It has failed to do for our time what Marx did for his.

The majority of Americans will probably function in terms of givenness and continuity as long as possible. The problem is: this doesn't make sense any longer; in the future, it will make even less sense out of what is happening around us. If and when someone realizes this, where can he/she turn for another option? Here our religious background may be of some value to us. However acculturated Christianity in America has become, it still keeps us in touch with a tradition which reflects on human experience in terms of death and resurrection and looks at present reality in the light of the coming Kingdom of God. Theological statements about eschatology will not contribute much to a transformation of perspective. But if we take that tradition more seriously as we become more involved in working for change in our society, we may find ourselves thinking and responding in a new way. Here I can only state what this means for me.

I do not believe in some law of history which guarantees the emergence of a new social order out of and beyond the advancing contradictions of the old order. A society may lose its power for creative response and still hang on for a long time, producing stagnation and slowly killing off its members yet surviving indefinitely. I do believe that human aspirations—a persistent drive in women and men for a richer and fuller life—do constitute the dynamic of history. I believe that, as social structures develop, they arouse aspirations that cannot be contained. "Once you wake up the human animal you can't put it back to sleep again."[6] I am also convinced that such structures can block these same aspirations. To struggle to overcome this contradiction by envisioning and fighting to create a form of life that transcends it becomes our historical vocation.

If we dare to undertake this task, we may make one further discovery. As we become aware of our own deepest aspirations and those of others, we can also develop them further by projecting, into the future, the way of life for which we yearn. Likewise, we need not be content with a growing awareness of the dominant trends around us which work against the fulfillment of these aspirations. We can also project those trends into the future and get a clearer picture of what their continuation is likely to produce.

In reflecting on my own experience in this regard, I have found that whenever I failed to perceive where the trends around me were leading and was unclear about the future I wanted, I delayed making major decisions; and the longer the delay, the more limited my options became. On the other hand, to the extent that I was able to identify and project trends into the future—trends in personal relationships, in the institutions to which I was related, in the developing sense of my own vocation—and make early decisions about what I wanted to become, to that extent my life has been open and growing. I've never been particularly good at this. But my recognition, rather early on, of the paternalism inherent in our relationships with people of the Third World has opened the way for exploring patterns of solidarity which have been especially rewarding; the conclusions I came to ten years ago about the bankruptcy of our educational institutions and of so many of our intellectual efforts led me to try out other educational processes and team work with my more creative students, ventures which have kept me going in barren times. I have also observed the same process at work in social structures. Out of such a convergence in our personal and social experience, we may eventually find resources for a new political approach.

Frustrated Aspirations—And a Possible Breakthrough

I would like to see us develop such an approach, not in abstract conceptual terms, but in reflection on the experience of people in our society today. In my own attempt to do this, I have chosen one of the most fascinating revelations of the longings and frustrations of men and women in America I have ever read. I refer to the stories people tell about themselves in Studs Terkel's book, *Working.* As I read these stories, I tried to perceive what these people were saying about the present order. What it is like and how it affects them. Their present ache as well as their sense of what could be. By following this procedure, I have arrived at several conclusions about the present state of affairs. I do not claim that any or all of the people from whose stories I quote draw these same conclusions. I would insist that they represent one possible interpretation of the experiences presented and offer a way out of the frustrations to which these men and women refer repeatedly.

What comes through in so many of these stories, in a powerful way, is the fact that participation in modern industrial society has produced a new awareness of what it means to be human in today's world and a longing for that quality of life. In Terkel's own words, "I was constantly astonished by the extraordinary dreams of ordinary people."

My wager is that this process of enlightenment will continue to grow; that it cannot be repressed for very long or destroyed; and that the established order is incapable of responding to it. Let me spell out what I mean:

1. We now know we don't have to be slaves of dull, boring, meaningless work;
   We now know we don't want to be; many of us simply won't tolerate it.

> It's so demeaning to be there and not be challenged. . . .
> I know I'm vegetating and being paid to do exactly that. . . .
> I feel like I'm being pimped for and it's not my style.
> The level of bitterness in this department is stunning.
>
> Nora Watson, p. 523

> There ought to be a reason behind what men do. We're not just machines, but some of us live like machines. We get plugged into a job and come down at nine o'clock in the morning and someone turns us on. At five o'clock someone turns us off and we go home. What happens during that time doesn't have any connection with our real lives.
>
> Jack Currier, p. 565

> The drones are no longer invisible nor mute. Nor are they exclusively of one class. Markham's Man with the Hoe may be Ma Bell's girl with the headset. . . . They're in the office as well as the warehouse; at the manager's desk as well as the assembly line; at some estranged company's computer as well as some estranged woman's kitchen floor.
>
> pp. xiii-xiv

Our present system is bound to produce and sell more and more; to produce it as rapidly and cheaply as possible. It is not free either to develop other types of work or to explore ways of reducing this burden of toil to a minimum for each of us.

2. Because of our fantastic economic growth, we don't have to be obsessed with making money any more.

> The almighty dollar is not the only thing in my estimation. There's more to it—how I'm treated. What I have to say about what I do, how I

do it. It's more important than the almighty dollar. The reason might be that the dollar's here now. It wasn't in my father's young days. I can concentrate on the social aspects, my rights.

Gary Bryner, President
Lordstown Local, UAW;
pp. 189-190

The present system can continue to function only by maintaining the myth that making money is all important.

3. We know that there is no reason to maintain—and feed our lives into—a productive machine that is more concerned about production than people, that exhausts the earth's resources, pollutes our atmosphere, creates unnecessary wants and induces people to buy worthless products. We know that when we serve such a machine we demean ourselves; something dies within us.

> *"I deplore the whole idea of commercialism. I find it degrading."*
> You begin to say, "What the fuck am I doing? I'm sitting here destroying my country."
>
> Walter Lundquist, commercial
> artist and industrial designer.
> pp. 525, 526

> I took on a foreman's job, some six or seven weeks and decided that was not my cup of tea. The one thing they stressed: production first, people second.
>
> Gary Bryner, p. 188

> I wouldn't want to see all the automobiles banned because they pollute the air. Yet I realize what the hell good is my livelihood if the air's gonna kill me anyway.
>
> Gary Bryner, p. 192

Our productive system has demonstrated that it cannot function without doing all these things.

4. Modern industrial society has given people a sense of their own worth and dignity; consequently, they want a chance to do something worthwhile with their time in their work situation, to be challenged to do their best and be proud of themselves. The massive structure of the industrial machine and of bureaucratic organizations denies all this to

large numbers; it is producing deep resentment and bitterness that will sooner or later explode.

> Jobs are not big enough for people.
> "I think most of us are looking for a calling, not a job."
> I realized: Okay, the road to ruin is doing a good job. The amazing, absurd thing was that once I decided to stop doing a good job, people recognized a kind of authority in me. Now I'm moving ahead like blazes.
> They expect less than you can offer.
>
> Nora Watson, pp. 521, xxiv, 522, 523

> I wanted to be a key man in the industry. Over the years I realized there isn't any key man—that every human is a commodity to be exploited. And destroyed and cast aside.
>
> Walter Lundquist, p. 525

Where is the present system doing anything to change this? How can it?

5. Our system has been so dynamic because it has been able to claim the energies of men and women; to claim their lives. Now with its success, it still calls for people's time, energy, and loyalty. At the same time it says: *You are dispensible*: through less opportunities for work for young people, growing numbers of unemployed, the facility with which people who have given the best years of their lives to a company or organization are dismissed, the trend toward retiring men and women at an earlier age. No system can rape and dispose of its people that way and survive as a human society.

> As the work force becomes increasingly younger, so does Willy Loman.
> Perhaps it is this specter that most haunts working men and women: the planned obsolescence of people that is of a piece with the planned obsolescence of the things they make. Or sell. It is perhaps this fear of no longer being needed in a world of needless things that most clearly spells out the unnaturalness, the surreality of much that is called work today.
>
> Terkel, pp. xvii, xviii

Until now many of us have assumed that radical dissatisfaction with the American system is something that is limited to marginal groups along with a small number of students and intellectuals. Studs Terkel's report, along with other studies, confirms my own experience as I have been in contact with diverse groups of people over the last couple of years: dissatisfaction with the present state of affairs is very widespread. An increasing number of people from many different backgrounds are deeply frustrated and are calling into question not only the way our society is functioning but some of our most basic values. To be sure, they are often confused; their analysis is a strange bag of contradictions. They have believed the promise of our industrial society that we were headed toward a new stage in human emancipation and self-realization; their experience shows that it has betrayed this promise. They have given their lives to serve a productive system which assured them that in doing so they were creating a society of increasing economic advantage for all. Now they know that it has failed to provide for the most basic needs of a significant proportion of the people of this country. Given the crises in the Third World and in our relations to it, as well as the possibilities of imminent exhaustion of the world's natural resources, this expectation is becoming a rapidly vanishing dream.

They were promised a rich and rewarding life if they sold their souls to this system: upward mobility, satisfaction through status and success, competitive achievement and more money. What they now experience is the loss of any real power over their lives; the dissolution of self in jobs and roles; a competitive struggle that leaves them diminished and deprived. The promises vanish but aspirations remain and increase. As the mythology collapses, people have greater freedom to look rationally and critically at the mess they are in; they also suspect that there is no way out.

Frustration may be the dominant mood of the moment; it does not have to continue forever. As some of us begin to see the impotence of the old order to produce the society we want, we can begin to break out of the defeatism its decline has produced. To the extent that we get more in touch with our unfulfilled aspirations, we may begin to see how the present situation is creating conditions for a new order of life and seize the opportunity to have a part in creating it. This shift in perspective can happen to us at any time and represent a sort of conversion experience. With it, at least two major changes may occur in our outlook:

1. The first will have to do with our whole attitude toward the productive society, its structure and assumptions. We will realize that we can harness our industrial machine—the production and distribution of goods, the development and use of technology—to meet the most basic needs of all people. We may not yet know how to do this; we do know it is

a task we must undertake. As we succeed at it, we will find ourselves, of necessity, moving in the direction of a more egalitarian society.

To accomplish this, we must demythologize our industrial society and look at it in the same rational way we look at other areas of our common life. We can also give it much less importance than it has enjoyed until now. If it stole the center of the stage for the last several centuries, that is no reason it should continue to do so. Until now the entrepreneur and the business executive have occupied positions of prestige and power in our society. All of us have been inclined to judge our worth, to some extent at least, by our place in the productive process.

That era will soon end. The time is coming when those who struggle to transform our industrial society to serve human ends and those who provide us with models of creative activity in other areas will receive more recognition. And our sense of our own worth will be defined in other ways. In the Middle Ages, the members of the religious hierarchy held people's world together. They had trememdous power and enjoyed great respect. In traditional Brazil, the *fazendeiro,* the large plantation owner who cared for and exploited all those on his estate, was in a similar position. In both instances, these men occupied their positions because of the values dominant in that particular time and place. They retained their power and shaped the ambitions and goals of those around them only as long as that world remained intact.

I can see a time coming when men and women will take a very rational approach to the production and distribution of the basic material necessities of life. This will be seen as something that has to be done, a burden to be shared by all—in order for all to have the freedom, the time and the energy to be engaged in more interesting and important things.

On a very small scale, something like this is beginning to happen with some families I know. Buying food, preparing meals, washing dishes and clothes, cleaning the house, caring for small children: these are no longer *the responsibility* of the woman of the house, by which she gains recognition and convinces herself of her own worth. They are responsibilities to be shared, and shared equally, by all adults and young people in the home. For this to happen takes time and effort, and a great deal of communication among the members of the family. It may not produce many gourmet meals and the house may not look quite as elegant as it did before. But one or more persons is freed in each instance to find a richer life; and the atmosphere around the home becomes more human. People discover ways of making their chores less of a burden; and from time to time one or another member of the household finds a special pleasure in preparing a meal or making the home attractive. To work something like this out in the economic realm represents a qualitatively different task. Today it is an urgent necessity, not a utopian dream; a major challenge to our creativity; an alternative to the loss of our humanity.

2. As we demythologize our present economic order and begin to structure it to serve human ends, something even more significant will happen to us. We will get more in touch with our aspirations for a richer life; we will also begin to realize that the development of our industrial society has intensified these dreams, while its decline makes their achievement a historical possibility for the first time.

Our material progress and the rewards it has offered us have left us with a yearning for something more that will not go away. The early stages of industrialization required discipline and repression: sublimation of sexual and other feelings, the rejection of present satisfaction for the sake of greater achievement and wealth in the future. It also called for the regimentation of men and women and the disciplining of human energies in order to get the productive process moving. Today that sort of repression is no longer needed. In fact, to the extent that it is maintained, social transformation is blocked and our most intimate self violated. Repression is no longer the necessary accompaniment of revolution; overcoming repression is now central to the revolution itself. The creation and consolidation of the nation-state demanded cultural integration. Today the nation-state is obsolete in face of economic, political, and social realities that are worldwide in character. But the mentality produced by it, coupled with the impact of modern technological development, produces sterile homogenization and uniformity. The alternative open to us is the encouragement of the richest diversity in personal life styles and in culture, based upon the growth of strong, free, and creative human beings.

These diverse elements come into focus when we take into account the fact that our Western cultural tradition, which held life together in a satisfying way for more than 1500 years, is now falling apart. Its disintegration has a profound effect on all of us. No longer is our structure of selfhood determined by an overall world view into which we can fit securely and find acceptable and accepted tools for thinking abour ourselves and our world. No longer do we have any absolutes which can serve as trustworthy points of reference for us. All structures external to us, on which we have traditionally relied to *give us* our selfhood and a framework of meaning, have let us down.

Our first reaction to all of this may be a deep crisis of self-identity. We may discover that all the connections we have had with self, with others, and with our world are being broken. We have no secure place to stand, no structure of self, passed on from one generation to another, in which we can feel at home. At the same time, these very elements contributing to a loss of self provide a unique occasion for human creativity. We can begin to discern a form of life in the light of which the secure and structured world of the past appears all too limited and confining. Once again we have before us an open horizon challenging us to an act of defiance, a drive to break all limits. To accept it means to create space in which to live that new reality now as fully as possible and to discover the power such new life offers us for subverting the old order and giving shape to the new.

A New Way of Life: A New Source of Power

We have arrived at a new stage in the struggle for human emancipation and self-realization. The focus of it: a new subjectivity which holds the promise of breaking the stranglehold of the forces of death around us. Not the rational autonomous individual of the Enlightenment. Not the privatized self, withdrawn from the world and from others, "trying to get it together." But the precariously centered self that grows and changes in the process of developing relationships, the shape of which is largely unknown at present. Relationships with others—which now seem impossible. Relationships with the world around it—which threatens to destroy all it hopes for. Relationships with a power for living not its own—the God we are now incapable of naming without binding ourselves and God to a dying order.

I have no adequate conceptual framework within which to describe what is going on in the striving for selfhood today. I know of no theological description of self-realization that is of much help to me. Nor am I interested in finding a psychological interpretation around which to construct a theology of personhood. I choose to look in a quite different direction for the resources I need: to an evolving new experience of selfhood and to the search for a new language capable of describing it and enriching it.

Perhaps I can get at this best by speaking in personal terms of the imagery that has broken through to me as I have been in contact with those whose experience has been richer than my own. It began with the dawning awareness of what it means to be more *in touch with myself*, after years of being largely out of touch with my emotions and feelings, after years of suppressing my own dreams and longings. This has meant a clearer sense of who I am, as a real person, over against the masks I use and the roles with which I am identified. As this happens, I develop a sense of respect for who I am, a new freedom to affirm myself without hesitation or apology.

This, I confess, has been very hard for me precisely because of my Protestant background. My sense that I was a sinner, even though a forgiven one, and my belief that to be a Christian I must "deny myself," combined to produce a very negative self-image. Whatever this emphasis may have contributed in the past, it is now bankrupt. It has little to offer a new generation of those who are striving to find a center for their lives as their world is disintegrating around them. It can, on the other hand, be easily used by those who want to break the self down even further in order to impose an external authority as a means of domination and control. This can happen as easily in the religious as in the political spheres.

In the Christian context in which I now live, self-acceptance means self-affirmation in the processs of growth and change. I can look at myself that way because I know that what I am is going to be transformed. Here is where a Christian sense of what it means to be human can break through with power. As I get more and more in touch with what is happening in me, and find ways of integrating and giving meaning to such an experience, I discover that *self-realization is a constant process of Becoming*. My religious heritage helps to produce a constant but creative tension between what I now am and what I want to become.

Our industrial society has also placed a strong emphasis upon living for the future. But that was something quite different. It was a matter of *not* living in the present, of depriving ourselves of material things now in order to have more material things and enjoy a higher status later on. What I am getting at is an orientation toward the future that reveals *present* possibilities to us. Being more alive is a matter of growth, not accumulation; of increasing awareness of who we are and what we experience by sharing our lives with others, not of the position we attain in competitive struggle. In the tension between what I am and what I can become, I realize that at certain times I can grow only as I die to my present self and risk a process of radical transformation. To be free to go through such a death experience in the expectation of resurrection to a richer life is, for me, the ultimate test of the power of Christian faith.

As self-realization goes on in these terms, it creates a milieu out of which we emerge with a new sense of who we are, in touch with a growing power within ourselves for life and for change. We discover that we are beginning *to dance to our own rhythm.* What a revolution this represents in the center of our existence! In past centuries, men and women have danced to rhythms other than their own: to the rhythm of nature; of God; of institutions and structures assumed to be divine and thus possessing authority over them. Our modern world has broken the power of these absolutes, leaving us with little more than the yearning for freedom, while we dance to the rhythm of the machine: industry, technology, bureaucracy, and the role definitions within which we are supposed to fit our lives in the various institutions with which we are related. The result is external conformity accompanied by inward chaos and pain. The often inarticulated longing to dance to one's own rhythm cannot be blotted out; it also cannot come to fruition in a culture which blocks its realization and provides no resources for its development.

In this situation, many forms of modern religiosity become the only escape from the turmoil of the frustrated awakening self—and the ultimate block to a breakthrough to authentic selfhood. Fortunately, even this refuge will not hold up very long for sensitive souls. Fortunately also, we can find some small space in which to begin to dance to our own rhythm. The stronger our sense of who we are, the more aware we are of our own uniqueness. Each of us has his/her own blend of experiences. We put our world together in our own unique way; we follow our own process of becoming, at its own pace, with its own time. In the midst of all this, to be authentically ourselves is the important thing; authenticity is life and power.

Self-realization also means: *we name our own world; we create our own meanings.* When we dance to our own rhythm we can no longer live by definitions; abstract doctrines, overall world views, linear logic—none of these connect with our experience or help us. We move in a quite different realm in which we relate to and respond as full human beings to the richness and diversity in our environment. We draw on symbols from our past and present, from many different articulations of experience, from religion and culture, to put our world together. The meanings which order our lives grow and change as we live them out; in the crucible of our historical experience they are tested and transformed. Out of this we develop a sense of direction which sustains and gives purpose to our lives in its very openness to the future.

Ultimately, self-realization today is a matter of becoming *subjects of our own life and destiny.* The struggle of people over the past several centuries to become subjects of their own history has moved toward increasing personalization and differentiation. Human emancipation now means the struggle to overcome all hierarchies, all patterns of domination and subordination, all that robs each person of the opportunity to take increasing power over his/her life and choose what he/she wants to become. To the degree that this happens, our sense of personal worth and meaningful existence will not be given to us by any external authority, nor can it be taken away by any power outside ourselves. It will not depend on where we stand in comparison or competition with others, but on the worthwhileness of our struggle to shape our own life and destiny.

Exploring New Connections

What I have just said can easily be dismissed on two counts: "This is nothing but another way of speaking about the old rugged individualism that has plagued us in America since the beginning." Or, "this is anarchism. Follow it and there's nothing to prevent our whole society from disintegrating." In response to such possible accusations, several things need to be said: When I see the little selves and the caricatures of humanity being produced in our closed world today, I have a new admiration for the person who has a strong sense of his or her individuality. I also think the anarchist has an important contribution to make in times like these. If I reject both of these options, I do so in the recognition that their appeal is directly related to the sickness of the present order. The newly awakened self is inclined to "do its own thing" whenever it finds no patterns for authentic relationship to others and to the world around it. Anarchism makes sense when our perception of the human is confronted at every turn by thoroughly dehumanizing structures.

As a matter of fact, I do see both individualism and anarchism as serious deviations from the path to self-realization. But they can be countered only as newly awakened selves perceive and find opportunities to explore new connections. These connections are first and foremost, connections with other human beings. How different they can and must be from those to which we have been accustomed until now! Many women, blacks and persons from the Third World are helping us to discover new possibilities for human relationships:

In the encounter of people who, from positions of inner strength, can be there for each other;

In relationships of equality and freedom, in which each becomes
  stronger and more alive as interdependence grows;
In the exhilarating contact of two or more people who are growing and
  moving, *and whose paths converge*, for a longer or shorter period of
  time;
In the discovery that conflict can be creative when those who fight,
  learn to accept and forgive each other as they are changed;
In the experience that love can replace domination and repression as
  the motivating and integrating power in our time;
When we discover real power and the satisfaction it brings—not as
  power *over* other people, but as the experience of men and women
  empowering each other to grow and respond to the world around
  them.

Essentially the new historical possibility open to us is this: to discover
that relationships are more rewarding and that we are more alive when
we share our lives with each other and help each other to grow than when
we compete. If we are even to begin to experience such a profound
transformation of relationships, we will need all the help we can get. The
more I venture into this area, the more I find myself drawing new
insights and strength from my Christian history. It is there that I know
the freedom to risk relating, given all the problems we have with it today.
I am encouraged to take the risk of trust, to expect to experience grace
when the going is the toughest; to forgive and to receive forgiveness
from others.

As I remain in contact with the Christian story, I find that relationships
have more space in which to develop. No matter how significant a
relationship may become, I don't have to hang on to it. I can let go and
allow it to become all that it can become. I can risk making the most of
convergence with others to the extent that I am free to face an open
future.

A new subjectivity, nourished in a community of subject-subject
relationships, will be compelled to create qualitatively different connections with the world around it. If we human beings become most alive
when we respond to each other, not when we treat others as objects or try
to dominate them, then our growing awareness of this will demand
expression in other realms: in our relation to our work and to nature, to
society and history.

To take this seriously would imply a major revolution in each of these
areas, a revolution the shape and consequences of which we cannot

foresee at present. Here I can only give a few clues as to what may be in store for us. In the world of work, it will drive us to create tools for self-expression and for creative use of things in response to human need. It will lead us to develop non-bureaucratic ways of relating to each other in order to undertake specific tasks, solve problems, and provide human services. In the so-called serving professions, it will shatter our present role relationships, call into question our paternalism, and lead us to work and share with others so as to capacitate them to take more and more responsibility for themselves.

We are no longer bound to the rhythm of nature; but we cannot continue to treat it as an object to be exploited ruthlessly, without making human life on this planet intolerable. It is now our historical task to develop a new sense of its rhythm and beauty, of the life it gives to us and of the urgent necessity to work out a new balance in our relationship to nature. In other words, to take seriously whatever it may mean *to respond* in this area as well as others.

Likewise, the subjectivity of which I am speaking offers us the possibility of transforming our relationship to society and to history. Because of it, we can no longer look at the social order as an object, external to us, an object to be dissected, analyzed, and fit into one or another ideological scheme. It is rather a realm in which *we also are situated,* developing our sense of who we are and where we are going in interaction with and response to other people and institutions. What is crucial for us, in these circumstances, is not to find new categories to explain and/or order the world. The important thing is the emergence of new human beings as they seek to transform themselves and the world. As they do so, they can explore new ways to articulate and clarify this process.

To the degree that this way of relating to our world around us overcomes our objectification of it, we will be surprised by a rebirth of wonder and mystery. We will no longer need to seek this experience in an escape from history—into ourselves or some esoteric realm. Wonder and mystery will surprise us in the midst of our day-to-day relationships to people and to the decaying structures around us. To be open to dimensions of life of which we were formerly unaware; to discover an open future before us on the other side of the dead ends in which we are trapped; to know a power not our own at work in our midst; to have a new sense of the wholeness and integration of an open-ended life in the midst of constant change: these are the experiences which await us.

What this all adds up to, for me, is the recognition that we are being addressed, that life is given to us as we respond to a call coming to us in and through the events around us. In earlier centuries new power was let loose in the world for personal and social transformation as men and women surrendered themselves in obedience to the God who called them. In our industrial society, the power released in the world has come primarily from the striving to achieve and succeed in a competitive society. We are now on the threshold of an era in which the self as subject, growing and changing as it gives shape to the future in the present, will let loose a similar power in the world. Out of that may well come a new symbolic language of response.

This may be within the range of historical possibility. But what are the chances it will happen? At this moment, they certainly look slim. Those who are moving along the road we have just indicated realize that their historical perspective on change must be radically altered: they find themselves at the very beginning of a long term process. They may be very clear about the bondage from which they want to escape; they are much less clear about an alternative to it or how to arrive there. In addition to this, every new experience of liberation also carries with it a break with internalized values, and the feeling of guilt that goes with it. To overcome this means a constant struggle.

The formation of a new self; the development of new patterns of relationship: these tasks in themselves are overwhelming. They seem impossible, given the power of the old order that stands over against them, waiting to destroy them. Any woman who has tried to give authentic expression to her new awareness of self, any Black or Third World student who has insisted on an educational experience in line with his or her own rationality and cultural heritage, feels acutely what any of us sooner or later discover when we attempt to live out what is becoming most authentic for us. Structures which cannot open the way to a new future or offer new life can do a great deal to destroy fragile signs of future life. And very often those most in tune with an emerging new order are least prepared to cope with the destructive power of the old.

Given these formidable obstacles, it is not surprising that so many people concerned about radical social transformation have accepted Marx's position on how to bring it about: concentrate all energies on getting control of the means of production and establishing the dictatorship of the proletariat. Take power first; then you can move toward deeper changes in culture and in the self. Without ignoring what is happening in Cuba or China, I challenge this approach. That strategy has not worked in any major industrialized country. In the countries where

Marxism has been established, it has failed to move on to what Marx characterized as the second stage of social transformation—which is very close to the process of self-realization we are getting at here. Aside from this, we are faced with the fact that, in our present situation, the transfer of power from one group to another is no longer a revolutionary event. More than that, the psychically deprived, humanly diminished men and women of a post-industrial society simply do not have the vision, energy, or sustaining power to pull off such a struggle.

Today we have arrived at the point where the Marxist position must be reversed. Only a new self as subject, born in the context of life-giving relationships, can perceive the type of social transformation now possible and necessary. Only such individuals and communities can take on the creative task now facing us or develop the drive to sustain such a long term struggle. The waves of revolution will move out in concentric circles from the newly emancipated and empowered self. Starting in areas which are most crucial for the type of transformation now called for and in which we have a relative freedom to develop a radically different way of life, we can gradually get a clearer picture of where we are going and gather strength for the struggle where it will be most difficult.

Establishing Beachheads of a New Order

"Jesus stands at the most extreme front of human possibilities."[7]

We die when we settle for the limited possibilities of a dying order. We come alive and become agents of transformation when we begin to live now the as yet unrealized possibilities around us, whose time has come. Possibilities unseen, denied, and resolutely destroyed by those who are bound to and defend the *status quo*. Possibilities we wager are being opened up for us in the midst of the crisis we are living. When those who are becoming subjects of their own destiny seize these opportunities, they begin to experience a new world, to live with wider horizons of expectation and participate in a dynamic of growth and struggle they could not have imagined before.

I would like to have time and space to present and discuss a variety of such adventures among people I know today. But time and space have run out. I can only try to state very quickly what I mean by the above paragraph, by referring to two areas central to the experience of all of us.

1. *New Life in Intimate Relationships.*   I am very much concerned by the profound skepticism I find almost everywhere about even the pos-

sibility of life-giving relationships of intimacy today. I can easily understand why this is the case. The nuclear family creates a devastating psychic scarcity among adults who in turn pass it on to their children. No wonder they hardly dare risk in-depth relationships. As an increasing number of women—and men to a lesser extent—get in closer touch with who they are and develop a stronger sense of being subjects, intimate relationships tend to become even more difficult—*as long as we continue to situate ourselves within the perspectives, values, and patterns of the old order*. Once we look at and begin to experience all this as the first signs of a new era in human relatedness, the picture changes. We are caught up in exploring the new possibilities we begin to perceive. Along that road, what now appear as insurmountable barriers are transformed into problems we can work through.

Those women and men who are constantly growing in response to the world around them discover relationships of intimacy in which each finds resources to develop her or his own potential while, at the same time, contributing to that growth on the part of the other. For such persons, life is a journey, and the richest relationships are the ones that occur when paths converge, when they share their aspirations and struggles. In a recent article on the future of man-woman relationships, Herbert A. Otto writes:

> The major ideal model in the society of the future will not be marriage, children, and a house in the suburbs but rather the experiencing of a series of deep and fulfilling relationships and varied environments, viewed as a continuous adventure.[8]

Two people cannot be everything for each other; neither one can meet all the needs of the other. Abundance comes when each of two people, who share deeply with each other, has a full life of his or her own and participates in an expanding circle of relationships, of varying degrees of intimacy.

As more authentic relationships of intimacy develop, we rediscover the pleasure and power of sex, and this in turn contributes to the revitalization, enrichment and transformation of relationships. The religious community is still, by and large, trying to control sex, as if it were some demonic power threatening the social fabric. What we should be concerned about is its banalization; the fact that for so many today it is either boring or not worth the hassle—when we face the possibility of conflict. If Christian faith has anything to offer in this area, it is in freeing people up to run the risks of intimacy and, as they do so, to work out patterns of sexual relationships that are enriching and rewarding.

All this suggests that we insist on beginning with explorations in intimacy and move from there to the consideration of alternative structures for the new era we are entering. A variety of such alternatives are already being tried out. Much more experience will be needed—with its accompanying joy and pain—until we begin to have models for the future.

In a church and middle class society obsessed with the preservation of present structures, this stance we are suggesting is of fundamental importance. If we choose it, we may soon be forced to recognize that what happens in this area is not a private matter. People most committed to preserving the old order are especially threatened by any questioning of present patterns of family life—and rightly so. The sterility of human relationships is intimately tied up with the sclerosis of present institutions and structures, and the internalized values they have imposed on us. A new quality of life in primary relationships could contribute a great deal to breaking their hold over us, offer us a new paradigm for social organization, and become a subversive force within the given order.

2. *Work as an Occasion for Self-Realization and Service.* Here too events have pushed us to the threshold of a new era from which we can begin to live in the present. What work once was, it no longer is. The satisfactions it once offered are less and less apparent. We are free to transform radically the type of work we do and its significance for us. But if that is to happen, we must create it for ourselves; the present system will not do it.

Ralph Helstein, president emeritus of the United Packinghouse Workers of America, recently made a statement which hints at this in a dramatic way. I consider it especially significant coming from someone who has spent his life in the labor movement, which has fought until now for quite different goals:

> "Learning is work. Caring for children is work. Community action is work. Once we accept the concept of work as something meaningful— not just as the source of a buck—you don't have to worry about finding enough jobs. There's no excuse for mules any more. Society does not need them. There's no question about our ability to feed and clothe and house everybody. The problem is going to come in finding enough ways for man to keep occupied, so he's in touch with reality."[9]

Work today: creative activity, the expression of a growing self; the utilization of the gifts and skills we have or can develop in response to human need and for social transformation. To the extent that our work can become our own particular combination of these elements, to that extent the new era will become a reality for us now.

If individuals and groups express this possibility for work, they will not solve the problems we alluded to earlier. They will not change our economic system nor the type of work people are forced to do. Rather they will create new problems and intensify those we already have. This is something we badly need at the present time. Only as our society is confronted by people who have the vision and courage to develop alternatives to present forms of dehumanizing labor will it be compelled to make room for change.

The agenda is clear: to decide what we want to do and can do in relation to the needs of the world around us and then figure out how to get on with it. The horizon is an open one, given the vast number of things we want to do but cannot be employed to work at, and the increasing number of urgent human and social needs not being met. Each of us could easily make his or her own list of such tasks:

Opportunities for people of all ages and classes to learn and to teach;

Human needs not being met by any agency: care of the elderly, child care and recreation, etc.;

Various forms of advocacy for those most needing it: prisoners, the elderly, the very poor;

Encouraging those who have no place and no power to organize for action;

Performing tasks which a professional elite is supposed to do, but which are poorly done or simply not available to large numbers of people;

Finding ways by which people with different skills and experience—from plumbers to physicians—can provide services for each other outside the present professional and institutional framework;

Creative expression of individual talents and gifts in arts, crafts, etc.

Here is an open arena in which people of all social classes—those who have never been to school and those with doctoral degrees; those most highly skilled and those who have yet to discover what they can do well—can come to a new realization of what it means to be subjects of their own destiny as they create their own work.

Who has the freedom to do this? Here again we face an interesting fact arising out of the contradictions of a post-industrial society: a system which attaches supreme value to work is incapable of providing it for increasing numbers of its members. Those who have no chance to work in the productive machine—and consequently have little to lose—can be the vanguard: The growing army of the *unemployed*, whose number has risen in the last two years from 4.9% to 8.4% of the work force—7.8 million people (*New York Times*, September 6, 1975). The *retired*, whose number is growing rapidly, and many of whom are being retired at an earlier age with great vitality, skills, and experience. *Young people* who by necessity and/or choice are free to enter the job-career game some years later than was expected of them earlier.

People in each of these groups are free to pursue a course in the area of work radically different from the one we have followed since the beginning of the industrial revolution. Whether they are able to take advantage of that opportunity and discover their vocation will depend upon two things: (1) their experience of a change of values which allows them to identify their self-worth with their new vocation, not with their ability to make it in the old competitive productive society; and (2) their capacity to imagine—and work together with others to find and give form to—specific work opportunities in line with their interests and skills.

The same applies to those who have independent means and thus do not have to take a job to survive; as well as those who, by reducing their needs and sharing incomes with each other, can be relatively free to concentrate much of their energy on creating their own work.

Those who have nothing to lose occupy a privileged position as innovators in this area. The rest of us are not, however, excluded. If we have more options open within the present system, that only means we have to *decide* what we will do. Among the possibilities are these:

To choose something we very much want to do, and go about it singlemindedly, trying to figure out how to survive in the process.

I know one young woman whose consuming passion is to communicate what is important to her by means of films. She has worked, singlehanded, at this for the past ten years against all kinds of obstacles. Only once has she taken a regular job, and that for a limited time. She is doing some very creative things and may eventually be able to make it as a free-lance film maker.

To join with a few other people who are willing to share their incomes and help each other to find more favorable work opportunities.

I spent five years as part of one such group in which this happened. I know it can be done. The members of this group were able to create space for each other—to work part-time, to concentrate on what they wanted to do for a period of time without worrying about money, to take time to find the type of work they wanted as well as to run risks in the positions they occupied.

To rediscover what it means to work in a particular job or profession as a *vocation*—according to the terms set by what one is called to do, not by the usual expectations that go with that job or profession.

This is not easy. It has, in some cases, severe limitations; in others, unusual possibilities. But many of us have little idea how far we could go in breaking out of the usual limits. As a teacher I have tried to do this by setting my own priorities: experimenting with new learning processes, encouraging innovation; being present for those students who are most uneasy with things as they are. I know how easily all such efforts can be co-opted. I am also convinced that much more could happen throughout our society as women and men participate in their jobs while dancing to a different drummer, and function as agents of subversion and transformation.

Is all this a pipe dream, given the fact that we are living in a very private time, when those people who are most involved in experiencing a new subjectivity—together with a search for alternative patterns of relationship and meaningful work—seem least interested in assuming responsibility in the larger political arena or fighting the given structures at any point? I don't know. I happen to believe that, sooner or later, the approach I have here outlined will appeal to some who until now have had a more limited outlook. In the meantime, those who share this vision have an important task ahead of them: to establish contact with each other and work out, in small groups, the political implications of their new perspective and experience.

Three

Toward a Nation Transformed:

In the Apocalypse

As some spoke of the temple, how it was adorned with noble stones and offerings, he said, "As for these things which you see, the days will come when there shall not be left one stone upon another that will not be throwndown."

"Nation will rise against nation, and kingdom against kingdom; there will be great earthquakes, and in various places famines and pestilences; and there will be terrors and great signs from heaven. . . . You will be delivered up even by parents and brothers and kinsmen and friends, and some of you they will put to death; you will be hated by all for my name's sake."

"Now when these things begin to take place, look up and raise your heads, because your redemption is drawing near."

Luke 21:5-6, 10-11, 16-17, 28

In these pages I have sketched an apocalyptic picture of America. That is not what I started out to do; now that it has happened, I cannot escape it. For me, the apocalypse is not something that may happen to us in the remote future. It is my experience in the present; the future that has already begun.

The end of the war in Vietnam has not ended my sense of horror at the consequences of our political and economic domination of the Third World—and the increasing resentment and bitterness of those who are victims of it. As mass starvation becomes more visible and more extensive (it has now reached ten to twelve million people each year), the suffering and social upheaval it will bring may well defy any of our powers of description at the present time.

The suffering produced by the failure of the world's most powerful economic system to meet basic human needs has already reached apocalyptic proportions: for one-fifth of our nation below the poverty level, for the unemployed and those condemned to demeaning work, for those who are paying the price of the collapse of our major urban centers. I see no reason to expect that situation to improve in the years ahead; it will quite likely get worse. Our major institutions have lost their creative potential at the very moment when they are faced with new challenges. The emptiness, frustration, and mounting insecurity of those in middle life is matched by the suffering of the abandoned elderly and the crisis of values and of life goals among the youth of our land. In each of these areas, the more desperate the situation becomes, the more incapable those in power are of coming up with solutions.

By circumstance as well as by choice, I find myself in constant contact with people of the Third World as well as the more deprived in our own society. As I move back and forth between their world and my own, I become more aware of what our system is doing to them and to us. I contemplate the imminent end of a way of life that once offered security and satisfaction; I have some sense of the suffering accompanying such a crisis. To the extent that it becomes a daily reality for me, I can no longer think about myself or my world in the terms I have been accustomed to nor go about business as usual.

As most of what I have lived by and counted on is threatened if not consumed by apocalyptic fire, my perception of what is happening around me begins to change. What remains and is transformed takes on new importance in the space cleared by the flames of purgation. Despair is somehow transformed into hope as I get some idea of what St. Paul may have meant when he spoke of those *saved . . . as through fire.*[1]

I began my story confessing my loss of faith in the American dream. The time came when I could no longer believe that by working at what most concerned me through my profession and in the social and political realms, I was struggling for a better world and contributing to a better future for my children. That myth vanished as I saw my participation in these spheres contributing more to death than to life. As a result, I spent many years living abroad and later as an exile in my own land. Now, as the apocalyptic fires burn brighter, I experience a strange transfiguration of America and of my place in it. I am once again at home. The over-whelming forces of destruction in the old order loom larger than ever before. They will probably wreak destruction on millions who become their victims—and on those of us who dare to defy them. But in the perspective of the apocalypse, their power is broken. This makes room for a new vision of America to emerge out of the ashes.

The apocalypse is thus the occasion for the resurrection of the American dream. Situated as we are on the front lines of development of our modern industrial-technological society, we are in a position to perceive its essential contradictions, to envisage and begin to give shape to a new historical era opening up on the other side of its collapse. What I see ahead is no longer the darkening and widening shadow of a dehumanized industrial society but an immense stump out of which a small tender branch is beginning to grow. That branch is a resurrected America, bound in solidarity to the rest of the world; using its tremendous technological and industrial potential to meet elementary human needs—and discovering how to survive as a more egalitarian society. It is a nation in which new human awareness, expressing itself in richer and deeper relationships, is beginning to provide a more rewarding way of life and subvert present institutions. When women and men begin to experience the energy and excitement that comes through such transformation, they discover, once again, that their lives have meaning and purpose as they become involved in a variety of struggles to transform society in line with that vision.

At a time when our major institutions and their leaders are trying to convince us to settle for the ever more limited possibilities of our narrowing world of givenness, awareness of the apocalypse leads me to defy these limits. I choose not to settle for the terms of a dying order or restrict my energies and loyalties to institutions which have no future. I would rather use them in attempts to perceive and give form to patterns of life and relationship that do not yet exist, but which can be created on the margin of these institutions: the school, the church, one or another of our present political organizations. Out of such struggles new relationships may develop which will someday produce new institutions.

This dream of a resurrected America and my wager that I come alive as I fight for it, is not the result of careful empirical calculations of our prospects for the future. It is a perspective on life and history that has compelling power for me because it has grown out of my life experiences. As I have, over the years, faced one dead end after another, something out of my Christian history and its symbolic language has enabled me to accept failure and loss—and to be surprised by an open horizon on the other side. Because this experience has been so compelling, I cannot avoid making it the central paradigm for my understanding of what could happen in human institutions and in this nation as well. As I have read and re-read St. Paul's witness to the death and resurrection of Christ and his own "dying daily" yet living, I know that this vision of the world and of the development of history is the one thing that makes sense out of my situation as well.

From this stance, the questions that concern me also begin to change. What I do does not depend upon an affirmative answer to the question: is there a chance that this vision of America transformed can become reality? Our nation may well choose to follow the path on which it is now going to the *end*. What does concern me is that men and women today— and their children—have a choice: the choice not to die with a dying order, not to be passive victims of the creeping dehumanization around them; that they have other options visible and available to them. To the extent that groups of people begin to appropriate and live that vision, we will have a future, no matter how far the fires of the apocalypse may go.

If this is the focus of the task before us, it calls for a radical shift in priorities, especially in the political sphere. The pressing issue is not to come up with a new ideology and strategy for social change; it is rather to create conditions for a new politics. This, in turn, is a matter of a fundamental change in our approach to our own history, the re-working of our story of America and our place in it. As several anthropologists have put it: we now need a new redemptive process, a new way of putting our lives and our world together. Consequently, those of us committed to social transformation must turn our attention to the development of communities in which perspectives are changed, values and goals re-defined, and new energies released for imagining and putting to the test new political strategies that are not available to us at this time.

Where will this happen? No political party or movement is close to perceiving, much less taking on, this task. None of our major institutions is oriented toward it. Only in the religious sphere are these questions even supposed to be of basic concern. Only there is the creation of community as a source and sign of a new social order at times acknowledged as a major responsibility. *The question of politics has now become a religious question.*

You may find it difficult to accept this thesis. Let me try to illustrate what I mean by telling the story of one group I've been working with in recent months. Its significance for me is due in part to the fact that it has been repeated on numerous occasions over the last several years. This particular group of young men and women are trying to decide where to go now that they have realized that they see no solutions for some of our most pressing social problems. Most of them have read the Club of Rome report on *Limits to Growth*, and one or more studies on the world food crisis. They are also becoming more aware of the crises in our own society and of their frustrations in the face of them. After several weeks of discussion, they agreed to divide up into task forces to look at trends in certain specific areas, project those trends into the future, and see how that would affect their own decisions now.

One group worked on developments on the political scene. They came up with the prediction that a new conservative party will soon be organized, composed primarily of "the producers" in our society: businessmen, blue collar workers, farmers. They calculate that within ten or twelve years it could control the choice of the president and play a major role in Congress. They are also convinced that this new alliance will move our country toward a much more authoritarian government. As one example of what this might mean, they predict we will eventually have an oath of loyalty "to the traditional American values that have made our country great"; an oath to be sworn to by public employees, teachers, and others.

Another group took a statement made by Robert Heilbroner in *An Inquiry into the Human Prospect,* to the effect that industrial production—and the consumption of natural resources—in the developed world doubles every ten years. On this basis they drew quite a disturbing picture of what our situation will be in 1986. Another group presented a dramatic picture of the number and types of people whose lives may be destroyed over the next ten years by gradually increasing unemployment and poverty, retirement at an earlier age, and intensified frustration with meaningless work. Still another task force projected into the future the present divorce rate and other signs of disintegration of the American family and suggested some radical alternatives as the only hope for the future.

As this picture has begun to take shape, members of the group have reacted in different ways. Several have developed a much greater sense of urgency about political action and are trying to organize people to bring pressures for change within the present system. They know this has limited possibilities. But as they have said: "These are the only structures we have in which to work for change." Two members have concluded that what we most need is a radical analysis of the functioning of our capitalistic society and a strategy for moving toward socialism. They have joined a Marxist study and action group. Several others have been completely overwhelmed by their new awareness of these problems. Their reaction has been: We can't change the system; we can change our own life style and hope that in the long run it will make a difference. They are looking for a farm in an isolated rural area.

I am much more interested in the members of the group who are moving in another direction. Even though they are more aware than before that they have no solutions for any of our major social problems, they are more committed to the social struggle. As one of them put it: "To drop out is to commit suicide at the same time that we sentence our children to death." But their sense of what constitutes the struggle at this precise moment has focused on a number of new tasks: to undergo themselves, and facilitate for others, a fundamental change in their perception of what is going on in the world around them; to be prepared for any small opportunity to act for change in the midst of the advancing apocalypse; to continue to question their way of life centered around production and consumption, competition and status, and explore other roads toward a fulfilling life; to relate to all sorts of people whose growing social awareness can lead to the acceptance and acceleration of a similar process of transformation.

Most of them happen to be from a religious background but have seen little or no connection between their earlier religious experience and their present political commitments. Some of them are somewhat surprised to discover that, as they work on the new questions they are raising, they are turning to religious language in order to understand and work through these issues. They are talking about how they can find resources for living with insecurity, how to exorcise the demonic power of old and obsolete values, how to celebrate new life as it takes precarious shape. They are more aware of their need for symbolic language, especially when they are describing an apocalyptic situation or searching for life out of death. They are also aware that putting their world together in the midst of their social involvements calls for a community in which personal and social issues are faced and worked through, a community which offers a type of ongoing support they have not yet found anywhere.

Most of them have no clear ideas as to how to make any new connections with their religious history or how to give shape to the sort of community for which they yearn. But a significant shift in direction has occurred. Whatever happens to this particular group, its experience is, for me, paradigmatic.

Even if we agree that the political question has become a religious one, we face a formidable problem: what religious movements in America are in any way prepared to take on the task I have just outlined? I confess I see none. In my judgment, these movements are about as prepared to live out what they have been mouthing about death and resurrection as the Grand Inquisitor was to welcome the return of Jesus of Nazareth. But the Grand Inquisitor did not have the last word. Nor will the future of the church be determined by those who sustain its present structures.

Nothing would please me more than to be proved wrong in this assessment of our religious organizations. In the meantime, I must decide where to invest my time and energy. I can't count on the liberal religious establishment to meet this challenge. To be sure, many within it are aware that something is wrong and would like to see a change. But they rarely are able to recognize the depth of the crisis or take the sort of radical action necessary to arrive at a breakthrough. To do that would mean to question persistently and work to transform the very values they have affirmed until now, values most of them as well as the membership of the church largely accept. It would mean facing the fact that existing patterns of ministry are based on these same values; that, as an institution, the church is part and parcel of the old order.

As long as the mainline churches continue to be so culturally bound, they will be victims of increasing frustration and turn to one fad after another to keep going. With the erosion of a compelling vision, the exercise of a professional role will become the important thing for the minister; the maintenance of an efficiently functioning institution, the unspoken *raison d'être* of the church, together with its seminaries, judicatories, and bureaucracies. As the cultural situation disintegrates, we can expect the various church institutions to become more cautious and conservative. We can also expect a small minority of clergy and lay women and men to break out of the dominant pattern and give form to communities of transformed life on the fringes.

I cannot look to the new religious conservatism for a significant response to the calling we now face. For those men and women of all social classes who are becoming more and more scared by the crisis enveloping them, the conservatives will be out in full force. They will be all too ready to offer divine sanction to shore up those values and institutions which have become most problematical. In the years ahead, we can expect continued growth among these movements. If and when authoritarian political forces take control of this country, some of these churches and movements will constitute a major source of ideological and political support for them.

Within some of these movements, a new evangelicalism is giving life and power to many. It is also arousing a concern for those who are suffering, and a longing for community; it is bringing people into touch with the Bible and with Christian history. Out of this may well come, for some, a new experience of freedom and a new historical language of faith which sooner or later will lead to involvement in the social struggle. Those who make this discovery may be rejected by their own religious communities. To the extent that they are able to rework their religious experience, they may become a significant force for change in our society in the next decades.

I also expect to be surrounded by all sorts of exotic religious movements. Some will represent specific elements in our Christian heritage, largely ignored by the established churches; others will draw on Eastern religious philosophy, new developments in psychology and para-psychology, or a blending of these and other elements. And most of them, from Jesus movements to transcendental forms of meditation, will have their hour and decline as rapidly as they arose.

Their appeal is the source of their ultimate failure. Most of them offer cheap religion, a way out that appeals because it is so simple, so uncon-cerned with the ambiguity and tragedy of life. A few will survive and grow because they offer a life that transcends and tries to escape the dilemmas and tragedies of history. While I reject them for this very reason, I admit that they too have a contribution to make—through those who are turned on by the experience they offer and later turn away in search of something more.

The Christian Church, as a religious institution, has an almost unbearable—and inescapable—tension built into it. Its central message is that of the resurrection of the crucified Christ. The End is the Begin-ning. Life arises out of death. As the bearer of that message it becomes an institution. It develops patterns of relationship, doctrines, and struc-tures to which it holds on like any other human institution. In fact, because it is religious, it has a tendency to become even more rigid; it assumes that its forms have divine sanction. Christian institutions be-come easily acculturated, tend to absolutize their own values and those of the social order of which they are a part, and demand loyalty of their members. At the same times, they are bearers of a message which questions those values, defies their pretensions and upsets their own claim for loyalty. They kindle, in their members, a sensitivity to the human situation and a concern for the future that becomes much more compelling than the demands of a religious organization. Consequently, those who take that message most seriously are more concerned about what happens to human beings than they are about the church. The dynamics of their response is determined by a call from beyond themselves, fraught with urgency in the face of what at times is a desperate human situation. To respond is to affirm boldly, "Here I stand!", often in defiance of ecclesiastical as well as civil power. Anyone who does that is part of a long and noble tradition which no Christian institution can completely suppress.

This built-in tension produces different responses in different historical situations. For me, living this tension today means two things:

1. I refuse to cut myself off from my own religious history or from a wider community of faith because religious institutions may be bankrupt. I know this stand is not popular among many who have served the church faithfully and, in the process, become disillusioned with it. Their experience in the church has been so negative that they rejoice to be free from its burdens. They have been and remain Christians, concerned to live out what is most important to them in their day-to-day life in the world. But, they ask, why do more than that? Why be concerned with maintaining contact with Christian history, its symbols and traditions? Why take on the extremely difficult task of re-creating community?

I sympathize with those who have arrived at this point. I cannot stop there. I have experienced life out of death—personally and in various spheres of social existence. I know that that experience and the symbols, language, and relationships that have been the bearers of it have provided me with insights and power for living I have found nowhere else. Consequently, I refuse to allow an impoverished, decadent institution to monopolize that story or continue to pervert it, to hide the power of its symbols or co-opt them for its own ends.

More than this, I am convinced that these symbols cannot and will not be controlled and co-opted for long. They, and the historical experience they interpret, have a strange power to break out again and again from the bondage in which they are held. To live by faith is to trust that this will happen in our time as well. Many of us can find no community in which to live this contact with the tradition or experience its power. We cannot escape a sense of the priority of this search for community and the need to find others inclined to do the same.

2. My response to the present situation in the church is a response *in freedom*, response to a calling, to One who addresses me. I am not bound to begin my reflection on faith with any doctrinal system nor limit my experience of Christian community to the terms set by a religious institu-

tion. In fact, when religious language has largely lost its power and meaning, when it limits our world of experience rather than breaking it open to wonder and mystery, when it is set in the context of conceptual frameworks which are products of a previous form of consciousness and rationality, then our concern for the reality of which that language was once the bearer compels us to reject it. Likewise, to experience communion with others in our journey of transformation may lead us to give form to a new network of relationships that is possible only if we do not fit into any of our present religious organizations.

As I look at the institutional church and religious organizations today, I have the image of an immense tree with a large number of branches. Many of them are stunted or have stopped growing; others are dead. On many more the leaves have dried up and there are few signs of life. But if my wager regarding the church is correct, then we can expect to see new green shoots sprouting out all over the tree and showing fascinating signs of growth.

They will represent a new social reality, *new life in community, among those who are deeply involved in the transformation of all aspects of our national life.* As the incarnation of new life through death and resurrection, they may provide us with models for processes of social transformation. For those of us who are floundering around in a church that claims our loyalty but offers us no compelling vocation, here is a New Starting Point. In more traditional terms, Christian obedience becomes a matter of response to the work of the Spirit in our midst. Such communities will offer us a new context to work out our social responsibility in an apocalyptic time. In my judgment, they will represent the major contribution of Christian faith to society. To rediscover and give shape to such communities of faith in the midst of our social and political involvements can become our primary vocation, a task worthy of our best efforts for the foreseeable future.

One of the most striking examples of what I am getting at is offered by groups of Christians in Korea. When we think of Korean Christians, we do not usually think of them as political revolutionaries. And yet, we now see them in the vanguard of the struggle against the Park regime and in the attempt to create a more just social order. Much of the ideological and political leadership of the movement has come from among their numbers. And they have become a point of reference and support for many others involved in this same struggle. How has this happened?

The story goes back two hundred years. It has to do with the long experience, on the part of the Korean people, of internal oppression and colonial domination. In the face of this, Confucianism had little to offer. It was closely tied to the ruling forces in Korean society and provided a religious validation for what they were doing. Its perspective on society strengthened the givenness of the established order; it structured the most basic human relationships according to a hierarchical pattern of domination and submission.

In this context, Catholic ideas entered Korea and eventually contributed to the formation of a strong indigenous religious movement among the people, known as Tonghak. Out of this arose the Tonghak Revolutionary Movement of 1894. Toward the end of the nineteenth century, Protestant missionaries arrived. The Bible was translated into the language of the people and a rapidly growing church was established. From among its members came a widespread community of pastors and laymen who were at the center of the March First Independence Movement of 1919.

In both instances, Christianity introduced a messianic and utopian vision and language. It identified with the people in their suffering, arousing in them a desire to be subjects of their own history and to become involved in a struggle for historical transformation. In each case, this happened as small groups of men and women carried their religious experience into the center of the political struggle and offered a new perspective. They developed a new messianic language of transformation for their society. As Yong-Bock Kim, a brilliant young Korean theologian, has pointed out to me, this community of faith, which he calls the *koinonia*, brought about an axial transformation in the history of the Korean people as a result of their participation in the March First Independence Movement.[2]

Given this history, it is not surprising that the Christian koinonia occupies an important place in the present political struggle. Over the last several years, small groups of Christians associated with the Urban Industrial Mission became engaged in organizing the poor and helping them to discover their role in the struggle against oppression. Students associated with the Student Christian Movement went into the factories and the slums, motivated by this same messianic vision and their sense of vocation in the struggle for national liberation. They also took the initiative in forming groups of university students with this same vision and commitment.

The results are now evident. In a church noted for its theological conservatism and pietism, a growing number of pastors and lay men and women have come together around their political involvements. Because of their faith, they have become the bearers of a dynamic of transformation which is contributing to the creation of a new political language and empowering as well as orienting a new peoples' movement.

Our intellectual and spiritual climate in America today is not so different from that of Confucian society in Korea when Christianity was introduced. Our dominant ideologies sanctify the established order. They assume the givenness of our present structures and the trends they have set in motion. They validate hierarchical relationships. But there is one basic difference. Christianity is not present in this culture as a *new* force. It is not the bearer of a messianic and utopian language, of a vision of life that turns our world upside down. Consequently, to the extent that American Christianity has become acculturated, the koinonia can come into existence only as we rediscover a *lost* heritage and express it in a language and in forms of community which are sharply defined over against that acculturation.

I have no model for such a koinonia. I do know that it is beginning to happen:

When two or three people really meet, discover a surprising convergence in their personal journeys of transformation and find ways to facilitate continued growth for each other as they risk living out a new way of life;

When a few men and women scattered across the country—or around the world—become aware of their shared commitment to create a new world, and begin to build a network of communication and solidarity with each other;

When a group of men and women on the fringes of a particular institution—a school, a church, a business organization, a political movement—find each other in their alienation and explore together how to imagine and work out concrete new options where they happen to be;

When a few people dedicated to a common task take specific steps to live in community and work through together the problems and opportunities this offers for a new way of life in confrontation with the established order.

I cannot predict what will come out of this sharing of life under such circumstances. The next stage is for those of us who are participating in the formation of such koinonias to begin to tell our stories to each other.

As we do this, we may be able to articulate what we are experiencing, the next steps we can take, and what we can learn from each other. In conclusion, I would like to suggest three areas in which we can expect a significant breakthrough to occur along that road.

1. *A new discussion of our strategies for political action.* Most of us get politically involved as agents of change when we are confronted by a desperate situation of poverty and injustice and feel compelled to do something about it. But we will be able to continue such action only as long as we believe what we are doing is going to make a difference. Here serious problems soon arise.

If, for example, we become concerned about world hunger, we start out by contributing to CROP or some other relief organization and trying to get others to do so. Eventually, we realize that, to do anything effective, we must exert pressure in Washington to influence government policy. We shift our efforts to Bread for the World or some similar political pressure group. Before long, we face the fact that hope for any solution depends upon a fundamental change in our economic system and in the structures of our relationship with the Third World. This involves a major change in our American system of values and way of life. Overwhelmed by this picture, we soon give up. Or we find that all of our energies are tied up in one or another of these efforts so that we are not free to think about the more basic issues or explore possible actions in relation to them. Or, as often happens in small radical groups, we start out with an ideology about the transition from an imperialist capitalist society to socialism. We then concentrate our efforts on gathering information about how our present system operates and form small action groups among those we count on to be agents of structural change. This too tends to consume all our efforts and sooner or later leaves many frustrated and exhausted.

Any one or all of these activities may be very important. The question is that of the context in which they are set. If life in the koinonia is in the center of our struggle for social transformation, certain things gradually become clear to us:

Given the bankruptcy of our political thought and strategies, new possibilities for creative politics will most likely come out of the tension between political ideologies and powerful symbols of transformation, out of the tension between political movements and small groups of men and women who find ways of transcending the limits of their present perspectives and strategies;

Only as we experience a radical transformation of our value system and create patterns of relationship which make life worth living now will we have the vitality and courage to maintain a long term struggle or encourage others to do so;

In a rapidly changing and increasingly apocalyptic world, creative leadership for change comes from those who are free to accompany such an evolving situation, identify new points of contradiction as well as those of imminent collapse, and come up with new responses all along the way;

Within this outlook, we are free to live without answers, and create and discard strategies time and time again. To the extent that future possibility becomes present reality, even in a very limited way, we do not need to see immediate results from our political efforts.

When the koinonia is able to live at some point where the battle between future and present is joined, everything it is and does has political significance. If it creates a context in which new human relationships are developing, its life becomes a model for the institutions and organizations around it. When it becomes involved in many different types of political action with an increasing awareness of the structural factors at work, whatever it does in response to specific human needs contributes to an ongoing process of radicalization among those with whom its members are working. In a society which has lost the capacity for creative response to new problems, few things are more important today or more subversive than groups of people who are able to offer new approaches, propose new options and begin to work them out. Out of experiences such as these we can expect new political language, strategies and movements to emerge when their time has come.

2. *A new type of ministry.* I have not forgotten that these lectures are addressed, first of all, to seminary students. All that I have said is directly related to my search for a compelling form of ministry for this time. You can now see where I am headed. For me, ministry centers around creating conditions for the advent and growth of the koinonia. I know of no task more difficult or demanding, for everything remains to be done. I know of nothing more rewarding: to be engaged in creating a network of relationships which can give life and sustain it in the midst of a dying order, to be a point of reference for those who are ready to break loose from that which imprisons them and explore a new life in freedom, to contribute to the shaping of a network of mutual learning and solidarity among those who accept that calling, to create conditions for life-giving relationships which can serve as paradigms for our society and be a source of strength for ongoing transformation—in persons and in social

structures. From all that I have said, it should also be clear that I am proposing a type of ministry for which we have few models at the present time. It may not be welcomed by the church; it may have to be carried out on the fringes of or outside the present religious institution.

To choose this vocation means ultimately to risk setting your own terms and finding your own way in greater or lesser tension with the institution preparing you for ministry. In this sense, the seminary becomes the place where you can take the first steps toward discerning what it may mean and where it will lead you. This puts us once again in touch with our Puritan forefathers from whom we can learn a great deal as we study their relationship with the established church of England. In dialogue with them we may understand much better what it means to be the koinonia and the price we may have to pay to be faithful to that vision. We may also be encouraged by the recognition that, in certain periods of history, those who choose this path are giving expression to the heritage of faith and opening new horizons for the next generation.

3. *An alternative approach to the theological task.*   While I find many seminarians and ministers who are going through a profound crisis of faith today, I am astonished by the rekindling of faith among members of the koinonia—men and women who have put their lives on the line and are wrestling with important human problems. These people are becoming aware of the fact that their religious heritage makes a difference in their pespective on the present situation as well as in the way they live. I will attempt, in the next chapter, to look more closely at this development and explore its implications for those of us who are committed to the task of theological reflection.

Four

The Liberation of Theology: Reflection on the People's Struggle by Those Involved in It

A new Christian consciousness is beginning to create a new type of theological reflection. Its development is intimately tied up with the emergence of a new human consciousness. But to the extent that it is shaped by the Christian story, this Christian consciousness affirms and questions, develops and transforms secular perspectives on life and the world. It challenges the theological establishment by raising once again the question of the nature of Christian thought; it also places an emphasis upon creativity that exposes the bankruptcy of the dominant intellectual and cultural ethos.

This theology, as reflection in response to the God who is making all things new, represents a willingness and an eagerness to find new paradigms with which to deal with new human problems. Grounded in the struggle of women and men to be transformed and to transform their world, it questions those intellectual efforts that function primarily in the realm of objective conceptual frameworks, isolated from the human struggle. It reaffirms a relationship to the past flowing out of response to a new future and from there creating new linkages with history; a discovery of continuity on the other side of a decisive break with trends set by past experiences and responses now holding us in bondage.

Such reflection, on the part of a new Christian consciousness, leads us directly to a rediscovery of our origins and of what it means to think theologically in a time of social and and cultural disintegration. Those of us who are heirs of the Reformation are called to do, for our time, what the Reformers did for theirs. Luther and Calvin were professors of theology, but that did not lead them to salvage the scholastic system, nor to provide a new rationale for the powerful—and for centuries tremendously satisfying—sacramental order. Whatever the equivalents in their time of declarations such as those of Hartford and Boston, they had no part in them. They perceived all such struggles as battles *within* a system of thought that had its day, battles that prevented those involved from facing the depth of the crisis in which they were immersed and from risking a new wager of faith. Faithfulness to the gospel meant, for Luther, posting his ninety-five theses on the church door of Wittenberg, thus provoking an upheaval in the theological world.

Luther experienced, in the center of his existence, the crisis of values and structures of his time. Identified with and overwhelmed by the new consciousness emerging around him, he lived with the loss of everything that had once ordered his life—until the Christian story broke through to him in a new way. Out of this experience, he began to give expression to a new Christian consciousness. In doing so, he spoke with power to the human predicament and his thought became an explosive force throughout Europe. It described the appearance of new life out of death, and this experience became the starting point for a new type of theological reflection and a new form of Christian existence.

In touch as he was with various expressions of the new subjectivity of the late Middle Ages, Luther affirmed it at the same time that he provided a firm foundation for it and transformed it. Justification by faith opened the way for an immediate relation of the soul to God, bringing with it a new sense of freedom and responsibility. The powerful structures of security, which offered cheap grace within the depersonalizing orders of medieval incorporation, lost their hold over men and women who knew what it meant to trust in a gracious God.

Likewise, the seething unrest under multiple forms of hierarchical domination was radicalized as it too was provided with a new foundation and transformed. An unknown monk, a "nobody" in the hierarchical religious structure, declared every Christian a priest, and lived this out as he confronted emperor and princes, bishops and abbots, as their peer. He challenged all of them by setting new terms for dealing with religious and social issues. Those who knew the barrenness of scholastic theological speculation were offered the excitement of a "new learning" in dialogue with St. Paul and Christian history. As they explored the meaning and implications of justification by faith, they were free to discard a nine-hundred-year-old theological method. Thus, they broke the spell of what had once been perceived as the highest achievement of Christendom and declared that the Middle Ages had been a time of "densissimae tenebrae."

If few of us today dare to risk such a radical break in the expectation that the Christian message will come through to us once again with power, this highlights both the extraordinary daring of Luther and Calvin and our own lack of faith.

Whatever the originality, creativity, and power of the thought of the Reformers, we can no longer be content to develop, interpret, and reinterpret what they have passed on to us. For the Reformers and their descendants in succeeding generations failed to follow through on the Revolution they started.

The intensity of their struggle for survival and their fear of disorder and anarchy led them to settle too quickly for too little: to replace the Roman Catholic hierarchy with new structures of ecclesiastical domination; to fail to work out the implications of their radical faith for the social structures around them. Having bought the whole culture package of their time, as Paul Lehmann once put it, they were incapable of developing a theological method that took seriously the people as subjects responding to the Word of God. And they did not realize the extent to which their God language itself continued to affirm and sustain structures of intellectual, religious, and social domination. The struggle of men and women to be subjects of their own life and destiny, which was initiated so dramatically in the time of the Reformation, continued in the Western world. But from the French Revolution to contemporary Marxist Revolutions, it has found expression primarily in secular political movements—movements that have been, to some extent, secularized versions of Christian anthropology and eschatology.

Today, the new consciousness taking shape around us calls upon us to continue the revolution which began in the sixteenth century. The vision that inspires it is that of *every woman and man a Subject, living out new relationships of growth, sharing, and equality throughout the structures and institutions of one interdependent world.* If Chrristanity has failed to keep up with this development, so also have the secular religions of the last century or two. All of us who are products of these various revolutions, whether Christians, Liberals, or Marxists, have been, to some degree, bypassed by events. In this situation, those of us who dare to relate to what is happening around us and at the same time explore our heritage of faith with new freedom and earnestness, may have a unique opportunity open before us. Out of this interaction within ourselves between a new historical experience and a broken-down tradition, new life and insight may break out to surprise us. Our encounter with those in the past who lived out a Christian messianic vision may help us to look at our world in a similar light; in our contact with Christians who brought the death of an old order into the midst of their lives and were surprised by resurrection, we may be encouraged to risk doing the same.

Now, as in the time of the Reformation, a radically different experience and understanding of the nature of God's relationship to men and women can radicalize, provide a foundation for and transform the struggle of people to become Subjects. At the heart of this is not a theological affirmation comparable to justification by faith but a new Christian consciousness, a consciousness taking form as it discovers and responds to Christ, *the one who became incarnate in the struggle of people to be Subjects.* The Creator of heaven and earth, the God of mystery and power, the Lord of history, comes to us incarnate as a humble carpenter of Nazareth, belonging to a people who have no place in the great world of nations. This God empties himself to come into and be present in the world in those who are "nobodies," who have nothing and no place. God becomes weak, exposing himself to death by crucifixion in order to affirm, raise up, and give responsibility and a destiny to the "wretched of the earth," liberating and empowering them to follow an endless road of becoming in a dynamic relationship with him.

The Subject who addresses us in and through the mystery of our world and our history, of life and relationships, is the One who affirms us and calls us to be subjects, transferring his power to us.

Forty years ago, Eugen Rosenstock-Huessy gave expression to this vision in *Out of Revolution:*

> In the Sistine Chapel of the Vatican, Michelangelo shows God creating Adam, and keeping in the folds of his immense robe a score of angels or spirits. Thus at the beginning of the world all the divine powers were on God's side; man was stark naked. We might conceive of a pendant to this picture; the end of creation, in which all the spirits that had accompanied the Creator should have left him and descended to man, helping, strengthening, enlarging his being into the divine. In this picture God would be alone, while Adam would have all the Elohim around him as his companions.[1]

Here, as with Luther, we have a breaking of all molds, a paradigm which sets the terms for a new order of human relationships. Those who are "nobodies," who have no place, come to the center of the stage of history. The power of all elites, all hierarchical structures, all forms of domination, is broken, making room for peoples' movements. Those who are most impoverished, despised, and marginalized discover that they can stand on their own feet, create fulfilling relationships, and challenge all those who would exercise dominion over them. New subjects begin to question all intellectual systems, including theological systems, which diminish them and violate their being and their growth, all types of rationality which force them to think in terms alien to them, all conceptual boxes into which they have been fit and which deprive them of life. Women and men become creators of their own meanings as they are empowered, in their interaction with God and with others in the community, to put their world together in new ways. A new subject is free to see how the structures of a technocratic society operate and live in defiance of its rules, finding life in that struggle.

This consciousness, whatever form its articulation may take at a particular moment, is, I contend, a legitimate outgrowth of the Reformation; at the same time, it calls for a new paradigm of theological reflection which will represent as radical a break with the immediate theological past as that which Luther and Calvin took. In fact, our freedom to search for and work from such a new paradigm today may be the test of our faithfulness to our own origins.

I believe that this new Christian consciousness is already a reality among many more women and men of faith than we now imagine, *and*, for some of them at least, it has begun to find expression in a process of theological thought, a process that defines a new and challenging theological task. At the same time, it identifies certain theological approaches which must be rejected in order to move ahead:

1. Once again, it becomes imperative that *faith* be the starting point for our theological efforts, *faith seeking understanding*, to use a classical phrase. This was certainly the case with the Reformers of the sixteenth century, a fact that Kierkegaard captured well when he declared: "There is only one relation to revealed truth: believing it."[2]

It is ironical that those of us situated firmly in the tradition of the Reformation have to be reminded of this point. But none of us can avoid asking ourselves if, as theologians, we really function that way. I find myself surrounded in the seminary by men and women who have come here because they have been surprised by the gift of faith. They have some sense of its meaning and power; they came here expecting to find a community of teachers and students eager to listen to their stories and help them to deepen and broaden that faith at the same time that they work out its implications for their lives. Many of them are very quickly disillusioned. As one student said to me recently: "I am surrounded by faithful people who have no faith." We theologians may be people of faith, but very little of what we do in the classroom offers any evidence that we are willing to take these stories of our students as the starting point for theological reflection with them. Until we do, most of our teaching of theology will have little meaning or power; at the same time we may, without knowing it, alienate such students from theological studies and diminish or push aside precisely those experiences that are so rich in promise for the articulation and development of a new Christian consciousness.

2. For those who share this consciousness of which I speak, a stance of faith means involvement in and commitment to the struggle of liberation, the struggle to become subjects over against a system—with its ethos, its structures and institutions—which denies them this possibility. As one group with which I am associated put it recently: "What we are doing is grounded in our personal and common struggles, not in our reflective processes. The question before us is how to get on with our struggles; how to generate power as two or three are gathered together, not how to inherit power." It is in the midst of this struggle that new understanding emerges. At the cutting edge of it, theological language names and interprets our struggle and thus provides power for it.

All we need to do to grasp the shift that is here called for is to pick up almost any recent work in systematic theology, even one presenting us with a theology of liberation. However sensitive an author may be to what is happening in the world, when he or she attempts to work theologically there develops an overall conceptual framework in which the thought is developed, a finished product to be passed on to others. And we cannot understand why some of the more sensitive students of theology are not turned on by it.

More than two decades ago, seminary and university students in Brazil forced me to face this problem. I thought I was offering them a theological frame of reference within which they could better understand and participate more courageously and critically in their revolutionary struggles. Eventually I was forced to face the fact that what I had been doing was no longer happening. One day two students who had studied with me for several years came to me and said something to this effect: "For a time, your theology provided us with resources for better understanding ourselves and what was going on around us. But it functioned for us only as we stepped out, so to speak, of the day-to-day reality in which we were involved, and entered into the theological framework, and then stepped back into our world of experience to apply our new insights. That once worked for us; it doesn't any longer. We are now immersed in a demanding historical struggle; we want to think seriously about it, to understand it, and find our way. We still have some hope that theology may help us. But if it is to speak to us, it must provide us with insights in the midst of our daily struggle, in terms which make sense of it and illumine it for us."

A few months ago, a Princeton student expressed the same thing in quite different terms: "I've been trying," he said, "to understand why I can't read books on theology or sit through most lectures in systematics. Maybe it's because my generation and I have been brought up on television; maybe it's because something else I don't understand has happened to me. But I know one thing: no matter how hard I try to work intellectually on problems of faith or issues of life and death being raised in my society, any approach that begins with some overall conceptual scheme and asks me to fit into it in order to think about life and the world simply says nothing to me. The question for me is not so much one of truth as of meaning. Whatever the search for truth is all about today, it cannot go on unconnected with my attempts to make sense out of what is happening to me and around me." Once I realize that, I know that traditional theological formulations belong to another time and place.

When this happened in Brazil, I could only stand by and watch as students one by one gave up theology to embrace one or another political ideology. Today, in America at least, there are no political ideologies waiting in the wings; more important is the fact that some of the students posing this question for us are doing so from a stance of faith and are already beginning to explore other theological approaches. The question they are raising is that of where they can turn for encouragement and help to pursue this task while it is still a compelling one for them.

To say the same thing in other terms: this new Christian consciousness is a historical consciousness; it demands that the language of theology be a historical language. I have no clear idea of what the eventual implications of this may be. I do know that we can find ways to begin to respond to this demand. Those of us who are fully immersed in a theological tradition can deal with concrete human problems and discover how the resources of that tradition speak to them; those who may not have a thorough theological training are often in touch with their own Christian history and can discover how to draw on it for insight and power as they struggle with such problems; in fact, as some of us have discovered, when we are struggling to become subjects over against the dominant culture, biblical stories and biblical language come to our minds quite spontaneously. They often speak to us in a way no other language does.

This is not anything especially new. For a number of years, some of those who have been working on social and psychological problems have come up with a variety of methods for doing what we are calling for. The problem is that, in the eyes of the systematicians, what they are doing may be interesting and worthwhile; it is seldom taken seriously *as theology*. The time has come to challenge this assumption and dare to insist that such efforts should have their place *at the center* of the theological enterprise.

3. For centuries we have assumed that one particular *form of rationality*, developed in the West over a long period of time, is *universal*. We are now confronted by massive evidence that it is not. And in the face of this fact, we can no longer go about our theological business as usual.

Over the years, more and more students have been saying to me: "It's not just *what* you say theologically that makes no sense to us; we don't think the way you do." A number of women students have clearly demonstrated to me that their thinking about life, experience, and faith is rich and profound; often I have to admit that it goes deeper and is more insightful than my own. But it represents a different type of rationality; a way of thinking that is more organic, more intuitive, less subject to reification, and less affected by the Cartesian subject-object dichotomy than mine is. Several black students have shown that they have a way of perceiving the world that is authentic for them and often quite creative, but it is very different from anything I have known until now.

What is going on here? Dr. Lalla Iverson, a brilliant explorer of contemporary forms of rationality, identifies two new types of reflection widely dispersed through our society. One of these she has found especially among Afro-Americans. She calls it *immediacy*: "a highly sophisticated form of immediate recall of great ranges of hidden data; . . . the total, or selectively coded, immediate perception of and response to the contiguous event or environment." Another, *unity-in-change*, is more evident among young people subjected to rapid change in urban society: "the ability to unify new or unrelated elements from several different categories of experience without prior arrangement into objective groups."[3]

A few months ago I got a sense of what she means by this in a small seminar of younger students. Over several weeks, we told our stories to each other. Early on, I realized that their stories were quite different from my own. I organize my experience within certain conceptual categories in order to make sense of it. They do not. They often experience what is happening in them and around them more profoundly than I do; some of them make room in their thought for more of the richness of experience than I do. But somehow they bring it all together without arranging it ahead of time in the rational categories—in the conceptual boxes—within which I function. When I asked them to read certain theological works that had been meaningful to me, they declared that what they read was like a foreign language to them. If I insisted that they think in the terms found in these writings, I violated their rationality. If they tried to do it, they felt inadequate. I soon realized that if I persisted in this, I would not only destroy their potential for creativity but also deprive them of resources of faith which might otherwise be at their disposal.

Many people in this country and in other parts of the world are finding that the language of the Western theological tradition *is not their language*. It will not and cannot name their world. More than that, whatever the content of it, it is a language of oppression, not of liberation.

No one has pointed this out to me more sharply than Timothy Njoya, a student at Princeton Theological Seminary, in his doctoral dissertation, *Dynamics of Change in African Christianity*.

In it, he shows how Western thought and the theological systems that have grown out of the experience of Europeans and Americans over centuries, have been imposed on Africans—to whose historical experience they are completely alien—since the beginning of the colonial period. They have sustained and validated a world view that makes African ways of thought as well as African culture inferior in comparison to the rationality and culture of Western nations. On many occasions, Western theology has been used to justify or at least condone the structures of oppression established by the West in Africa and elsewhere. More than that, Western theology itself has been one form of colonial domination.

Gustavo Gutiérrez and other theologians want to reinterpret a theological system arising out of the development of Christianity in the West, in order to put Jesus and Christian faith on the side of the struggle for liberation. What they have not yet realized is that, to accomplish what they set out to do, they will have to break the hold of one particular formulation of the theological tradition. Only thus can they relate to Africans and Asians who are determined to develop their own theological histories just as we have done in the West. *No reinterpretation will suffice.* To go even further, a new Christian consciousness among various groups of people in the West is beginning to discover that it must follow the same route. No amount of reinterpretation of a tradition created in and through the development of Western Christendom holds the key to the future—*for the people of Asia and Africa or for us in the West.*

4. In the contemporary struggle of the disinherited and the powerless to become subjects, only a theology "of the people, by the people, and for the people" can be the bearer of the Christian message. Only as theologians are open to the moving of the Spirit among the poor and dispossessed people of God will they be able to contribute to a theology of liberation.

Recently I became aware of the urgency of this shift by my experiences in the seminary. New students arriving here are confronted with an alien but impressive terminology, by clearly defined theological categories, and by a type of thought that moves easily within this framework as it fits such categories neatly together. The more they come in contact with all this, and the more prestige it has in the seminary community, the more aware they are that they are ignorant. Only the professional theologians are intelligent. Students listen and learn to appropriate and feed back to their instructions what has been given to them, whether it connects with their life experiences or not. Hopefully, some day they will also arrive at knowledge and then be able to pass on these concepts to the theologically illiterate lay men and women in their congregations.

For the last several months, I have been meeting regularly with a group of students who refuse to buy this myth. All this, they contend, is a type of elitism that has little to do with serious reflection on the meaning of faith. So they have gotten together with another professor and myself to tell their stories to each other and reflect upon them. Week by week, the same thing happens: as they get enough courage to be in touch with their experience of faith and their own way of expressing it, all of us find ourselves engaged in a depth of theological exploration we have not known for a long time. Traditional relationships between professor and student have broken down and have given way to a process of interaction in which we all learn from each other. And as each student gains a new self-confidence, we all cultivate a capacity to draw on our theological heritage and to gain new insights into our faith which carries us beyond anything we have been able to do until this time, working individually.

If this is what happens with a group of seminary students, you can well imagine the situation of the average lay person in the church or of the "uneducated" men and women whose potential for theological reflection has been ignored until now. Many of them have moved through great experiences from which they have learned much—about themselves and about the power of faith. They often have profound insights, extraordinary dreams, and striking intuitions about the meaning of the gospel. But as long as we maintain our present attitude and theological methods, we will never be able to make room for this type of learning nor overcome the structures of elitism and paternalism we have allowed to set the terms over the centuries.

In his very brief conclusion to *A Theology of Liberation*, Gustavo Gutiérrez says:

> In the last instance we will have an authentic theology of liberation only when the oppressed themselves can freely raise their voice and express themselves directly and creatively in society and in the heart of the People of God, when they themselves "account for the hope," which they bear, when they are the protagonists of their own liberation.[4]

The question he does not deal with is: how can this happen? I believe the answer is a very simple one: it will happen when the theologian follows the path of incarnation and takes the same risks God does in doing so. Until then, our theological efforts will block rather than contribute to this goal.

5. If the shift in human consciousness of which I have spoken has any validity to it and if Christ incarnate in the dynamics of the struggle for liberation is the foundation of our theological reflection, then we are compelled to make room for an *evocative* theology. As each person in her or his own unique situation and each group in its own particular historical and cultural context strive to put the world together and make sense of the struggle, in which they are engaged, we will once again discover that theological language is symbolic language. Its unique power lies in its capacity to integrate and thus make sense out of our experience, to open our thought and lives to perceive and give form to the kingdom already breaking into the present. The presence of Christ in the dynamics of change frees us to rejoice in each new experience of meaning and integration given to us along the way, without hanging on to it or transforming it into a new authority for us. We will realize that the road toward greater understanding follows the pattern of integration, breakdown, new integration, etc.; that our security lies in an expanding history, in which our freedom to die to our past becomes the road to new life; our willingness to move beyond old formulations opens the door to richer and more profound understanding of the Christian story.

Let a New Christian Consciousness Set the Terms

For those whose experience I have attempted to describe, the theological task is that of following through, by means of an ongoing process of reflection, the Christian perception now taking hold of them: centered each in her or his own struggle of liberation, compelled to think about that struggle day by day in interaction with the Christian story—in its original forms and as it has been recreated time and again in Christian history, and compelled also to speak clearly to and fight with others engaged in similar struggles. To speak authentically about the nature of the theological task in this context is not to lay out a program for the next decade, but to report on what is beginning to happen as people move in this direction and as new energies for theological work are released. In concluding this chapter, I can only give a few hints as to what this entails for me and for several small groups with whom I am associated.

1. It means, first of all, our willingness to trust the perception we have, to dare to follow it wherever it leads, however sharply we are forced to define our position over against the theological establishment.

We need not—in fact, we cannot—function any longer primarily in reaction to dominant theological systems around us. The new consciousness with which we identify is that of women and men struggling to become subjects in a world of non-persons. But the central thing for us is the fact that it is a new *Christian* consciousness. In the midst of this struggle, a new experience of faith has become the primary source of our understanding and of whatever power we have. And we need not apologize for our inability to come up with a striking statement of that faith in coherent conceptual terms. We know that an articulation of it is taking shape as we struggle together. We can rejoice in and make the most of any clues found for us by companions on the journey. I find Timothy Njoya's dissertation, cited earlier in this chapter, particularly helpful, with its central theme: *Christ becoming incarnate in the dynamics of change.* I also connect with Rosenstock-Huessy's declaration in his short preface to *The Christian Future,* written 30 years ago:

> The crux of my life and of the life of the young has been the same: to break the impasse between the tradition of the Holy Ghost and the workings of the spirit of the times in the courage and faith of simple soldiers.[5] (I would reinterpret the word "soldiers" to refer to those around the world engaged in contemporary struggles for liberation.)

We know that faith empowers American Blacks, women, young

people, the people of the Third World—as well as those of us belonging to the established order whose former world of meaning has broken down—to stick with the issues raised in their struggles; trust their different forms of rationality; and strive, each in his or her own way, to make connections with Christian language and symbols. Whether we be lay people in the church, students in a theological seminary, or professional theologians fighting on a new frontier, *we know that no one else can do that work for us*. We already have some taste of the richness of reflection which comes as our deepest and most authentic experiences are illumined and integrated by symbols out of our heritage, especially among small groups seeking to find their way; we are also aware that this type of thought means the future breaking into our present, rather than boxing us into containers produced by the past.

If those most conversant with the Christian tradition in one discipline or another refuse to take that risk, they will remain victims of their own fears, but they cannot impose those fears on us. If systematic theologians insist on functioning within traditional conceptual frameworks—or fitting into new ones imported from other parts of the world—they are free to impose structures alien to their experience on themselves, but not on us.

Until now, those of us struggling to give expression to a new theological paradigm have often allowed ourselves to be intimidated by theologians who have attacked us for not being critical enough of our own positions—meaning that we have not paid enough attention to their criticism arising out of the paradigms we have been forced to abandon. The time has come for us to challenge such attacks by demonstrating that it is our openness to criticism and intense conflict that calls *them* into question. To start with the incarnation of Christ in widely different struggles for liberation means to expose ourselves constantly to disagreements which are inevitable, given our diversity of backgrounds and experience as well as our different approaches. It also means that all of our perceptions, perspectives, and language are open to questioning, for we are learning that we grow and arrive at greater insight only as they break down and are recreated time and again—from the extent that the professional theologians are vulnerable in this regard, to that extent critical interaction can take place. Those who refuse to become vulnerable exclude themselves from the dialogue.

2. To the extent that the new consciousness arising out of our struggle to become subjects becomes a *Christian* consciousness, something else happens. Certain elements of the Christian story, more or less peripheral

to our major theological systems, speak with particular relevance to our situation; other elements are rediscovered and reinterpreted, and thus take on new meaning. In both instances we come alive and are transformed in our encounter with the experience of previous generations and our theological reflection grips us as it opens a new world to us.

Ten years ago, in *Containment and Change*, I spoke rather timidly of the importance of a messianic vision. Today I would affirm it much more boldly and insist on giving it a central place in our life and thought. Over the last decade I have become much more aware of the barrenness of so much of our reflection on the state of our major institutions, our national life, or the experience of the oppressed, when a messianic perspective is lacking. I also have come to a much stronger sense of the power of messianic language in the historical experience of the Korean people as portrayed by Yong-Bock Kim,[6] and in our historical development as Americans. Most significant of all, I now realize that this messianic vision is central to my own self-understanding as a Christian, shaping my perception of this present moment. I came to understand this better in a discussion I had recently with a scholar with whom I have worked over many years. As we were trying to talk to each other, with a great deal of difficulty, he said: "There's a basic difference between us. I look critically at all the institutions I'm a part of. I identify the limited possibilities they offer me and then try to make the most of them. You're never willing to do that. You're always restless. You're always looking for something better around the next corner."

That's true. And, I would contend, that response is at the heart of my Christian perception of the world. It is confirmed when I see it arise, time and again, as small groups of people from a similar background attempt to define their stance in the present situation. I hope that more of us who are theologically oriented—and deeply involved in one aspect or another of American life today—will perceive more clearly the meaning of this element in our heritage and discover more of its power to break open our closed world and shape our reflection on it.

Throughout what I have written about the American dream, the themes of death/resurrection and apocalyptic have appeared time and again. I want to call attention here to the rich resources for reflection on our struggle today, waiting to be uncovered by further theological work. And I want to underline the word *further*. I am convinced that much of the discussion thus far of these themes arises out of an "objective" analysis of what is assumed to be an *archaic* world view, rather than the exploration of a form of historical consciousness which contributed to a breakthrough in understanding during the first century and can do the same in our thought about life in America today. Two things are at stake here: (1) the validity of a perspective by which the present is perceived in the light of a future which breaks the domination of principalities and powers looming as formidable obstacles in our struggle for liberation— and thus frees us to take on the task of overcoming present conditions; and (2) the power of an apocalyptic historical consciousness to transform our theology.

I have been greatly helped in my understanding of this by Joseph Nyce, a doctoral student at Princeton, who has recently written a paper on "The Apostle Paul and the Transforming Gospel of Christ." In making this point regarding Paul's apocalyptic consciousness, Nyce interprets Paul's experience in a way which defines sharply what it might mean for us to explore theologically this form of consciousness. As he puts it:

> As a persecutor of Christians before God in the form of Jesus, Paul's religious zeal now stood out as the vilest of sins. Seeing Jesus, the one cursed by the Law, now resurrected and assuming the form of God, all the promises of righteousness expected through striving to obey the Law collapsed into a heap of perverted notions of self-justification. And all the wisdom that mankind had amassed and so effectively used to form religious and social structures of order and division suddenly became chains binding his hands and feet and blinders over his eyes. But yet, in the midst of this broken and shattered world, Paul found himself called to be an apostle . . . . Here in the ruins of the old world, Paul, an unworthy sinner, was justified by the grace of God alone . . . .
>
> This is the apocalyptic situation Paul experienced on the road to Damascus . . . . The question was not primarily one of conflicting truth claims but of historical happenings . . . . He was not struck down by a truth claim, but by the radical contradiction of all his faculties for appropriating truth.

It is just possible that any theologian who dares to take Paul's historical consciousness seriously will conclude that her or his own response to the Christian story—at this point in the collapse of Western Christendom and of the institutions it has created and sustained—will be no less traumatic. And I would wager that the theologian who faces that possibility could be grasped by a word for our time that would be both powerful and world-shaking.

I maintain that, along this road, other elements of the gospel message that we have been mouthing for generations will take on new meaning for us as they are rediscovered and reinterpreted. Two examples will here suffice.

A young woman I know has, during the past year, gone through a series of profound crises. Over a period of a few months, she found herself breaking out of the structures of her rigid Calvinist theology, ending a marriage that was destroying her, and getting out of a work situation that had become intolerable. As this was happening she shared her struggle with a small group of friends and associates. As she did so, she discovered that they were present for her in a way she had never known before. She asked for answers to her problems but got none; yet somehow the assurance came through to her that she could continue to live the process of transformation she had begun and, along that route, find a security she had not experienced hitherto. A few weeks ago, I heard her tell the latest chapter of her story: her discovery of the sustaining presence of God in her life. In it, she said: "Now I can name the gift you transmitted to me. For the first time in years I can speak to anyone, in or out of the Christian community, of my experience of God. If, during those months when I was most desperate, you had talked to me about God, with the theological language you would have used, I would have turned away from you; and I would never have known what I now know. But because you mediated grace to me, because you demonstrated to me that I could live through incoherence without answers, I am today a woman of faith."

Another young woman found herself rejecting traditional theological language as she became increasingly aware of how it had been used over the centuries as an instrument of oppression of women. But as she slowly developed a new sense of herself and of the possibilities of life open to her, she discovered that that language, now reinterpreted, kept coming back to her to name her new experience of being alive. She found herself speaking of what was happening as a gift of grace. The language of sin and salvation became important once again, as the description of her former acceptance of herself as a non-person and her discovery of a power not her own opening up a new life for her.

3. As the Christian story illumines and transforms our struggle for liberation today, we perceive the outline of a theological method we are already using, a method that can become more explicit and be developed further as we move ahead.

Neo-orthodoxy performed a great service for the world by emphasizing the kerygmatic character of Christian theology. It is the articulation of a message, grounded in revelation, which makes a difference. Neo-orthodoxy was wrong in assuming that to be faithful to this perception, it had to continue to use the language of the Western cultural tradition in which this revelation had been expressed, with the type of Western rationality developed in that cultural context, and proceed to organize it conceptually and systematically. As a result, it produced a whole package which was accepted as the expression of Christian truth and could then be announced to and imposed on those willing to accept it. In doing this, neo-orthodoxy failed to take into account the nature of the biblical story, a story that cannot be fit into any such definitive scheme without excluding essential elements of it, without limiting and violating it. It also failed to perceive the extent to which all its own formulations were conditioned by the fact that they had arisen out of an encounter between the Christian story and a particular cultural history. In the process, much of the symbolic dimension of theological language was lost.

However important this emphasis was when first made, the insistence of theologians today to hold on to these formulations stands exposed, for many of us today, as a sign of lack of faith. As theologians, our starting point is our trust in the word of God, its power to speak to the human condition, whatever the limits of our theological systems. We are free to enter into the arena of human struggle, and witness, in our *weakness*, to the word which gives life to us. We can trust that word to interact with all other attempts to understand and transform the human condition, demonstrate its power to illumine our struggle, help us to put our world together in openness to a new future, and empower us to establish small beachheads of new life here and now. This means accepting the risk and rejoicing in the opportunity of day-to-day interaction of at least four elements:

   the missionary situation: the crisis of values and loss of world as it is
      experienced by various individuals and groups;
   the human sciences: the contributions offered by social analysis and
      psychological insight;
   autobiography: our attempts to put together, understand, critically
      evaluate and develop our own stories;
   the resources of our Christian history: theological language and sym-
      bols.

At this point, to concentrate on developing this method further in theoretical terms, or to describe a trustworthy process by which this can happen, would violate the method itself. If we dare to take it seriously, then our primary concern is to experience the interaction of these various elements in our lives, to reflect on what is happening as it proceeds, to speak with others who are trying to do the same thing in situations often quite different from our own—and expect to arrive at greater clarity about our method as it is worked out and transformed.

4. In his fascinating study of *Christianity and Classical Culture* (New York: Oxford University Press, 1944), Charles Norris Cochrane has shown how the crisis of classical culture became the occasion for a theological breakthrough that had a profound influence in shaping Western life and thought for 1500 years. Today, the crisis of classical theology could become the occasion for a new theological breakthrough, a breakthrough that could do, for our time, something of what the theologians of the fourth century did for theirs: provide a point of departure for a fresh experiment in human relationships, and offer a real hope for the fulfillment of the promise of secular life. The possibility of this breakthrough occurring will depend upon the willingness of theologians to let their conceptual frameworks and theological formulations break down time and again in order to move on to new perceptions, perspectives, and articulations. As they do this, they will give expression to a way of moving toward truth and thus open up, for our time, a new world of life and reflection on it. On various occasions I have spoken of this as an eschatological approach to truth; Timothy Njoya calls it the development of a transient epistemology.

Whatever the terms we use, we are affirming that the corollary to the theological method suggested above is an ongoing process of integration—incoherence—reintegration; and that out of such a lived history, we begin to create a new structure of thought, a new criterion for understanding our faith and our world. As we function more and more in the context of this history, we perceive that theological reflection need not be in the past tense; that our theological language provides us with resources for reflecting upon the present in the light of a new future as we make new connections with the heritage of faith as well as with our broader secular experience. If we risk moving through incoherence and find ourselves being empowered to put our world together again, a new type of reflection surprises us by its power. We need not move from one closed conceptual framework to another, from one container to another, but from a type of thought that is locked into containers of one sort or another to a process of reflection that does not need neatly worked-out conceptual boxes.

To the degree that this happens, theology once again becomes a challenge to secular thought. It confronts the Marxist, the Liberal, or anyone else struggling to preserve an intact system of thought with another alternative much richer in creative possibilities. It thus speaks directly to the new Christian and secular consciousness, supporting it, accelerating its development, and offering it criteria for constant critical self-evaluation.

5. Among those I know who have chosen to follow more or less the route I have outlined above, I find a new stimulus for serious in-depth study of various aspects of the Christian tradition: in biblical studies, the history of the Christian community, and the historical development of new theological perspectives in and through the struggle of Christian thinkers in times of personal and social disintegration. For some, this means a new interest in what happened during the first century of Christian history, or more specifically in the life of St. Paul; for others, a study of one or another messianic or millenarian people's movement; for others, attempts to understand better the Reformation of the sixteenth century or the evolution of the conversion experience of African Christians over several generations. In all these instances, two things stand out: (1) The approach is essentially *dialogical,* as men and women of faith struggle today to respond to their historical situation in interaction with those who have been deeply involved in a similar struggle in other times and places. (2) The aim of such historical studies is not to learn how others responded and then *apply* this learning today. It is rather to enter into the experience of others in such a way that we can draw upon it to interpret our own experience and find strength to continue to respond more faithfully in solidarity with each other. We may not have any clear explanations of how this happens; we do know that, as we are more in touch with our aspirations for a new future and at the same time live this dialogue with our Christian past, we are better prepared for the task before us and empowered to go about it.

If what I have said in this chapter makes any sense, then one conclusion is obvious: my primary concern is not to develop this approach further but to continue to put it to the test and see what comes of it. The perspective I have outlined has grown out of my attempts in recent years, and those of a few associates, to identify the way in which our own Christian history and the Christian story are functioning in our struggle for personal and social transformation; and the shape of the theological adventure on which we are now embarked. In other words, we have not set out to develop a new theological method or system; our starting point is our awareness that our faith is shaping our struggles and that a process of theological reflection is going on. We want to identify, clarify, and develop it further as we work at the tasks to which we are committed. Hopefully, some of you who read these pages will connect with this and be interested in sharing with others what is happening to you. The next step, as I see it, is to build a wider network of sharing and solidarity and discover how we can learn more from each other. It is out of such supportive and critical interaction that a new Christian consciousness can arrive at further insight into the meaning of faith, the nature of its struggle, and the resources now available for it.

I originally set out to write a critique of liberation theology. I soon discovered that I could not do it. That theology thus far has grown out of the specific struggles for liberation now going on primarily in the Third World. For me to enter into dialogue with those so involved, it is essential that I speak out of my struggle for liberation in my own country. That is what I have tried to do. The most important thing that has happened to me as I have done this is to discover that it pushes me toward a *radical transformation of my whole theological approach*. If I have anything to say to theologians of liberation in other parts of the world, it is to spell out what this means, why it has happened, and the questions it has forced me to deal with. That is all I can do at this point. If the dialogue is to continue, it will have to focus on some of these questions. To the extent that they are valid, it will go on first of all with those who consider it worth their efforts to respond to them, from where they stand, however different or critical their reactions may be. The first consequence of this may be our recognition that we can no longer try to fit each other into our own theological frames of reference and criticize each other that way. It may lead us to question whether or not we can even enter into dialogue with each other or work together. It could also lead us to a new stage of theological encounter in which we learn how to listen to and respond to each other taking this radical divergence into account. If and when this happens, we will be further along the road to a new era in creative theological reflection than we now imagine.

Response by

Gustavo Gutiérrez

The dialogue with Professor Richard Shaull and the community of Pittsburgh Theological Seminary, which is reflected in this book has been of great use to me. In regard to the conversations that we had, I would like to make some final observations. In the first place, I consider it necessary to underline some ideas which we discussed. Also, I would like to make some observations and reflections on the work presented by Professor Shaull.

First, the connection between salvation and liberty has always been centered in a political contest, and the theological reflection on these questions has placed itself in this framework. The perspective during the Middle Ages was that of a political power in a society which considered itself Christian, but which suppressed the social and religious dissension. The bourgeois situation puts things in another way. Although the Christian churches in Europe were forced to enter little by little into this pattern of thought, the notion of political power in opposition to an ecclesiastical power was not yet the unifying factor in the society. The theologians began to talk about the relation of the civil society to religious society, or the Church and World. The ideology of the bourgeois class expressed itself in the movement for the modern liberties and this ideology became the dominant voice in European and North American progressive theology.

In the second chapter of my work, the process of this challenge with theological answers was sketched. These answers were prevalent at Vatican Council II and during recent theological thought. These answers addressed the unbeliever, the secularized world, and in the last instance, the bourgeois class and its liberal ideology.

For the Christian progressive theologians of the modern countries who blossomed during this favorable movement for democratic liberties, it is difficult to understand what the reverse of the history means for the "absentees" of this history.

Among the lower social classes and the poor countries, the new and powerful bourgeois class exercised hegemony to its advantage. What, for some was modernity, democracy, and free exercise of reason, for others was a form of exploitation, an aspect of democracy and deceit on the part of the dominant national classes which were allies and servants of the interest of the capitalistic system.

In Latin America, the interlocutor and the most respected of the theological endeavors is not the skeptic or incredulous bourgeois; it is rather a person, who is not even considered a human or an important being; he or she belongs to the exploited races, the despised cultures. In evangelical terms the interlocutor of this theology is the poor. This perspective goes way back to the sixteenth century in Latin America. For instance, the Indians, who became the objects of exploitation by Western civilization, of those who called themselves Christians and who were motivated by the Christian faith and their contemporary theology.

This is the case of the actual theology of liberation. This theology is not exactly as someone said, "the political theology of Latin America." It is not a theology of the left, but runs along the same lines as that of European theology. Its origin is different. Here, the interlocutor is the oppressed, not the interlocutor of the progressive theology. The difference between progressive theology and the theology of liberation is political before becoming theological. Without an analysis of the classes it is not possible to understand this contradiction.

For this reason, we are talking of the process of liberation as a conquest of real liberty. For this reason, we have to refer to Europe and North America when we speak of our own historical reality. The popular classes in those countries some time ago, and the crowds of people dispossessed today in the poor countries are like the opposite side of the coin of a history written by the dominant sector of the rich countries as well as the oppressor class of the poor countries.

Before presenting some observations on the work of Professor Shaull, I would like to say that it has been a personal pleasure for me to meet him. I feel like I've known him a long time because of references to him by my Brazilian friends and companions who have been talking so much about his friendship. I also know him through his writing.

Ten years ago, on the occasion of an encounter of the World Council of Churches, Professor Shaull brought up the need for thinking theologically in a different way. "We are," said Professor Shaull, "in a revolutionary period, where old theological ideas are not satisfactory, therefore, we must start thinking in a different way." Today, we find Professor Shaull faithful to these first impressions and always in search of them. Professor Shaull has been speaking to us during these days of the necessity of a liberation of the theology, or as he preferred to put it, of a transformation of theology in order to beget a theology of transformation. Basically, I agree with this necessity, although I am expressing myself in a different way.

Professor Shaull was saying too, that as a missionary in Brazil, he has learned the importance of the revolutionary commitment to this theological task. It is, moreover, from this task that it will be possible to evaluate the quality of a theological reflection.

The texts of the work presented by Professor Shaull are: "Any progress I have made in this direction has come from one primary source, the indirection within myself, and between my Christian experience and historical memory and my experience of contemporary crisis," and the second text: "For what the theologian has insisted again and again is that our intellectual efforts have to be tested by their capacity to clarify our struggle for a more humane future rather than by their conceptual integrity or epistemological fitness."

It is comforting at this point to know that my impressions correspond to my own experience and, therefore, I basically agree with Professor Shaull. But, I also have to disagree with the Professor, perhaps because I do not completely understand his thoughts. I think his idea of a revolution is too broad. Is this the reason why he prefers to talk of transformation instead of liberation? This amplitude presents a problem: confusion. It seems to me, there is a need for a clear and concrete explanation of the contemporary revolutionary process. I think that it will be difficult to find a new language and theological rationality as Professor Shaull would like to find, if this language and rationality do not come from a transformation of the history of those exploited peoples, the "condemned of the earth," or if this language and rationality do not come from those who convey the evangelical message.

These points of contact and reflection raise some issues involving the theological task. The first is that the poor, according to the Bible, are understood from our perspective as the exploited social classes, the suppressed races, the despised cultures. Second is the necessity of new channels for theological reflection.

Today, these two first issues are still the most important and they are closely related. The new roads for theological reflection must be marked by the political and theological experience and way of thinking of the "absentees of history."

Theology is an understanding of faith. It is a rereading of the word of God as it is lived by the Christian community in history. The way the faith is lived, expressing the interests and aspirations of the exploited classes, is the foundation for their understanding and profound acceptance of Christ, their liberator. Consequently, fruitful theological reflection begins here.

The theology comes later. It is a second act. "Credo ut intelligum." St. Anselm said, "I believe to understand." This theology will be marked by the experiences of a people whose conscience tells them daily to be true actors of history. This theology will then be marked by the categories that the poor and the exploited use to understand and transform this history.

This theology is a way of communicating the faith. The theological function is oriented toward the announcement of the gospel, the gospel as interpreted by the exploited and oppressed of Latin America. The cry proclaimed by them will be a restless gospel—restless and threatening to the big and the powerful of the world.

Yes, the situation of theologians has changed. Theologians can only accomplish their goals in the Christian community if they have included themselves in the process of liberation, and involved themselves with the poor and the oppressed. Difficult questions are raised for theological reflection, making it quite clear that it is impossible to separate the theory from the social process. The theologian is not an idle spectator in this historical setting, watching it pass by, but a person who has an important living place in society among the social classes that confront him or her. From this central point one thinks and lives one's faith, and this condition enables the theologian to make the word a more understandable reality in history, where this word of God became Flesh. Robert McAfee Brown in Nairobi last year put it so very well when he said, "Jesus is the Liberator, the Standard, as well as the Divider, and because he divides, he liberates and unifies."

Notes

Freedom and Salvation: A Political Problem
Gustavo Gutiérrez

CHAPTER ONE

[1]Cf. the histories of this period of the Church. As is known, the socialist writers were interested in this matter. Cf., for example: Karl Kautsky, *Foundations of Christianity* (New York: Monthly Review Press, 1972). See also the writings of Friedrich Engels and Antonio Gramsci.

[2]Tertullian, *Apologeticum*, Onorato Tescari, ed. (Turin, 1951), XXIV, 7, 9, p. 159.

[3]On the concept of tolerance and religious freedom in Roman juridical institutions, cf. for example: G. Bossier, *La religion romaine d'Auguste aux Antonins.*

[4]*Apologeticum*, XXI, 30, p. 137.

[5]*Apologeticum*, XXIV, 6, p. 157.

[6]"It is of human law and natural law that each one can adore what he wants. The religion of one person neither helps nor hinders another. It is not of religion's nature to force religion. Religion should be spontaneously adopted, not by force since sacrifices have no value unless they are offered willingly. Therefore, if they oblige us to offer sacrifices, you give nothing to the gods, they have no need of sacrifices offered against the will." "Liber Ad Scapulam," Article II, *Patrologia Latina* (hereafter *P.L.*), Jacques Paul Migne, ed. (Paris: Garnier, 18[?]-18[?]), I, Col. 777.

[7]*Apologeticum*, XLVI, 2-4.

[8]*Apologeticum*, XVII; 1-4, pp. 107, 109. For Tertullian's doctrine on this and related matters consult Charles A. H. Guignebert, *Tertullien, étude sur les sentiments à l'égard de l'empire et de la société civile* (Paris: Ernest Leroux, 1901).

[9]Lactantius, *Divinarum Institutionum*, V, 21, 3-4; *P.L.*, VI, 618.

[10]*Ibid.*, II, 3, 20-25, and V, 16.

[11]*Ibid.*, V, 21; *P.L.*, VI, 619-620.

[12]*Epitome divinarum Institutionum*, 54; *P.L.*, VI, 1061. (Blaise Pascal comments on this test in his 12th Provincial Letter.)

[13]*Divinarum Institutionum*, IV, 30, 6, 9. The Alexandrian school had strongly instituted this idea: as the Law was for the Jews, philosophy leads the pagans to Christ.

[14]According to Louis Capéran, "no one has underlined with more insistence the means employed by God to win men; within the heart of paganism itself there is a kind of independent revelation." *Le problème du salut des infidèles* (Toulouse: Grand Séminaire, 1934), I, 74.

[15]Cf. the texts of Athenagoras, Tacianus, Minucius, Felix, and Justin collected by J. Rivère, *Saint Justin et les apologistes du second siècle* (Paris, 1911). See specifically Chapter Four: "Le christianisme et l'Etat," pp. 71-86.

[16]The texts of Lactantius were quoted, for example, in the declaration on freedom in religious matters in Vatican II.

[17]Hippolytus, *Coment. in Danielem* III, 200,25, 31; and other texts in the same work.

[18]Justin the Martyr affirmed this very early calling on a text from sacred Scripture which in the future will frequently be cited but not always in the same sense: "Render to Caesar what is Caesar's and to God what is God's." *Apologia*, I, 17.

[19]In this respect see the texts collected by Hugo Rahner, *Abendländische Kirchen Freiheit* (Einsiedeln, Cologne: Verlagsanstalt Benziger & Co. AG, 1943), pp. 45-64.

[20]Tertullian will say with sarcasm: "Whoever says the emperor is God denies the imperial dignity since if he is not a man neither will he be emperor." *Apologeticum*, XXXIII, 34.

[21]Cf. St. Irenaeus, "Adversus Haereses," V, 24, 2 in *Patrologia Graeca* (hereafter *P.G.*), Jacques Paul Migne, ed. (Paris: Seu Petit-Montrouge, 1857-1866) VII, Col. 1187.

[22]The Edict of Milan was known and frequently cited. For example, it was found in *Lo Grasso Ecclesia et Status, Fontes selecti* (Rome, 1952) notes 3-7. As we know, this text is from Eusebius and Lactantius, but the existence of a true edict has been debated. Cf. Paolo Brezzi, *Christianesimo e impero romano* (Rome: Casa editrice A.V.E., 1944), pp. 263-264, which have a bibliography on the subject.

[23]Licinius was a pagan and Constantine had been recently converted to Christianity. Constantine's Christianity has always interested historians. Really it is important for understanding the context of his action in favor of the Church. In addition to the pages which are devoted to him in the general historical studies of the times, see Ch. Martin, "L'Empereur Constantin fut-il un chretien sincère?" in *Nouvelle Revue Théologique* (1956), pp. 952-954; and the data presented in the more recent study of Salvatore Calderone, *Constantino e il cattolicesimo* (Florence: Pubblicazioni a cura dell' Istituto di Storia dell' Universita di Messina, 1962), Vol. 3.

[24]Cf. the old but penetrating study of Pierre Batiffol, *La paix constantinienne et le catholicisme* (Paris: J. Gabalda, 1914), pp. 188-201.

[25]"The privileges which have been granted out of respect for religion should only favor the followers of Catholicism. . . . We desire that the heretics and schismatics not only be denied these privileges but also that they be subject to punishment." Latin text in Theodor Mommsen, *Theodosiani libri* XVI (Berlin: Weidmannos, 1905), Vol. I, part II.

[26]"We desire that all people justly governed by Our Grace follow this religion. . . ." Those who do not do this "should be punished not only by divine vengeance but also by the power which the heavenly will has granted us." *Ibid.*, p. 833.

[27]Here we have an example, a text from the year 438 by Theodosius which reflects well this mentality: "the first preoccupation of the imperial majesty should be the protection of the true religion to whose cult the prosperity of human undertakings is linked."

[28]Cf. Christopher Dawson, *The Making of Europe* (London: Sheed & Ward, 1934), pp. 43-44.

[29]"De fide," *lib.* II, Ch. 16, note 139 (*P.L.*, XVI, 588).

[30]At the beginning of this period we find a text from which a sane doctrine on religious freedom could have been deduced. It is the Synod of Sardica (343-344). This text asked that "each one, free from all coercion, live his religious life in full freedom" (*Corpus Scriptorum Ecclesiasticorum Latinorum* [CSEL], 65, pp. 182 ff.). However, this text had no followup, and also its interest diminishes somewhat if we recall that it was written for Constantine who

was intervening openly in the argument between Catholics and Arians, favoring the latter. Therefore, just as before the Edict of Milan, the text faced a hostile authority in demanding respect for freedom in religious matters.

[31]"Historia Arianorum," 67, (*P.G.*, XXV, 773).

[32]"In Joannem," XXVI, note 2 (*P.L.*, XXXV, 1607). This is a frequently cited text, but it does not point out that it dates from 416. That was the time during which Augustine's position on the matter had become very hard. This proves to us that the defense of the freedom of the act of faith is not incompatible with certain forms of religious intolerance. Augustine's case is instructive, but it is not the only one.

[33]Augustine, "Contra litteras Patiliani," II, 183, 184 (*P.L.*, XLIII, 315).

[34]It was due in great part to the conversions achieved by the Imperial Edict of 405 which abolished the schismatic church and obliged all to return to unity under pain of grave sanctions, that Augustine saw the advantageous side of these measures, and this worked in him a change in the matter of religious freedom (cf. "Retractatio," II, 5, *P.L.*, XXXII, 632). Centuries later, Bernard of Clairvaux, Bruno of Querfurt, and Thomas Aquinas himself justified in this way the measures of force: it was a matter of combating an obstacle, that is to say, the domination of the devil and not a matter of imposing the faith. Indeed, all of them were strong defenders of the freedom of the act of faith.

[35]Ambrose of Milan, "In Rom." X, 17-18 (*P.L.*, XVII, 153).

[36]*Ibid.*, II, 16 (*P.L.* XVII, 68-69).

[37]Cf. "Contra epist. Manichei vocant Fundamenti," notes 2, 3, (*P.L.* XLII, 174-175).

[38]"Epistle" 93, 5, 7; y "Retractatio," II, 5.

[39]This small work is of a complex interpretation, but it seems to offer in its fundamental part (the first chapters) a doctrine of great amplitude on the question of salvation trying to explain the text "many are called but few are chosen."

[40]"De gubernatione Dei" in *CSEL*, VIII, pp. 41, 20; 86, 25; 103, 24.

[41]How can this isolated testimony be explained? This would corroborate some of the ideas I wanted to underline to emphasize the influence from Tertullian. Jean Pierre Waltzing, a specialist in this area, has indeed shown that Salvian is dependent on Tertullian and even has plagiarized in other passages of his work. Cf. "Tertulien et Salvien" in *Le Musée belge*, Vols. XIX-XXIV (1920), 39-43.

[42]Cf. a letter to Emperor Gratian (Epistle 17, 1,2, *P.L.*, XVI, 1005A). Ambrose exercised a great influence on the emperor. Cf. Claudio Morino, *Chiesa e stato nella dottrine di S. Ambrogio* (Rome: Pontifica Università Lateranense, 1963).

[43]Cf. "Epistle," 21 (*P.L.*, XVI, 1002-1007).

[44]In effect, this was accepted by Catholics as well as by heretics and schismatics. Cf. V. Monachino, "L'impiego della forza al servizio della religione nel pensiero de S. Agostino," in *Nova Historia* (1959), pp. 13-38.

[45]"Epistle," 156, c. 3 (*P.L.*, LIV, 1130), Lo Grasso, note 104, pp. 48-49. The same idea in another letter: *P.L.*, LIV, "Epistle," 152, 1122.

[46]See the text in Lo Grasso, notes 108-112.

[47]However, we should not exaggerate the reaches of this famous text. G. Soranzo has even brought out the hypothesis that Gelasius distinguishes between the "*auctoritas sacrata pontificum*" and the "*reglais potestas*." The first would be the grounds of the second which would be limited to being its executive force. ("I precedenti della cosidetta teoria gelasiana" in *Riv. stor. Chiesa in Italia* [1947], pp. 3-21.) Soranzo goes so far as to claim that this would be the only "new element" in the Gelasian text. Marcel Pacaut picks up the same idea but without referring to Soranzo. *La théocratic* (Paris: Aubier, 1957), p. 24. The truth is

that the Church at this time was in difficulties with the emperor. This led the Pope to put the accent on aspects which gave his text an unexpected equilibrium. This, however, did not mean a mentality which was radically different from that of his times as often is claimed.

[48]"Until Aquinas it is not possiole to find in the area of orthodox thought a univocal and constant doctrine on the matter of religious tolerance." Mario Condorelli, *I fondamenti giuridici della tolleranza religiosa nell' elaborazione cononistica dei secoli* XII-XIV (Milan: Università di Catania, Pubblicazioni della Facoltà di Giurisprudenza, 1960), no. 36, p. 5.

[49]*Summa Theologiae* (hereafter *S.T.*), q. 66, a. 4, ad. 2. In another passage he will speak of *"tolerantia adversorum,"* (I, II, q. 102, a. 4, ad. 8). Cf. also, II, II, q. 73, a. 4; q. 108, a. 1; II, II, q. 136, a. 1, ad. 2.

[50]It is clear that for Thomas what is tolerated is something morally evil or at least not acceptable and that the attitude of tolerance is only a virtue when directed towards some good.

[51]*S.T.*, II, II, q. 10, a. 11.

[52]This expression is inspired in Thomas Aquinas and is found in Pius XII's speech to the Italian jurists on December 6, 1953.

[53]*S.T.*, II, II, q. 10, a. 8.

[54]*Ibid.*, a. 12.

[55]*Ibid.*, q. 11, a. 3.

[56]*Ibid.*, ad. 1.

[57]*Ibid.*, II, II, q. 10, a. 8, ad. 3.

[58]In IV *Sent.*, dist. 13, q. 2, a. 3.

[59]"Scito teipsum," *P.L.*, CLXXVIII, c. 657.

[60]In II *Sent.*, d. 39, a. 1, q. 3.

[61]*S.T.*, I-II, q. 3.

[62]Joseph Lecler in *Histoire de la tolérance* (Paris: Aubier, 1955) Vol. I, p. 121, note 116 limits himself to recognizing that Thomas Aquinas does not exactly answer the question which he himself is asking. B. Olivier, "Les droits da la conscience, le problème de la conscience errante" in *Tolerance et communauté humaine* (Paris, 1952), p. 173, note 116, confronts the question more frankly. Eric d'Arcy sharply criticizes Thomas Aquinas' position in *Conscience and Its Right to Freedom* (London: Sheed & Ward, 1961), pp. 112-122.

[63]*S.T.*, II, II, q. 10, a. 10.

[64]See, for example, the testimonies brought by Joseph Lecler, *op. cit.*

[65]On the concept of "political religion" and its modern forms cf. Jürgen Moltmann, "Theologische Kritik der politischen Religion," in *Kirche im Prozess der Aufklärung* (Munich: Kaiser, 1970), pp. 11-51.

[66]Indeed, we would also have to follow "the path of the poor" in the Church of the Middle Ages. The theology which springs from there will have different accents from those we are remembering.

CHAPTER TWO

[1]Concerning the Industrial Revolution, one can consult the classical works of Paul Mantoux, *The Industrial Revolution in the Eighteenth Century* (London: Jonathan Cape, 1961)

and Eric J. Hobsbawn, *The Age of Revolution, Europe 1789-1848* (London: Cardinal, 1962) and by the same author, *Industry and Empire* (Baltimore: Penguin Books, 1969).

[2]In a less explosive way, the movement is already felt in the eighteenth century in England, and a few years before the French Revolution, in the North American revolution. However, strictly speaking, the democratic ideas do not spring up in North America but rather under the impact of what happened in France: "Before the French Revolution the American mind had been curiously sensitive over the term democrat; even Samuel Adams had been driven by expediency to reject the word, and amongst the radicals, few had the boldness to avow themselves democrats. By common consent the term had been covered with opprobrium; democracy was no other than a *bellua multorum capitum*, the hydra-headed monster of earlier Tories, licentious, irreligious, the very spawn of anarchy. But now the old conceptions were rapidly swept away, and democracy was accepted by liberals as the ultimate form of political organization, to which the American experiment was to be dedicated." Vernon Parrington, *Main Currents in American Thought* (New York: Harcourt Brace Jovanovich, Inc., 1954), I, 328.

[3]Concerning the difference between the freedoms of antiquity and those of modern times, cf. Umbertoni Cerroni, *La libertà dei moderni* (Bari: De Donato, 1968), pp. 75-81.

[4]As is known, this will be one of the great themes of reflection for Jean Jacques Rousseau.

[5]Immanuel Kant, "Que es la Ilustración," in *Filosofía de la Historia* (Buenos Aires, 1964), pp. 58, 60, 66.

[6]Francis Bacon will play an important role in this. Cf. Benjamin Farrington, *Francis Bacon Philosopher of Industrial Science* (London: Lawrence & Wishart, 1951).

[7]Georg. Wilhelm Friedrich Hegel, *Leçons sur la philosophie de l'historie* (Paris: J. Vrin, c. 1963), p. 320.

[8]Christopher Hill, *Reformation to Industrial Revolution* (Baltimore: Penguin Books, 1969).

[9]Cf. Max Horkheimer and Theodor Adorno, *Dialektik der Aufklärung, Philosophische Fragmente* (Frankfurt: Fischer, 1969). Tocqueville had already observed the contradictions of the movement with modern liberties.

[10]Willi Oellmüller, *Die unbefriedigte Aufklärung* (Frankfurt: Suhrkamp, 1969).

[11]A. Alvarez Bolado in *Dios y la ciudad* (Madrid, 1975), p. 36.

[12]Karl Marx studied this process extensively. Cf. for example, the chapter on "The accumulation of capital," in *The Capital*, Vol. I, Friedrich Engels, ed., Samuel Moore, trans. (Chicago: Encyclopaedia Britannica, 1952).

[13]Adam Smith will be the great theoritician of this free economy based on the free play of each person's interests. Within the limits of capitalism, David Ricardo will be the most attentive to the internal contradictions of the system.

[14]This will be an important theme of reflection for J. J. Rousseau and is one of the reasons for his critical attitude towards liberalism, a more critical position than that of his contemporaries.

[15]Guido de Ruggiero, *Storia del liberalismo europeo*, second edition (Milan: Feltrinelli, 1966), p. 43.

[16]This will be one of the points that Marx criticizes. For him there is a real inequality in the buying and selling from the moment when the majority of the population begins to sell its own work force for a salary.

[17]Hegel, *op. cit.*, pp. 336-342.

[18]Lucien Goldmann, *La ilustración y la sociedad actual* (Caracas: Monte Avila, 1969). Many of the observations we have made concerning the Enlightenment were inspired by this work.

[19]Cf. Joachim Matthes, *Religion und Gesellschaft. Einführung in die Religions-soziologie* (Hamburg: Rowohlt, 1969), I, Ch. 2.

[20]Cf. Ernst Cassirer's classic work, *Die Philosophie der Aufklärung* (Tübingen: Mohr, 1932), Ch. 4.

[21]Kant and Hegel try to respond to this problem. Thanks to Rousseau, Kant is able to distinguish between the cultured man and the moral man. Hegel affirms the Christian religion that the people practice and express, at the level of representation, the same spirit present in the history which "absolute wisdom" will present in clear and conceptual terms.

[22]Max Weber, *The Protestant Ethic and the Spirit of Capitalism* (New York: Scribner's, 1958).

[23]This is what Pius IX maintains. For example, cf. *Les actes pontificaux cités dans l'encyclique et le Syllabus du 8 Décembre, 1864* (Paris: Poussielgue, 1865), p. 698.

[24]Leo XII, Bullarii *Romani Continuatio* (Prati, 1854), VIII, 53. In his first encyclical, Pius VIII states that "the sophists of this century claim that the gate of salvation is open to all religion, thus giving the same praise to truth and error, to vice and virtue, to honesty and immorality." The complete text in Artaud de Montor, *Histoire du Pape Pie VIII* (Paris, 1844), pp. 67-78.

[25]A year before the *Syllabus,* Pius IX had recalled the "no one can be saved outside the Catholic Church," Encyclical "Quanto conficiamur," August 10, 1863.

[26]The acts of the French Assembly were qualified as heretical by Pius VI, and Pius IX presented his encyclical "Quanta cura," as being motivated by "the salvation of souls," and concerned with discovering and condemning all heresies and errors contrary to "the Church and civil society."

[27]See text in I. Lo Grasso, *Ecclesia et Status. Fontes selecti* (Rome, 1952), no. 697.

[28]Quoted by Artaud de Montor from Leo XII, *Histoire du Pape . . . ,* p. 363.

[29]Bull, *Romani Continuatio* (Prati, 1850), VII, pars prima, 1719a. The reference to this famous text of Leo I is still found in Pius IX, but it is significant that, as far as we know, it is not found in Leo XIII.

[30]Pius VII, Bull, *Romani Continuatio* (Prati, 1852), VII, pars secunda, 1167-1168.

[31]Leo XII, Bull, *Romani Continuatio,* VIII, 53.

[32]Pius IX *Quanta cura,* in Lo Grasso, *op. cit.*

[33]"There is no Catholic who does not know that Jesus Christ, in instituting his Church gave the apostles and their successors a power independent from all other." (*Quod aliquantulum,* March 10, 1791). A year earlier he had condemned a doctrine that considered that "religion should be submitted to and serve political interests." (*Op. cit.,* p. 3.) John Courtenay Murray has underlined this defense of the Church's liberty faced with a totalitarian regime. Cf. "The Church and Totalitarian Democracy," in *Theological Studies* (December 1952). However, it seems to us that this is an ambiguous use of the texts in that he does not sufficiently point out that this defense by Pius VI is bound to an affirmation of the spiritual primacy of the Church, a primacy that should be translated in a determined social order. It is certainly a question of the ancient regime which guaranteed the mission of the Church as exclusive holder of religious truth. For this reason, Pius VI will call upon the authority of Thomas Aquinas, and he refers critically to the Edict of Nantes.

[34]Pius VI, *Brefs et . . . ,* p. 131; cf. also, p. 125.

[35]This was one of the objectives of Vatican diplomacy of the time. This explains the presence of representatives of the Holy See in the Congress of Vienna which sought to restore the ancient regime. This also explains the importance of Metternich, promoter of the Holy Alliance, in Rome during the pontificates of Pius VII and Gregory XVI.

[36]Cf. Jean Leflon, *Monsieur Eméry* (Paris: Bonne Presse, 1945), I, 251. Cf. also, J. Mailloi, *Pie VI et le sermont de liberté-égalite* (Paris, 1915).

[37]Bull, *Romani Continuatio*, XIV, 363 ff.

[38]Cf. the studies of the historian Alois Simon; see, for example, "Le Saint Siège et la Constitution belge," in *Coll. Mech.* (1947), pp. 495-525.

[39]Alois Simon, *L'hypothèse liberal en Belgique* (Wetteren: Éditions Scaldis, 1956), p. 28.

[40]Felicité de la Mennais (1782-1854) was ordained a priest in 1816. He was a polemicist and writer and was elected deputy to the French Assembly in the republican period of 1848-1849. He is one of the important persons in French socialism in the first half of the century.

[41]In Ireland a liberal movement was already forming in Catholic groups centered around O'Connell.

[42]Cf. Lamennais, *Des progrès de la révolution et de la guerre contre l'Eglise* (Paris: Belin-Mandar et Devaux, 1829). This is a transitional work in the evolution of Lamennais' thought.

[43]*Ibid.*, pp. 31-32.

[44]"L'Avenir," October 16, 1830, in Lamennais, *Oeuvres complètes* (Brussels: Société belge de librairie, 1839), II, 411.

[45]*Ibid.*, p. 424.

[46]*Ibid.*

[47]"Nothing can stop the process which God put in germ in each one of his creatures and which draws them to him through a continuing movement of ascension . . . human society rejects the old institutions and seeks to build itself with new forms . . . [of which] liberty is the most fundamental." *Ibid.*, p. 460.

[48]"The tendency to withdraw the spiritual order, the order of thought, and consciousness from the authority of the governments not only is legitimate in itself but also a great progress . . . and Catholicism's greatest conquest." *Ibid.*

[49]*Ibid.*, p. 474.

[50]*Ibid.*, p. 422. Lamennais demands "Freedom of conscience which is full, universal, without distinction as well as without privilege." *Ibid.*, p. 429.

[51]*Ibid.*, p. 422.

[52]However, it is not correct to claim that Lamennais "in 1830 above all proposed the Catholic thesis . . . the traditional doctrine," that is to say, "the union of Church and State." J. Leder, *L'Eglise et la souverainité de l'Etat* (Paris, 1944), p. 228.

[53]Christian Maréchal underlined the importance of this aspect in Lamennais' work. Maréchal even thought that the break with the Church took place more out of fidelity for his doctrine of common reason than out of defiance of the condemnations of his ideas on religious freedom. Maréchal presented this opinion towards the end of his life, and it was taken up by Aubert, Duroselle and Semolo. "Le libéralisme religieux au XIX s," in *Relazioni del X Congresso Internazionale di Scienze Storiche* (Florence, 1955), V, 310. However, in fact, both aspects of Lamennais' thought, freedom, and salvation, seem to be closely related.

[54]For this reason, he has been likened to the thought of Bonald and finally with pantheism. However, there are some points that are not clear. The great student of Lamennais, Christian Maréchal in "Lamennais, Descartes and St. Thomas," *Revue Philosophique* (October 1947) and "La vrai doctrine de Lamennais: le retour a la raison," *Ibid.* (July 1949), maintains that the author of the "essai" has been falsely considered a traditionalist. This affirmation is refuted by L. Foucher, among others. *La philosophie catholique en France au XIXe siècle* (Paris: J. Vrin, 1955), pp. 42-50.

[55]Lamennais, *Essai sur l'indifference en matiére de religion* (Paris: De Méquignon Fils Ainé et Boiste Pére, 1823), III, 256-257.

[56]"How beautiful is the tradition which begins with the world and which, in spite of innumerable errors, perpetuates itself without interruption in all peoples." *Ibid.*, IV, 59.

[57]*Ibid.*, III, 200.

[58]*Ibid.*, II, 482. Lamennais here calls upon the testimony of the Church Fathers: Irenaeus, Justin, and naturally he refers to Tertullian's famous text on the soul which is "naturally Christian."

[59]*Ibid.*, IV, 498-499.

[60]Paul Dudon, generally speaking not very objective in his study of Lamennais, is correct in pointing out the differences between Lamennais' conceptions and those of Leo XIII. The author says that Lamennais, contrary to the Pope, defends common law for the Church *"non comme un pis aller imposé par des circonstances regrettables, mais comme la conséquence heureuse d'un systeme social en progres sur l'organisation de l'ancien regimé"* in *Lamennais et le Saint-Siège* (Paris: Librairie académique, 1911), p. 383. Even when his interpretation of Leo XIII's doctrine is somewhat rigid he is correct in denying that the Pope had been *"une sorte d'exécuteur testamentaire des plus grandes initiatives du fondateur de l'avenir, dont le malheur fût dit-on devancer son époque."* (*Ibid.*, p. 382.) Actually, in spite of his efforts, Leo XIII could not overcome a problem which was very "traditional." Lamennais' attempt, even though ambiguous, went much farther. It was necessary to wait until Vatican II to see more clearly into the question.

[61]Cf. Karl Marx, *The Class Struggles in France, 1848-50* (New York: International Publishers, 1934).

[62]*Op. cit.*, pp. 312-313. The subtitle of this text is significant: "The accord of Catholic Doctrine with the Form of the Modern Governments."

[63]Letter of July 27, 1859 published in *Le Correspondant*, 243 (1911), p. 859.

[64]*Ibid.*, pp. 70-71.

[65]*Ibid.*, p. 73.

[66]Cf. Montalembert, *L'église libre dans l'etat libre* (Paris: C. Douniol, 1863).

[67]This attitude, after a moment of euphoria, will lead Montalembert to take refuge, without much elegance, in the distinction between principles and circumstances.

[68]Quoted in Edouard Lecanuet, *Montalembert* (Paris: C. Poussielgue, 1903), III, 365.

[69]The article is not signed. However, in consulting the archive of *Civiltá Cattolica*, one finds a copy signed by C. M. Curci, a Jesuit priest.

[70]"Il Congresso Cattolico de Malines e le libertà moderne" in *Civiltá Cattolica* (October 2, 1963).

[71]Cf. *La convention du 15 septembre et l'encyclique du 8 décembre* (Paris, January 1865). In spite of what is often found in studies on this theme, the distinction between thesis and hypothesis is not original with Dupanloup.

[72]*Inmortale Dei.*

[73]*Ibid.*

[74]Cf. his encyclical *Libertas.*

[75]On the "politics of Leo XIII," consult the severe article of Pierre Thibault, "Savior et pouvoir," *Philosophie thomiste et politique cléricale au XIXe siècle* (Quebec, 1972).

[76]Cf. Roger Aubert, *La théologie catholique au milieu de XXe siècle* (Tournai: Casterman, 1954).

[77]In this respect, cf. Roger Aubert, *Le problème de l'acte de foi* (Louvain: Publications Universitaires, 1950).

[78]"The Problem of State Religion," in *Theological Studies* (June 1951). Murray will be one of the writers of the conciliar declaration on religious freedom, a problem many considered to be "the North American question in the council."

[79]A distinction made by Leo XII. Cf. *Inmortale Dei.*

[80]Cf. Gustavo Gutiérrez, *A Theology of Liberation* (Maryknoll, New York: Orbis Books, 1973), Ch. 9.

[81]Cf. Yves Congar, *The Wide World My Parish: Salvation and Its Problem,* Donald Attwater, trans. (London: Darton, Longman, & Todd, 1961).

[82]J. C. Murray, on the contrary, places himself on a more juridical level.

[83]Encyclical, *Non abbiamo bisogno* (June 29, 1931).

[84]Cf., for example, Pius XI's encyclical *Quadragessimo anno, Divini Redemptoris,* Pius XII's encyclical *Summi Pontificatus,* and especially his Christmas message in 1944.

[85]*Non abbiamo bisogno.* The same in Pius XII *Summi Pontificatus.*

[86]*Actes de Pie XI,* V, 129.

[87]Cf. Pius XII, Discourse on February 10, 1952 and the Message of March 8, 1952.

[88]We are referring to the so-called promotion of the laity by means of Catholic Action.

[89]Discourse to the Italian jurists, July 6, 1953.

[90]This distinction reminds us of the one Lamennais established between the "sentiment of freedom" and "a philosophical theory."

[91]This concerns Chapter IX, "Relations Between Church and State and Religious Tolerance," from the *Outline of the Constitution on the Church.*

[92]We are referring to the schema prepared by the secretariat for the unity of Christians called "Constitution on Religious Freedom."

[93]For a history of the conciliar schemas and debates consult Matias Garcia's excellent work, "Análisis historico" in *Vaticano II, La Libertad religiosa. Texto y análisis* (Madrid, 1966), pp. 45-217.

[94]This is what was maintained by the narrator Mons. de Smedt as well as by two of his most influential writers: J. C. Murray in "La déclaration sur la liberté religieuse," in *Nouvelle Revue Théologique* (January 1966), pp. 41-67, and Paven, *Libertà religiosa e pubblici poteri* (Milan, 1965).

[95]In an extensive document distributed at the beginning of the fourth conciliar session, the *Coetus Internationalis Patrum,* Leo XII points out two fundamental errors in this schema: the attempt to consider the problem in a "merely juridical" form and the affirmation of the incompetence of civil authority in religious matters.

[96]Carrillo de Albornoz considers this to be the most important point of the Declaration. Cf. "The Ecumenical and World Significance of the Vatican Declaration on Religious Liberty" in *The Ecumenical Review* (January 1966), p. 81.

[97]In these pages I refer to an earlier work on the declaration: Gustavo Gutiérrez, "Libertad religiosa y diálogo salvador" in *Salvación y construcción del mundo* (Barcelona, 1968), pp. 17-43.

[98]Consult the presentation that A. Alvarez Bolado makes concerning the political theology in the article I mentioned.

[99]Cf. Willi Oemüller, *Die unbefriedigte Aufklärung.*

[100]Dietrich Bonhoeffer, *Resistence et soumission* (Geneva: Imprimerie Atar, 1963), p. 145. See also p. 162.

[101]*Ibid.,* p. 142.

[102]*Ibid.,* p. 124.

[103]*Ibid.,* p. 166.

[104]*Ibid.*, p. 162.

[105]Cf. R. Gibollini, *La teologia di Jürgen Moltmann* (Brescia, 1975).

[106]Cf., for example, "Fe y política" in *Diálogo Ecuménico* (1974), no. 33, p. 37. "Political theology," says Moltmann, "sinks its roots in the theology of hope." (*Ibid.*, p. 40) Concerning Moltmann's rapprochement and contributions to political theology as well as the whole of his work, see the excellent and complete work of R. Gibollini mentioned in the previous note.

[107]In *A Theology of Liberation*, I make a presentation and criticism of the first version of the new political theology.

[108]"Questioni scelte e prospettive." This article should be published in the *Editorial Queriniana* (Brescia, Italy) towards the end of 1975. The texts from Metz which I quote without footnotes come from this article.

[109]In the sense that this is presented in the famous work of Carl Schmitt, *The Necessity of Politics*, E. M. Codd, trans. (London: Sheed & Ward, 1931).

[110]See a perspicacious presentation and criticism of this Lutheran doctrine in Jürgen Moltmann's article mentioned above.

[111]Cf. Johannes B. Metz, *Zur Theologie der Welt* (Mainz: Matthias-Grünewald, 1968) and Jürgen Moltmann, *Der gekreuzigte Gott* (Munich, 1972).

[112]Cf. J. B. Metz, "Breve apologia de la narration," *Concilium* (May 1973), LXXXV, 222-238.

[113]J. B. Metz, "Iglesia y pueblo," in *Dios y la ciudad* (Madrid, 1975), p. 141.

[114]Metz's ideas have led to important reflections concerning the Church in its social function. Cf., for example, Marcel Xhaufflaire and others, *La practique de la théologie politique* (Tournai: Casterman, 1974).

[115]In presenting the texts of the two conferences of Moltmann and Metz in Madrid in 1974, A. Alvarez Bolado and Gómez Caffarena point out that the confrontation with liberation theology was present in the audience as well as in the speakers. Gómez Cafferena writes: "It can be said that liberation theology formed the ground work of that which many who assisted at the conferences instinctively contrasted with the new version which the Germans gave to their theology. . . . If it is possible, therefore to sum up in two traits the newness of the contributions, perhaps it would have to be said: Moltmann opted for a systematic reaffirmation, even though it is more clear and nuanced (in this way it was also able to confront situations such as those of Latin America or Spain, in any event trying to do this with more maturity than liberation theology). Metz chose to strongly underline an aspect of his theology which had been less emphasized up until that time. (In this way his theology also was able to confront situations such as those of Latin America or Spain, trying to do so with greater *authenticity* than liberation theology.) He emphasized the relevance of the people (pueblo) as an active subject." (*Dios y la ciudad*, pp. 14-15.) R. Gibollini points out that Moltmann was the first to pick up and take into account the questions posed by liberation theology. *Op. cit.*, p. 259.

CHAPTER THREE

[1]Cf. V. D. Sierra, *El Sentido Misional de la Conquista de América* (Buenos Aires: Huarpes, 1944).

[2]The texts of these bulls can be found for example in Silvio Zavála, *Las instituciones jurídicas en la conquista de América* (Madrid: Imprenta helénica, 1935).

[3]"Del único modo . . . ," (Mexico: Fondo de Cultura, Económica, 1942), p. 7.

[4]Bartolomé de Las Casas, "Historia de las Indias" en *Obras escogidas* (hereafter *O.E.*) (Madrid, 1954); See *Biblioteca de Autores Cristianos II*, p. 124. Cf. also, an excellent selection and introduction in J. B. Lassègue, *La larga marcha de Las Casas* (Lima: Centro de Estudios y Publicaciones, 1974).

[5]Enrique Ruiz Maldonado, an excellent scholar of de Las Casas' thought, suggests that in the "Apologia," a work as yet unpublished, de Las Casas seems to accept the possibility of salvation within the indigenous religions. "La justicia en la obra de Fray Bartolomé de Las Casas," in *Libro Anual del Instituto Superior de Estudios Eclesiasticos* (1974), part 2, p. 24, note 30. In another approach to the subject, Pérez de Tudela says that a doubt about the traditional doctrine of salvation is present in other works of de Las Casas. "Estudio preliminar" in *O.E.*, I, p. cxi, notes 279, 281. The position of de Las Casas on black enslavement is very difficult and not clear. On this point as on other points, de Las Casas is a man of his time. Today from our ethical perspective we would be critical of him.

[6]"Memorial al Consejo de Indias," (1561) *O.E.*, V, p. 537.

[7]"Del único modo . . . " p. 545. That was already the meaning of the famous sermon of Father Antonio de Montesinos, in 1511, which initiated the "Controversy on the Indies." In this sermon he denounced the oppression to which the Indians were subjected. Cf. the note in this respect in *Libro Anual . . .*, p. 113-117.

[8]"Petición a su Santidad Pio V," (1566), *O.E.*, V, p. 541.

[9]"Entre los remedios," (1542), *O.E.*, V, p. 118.

[10]*Loc. cit.*

[11]Concerning this point, see E. Hoornaert, "Las Casas o Sepúlveda" in *Revista Eclesiastica Brazileira* (December 1970), pp. 850-870.

[12]"Del único modo . . . ," pp. 475, 493-497.

[13]"Thomás de Aquino, Bartolomé de Las Casas y la controversia de las Indias" in *Libro Anual . . .*, p. 100.

[14]To proceed otherwise would mean "asserting that the evangelical law, full of sweetness, frivolity, softness, and gentleness, should be introduced as Mohammed introduced his law." "Tratado sobre los indios que se han hecho exclavos," (1552), *O.E.*, V, p. 259.

[15]*O.E.*, V, p. 539.

[16]"Tratado . . . ," *O.E.*, V, p. 281.

[17]The *encomienda* consisted in giving the colonizers rights over the land and over the Indians that occupied the land, and it was orientated towards the exploitation of these lands by means of the unpaid work of the Indians. In exchange for this economic benefit, the *encomendero* was obliged to provide for the Christianization of the Indians.

[18]"Memorial de remedios," (1542), *O.E.*, V, p. 121. De Las Casas' action brought about a law in 1549 which prohibited new conquests in the Indies. Juan Friede considers this to "have been the outstanding achievement of de Las Casas' movement." *Bartolomé de Las Casas: precursor del anti-colonialismo* (México: Siglo XXI) p. 200. However, this law was revoked in 1556.

[19]"Entre los remedios," *O.E.*, V, pp. 60, 98.

[20]J. Friede, *op. cit.*, has underlined this political and activist aspect of Bartolomé de Las Casas, in this way, combating the image of "idealist" with which he is often presented.

[21]"Carta al Maestro Fray Bartolomé de Carranza," (1555), *O.E.*, V, p. 436.

[22]Ginéz de Sepúlveda (1490-1573) studied theology in Rome under the famous Cardinal Cayetano. He wrote the "Democrates alter" in which he defends the rights of the conquest and colonization.

[23]Cf. for example, V. Carro, "La teología y los teologos-juristas espanoles ante la

conquista de América *Consejo Superior de Invetigaciones Científicas* (Madrid, 1944) and L. Hanko, "El prejuicio racial en el Nuovo Mundo," (México: Sep Setentas, 1974).

[24]"Aquí se contiene una disputa o controversia," (1552), *O.E.*, V, p. 293.

[25]For example, this is what V. Carro does, *op. cit.*

[26]*O.E.*, V, p. cxxxix.

[27]Cl. Matiollo asks, "Was Francisco de Vitoria a precursor of the theology of liberation?" in *Stromata* (July-September 1974), pp. 257-294, (October-December), pp. 471-502. In spite of the interest in this article, our answer is no.

[28]"Historia de las Indias," *O.E.*, II, p. 356.

[29]*Ibid.*, p. 511. It is important to note that even if de Las Casas assumed the Indians' cause, he also defends the poor Spaniards in respect to those who have power in the Indies. See J. Friede, *op. cit.*, p. 105.

[30]Concerning these points, consult the works of Osvaldo Sunkel and Pedro Paz, *El subdesarrrollo latinoamericano y la teoría del desarrollo* (México: Siglo Veintiuno, 1970); Celso Furtado, *La Economía Latinoamericana* (Santiago de Chile: Editorial Universitaria, 1969); and from a more historical point of view, Tolio Halperin, *Historia Contemporánea de América Latina* (Madrid: Alianza Editorial, 1969).

[31]Cf. Sergio Bagú, *Economia de la Sociedad Colonial* (Buenos Aires: El Ateneo, 1949), Andre Gunder Frank, *Capitalism and Underdevelopment in Latin America* (New York: Monthly Review Press, 1967).

[32]A good example is the Argentine liberal, Domingo Sarmiento, author of a work called *Civilización y Barbarie* (Buenos Aires: Editorial Universitaria de Buenos Aires, 1961).

[33]This type of politics is well-known. Concerning the image that the new North American society has of the Indians, one can consult Jack D. Forbes, *The Indian in America's Past* (Englewood Cliffs: Prentice Hall, 1964).

[34]Jürgen Moltmann, in an open letter to J. Míguez-Bonino, is worried about what he considers to be too little an interest on the part of the theology of liberation, for the achievements of liberalism and democracy. What happens is that our historical experience is different and this leads us to think of the paths that the "popular" classes must take in order to conquer an authentic freedom.

[35]Cf. José Míguez-Bonino, *Doing Theology in a Revolutionary Situation* (Philadelphia: Fortress Press, 1975), p. 10.

[36]Cf. Enrique Dussel, *Historia de la Iglesia en América Latina* (Barcelona: Nova Terra, 1974).

[37]In those countries, Maritain's thought was very much discussed in circles of Catholic intellectuals. Cf., for example, F. Martínez Pas, *Maritain, política e ideología* (Buenos Aires: Editorial Nahuel, 1966), and Javier Castillo, *Las fuentes de la democracia cristiana* (Santiago de Chile, 1968).

[38]That was the role of Christian democracy in Chile during Allende's popular government. Today, some sectors of this political party seem distant from General Pinochet, but before they gave a strong support for this fascist group.

[39]In this theological perspective, the work of Yves Congar was very influential in the most progressive sectors which were bound to the lay apostolic movements. This was the case in countries such as Uruguay, Peru, Argentina.

[40]The most typical case is that of Chile. In this country, the Christian democracy captured, until a few years ago, the political interests which awakened in the Christian groups. But this is valid also for some other countries in Latin America.

[41]In this line we find, for example, Juan Santos Atahualpa who led an indigenous

rebellion in the mid-eighteenth century, and also in some way Tupac Amaru who rebelled at the end of the same century.

[42]Cf. the studies of Engels on the war of the peasants in Germany in the sixteenth century and Ernst Bloch, *Thomas Münzer als Theóloge der Revolution* (Munich: Kurt Wolff, 1921) and his more recent *La filosofía del Renacimiento.*

[43]We are thinking of the notable and isolated figure of Don Clotario Blest, founder of the Central Unica de Trabajadores de Chile at the beginning of this century.

[44]Cf. Gustavo Gutiérrez, *Hacia una teología de liberacion* (Montevideo: MIEC, 1969). This text reproduces a conference given in Chimbote, Peru in July 1968; a report presented in a meeting organized by SODEPAX in Cartigny, Switzerland in 1969, *id.*, *Notes on Theology of Liberation.* Varios: *Liberación, Opción de la Iglesia latino-americana en la décade del 70* (Bogota, 1970), prepatory texts for a symposium on the theology of liberation held in Bogotá in March 1970. Hugo Assmann, *Opresión-liberación, desafio a los cristianos* (Montevideo, 1971), (reprinted under the title, *Teología de la praxis de liberación* [Madrid: Sigueme, 1973]). Gustavo Gutiérrez, *Teología de la liberación* (Lima, 1971).

[45]Concerning a vision that all have in common on this question and on ways sought by contemporary theology, see the interesting reflection of Claude Geffre, *Une nouvelle age de la theologie* (Paris, 1972). See also, Henri Bouillard, "Exégèse, herméneutique et theologie. Problèmes de méthode" in *Exégèse et herméneutique* (Paris, 1971), and the fine analysis by Jean Pierre Jossua, "Ensemblement du discours chrétien," in *Christus* (June 1973), pp. 345-354. Cf. also, the recent works of Edward Schillebeeckx about theological method.

[46]Cf. the essay of J. Guichard to underline these questions: "Foi chrétienne et theórie de la connaissance" in Lumière et Vie (June-August 1973), pp. 61-84.

[47]In this framework, we must perhaps rethink the reflections of Duns Scotus about Praxis (and not only action), God as *cognoscibile operabile,* and theology as practical science. Cf. also, but in modern perspective, Frans V. Ouderijn, *Kritische Theologie als Kritik der Theologie* (Munich-Mainz, 1972).

[48]That means that the theologian must be a person committed to the process of liberation. It is a condition for a work not only concrete but also truly scientific.

[49]This manner of perceiving theology is one of the first intuitions of the theology of liberation. Cf. Gustavo Gutiérrez, *La Pastoral de la Iglesia en América Latina* (Montevideo: Análisis Teológico, 1968) and *id., Notes on a Theology of Liberation* (Lausanne, 1970).

[50]Justice no. 3 in Conference of Latin American Bishops, Medellin, 1968.

[51]The articles of the review, "Tierra Nueva" (Bogotá, Colombia) lead to those simplistic and distorted presentations of the theology of liberation. This publication is under the guidance of R. Veckemans. Mons. Alfonso López was one of its collaborators. A present collaborator is Eduardo Ibarra, author of "Le contexte de la théologie de la libération" in the co-authored work, *Théologies de la libération en Amérique Latine* (Paris: Beaudierne, 1974). With good reason, H. de Lavallette judges this work as "tendentious." "Bulletin de théologie politique," in *Recherches des Science Religieuse* (October, December 1974), p. 626. This is the least that can be said.

[52]There is, at present, a great effort to domesticate the theology of liberaton, for example, using its terms but emptied of meaning, or speaking of a noncommitted pluralism.

[53]J. C. Scannone has made important contributions to Latin American theological reflection, *Teología de la liberación y praxis popular* (Madrid: Sigueme, 1976). However, he works in a perspective different from the one we are trying to present here.

[54]Cf., for example, James H. Cone, *God of the Oppressed* (New York: Seabury Press, 1975)

and the promising work of Virgilio Elizondo, *Christianity and Culture* (Huntington: Our Sunday Visitor, Inc., 1975).

[55]The expression is from Leonardo Boff, a Brazilian theologian.

[56]M. Richard Shuall, in 1966, had already lucidly underlined the need to rethink the faith in a world revolutionary situation.

[57]In these lines, I am using expressions which spring from the reflection of Peruvian Christian groups referring to their liberating commitment.

Notes

The Death and Resurrection of the American Dream
Richard Shaull

INTRODUCTION

[1]Paul Lehmann, *The Transfiguration of Politics* (New York: Harper and Row, 1975), p. 7.

[2]In these pages I am going to use the word *America* frequently to speak of the United States, as well as the adjective *American*. I do so, with apologies to my friends in Canada and Latin America, because I am trying to get at our story as we have told it, and also because we do not as yet have a new language to speak of ourselves and our nation.

[3]Eugen Rosenstock-Huessy, *Out of Revolution* (Brunswich: Four Wells, 1964), p. 4.

[4]Page Smith, *A New Age Now Begins: A People's History of the American Revolution* (New York: McGraw-Hill, 1976), Vol. 1, p. 9.

CHAPTER ONE

[1]I regret that these volumes came off the press only a few months ago and that I discovered them long after this manuscript had been turned over to the publishers—when I was in the midst of pulling together a brief introduction. From a quick inspection of them, I am aware of how much a careful reading of this story might have contributed to what I am here trying to get at.

[2]Quoted in Michael Walzer, *The Revolution of the Saints* (Cambridge: Harvard University Press, 1965), pp. 10-11.

[3]*Ibid.*, p. 10.

[4]Leslie Fiedler, *Love and Death in the American Novel* (New York: Stein and Day, 1975), p. 37.

[5]Hans Morgenthau, "The Aborted Nixon Revolution," *The New Republic*, August 11, 1973, pp. 17-19.

[6]An interesting example of this is the book by Edmund Stillman and William Pfaff, *The Politics of Hysteria* (New York: Harper and Row, 1964). In it, the authors present a very critical evaluation of our foreign policy since World War II. Faced with the destructiveness of our Promethean efforts, the only advice they can offer us is this: "Skepticism and stoicism . . . are essential to arm men to endure the waste and perplexity of history; only they can save us from despair, or from the self-destroying recourse to a magical totalitarianism." Modern survival is, in the end, not merely a matter of wisdom and strength, but *"pas trop de zele."* P. 252.

[7]Edward Goldsmith, ed., *A Blueprint for Survival* (Boston: Houghton Mifflin Co., 1972) p. 3.

[8]For an interesting and valuable discussion of this goal of Marx, see Shlomo Avineri's article on "Marx's Vision of Future Society," in *Dissent*, Summer 1973, pp. 323-331.

CHAPTER TWO

[1]See especially *The Genius of American Politics* (Chicago: University of Chicago Press, 1953).

[2]*St. Louis Post-Dispatch*, July 20, 1975.

[3]Robert Heilbroner, *An Inquiry into the Human Prospect* (W. W. Norton & Co., 1974).

[4]*Ibid.*, p. 129.

[5]*Ibid.*, pp. 140, 141, 144.

[6]Studs Terkel, *Working: People Talk About What They Do All Day and How They Feel About What They Do* (New York: Pantheon Books, A Division of Random House, Inc., 1974), p. 527. Copyright © 1972, 1974 by Studs Terkel. All material from this book is used by permission of Pantheon Books.

[7]Adolf Holl, *Jesus in Bad Company*, Trans. by Simon King (New York: Avon Books, 1974), p. 64.

[8]Herbert A. Otto, "Man-Woman Relationships in the Society of the Future," *The Futurist*, April 1973, p. 60.

[9]Terkel, *Working*, pp. xxii-xxiii.

CHAPTER THREE

[1]"Each man's work will become manifest; for the Day will disclose it, because it will be revealed with fire, and the fire will test what sort of work each one has done. If the work which any man has built on the foundation survives, he will receive a reward. If any man's work is burned up, he will suffer loss, though he himself will be saved, but only as through fire." 1 Cor. 3: 13-15.

[2]I am greatly indebted to Mr. Kim, with whom I have been engaged in discussion of these issues over a number of years, not only for this story, but also for other insights into the relation of Christian faith to social transformation which have come to play a central role in the formulation of my own position.

CHAPTER FOUR

[1]Rosenstock-Huessy, pp. 727-728.

[2]Søren Kierkegaard, *Attack Upon Christendom* (Boston: Beacon Press, 1956), p. 271.

[3]*Experiments in Thought and Modern Form*, p. 4. Unpublished manuscript.

[4]Gustavo Gutiérrez, *A Theology of Liberation: History, Politics and Salvation*, Sister Caridad Inda and John Eagleson, eds., trans. (Maryknoll, N.Y.: Orbis Books, 1973).

[5]Eugen Rosenstock-Huessy, *The Christian Future or the Modern Mind Outrun* (New York: Charles Scribner's Sons, 1946), p. viii.

[6]See his dissertation, *Historical Transformation, People's Movement and Messianic Koinonia: A Study of the Relationship of Christian and Tonghak Religious Communities to the March First Independence Movement in Korea* (Princeton Theological Seminary, 1976).

the **method** method

the
method.
method

7 obsessions

that helped our scrappy start-up
turn an industry upside down

ERIC RYAN
+ ADAM LOWRY

with Lucas Conley

---

portfolio / penguin

This book is dedicated to all of the **People Against Dirty** who made Method possible. To our team members who have given us ten great years of unwavering passion, courage, and hard work, to our advocates who brought Method into their homes and helped spread our revolution, to our families who never laughed at us and who made personal sacrifices to support our dreams, to the investors who put their money where their mouth was, and to every retailer who supported Method by putting our little bottles of goodness on their shelves. This book is for you!

INTRODUCTION

HELLO. AS YOU PROBABLY GUESSED FROM LOOKing at the cover, this is a book about Method, that quirky, California-based maker of environmentally friendly and stylish cleaning products for the home. But before we get all excited to share all about what goes on behind the scenes here (but sorry, we can't share the photo booth pictures from last year's prom), you should know that this is much more than our story. *The Method Method* is packed with innovative ideas about business—the very same ideas that led to our ranking as one of *Fast Company*'s and *Time*'s most innovative companies in the world, earned us a spot on the Inc. 500 (we reached number seven), and won us a PETA Persons of the Year award, among closets full of other design, sustainability, and product awards. (Forgive us for bragging, but our editor said this would give us more credibility). Tips, case studies, favorite quotes, embarrassing mistakes—we gathered everything we've learned in ten years of building our brand and crammed it all into these pages. In the process, we learned something new, too:

Everything we know, we learned from you.

It's true. Just by picking up this book—if you haven't bought it yet, go ahead . . . we'll wait—you have joined a community of millions of customers who engage with our brand every day, teaching us how to do our job better in so many different ways. And we've been listening. In just ten years, you've helped us grow Method from a two-man, four-product outfit operating out of the back of our car into an international brand at the vanguard of a new category of environmentally and socially driven companies changing how business is done. So, yeah, we owe you one.

Taking stock this year on our tenth birthday, we decided to show our appreciation by sharing everything we've learned in one nice little package. The good stuff, the bad stuff, even the proprietary stuff that made our lawyers squirm. We're not worried that you're going to steal our ideas and go try to mimic us—we trust you, and besides, our obsessions are easier said than done. We do hope that, no matter what industry you're in or what position you hold at your company, you'll be able to learn something from our ideas and possibly make them your own. We also hope you'll be able to avoid some of the mistakes we've made—and trust us, we've made plenty.

At the core of it all are our seven obsessions, the rules we live by. Other businesses might refer to these as strategies, but *strategy* is a tired corporate word for something you do for your boss. Obsessions are bigger. Obsessions are something you take home with you, something that drives entrepreneurs to think deeper, work longer, and change entire industries. Some we've followed from the beginning; others we've learned the hard way. Reflecting on the past ten years, we understand now that our obsessions are actually rules written by our younger selves, holding us to the ideals we shared when we first decided to launch the company.

It hasn't always been easy. Consider our competition: Soap companies were the world's first multinationals and the first to pioneer mass media ("soap opera" anyone?). Not only did they have a hundred-year head start on us, they had tens of thousands of employees and millions of loyal customers on their side! People told us we were committing entrepreneurial suicide, but we saw plenty of room for improvement in this rather stagnant industry, and so we decided to take it on. To succeed, we knew we couldn't launch just one groundbreaking innovation or change just one rule—we had to redefine the battlefield as much as possible, turning their weaknesses into our strengths. They have size and power, but we have speed and agility. They follow Six Sigma, but we built an imaginative, irreverent culture that allows our people to create and express themselves through their work. They try to be all things to all people, but we inspire a small group of advocates dedicated to evangelizing our brand to anyone who will listen. Devoting one chapter to each of our seven obsessions, we explore why they matter, how we live up to them, where we've gone astray, and what we've learned from each along the way. Admitting that we could never have done this without a lot of help and inspiration, we also spotlight someone (our "muse") in each chapter who embodies each obsession even more than we do.

If you're like us, you're impatient to revolutionize the way business is done and to create positive social change in the process. Maybe you're a business leader—the MBA searching for ways to put your new ideas into practice. Maybe you're an aspiring entrepreneur—itching for an opportunity to disrupt an industry. Whether you're sitting in a cube farm at MegaCorp or in your underwear in your garage, we know where you're coming from because we've been there, too. Take it from us, change is possible—as long as you're ready to obsess over it.

Never before has the world of business evolved as quickly as it's evolving today. It's not just technology—everything about the world of work is changing: the ways in which we design, produce, ship, and sell goods; the means by which we find, gather, and share information; and how we assess value—not only on our balance sheets, but in our personal and professional lives. Each of these areas presents profound challenges to today's entrepreneurs, and each of our obsessions is designed to help you meet those challenges and exploit the cultural shifts behind them.

We hope the lessons in this book—real, unvarnished, battle-tested tales gleaned from years of outthinking our bigger and better-financed competitors—will help inspire you to see your job differently. We hope this book will help lay a path from the way most of us work today to the way we could work tomorrow—a model that aligns business interests, social interests, and environmental interests. We also hope this book does right by our partners, team members, and customers, celebrating them while attracting new allies, talent, and advocates in the process. Finally, we hope it makes our moms proud.

If this book does nothing else, it should dispel the myth of the lone entrepreneur. Our names may be on the cover, but what's inside represents the enormous efforts of loyal colleagues inside and outside Method, past and present. Getting this far took a lot of help from a lot of people, and to all those who helped us become what we are today, we are grateful. We couldn't have done this without your passion, long hours, personal sacrifice, courage, and heavy doses of weirdness. Thank you, people against dirty!

—Eric and Adam, friends and founders

CONTENTS

the **method** method

OUR STORY

THE FIRST TEN YEARS OF MAKING SOAP

from a dirty apartment to soap star

WE PROMISED THIS WOULDN'T BE A BOOK ALL about us, but in order to understand where we're coming from and the principles that drive our company, a little background is in order. Method's story begins in 1998 with a chance encounter between the two of us on a crowded flight from Detroit to San Francisco. Old acquaintances from school in Grosse Pointe, Michigan, we fell into easy conversation. While we'd sailed together on Lake St. Clair as teens, we'd gone our separate ways after high school—Adam, to the world of equations and fluid dynamics studying chemical engineering and environmental science at Stanford University, and Eric, to the University of Rhode Island and London's Richmond University, where he spent five years testing the patience of his business and communications professors. As we'd only seen each other on holidays over the years, it wasn't until that plane ride that we realized we were both living in San Francisco.

Heading back to California on that late-night flight, we discovered we were both at a point in our careers where we were asking ourselves, "Is this really what I want to do?" Working on climate research, Adam had grown weary of the environmental echo chamber. Compiling data for the Kyoto Protocol was compelling, but how fulfilling could it be if the only people reading his work were already convinced the environment was in danger? Working for advertising agencies, Eric could feel himself growing jaded. Most of the work he did never saw the light of day, killed by uncreative clients in bad golf shirts. And while crafting ad campaigns for brands like Saturn was fun, how was he supposed to stay engaged after it became obvious his only job was to sell a mediocre product—not help make it any better? As the two of us caught up, one thing became clear:

we were both looking to create something different and pursue our entrepreneurial aspirations. But what?

We had plenty of ideas—a modern interpretation of Pottery Barn? A healthy pizza chain?—but none of them were very compelling or made much sense. Though we left the plane without any great ideas, we were excited by the prospect of doing something truly different and worthwhile. A few months after reconnecting, one of Adam's roommates got married, so Eric moved in and our ambition to start something grew by the day. But *what to start*? Every bar-stool brainstorming session led us to the same conclusion: Keep our day jobs. But as it turned out, it was Eric's day job, which included creating a new toothpaste for a major brand (because the world *really needed* another toothpaste brand) that led us to our eureka moment. After spending countless mind-numbing research hours in supermarket aisles, Eric found himself imagining how he'd reinvent some of the products we use every day. He realized that rather than trying to create something out of thin air, it was much easier to find a proven but tired industry and identify a way to disrupt it. This is how you are trained to think in advertising: Look at a category and find the cultural shift or consumer motivation that the leading brands are not delivering on. The space in between is where you'll find the opportunity.

A few months later, we were both home in Detroit over the holidays and headed to northern Michigan for a weekend of skiing. During the five-hour road trip, Eric mentioned that the cleaning products industry might be the right place to dig. From Eric's point of view as a marketer, the cleaning category looked like a sitting duck. Think about it: The household cleaning aisle is huge, but every mainstream product more or less looks the same (like a relic of the 1950s), positions itself the same ("Cleaning will be a jiff!"), and works the same (with enough toxic chemicals, who can't get grass stains out of a T-shirt?). As a chemist, Adam saw vast room for improvement among the "green" alternatives—at that point, a handful of pious brands selling subpar products under the auspices of conservation and personal sacrifice. From our perspective, shopping for soap was like dating in a town with two options: Hire a so-called professional (a sure thing, even if it leaves you feeling dirty) or get stuck with a prude (and embrace austerity in the name of moral righteousness). Frankly, the choices sucked!

Yeah, we know. It sounds weird: two twenty-four-year-old guys not known for their home-cleaning habits idling away the hours lost in conversation about dish soap and disinfectant spray. But it didn't *feel* weird. On the contrary, it felt perfectly natural. Rather than design one innovative product, why not disrupt an entire category? The more we talked about it, the more convinced we became

▲ **FIND THE CULTURAL SHIFT.** Our methodology for disrupting mature categories.

that cleaning products offered the ideal opportunity to combine our passions and skills. Eric imagined bringing style to the category. If you could transform a cleaning product for the house into an accessory for the home—offering a playful piece of sculpture, say, in place of a plain old soap pump or spray bottle—people might just be inclined to leave it on the counter instead of hiding it in a cabinet or tossing it under the sink. Adam imagined bringing substance to the category. If you could replace the toxic ingredients with natural stuff that worked

THE POWER OF THE DUO

Look at any great company and you will find a combination of diverse skills, often springing from a pair of diverse leaders. Mickey Drexler and Don Fisher at Gap, Steve Jobs and Tim Cook at Apple, Steve Ballmer and Bill Gates at Microsoft—some of the most original ideas are the offspring of two opposite perspectives. Of course, many great companies are launched and run by someone flying solo, but it can only help to have a partner who complements your skills.

▲ **THAT'S NOT BEER.** Fortunately, our
products are nontoxic, so no roommates
were hurt in the making of this business.

well and smelled nice, people might feel better about what they were using in
their homes (and the impact it had outside them). It was the first and most powerful "yes, and" conversation in Method's history—our "peanut butter and choc-
olate" moment where everything just came together. Here was a major, mature
product category that had completely missed two profound cultural shifts.
Bringing style and substance together could potentially revolutionize the industry and change people's entire attitude toward cleaning. After five hours discussing the idea in the car, we arrived at the mountain more excited about soap than
skiing.

A few days later, after talking things over on the chairlift, we returned to San
Francisco and launched our research phase. This was about when our roommates
began suspecting we were nuts. What exactly was in all those beer pitchers
labeled DO NOT DRINK? Why the sudden interest in cleaning the toilets so often?
Every trip to the grocery store became a reconnaissance mission. Every weekend
errand, a market feasibility study. Hashing out our observations week after week
from our modest (and, ironically, very dirty) apartment at 1731 Pine Street, we
reached a couple of what Eric would call key consumer insights.

CULTURAL SHIFT #1: LIFESTYLING THE HOME

Eric's advertising background helped us see that even though the leading cleaning brands marketed their products like commodities—simple utilitarian solutions to use, throw under the sink, and forget about until the next cleaning day—consumers actually invested a lot of interest and emotion in caring for their homes. After all, our homes are extensions of ourselves. Moving into a new place, we pore over every last paint swatch and carpet sample. Settling in, we build fond memories of and strong feelings for every last mismatched coffee mug and hand-me-down end table. This cultural shift was increasingly evidenced by the explosion of shelter magazines, shows like *Trading Spaces,* and entire networks like Home and Garden Television. More than in previous generations, people were envisioning their homes as personal expressions. Home fashion and design was taking hold in the mainstream. No longer were consumers satisfied with Aunt Sophie's old dining room table and other passed-down relics—they wanted that chic new Seabury sofa from Crate & Barrel. And once they updated the couch, suddenly the rug looked tired. Then the window dressings, too. Accessorizing and stylizing the home with designer goods became a national obsession, giving rise to major chains like Pottery Barn, IKEA, and Room & Board.

The cleaning industry missed this shift entirely, positioning their products as solutions to everyday problems rather than complements to a lifestyle. Just as Vidal Sassoon and Williams-Sonoma identified ways to bring aspiration and a premium appeal to previously boring, solution-focused mass categories like shampoo and cookware, we saw an opportunity to leverage design and emotion to elevate the banal household cleaner into an accessory for the home.

So why is it—if we care so much for our homes—that we leave all the upkeep to that motley crew of uninspired jugs and spray bottles lurking under the sink? Tapping our expert research consultants (i.e., our friends and families), the answer was inevitably the same: Nobody really wants to think about cleaning products. At least, we try not to. Whenever they come up, we tend to regard them as a necessary evil—quick solutions to annoying problems. Granted, cleaning products should be easy, but couldn't they also be pleasant to look at or even fun to use? What if we were to design products worthy of a place on the counter, ones that we actually looked forward to using? This insight led us to our first mission: making cleaning fun.

CULTURAL SHIFT #2: OUR CHEMICAL ADDICTION

Tapping Adam's chemical engineering know-how, Eric was shocked to find how "dirty" the cleaning products on the market really were. Essentially, we were using poison to make our homes cleaner, surrounding ourselves with toxic ingredients and polluting our environment in the process. Worse, few consumers knew how bad it was. We'd been bamboozled into believing that the acrid whiff of bleach was the smell of "clean" and that the burning under our fingernails after scrubbing the counter was "hygienic." It didn't make sense to us that we pollute when we clean and use poison to make our homes healthier.

The second cultural shift in the category was that the consumer was putting more emphasis on natural health. Living in San Francisco at the time, you could see the natural and organic movement moving into the mainstream from a mile away. Yet while consumers were buying organic milk and strawberries in droves, they were still spraying pesticides throughout the kitchen in the form of antibacterial cleaners. We felt it was only a matter of time before consumers would care as much about what they put on their skin and in their home as they did about what they were eating and drinking. Sure, cleaning should be thorough, but

---

A NAMING METHOD FOR NAMING METHOD

It's a question we get all the time, and a valid one for any entrepreneur: "How do you come up with a name for your company?" Eric's background in branding and name development taught us to start by selecting a "jumping-off word," something that captured the spirit of the idea we wanted to communicate. In our case, we wanted to represent a whole new approach to cleaning—a smarter, more holistic process—a new way, based on great technique rather than brute force. *Technique* became our jumping-off word, and one evening while we were both in the bathroom brushing our teeth (yes, weird), Adam threw out the suggestion *method*. Eric yelled out, "That's it!" and we had our name. Claiming a common term hasn't exactly been easy (our lawyers advised against it), but we believe the name has made a difference in the success of the company, and we couldn't imagine it any other way.

---

shouldn't it also be healthy and safe? What if we were to design nontoxic products that didn't leave a legacy of pollution? This insight led us to our second mission: making cleaning actually . . . clean.

THE ELEVATOR PITCH: AVEDA FOR THE HOME

We said we were both searching for "something different" when we ran into each other on that plane back in 1998. When we sent out our first business plan, eighteen months later, we finally began to understand what *different* was actually going to mean. Picture the scene: It was early 2000, the NASDAQ was north of five thousand, and everyone and their kid sister in San Francisco had a dot-com dream. Sneaker millionaires were springing up as fast as you could say "first-mover advantage," lavish launch parties were the norm, and we were running around town with an earnest vision for soap.

Welcome to the proof-of-concept stage of a new business, the phase where you strap wings to your back and try to convince others to jump off a cliff and learn to fly with you. Before long, our roommates weren't the only ones who thought we were crazy. A cleaning products company founded on high-end design and an ethos of sustainability? Venture capitalists laughed off the idea. "Green" was a niche for puritan do-gooders willing to put up with substandard products. And design? When it came to washing hands and doing dishes, people only cared about function and price, not aesthetics.

It wasn't that we hadn't thought things out. To the contrary, we'd spent months honing our pitch before shopping it around. Our big idea—to bring a personal-care approach to cleaning—was clear and simple. "Aveda for the home"—a nod to the botanically based high-end beauty brand—was our pitch-perfect elevator pitch. The problem wasn't communicating the idea; everybody we approached understood what we were trying to do. The problem was, *no one thought we could do it.*

Maybe you know the feeling—that diffuse sense of panic that someone, somewhere, is about to steal your idea. In our case, there were seven multinationals with names like P&G and Unilever dominating this space. With their thousands of employees and millions of dollars poured into market research every year, how could they possibly miss the opportunity we saw? This scared us to death; there must be something we were missing if no one before us had done this. Then again, IBM missed Apple, Kodak ignored digital, and nobody knew

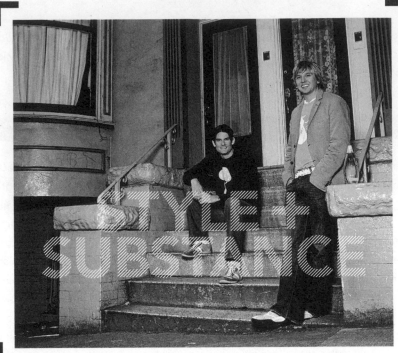

▲ TWO FRIENDS WITH TWO VERY DIFFERENT PHILOSOPHIES.
The birthplace of Method, a very dirty San Francisco flat.

more about coffee than Maxwell House, but they didn't see Starbucks coming. Big brands miss big opportunities all the time, and despite the skepticism, we still believed we had a great idea.

This is the awkward and insecure stage that makes getting companies off the ground so damn difficult. It's also where most business dreams die, only to be occasionally eulogized when a friend or family member asks, "Hey, whatever happened to that crazy idea of yours . . . ?" The fundamental problem at this stage is that you need money to launch the business and prove the concept, yet who's going to give you money when you haven't proven the business idea? This is the point when you find out how bad you want it, how thick your skin is, how much you're willing sacrifice to make it happen. You have no choice but to prove the business yourself and do it as quickly as possible with what little resources you have.

To get Method through the proof-of-concept stage, we crafted a plan to create a first line of products and distribute it to twenty local stores. The idea was to prove we could compete against the national brands—even with no employees, no salaries to support ourselves, no previous training, and with a very small amount of savings. We knew success during this stage was dependent on our ability to get others to share our vision and support it (either with an immediate cash investment or a pledge to help with some part of the business). Luckily, we were fortunate enough to get suppliers, designers, lawyers, accountants, manufacturing partners, and friends to offer free services in exchange for equity or payment—assuming we raised money down the road.

Over the next six months, we created our first line of products through a lot of quick experimentation and a heavy dose of borrowed expertise. Working on the formulation, Adam was able to convince local chemist Steve Deptris and the Royal Chemical Company to help us create and manufacture our formulas. We strived hard for nontoxic products that actually worked—no easy feat. Meanwhile, Eric focused on the product design and brand identity. Our first bottle was inspired by a camping fuel bottle found in Norway, and we convinced Michael Rutchik, a local designer, to partner with us on the graphic design. To help the bottle stand out on the shelf and reinforce our safe and human approach, our labels featured photographs of people cleaning the appropriate surface. The essential skill at this stage: infect others with your vision and passion. Make your mission contagious so that others will take risk and work with you, even if it's for very little up-front compensation.

With finished products in hand, we started the uphill climb to get them into stores. We can still remember walking into that first grocery store at 6:00 A.M., tracking down the manager, and launching into a nervous thirty-second pitch about why he should carry Method. We're still not sure why he said yes—was it the beauty and appeal of the product, or just his concern that we would keep coming back? Regardless, on February 28, 2001, Method landed its first sale at Mollie Stone's Market in Burlingame, just south of San Francisco! Imagine our feeling of awe as we watched the cashier scan our product right before our eyes: The bar code lined up, the register beeped, and the Method brand was born.

Over the next several months, we went door-to-door, pitching to every Bay Area independent market we could find. We settled into a routine, picking up product at the factory in the morning, delivering it to stores throughout the day, and counting up how many we sold by day's end so that we could build a sales story. To market the product, we held in-store demonstrations and passed out coupons, which also doubled as consumer research. Not only did sales start to pick up, but the product began striking an emotional spark with consumers! Our customer service number (actually Eric's cell phone) was on the back label of every bottle. As e-mails and calls of praise started to pour in, the business came to life. Consumers were raving about our unique products, like the cucumber bathroom spray cleaner. At first, we were sure it was our friends playing practical jokes on us, but (after hanging up on the first few callers) we realized our customers were actually excited!

Within a couple of months, Method products were available in thirty stores, and our confidence was building. But in order to keep growing after maxing out the number of local independent grocers, we knew we would need to start selling to bigger retail chains like Safeway or Albertsons. Fortunately, all that time spent getting our hands dirty (figuratively of course) was finally paying off; after months of selling directly to independent store managers, we were actually beginning to understand the ins and outs of the grocery industry. More important, we had some real sales data now, so we could actually sit down with the big buyers and properly pitch our line with some hope of getting in.

But we had one big problem. Our seed money was gone, and selling to grocery chains would require ramping up our inventory and shipping directly from a warehouse rather than hand-delivering product out of the back of Adam's mom's car. We needed a lot more capital, and while our proof of concept was strengthening, it was not strong enough to raise investments from venture capitalists or other professional sources. Despite our early success, we needed to make a big leap—and quickly!

Now, like it or not, the only way to get through this awkward entrepreneurial stage is to raise "angel" money (you could also call this part the Friends, Fools, and Family stage). Angel investors get their name for one obvious reason: they save you from death (or delay it, to be more precise). We set out to raise capital from anyone willing to believe in us—who in the end turned out to be our families, roommates, and a handful of friends. While everyone gave small amounts, it was enough to sustain the business and keep us on a path toward our next milestone: proving the business in major grocery store chains.

Many entrepreneurs struggle with the decision to take money from close friends and loved ones. The reality is that you don't have much of a choice. Before you've proven your idea, the only thing people can bet on is you . . . and, inevitably, the only people willing to do that are your friends and family. Of course, the upside to taking money from the people you care about most is that it puts a lot of pressure on your back. (No, seriously, this is a good thing.) You go from not wanting to let yourself down to not wanting to let your family down. It forces you to do everything you can to avoid sitting down at Christmas dinner saying, "Sorry, Grandma, I lost that ten thousand dollars you loaned me."

With friends-and-family money in hand, we finally achieved our goal of getting Method into the bigger grocery store chains—among them, Ralphs in Southern California and QFC up in the Seattle area. But while the business was growing, it was also burning through cash faster. Soon, not only were we working 24/7 to expand distribution across nearly two hundred stores and counting (a full-time job in and of itself), but we also began trying to raise professional money—venture capital. We were going big or going home.

This is the point where we should probably say something gritty and inspiring about triumph through ingenuity and perseverance. But the fact is, we were laughed out of every venture capital pitch meeting, we ran up $100,000 of credit card debt as the angel money ran dry, and after we quit our jobs to chase this harebrained idea, Eric's girlfriend dumped him. And that wasn't even the low point. Lower still were the nights waking in a cold sweat, fretting about how to pay back the money we had borrowed from our friends and family. Even lower was the spiraling nausea of nearly losing our first round of venture capital funding when the economy took a dive in 2001. (After all, who would want to invest in premium home cleaning products during a crippling recession?) At that point, our vendors began putting us on credit holds, freezing our production, and send-

▲ **GET YOUR HANDS DIRTY.** There is no substitute for hands-on learning by doing the selling and delivering yourself. (Adam holding our first invoice and Eric performing an in-store demo. Don't ask why we are in the liquor aisle.)

ing us scrambling to find a bridge investment. The lowest moment? Viewing a car accident as good luck because—with just $16 left in the bank—we could use the insurance payout to cover our rent and food.

Unlike most business success stories, this one fully acknowledges the role that *luck* played in tipping the scales. As when David Bennett, cofounder of Mollie Stone's Market, suddenly decided to buy all the home-brewed spray cleaner we'd managed to squeeze into our car. Or when the president of a major gambling company in Las Vegas floated us a bridge loan just big enough to keep us alive until a pair of enterprising VC investors named Steve and Herb Simon decided to risk half a million dollars on a pair of unproven kids in the midst of the (first) global financial meltdown of the century.

Ultimately, Eric got the girl back, Grandma didn't lose her nest egg, and the insurance company didn't ask too many questions. From the beginning—and at so many other points we'll never have the time or space to tell—luck often made the difference between success and failure. That said, the old cliché is true—sometimes you have to create your own luck. The recipe: a dash of opportunity and a whole lot of preparation. Getting a new venture off the ground requires busting your ass and envisioning multiple ways to win. Just remember to bring a valid credit card to the celebration dinner. Ours all got denied. Luckily, when we told the owner, a friend of ours at San Francisco's Caffe Sociale, why we were celebrating, he let us off with an IOU.

AIMING HIGH: SETTING OUR SIGHTS ON TARGET

Of course, luck only goes so far, and at some point, you have to rely on ingenuity and perseverance to make up the difference. Our lucky break with the Simons had only postponed the most dire financial consequences. (We know what you're thinking: *How much was that celebration dinner?*) While the first $500,000 check from the Simons was more money than either of us had ever seen, more than half of it went straight to impatient suppliers, overdue bills, legal fees, and an ever-expanding—albeit exceedingly friendly—phalanx of VC contract attorneys. As the champagne fog cleared from our heads the day after our fete at Sociale, we realized what was really giving us indigestion: With just $200,000 left in the bank, in order to continue our partnership with the Simons, we had ninety days to expand distribution to eight hundred stores.

Here's the deal: professional investors need to draw a line in the sand, to set some type of milestone that gives them the freedom to step away if things aren't moving in the right direction. Investors need safeguards to keep from indiscriminately pouring money into well-meaning but money-losing enterprises. Sure, your cousin's idea for an automated toaster-size olive press in every kitchen may be compelling, but at what point do you stop sending him checks and cut your losses? In our case, if we wanted the second half-million from the Simons, the contract stipulated that we had to ramp up distribution from two hundred stores to an astounding eight hundred in under three months.

The problem with such an aggressive distribution goal is that it creates an unhealthy incentive: any store at any cost. Inevitably, you wind up putting yourself in stores you shouldn't be in. But we didn't have time to sweat the details.

With just ninety days to achieve our goal, we abandoned every other activity and became full-time salesmen—knocking on every grocer's delivery door and competing with each other to see who could sign up more customers at retailing and natural-products conferences. Having exhausted the network of independent retailers in our area, we had started approaching buyers at the regional chains—Wegmans, Albertsons, Safeway—meeting after meeting, sharpening our pitch each time. As fast as the distribution agreements stacked up, however, our cash vanished faster.

It wasn't as if we were paying ourselves lavish salaries (or any salary, for that matter). We both believe strongly in investing in talent, so the two of us had been deferring our own salaries to pay our consultant, Alastair Dorward, competitively. But at the close of our Series A, we'd hired Alastair full time. The only one of the three of us with an MBA and real-world entrepreneurial experience, Alastair was worth every penny. But as our accounts had increased, so had our overhead—staff, rent, and operating costs were burning up more of our capital every day. Meanwhile, the rejections added up, the money dwindled away, and we got increasingly desperate—both at work and at home. Soon enough, we were back in the poorhouse, and our roommates were once again balking at covering our bar tabs. Grandma couldn't help us now. The only way forward was to scale up—dramatically—and the only way to do that was to land a national distributor.

From the very beginning—before we had any products to sell, before we'd even named the company—getting our new cleaning products into Target had been our ultimate goal. Not only was Target our best chance at mainstream credibility, it was a natural fit for our nascent brand. First off, Target was trend-forward. The retailer had already brought beautiful design into the home with designers like Michael Graves and Todd Oldham, and its "Expect more, pay less" motto was an obvious match for our style-plus-substance philosophy. And when it came to national distribution (something we'd promised the Simons), none of the other usual suspects were a good match. Kmart was flailing, and, in 2002, Walmart just wasn't the right place for a premium, design-based start-up to debut. No matter how we looked at it, we were destined for Target.

All of which is to say that, while the Simons may have lit a fire under us, we'd been networking furiously for a Target contact since our fateful ski trip, inquiring through friends, friends of friends, friends of acquaintances, friends of complete strangers . . . and at long last, we received our first promising lead in the fall of 2002. A manufacturer owned by a friendly VC fund was scheduled to discuss a private-label partnership with Target's head buyer. Were we interested in piggy-backing and making a quick pitch after the manufacturer was done (if there was time)? It wasn't the dream date we'd imagined, but a review with Target's head buyer was too tempting to pass up. Accepting the invitation with gratitude, we circled the day on our calendars in red ink.

It's difficult to justify in retrospect, but we were feeling halfway confident about our upcoming blind date with America's third-largest retailer. Devoting our time to closing hundreds of minor sales had boosted our confidence to an all-time high—and not without reason. In the weeks leading up to our rendez-vous in Minneapolis, Target's home base, we'd signed our biggest account yet (a two-state deal with Albertsons, the regional grocery chain), reached our goal of eight hundred stores (miraculously—and recklessly, as you'll see), and trig-gered the second half of our venture capital funding. We knew convincing any-one to take us national with only one product (our spray cleaner in four different variants) wouldn't be easy, but what choice did we have? In the rush to build our distribution, there simply hadn't been time to develop any new concepts. No matter: Our bank account was flush, our supply lines were overflowing, and our pitch was laser sharp. Setting our sights on Target, we actually liked our chances. Luck had gotten us this far, right?

Our chances, as it turned out, were less than those of a snowball in hell. At least, that's how Target's divisional head put it after a cursory look at our presenta-tion materials. Our product was ordinary. Our brand wouldn't have broad appeal. Go home. After weeks psyching ourselves up for our all-important pitch, we couldn't believe our ears. The buyer seemed annoyed with us for wasting his time.

We'd aimed high, failed big, and crashed hard. Going back to work was the worst part. We didn't want to be just another minor-league company stuck in some regional niche, neither growing nor shrinking. (Even if we'd settled for the minor leagues, sooner or later one of the big global brands was going to catch on and copy our model.) After months of seemingly boundless success,

Method had come to a screeching halt. We couldn't help asking ourselves, *What was the point?*

When you're in an entrepreneurial funk, you wind up questioning everything. What am I doing? How on earth did I think I could do this? Do I even want to do this anymore? Wallowing in this kind of mood, you start to think about all the opportunities you passed over along the way. Sometimes it was just an itch—perhaps a casual inquiry about job opportunities during lunch with an old colleague. Sometimes it was a fever—such as the overwhelming urge to drop everything, book a last-minute flight, and start over in some far-off, exotic corner of the world where no one knows your name. We were no different. This was—to put it mildly—a *delicate* phase in Method's history. It all could have gone one way or another.

HAVE THE RIGHT PEOPLE TO LEAN ON

When the going gets tough, especially early on, leaning on people who've been there before makes all the difference. These trusted advisers can be found anywhere, but the closer they are to you the better. We found just such a person in Jim Merlo. Jim is the CEO of one of our first suppliers, Trifinity Partners. Jim and his team were miracle workers, always willing and able to work with us to try something new. Jim, in particular, was the perfect blend of puckish ingenuity and unvarnished honesty. A proudly old-school Chicago manufacturer, whenever we had a problem Jim had seen it before—and "had a guy" who could take care of it. One day when it seemed like we weren't going to pull another rabbit out of our hats, Jim turned to a rather dejected Adam and, in his heavy Chicago accent, said, "Adam, just remember: we're not saving lives here. We're just makin' soap." Merlo's lessons have stuck with us. Always keep your mission squarely in your sights and strive for it like your life depends on it. But when times get tough—and they always do—have someone like Jim around who will take you for a beer and remind you that, luckily, it's not really a life-or-death situation.

THE FIRST SNOWBALL

No matter how much we tried to distract ourselves in the wake of Target's rejection, we couldn't ignore the fact that, without a national retailer, it was only a matter of time before our money ran out, our investors walked away, and everything came crashing down around us. To compete against Goliath, we needed scale, and Target was the best fit. There was only one option: regroup and take another run at Target.

Our first pitch had taught us that Target simply wasn't interested in our modest product line or our relatively unknown brand—yet. So we attacked the obstacles with zeal. Our spray cleaner wasn't intriguing enough? We designed an entire line of home cleaning products! Our brand wasn't famous enough? We enlisted the star power of Karim Rashid, one of the world's best-known industrial designers, commissioning him to create new bottles! We weren't worth the head buyer's time? We found time with somebody else!

Ask anyone in the retail business, and they'll tell you the same thing: Never, ever try to make an end run around a buyer. Even if you succeed by convincing some executive to intervene and put your product on the shelf (unlikely, at best), you'll have made the buyer an enemy for life. Nevertheless, when an old advertising-industry friend of Eric's offered to make an overture on our behalf, we happily allowed him to get us another meeting. Knowing full well what we were up against, he put a call in to the retailer's marketing department and said the magic words: *Karim Rashid*. Within minutes, we had a date on the books: April 10, 2002.

For those who aren't familiar with him, Rashid is the rare designer who believes in creating for the majority rather than the minority. He made his name transforming everyday products—the Oh Chair for Umbra, the Garbo Wastecan, perfume bottles for Issey Miyake—into icons. In short, Target wanted Rashid, and we were just along for the ride. And the ride wasn't free. Hiring Rashid to sketch up our designs and attend our pitch meeting exhausted the very last of our operating capital. This was going to be our Hail Mary pass, an all-or-nothing gamble for Method's survival.

The prototype—a bottle shaped like a bowling pin and cleverly designed to dispense dish soap through a valve in its base—arrived by FedEx just in time for the meeting, led by Eric and Alastair (Adam was scrambling to develop the prototype back in California). Simultaneously relieved and anxious, we filled the bottle with soap (not knowing if it would even work), filed into the packed conference room, and flashed a quick glance over our audience. Glaring right back at us, arms crossed, was Target's head buyer.

Mustering all of his willpower, Eric launched into his presentation—stilted at first, but gathering confidence as he explained our vision for the future of cleaning and home care. Naturally, we came prepared with product sketches,

▲ **PUTTING IT ALL ON THE
LINE WITH DESIGN.** Our first
attempt at disrupting dish soap,
designed by Karim Rashid.

mock-ups of potential in-aisle displays, and a theoretical marketing campaign, but—pinned down by the withering glower of the head buyer—Eric couldn't tell if any of it was hitting home. That is, until he watched the prototype bottle making its way slowly around the room. Reaching the head buyer, he picked it up skeptically, squeezed a stream of soap out the bottom, and exclaimed in wonder, "Oh my god, even I would use this!"

There are a few distinct memories after that—the senior marketing director declaring our product "on trend" and "perfect for Target's guests" (*guests* is Target-speak for customers), the room breaking into applause as we wrapped up our presentation, the head buyer agreeing to a ninety-day, hundred-store trial run—but the rest of the meeting is mostly just a dizzy, elated haze. An hour later (celebrating in a downtown Minneapolis bar), Eric and Alastair called Adam with the good news.

THE SECOND SNOWBALL

Back in California, Adam had been taking care of all the day-to-day operations: formulating the new product compounds, logging the shipments, engineering the Karim Rashid designs. Standing in a friend's backyard when the call from Minnesota came through that Friday evening, Adam could hardly make out what Eric was saying over all the hooting and hollering on the other end of the line. Pressing the phone to his ear, bits and pieces started coming through. "Target said yes" . . . "a hundred stores in Chicago and San Francisco" . . . "June 28th." The blood drained from Adam's face: The upside-down bottle was just a proto-type, built from a malleable aluminum mold and quick-dry adhesives. It wasn't production ready. Even if he started the production process the very next morn-ing, it would take months before the bottle was ready for market. Hell, the lead time on an injection mold alone was six months! But here was Method's crack sales duo, celebrating over cocktails after agreeing to the impossible: a multi-state retail test for a product that didn't exist, in less than ten weeks. Landing their biggest sale yet, they had effectively doomed the company. It was impos-sible. Outrageous. There was simply no way it could happen.

But, it *had* to happen.

Given a snowball's chance in hell, Eric and Alastair had somehow managed to land a deal with one of the world's largest retailers. Now it was Adam's turn to beat the odds. Hanging up on Eric, he immediately dialed Craig Sawicki, Method's manufacturing partner. Sawicki was Alastair's perfect foil. Whereas Alastair was British, refined, and always impeccably dressed, Sawicki was a salt-of-the-earth type who'd spent his entire career chain-smoking in the bowels of Chicago's industrial factories. Reaching Sawicki on his cell, Adam explained the situation. This was Method's chance to break through; everything was on the line. Meeting at Sawicki's office the next morning (after a red-eye to Chicago), they got right to work.

In the days and weeks that followed, Adam and Craig called in every last favor and twisted every last arm on the North Side of Chicago. If a supplier balked on the phone, they would show up at his factory and ask in person. If a fabricator had problems with a particular part, they worked alongside him late into the night to solve the issue. As Eric and Alastair worked the phones and crisscrossed the country in search of new business, Adam and Craig were hun-kered down in run-down factories and grimy machine shops.

Maybe it was because we were too naive to know that what we were asking for was absurd. Maybe it was because we were always willing to work as hard as or harder than anyone we worked with. In the end, it will always be a mystery to us why Craig was willing to pull out all the stops and give up all those nights and weekends for a pair of idealistic kids from Michigan. But he did—and as a result, we met our deadline with Target.

After a mad dash to fabricate and fill thousands of orders by the deadline, our idiosyncratic, upside-down bottles landed on Target's shelves on August 1, 2002. Suddenly, what had seemed bold and revolutionary in a designer's art-fully rendered sketch began to feel like a colossal mistake. Standing shoulder-to-shoulder with familiar brands like Dawn and Palmolive, our bottles clearly flouted every rule in the CPG (consumer packaged goods) handbook. The accepted dish-soap doctrine was to use the bottle as a billboard to attract attention in the aisle, resulting in flat form factors and large, loud labels. Ergonomics (how well the bottle functioned) and aesthetics (what it looked like on the kitchen counter, not the aisle) had long been ruled "secondary design criteria." Not only was our bottle aesthetically striking and ergonomically innovative, the label was more akin to that of a perfume bottle than the garish fifties-era bottles shouting for the customer's attention. Instead of an evocative brand name—like Joy, Cascade, or Sunlight—the label read simply, METHOD DISH SOAP.

Intrigued by the funky bottle, unique scents, and minimalist label, some shoppers bought the product on impulse. But while our sales figures were low, the response from those early adopters was encouraging. Letters started show-ing up at our San Francisco office. Did we make an all-natural shampoo? What about a line of nontoxic laundry detergents? Seduced by our style, consumers were becoming smitten with our substance! (Our employees later dubbed this Method's Trojan horse effect.)

Besides slower-than-expected sales, there was one other small problem: The bottles were leaking. Whether attempting to pop the cap in order to smell the fragrance, or simply curious about the mechanics of the weird-looking bottle, consumers were prying the bottoms loose and then returning them to the shelf, where they proceeded to drip over the entire Method display and pool in the aisle. While a tamper-resistant sticker would later solve the problem, this did not make for a good first impression with consumers or with Target. Armed with a store list, we abandoned our sales work and spent weeks navigating the suburbs of Chicagoland and Northern California (before GPS, mind you), visiting store after store to wipe up the gooey, sticky mess again and again and again. Sisy-phus had nothing on us. As we watched our weekly sales start to fall, our hearts sank. No matter how many coupons we passed out, no matter how many store managers we pumped up, no matter how many messy shelves we cleaned up, each week came up far short of the goal we needed to hit to go national. Out of sheer desperation, we even started buying product ourselves and passing it out for free in the parking lots to Target customers (who must have thought we were bonkers). It wasn't our proudest moment, but at that point we would have done anything to ensure our company survived.

Just as we were beginning to get desperate about our underwhelming sales, a new buyer took over our category for the chain. She was intrigued by our products and passionate about our mission. Instead of dismissing the test as a failure, sending us into a death spiral, she dug deeper into the stats—the sales "hurdle" we had been given was erroneously high and there was more to the story. While our unit sales were lower than that of many established brands, we were helping Target bring in new customers and driving greater overall profits for the entire category. When we returned to Minneapolis for our September check-in meeting, Target made it official: We were going national!

When Method's hand soap, our third product, launched the following spring, decorating the nation's kitchen countertops and bathroom sinks with a multicolored array of teardrop-shaped bottles, we had finally become too big for the big brands to ignore. Stirred by the excitement we were generating in the market, century-old brands roused themselves from decades of complacency and began responding with modern-looking, natural products of their own. At this point, we truly understood the multiplying effect of our mission and our belief in leveraging business as a social-change agent. One idea, nurtured by two guys, had grown into three product lines, dozens of retail partnerships, thousands of loyal customers, and millions in sales. More than a personal obsession, our style-and-substance philosophy was becoming a movement.

THE BIG SCALE-UP

Once we went national, the real growth began. Landing in Target gave us credibility to crack other national retailers throughout the United States. We continued to expand the product line to keep up with our consumers' desires for more Method in more parts of their homes, eventually making the leap to Canada, Europe, and even parts of Asia. (Admittedly, in part we just wanted to be able to use the phrase "We're huge in Japan!") Revenue soared, growing 50, 100, even 200 percent a year. Keeping up with our growth meant scaling quickly, and demonstrating scale was critical to proving we were an enduring brand, not a fad. We were overwhelmed with new employees, new partners, new infrastructure, and new ways of doing business (all of it learned on the job, of course). Outgrowing our original office in a Victorian house on Union Street in San Francisco, we moved to a second location down the street. Before long, we were moving again—to our current location on Commercial Street—and opening offices in Chicago and London. By 2006 we were the seventh-fastest-growing private company in the country, according to *Inc.* magazine. And we were doing it in consumer categories that had been flat or in decline for a decade or more.

This was a magical period when we operated the business with an entrepreneurial mind-set and our employees had a high degree of freedom to pursue new business opportunities. Within a few years, we started a show on HSN (the Home Shopping Network), launched an automotive brand called Vroom, created a entirely new body-care line, and launched an air-care line, which included our first foray into electronics. Nothing scared us, and the company approached every project with a can-do attitude. This wasn't your typical start-up growth; this was wild, uninhibited growth—the kind that affords all sorts of insights along the way (as we'll discuss later) and the kind that—at least temporarily—hides all your sins and bad habits (we'll get to those, too).

TURBULENCE DOESN'T MEAN YOU ARE GOING DOWN

For those of you who have studied entrepreneurship, it should come as no surprise that our biggest mistake was simply growing too fast and trying to do too much. Rapidly expanding into a number of areas, we grew naively, as if the good times would never end. In 2008 our mistakes started catching up with us. Ironically, that same year we hit the $100 million revenue mark after doing business for just 2,861 days, or a little under eight years. We reached this goal in less time than Powerbar, Ben & Jerry's, Nike, or Snapple.

Then we hit the perfect storm. Our first major product failure—an ill-advised venture into personal care called Bloq—coincided with a faltering economy and surging oil prices that threatened to further undermine our profitability. At the same time, Goliath woke up, and several of our competitors launched green products that took dead aim at our shelf space and came armed with marketing budgets fifty times the size of ours. (We later learned some of the companies launched these under the code name "Kill Method"—yikes!) Increasingly exposed, we were at risk of becoming a cliché—a premium, high-water brand

▲ **OWNED AND OPERATED BY HUMAN BEINGS.** Blurring the lines between our personal and professional lives rebalances life.

marooned by the recessionary low tide. We had successfully scaled up the business to $100 million at a record pace, but the reality sank in: To survive the recession and get Method to the next stage, we would need to change the way we operated. And do it fast!

Unlike just about all of the previous challenges we had faced, we were now too big to simply will ourselves to success. We couldn't just roll up our sleeves and work a little harder to solve the problems that we were facing. We needed to make some major cuts if we wanted to survive. These were grown-up problems with no easy solutions. And no matter how we crunched the numbers, we were facing every entrepreneur's worst nightmare: laying off colleagues who were more friends than employees.

We've always been open about our finances, and everyone on staff had known for months that we'd have to make cuts, but it was all somewhat abstract until we started naming names. That was truly agonizing. There's no greater test of an owner or manager than when you have to take someone's job—especially after experiencing all the rewards that come with creating those jobs. Without exception, the hardest thing we've ever had to do was take those jobs away. To this day, we remain deeply sorry that we had to do it, and we vowed never again to put ourselves or our colleagues in the same position.

Our culture helped us survive this period. After our departing colleagues removed their photos from the photo wall—our version of the family portrait—and everyone helped them pack up their desks, we all went out and had a drink together. It is in times like this that we truly appreciate the genuine strength of our culture (an obsession you'll hear more about in the next chapter). As each person left, every one of them heading home to break the news to their families, they looked us in the eye and told us they were sorry for what we were going through. Believe it or not—and we hardly could—they apologized to *us*. They felt they'd let us down as much as we felt we'd let them down. Having built the company as a family, the two of us had handled everything personally. Our employees understood what the necessity had done to us. While it probably sounds strange, we believe we're better, stronger people, and better, stronger leaders, having gone through that process.

In just twelve months, we killed two major product lines—body and air care—that had accounted for 15 percent of our business, laid off 10 percent of our staff, changed CEOs to bring in more operating experience, and said good-bye to our most unprofitable retailers. There was not much to be proud of, but if we're proud of anything, it's that we ripped off the Band-Aid quickly. Some companies retreat awkwardly for years, waddling gracelessly as they adapt to a new environment. But as the downward trend in late 2008 stretched from months into quarters, we resolved to get through the pain fast.

ONWARD AND UPWARD

The layoffs knocked us down for a while, but the stability that came as a result has encouraged people to reengage and enabled us to begin growing again—albeit in a far more disciplined way than we did in the past. On a certain level, today's 20 percent growth rate seems relatively placid, but we're different now—both as individuals and as a company. As we write this, we've been in business for more than ten years, emerged from the recession, built a stronger business, and reached record profitability. Though we had to change the way we operated in order to scale the business to the next level, we never abandoned our core values, obsessions, and beliefs. Recognizing the power of our obsessions after they helped us thrive through unprecedented challenges—and how many of our failures could be attributed to straying from our obsessions—only further reinforced them.

We've changed from seeing ourselves as doers to seeing ourselves as leaders. And as leaders, we have committed ourselves to saying what we intend to do and then doing it—setting the right expectations and delivering on those expectations. Leadership can be less concrete than cooking up cleaning formulas and hitting our sales targets. The obstacles are softer, more subjective. The problems are nebulous, easy to miss, and hard to articulate. In the beginning, challenges like launching that first upside-down soap bottle were clear and present. There was a romance to them because there was a job to be done and we knew what it was, even if not exactly how to do it. Now we understand that the job will never be done. It's a different way of thinking about work—an approach that draws on everything we've learned in ten years of business to deliver revolutionary performance with a purpose. It's our way of doing things. It's the Method method.

obsession

CREATE A CULTURE CLUB

use culture as a competitive advantage by branding from the inside out

IF YOU WERE TO ENTER THE METHOD OFFICES AT 637 Commercial Street in downtown San Francisco, walk past the guard dog (a green plastic pooch in the lobby), skirt the security perimeter checkpoint in the lobby (staffed by different team members each day), and penetrate the top-secret defense measures (so secret, there aren't any), you would find yourself at the heart of Method's headquarters—the nerve center where our products are designed and our decisions are made.

There, scrawled across a series of floor-to-ceiling whiteboards we call wiki walls, you would see our strategies, a detailed breakdown of everything we plan to accomplish over the next eighteen months. Our sales goals and financial forecasts, our media plans and product development cycles—all our whats, whens, and hows for the next year and a half, right there in erasable marker. The long lists of statistics and projections would all seem fairly familiar to an executive from any other company . . . all except the section titled "People and Environment."

Culture, as we refer to it informally, has a place on the strategy wall because it's the driving force behind everything we do. In fact, while few modern companies go to similar lengths to foster and measure it, culture is increasingly the driving (or draining) force behind everyone else's results too. While there are as many definitions of culture as there are companies, to us culture encompasses the shared values, behaviors, and practices of a company's employees. To put it another way, it's the code for how we all treat one another. Our goal was to create a culture that would inspire and enable us to do our best work while fostering a workplace that enriches our lives. A great culture is one that's aligned with the missions of the company, be it delivering superlative customer service (like Zing-erman's Deli in Ann Arbor), driving innovation (like Netflix), or being a low-price leader (like Southwest Airlines).

Most leaders underestimate the power of culture for reaching business goals, particularly when starting with limited resources. They'll say, "Fix the business first, and then we'll have the time and money to invest in culture." That's like a coach saying, "Once we start winning, we'll get everyone motivated and playing as a team." It just doesn't work that way.

TRANSPARENCY, AUTHENTICITY, AND CULTURE IN AN ALWAYS-ON WORLD

It's a little-known fact that the 1908 Model T averaged 21 miles per gallon (according to Ford's Web site). It would stand to reason that, a century later, automakers would have steadily advanced fuel efficiency ratings to grand new heights. Such is not the case. The big automakers' average in 2010 was 25 mpg—a measly 4 mpg improvement over more than a century, and the minimum required by law. While their advertising campaigns proclaim their commitment to innovation and the environment, auto industry lobbyists and lawyers are hard at work in Washington fighting efforts to raise fuel-economy standards. Though this type of corporate hypocrisy may have flown in the past, we are entering a new, transparent world where the consequences of saying one thing while doing another are beginning to exact a toll on businesses in the marketplace. As founders of our own company and the guardians of a thriving brand culture, the significance of this profound shift in consumer power and priorities was forever on our minds.

Today's corporations operate in an era of unprecedented transparency. The line separating public image and private behavior has all but vanished, eroded by the availability of information and the advance of social media. Pinstriped CEOs rub elbows with rank-and-file shareholders on Twitter; blue-collar factory workers publish candid blog posts about life on the shop floor; fervent brand advocates respond to customers about that morning's company news before the PR reps even hit the snooze button. No longer can corporations afford to talk out of both sides of their mouths, preaching one message to consumers while practicing another behind the scenes. In today's always-on business environment, authenticity is the universal language of successful organizations.

The nucleus of that authenticity—that binding energy generated by employees, customers, and the media alike—is a company's culture. Unbounded by cubicle walls or HR handbooks, culture is the x factor, the soul of the brand, the whole that's somehow greater than the sum of its parts. In contrast to other critical corporate assets, a vibrant company culture doesn't show up on a balance sheet. It cannot be inventoried, valued, or written off. Despite its nebulous nature, not only does everyone tend to agree on what makes a strong corporate culture, we canonize the best examples. Magazines rank corporate cultures in annual lists. Consultants celebrate cultures at industry conferences. Culture is the subject of seminars, books, and entire university courses. Why? We're glad you asked.

Below, a few reasons why you should give a damn about culture.

BECAUSE WHEN IT COMES TO INNOVATION, CULTURE WINS OVER PROCESS Process is about getting where you want to go quickly and reliably (think Six Sigma, business process reengineering, etc.) while innovation is about reaching new and uncharted territory. In our surplus economy, success depends on creating brands and products that stand out, and such innovations are best delivered through open, collaborative cultures. The only way to predictably reach the unknown is with the right culture. Take Google, for example, which is famous for giving its best engineers one day a week to devote to their own pet projects and has beta-tested and launched hundreds of innovative products and services through their Google Labs division as a result of this freedom.

BECAUSE WORD TRAVELS, AND SO DOES TALENT The talent war is heating up, and the winners will be those who deliver a great culture for their employees. According to the Bureau of Labor Statistics, today's average worker changes jobs every 4.1 years. In a media-saturated world, we all hear stories about companies, like the grocery chain Wegmans, that go above and beyond to support and encourage their employees. Whether your culture rocks or is on the rocks, your reputation will precede you. In an increasingly mobile society, the strongest employees need compelling reasons to stay.

BECAUSE THE LINES BETWEEN OUR PERSONAL AND PROFESSIONAL LIVES ARE BLURRING We spend the majority of our waking lives at work, and the texts, e-mails, and calls keep coming long after we go home. We are forever tethered to our jobs, allowing our professional lives to seep into our personal ones. Even our escapism is work-related! *The Office, Mad Men, The Apprentice*—our society is obsessed with workplace culture. There's no escaping work, so the best way to achieve work-life balance is to find a great professional culture that you don't mind letting bleed into the rest of your life.

BECAUSE STANDARDS FOR CULTURE ARE RISING Back in the day, a "casual Friday" policy and some corporate swag around the holidays were enough to stand out from the crowd when it came to culture. Not anymore. Companies like Pixar offer employees over one hundred courses through an internal Pixar University. Zappos offers new employees $3,000 to quit after their first week—97 percent like the new job so much they turn down the offer (and the ones who accept it probably wouldn't have been a good fit anyway). These days, fostering an exceptional culture requires effort and creativity.

For those companies fortunate enough to possess one, a winning culture provides seemingly endless benefits—from boosting employee satisfaction and retention rates to fostering a cohesive brand identity and a high degree of innovation. Companies with resilient cultures attract better talent, inspire more customers, and outlast their competitors.

Most important, a powerful corporate culture offers the ultimate competitive advantage because it's impossible to copy. Trade secrets can be stolen, best practices mimicked, but the many variables that factor into a company's culture—the odd habits of its working atmosphere, the peculiarities of its various hierarchies, the way everyone just gets along—coalesce into that "certain something" that cannot be replicated. Not by competitors seeking to duplicate it, and not by those unfortunate companies who let it slip and then struggle in vain to re-create it once it's gone. Yet by January 2006, we were on the verge of becoming one of the latter.

CAUSE FOR CELEBRATION

By January 2006, Method's success had far surpassed even our wildest expectations. We could hardly believe our good fortune. In just five years, we had become an industry sensation. Our artful designs and environmentally friendly products were all over the press—the brand had become an instant media darling. Our soaring growth, meanwhile, made us the envy of every competitor. We even had invites to the Playboy Mansion (only one of us swam in the grotto, but we'll leave it to you to guess who). Method was the world's first hip home-care brand, and we were making our presence known.

As in each of the previous four years, 2006 ushered in a new round of record-breaking sales figures and a flurry of headlines to accompany them. Our overall revenue had more than doubled the previous year, rocketing past $32 million.

▲ LIVING OUR VALUES. As PETA Persons of the year we always make our stance against animal testing clear. Even at Hef's house

Liquid detergent, up over 300 percent for the year, had cracked the industry top ten. Even some of our slower categories, like air care and dish soap, managed to increase sales by 200 percent or more. Sales, buzz, game-changing innovations—no matter how you looked at it, the brand was red-hot.

But with success came a whole new set of challenges. To keep pace with soaring demand, we evolved rapidly. New product lines were springing up as fast as we could imagine them, expanding the brand aisle by aisle and store by store to different corners of the market. New hires swelled our ranks, their make-shift workspaces overflowing into hallways and conference rooms. In the mad dash to keep up with staggering growth, we outgrew our home office three times in five years. New manufacturers, new suppliers, new distributors . . . we were bursting at the seams with start-up enthusiasm.

So why did we feel as though we were on the verge of falling apart?

Josh Handy, Method's Disrupter (aka vice president of innovation), sums it up well: "Everyone you met loved their job and the company so much, they evangelized it to a point of weirdness. But we were in danger of losing one-to-one personal contact—where individuals could affect the direction of the company and where everyone shared the work."

From tense intraoffice e-mails to fewer after-hours jam sessions, the reality was sinking in: Success was changing our culture. We knew our culture was our most valuable asset—it was the reason our employees came to work early and stayed late and the reason the best people in the industry defected from coveted jobs at stable competitors like P&G, Unilever, and Clorox to join us—but we had always thought it was something that happened organically, a serendipitous accident that arose when all the right forces converged. We'd never really thought about creating or maintaining a culture, and we soon realized we'd been ignoring it for too long.

As the excitement over January's superb sales figures waned, veteran employees and new hires alike began to sense the irony: Culture was at the root of all of our success, but success was unraveling our culture. Our challenge: Hold on to one without giving up the other.

PART LOGIC, PART MAGIC

When you're doing culture really well, you don't notice you're doing it at all. Unlike the cleverly designed products bubbling out of our labs, there was no ingenious formula behind our culture. Like many successful start-ups, the shared values and behaviors that motivated us were largely a happy accident—the by-products formed when passionate, young, like-minded entrepreneurs defy industry expectations, change the world, and have fun in the process. Cool products, a clear vision, strong camaraderie, and a sense of purpose—virtually everything about the company was the result of smart, irreverent, devoted people doing everything in their own smart, irreverent, and devoted way.

Nowhere was this start-up serendipity more apparent than in our thriving and collaborative work atmosphere. It just took care of itself. When we hired a bright new employee, we did so because we instinctively felt he or she was the type of person we could imagine working alongside for ten, twelve, maybe sixteen hours a day. The Astroturf-lined Ping-Pong room? The cereal and beer in the office kitchen? These weren't contrived creature comforts cooked up during some HR workshop in the name of employee retention; they were the offbeat inspirations of earnest employees writing their own rules for the workplace. In short, we were benefiting from the paradox underlying all corporate cultures: Despite most companies' best efforts, the best cultures tend to be effortless.

So happy an accident was our culture, we didn't even have an HR depart-

▲ **THE ANNUAL METHOD PROM.** People rarely excel at anything unless they're having fun doing it.

ment devoted to maintaining it. Why should we? We owed much of our success to our willingness to shrug off the organizational theories and procedures that preoccupy MBA students and traditional administrators. Something so stiff and corporate-sounding as "human resources" just didn't belong in a rebellious, freewheeling upstart brand that held its own mock proms and organized itself into *pods* (our name for cross-functional product teams). Spontaneity and ingenuity, unfettered by bureaucratic process, were our lifeblood. Everyone's practical needs, from dental benefits to hang-ups with delegation, were handled on an ad hoc basis by a handful of the company's leaders, like the payroll coordinator, the controller, even our CEO. The result: an informal, collegial atmosphere based on common sense, honesty, mutual respect . . . and a lot of luck.

But after years of taking our culture for granted, rapid growth was wearing all of us down. Once second nature, our sense of identity and purpose flagged. At this point, an established company might have retraced its steps and made some minor adjustments, but we had nothing to adjust! We never had a plan for Method's culture. Since founding the company, it was all we could do to keep up with our growth. Six years later, everyone agreed that culture was our secret sauce . . . but no one had the recipe.

The culture problem was unlike any we had ever faced. This wasn't simply a matter of recalling a leaky valve or tweaking the ingredients in a new product. Identifying employees' concerns and formally establishing the brand's core values would involve some profound soul searching. In order to evolve, we had to regress, returning to a simple question with a profoundly complex answer: Who are we?

Despite our breakneck production schedule and our far-flung workforce—with ninety employees spread through three offices, in San Francisco, Chicago, and London—we made the decision that January to call an all-company offsite devoted to culture. Retreating to the California countryside with the entire staff, miles from the hustle and bustle of San Francisco and our crowded urban headquarters, we opened our minds, our notebooks, and the floor to our employees.

Some asked for better communication among the ever-growing number of pods. Others believed new employees needed more training in how to do things the Method way. Encouraged to speak freely, employee concerns ran the gamut. People wanted more career development and more feedback. They said they could have been on-boarded a little better or that we could be helping them become better recruiters. In essence, we'd been ignoring that stuff.

"Basically, people were asking for more structure, more process," says Anna Boyarsky, president of the Method Fan Club (aka advocacy director). "Process wasn't as necessary when we were smaller—our touch points were closer and the company was young and growing."

Culturally, there was very little *method* to Method—though we had always dismissed this irony with a grin and a shrug. But as concerns about preserving the company's culture mounted at our offsite, the atmosphere changed from levity to one of frustrated gravity. Listening to our employees' appeals, we began to appreciate a new irony. Afforded every freedom, our colleagues were requesting formality. Pardoned from protocol, they pleaded for procedure.

The idea of so much liberty in the workplace might be difficult for most people to imagine. Daydreaming in our cubicles between boardroom briefings with superiors and conference calls with subordinates, most of us long for a *less* regimented working environment. "If only we spent less time dealing with quarterly employee reviews, boring HR e-mails, and all those notorious TPS reports," we gripe, "maybe *then* we'd finally have some time to do our jobs!" Right. The swivel chair is always comfier on the other side of the cubicle partition. We forget that the same structure and process we malign is responsible for keeping everyone oriented, motivated, and accountable. We forget that, far from limiting creativity, structure and process often channel it in the right directions.

As crucial as spontaneity and ingenuity had been to our culture, the time had come to begin formalizing our approach. We began with notes about what mattered to our employees. Notebooks full of notes. Distilling everything down to a few core values was the challenge. And reintroducing these essential values—building them back into the day-to-day operations of the company—would come next. But how would we institutionalize Method's best practices without squeezing the life out of them and making the company feel like, well, an institution? The offsite was over, but as we barreled south toward the city on the 101 that rainy Sunday afternoon, all of us understood that the greatest journey our company would ever undertake—the quest to capture and preserve our culture—had only just begun.

THE QUEST TO DEFINE METHOD'S CULTURE

Like the age-old riddle about silence—which expires the moment you say its name—culture defies cultivation. The latest HR theories can no more measure a company's culture than an MRI can isolate an individual's soul. No drab mission statement ever inspired anyone to put in extra hours on a side project, no weekend team-building exercise in the forest ever got executives and hourly workers to sit side by side at lunch on Monday, and the world has yet to see an employee handbook capable of boosting employee morale. The greater the effort to formalize it—to box it in with structure and guidelines—the faster culture slips away. Nevertheless, diligent HR pros devote dense manuals full of prescriptive theory to its creation, only to throw up their hands, exasperated, when it materializes spontaneously in the ranks of unassuming start-ups all around them. At Method, we understood that too much process would only be an impediment. The challenge was to institute process without suffocating culture—but how?

"Our challenge as a company was, how do you keep the magic alive?" says Rudy Becker, the Resinator (aka engineering director). "It's one thing to succeed when you're small, but how do you keep all the good stuff while you grow? We knew what got us where we were and we didn't want to lose that. If we did lose it, it would almost not be worth it anymore."

In the midst of countless aimless discussions about how to fix Method's cul-

THE MINISTRY OF CULTURE

Imagine: An esteemed and empowered division of the company charged with maintaining a strong workplace culture that inspires employees, drives profits, and changes the world for the better. Some fantasy, right? Be that as it may, corporate America is forever forming subcommittees, executive councils, governing boards, special task forces, and ministries devoted to overseeing workplace culture. Most are distracting, grasping aimlessly with endless memos and pointless exercises (like the Ministry of Information in Terry Gilliam's *Brazil*). Others stifle the professional atmosphere with narrow guidelines and heavy-handed edicts (e.g., the Ministry of Truth in George Orwell's *1984*). But a rare few strike just the right balance, fostering the right conditions while still allowing things to take shape on their own.

Take a moment to identify the best aspects of your life at work and imagine how a group of devoted caretakers might help those aspects flourish. If you're still in the business-plan stage, make a list of all the qualities you envision in your ideal workplace and how you might encourage them on a day-to-day basis. Don't worry too much about what's practical at this stage—rather than an actionable plan, think of this as the ideal.

---

ture, our Big Spender (or CFO), Andrea Freedman, had an epiphany. What if we were to establish a pod to build and maintain our culture—a kind of ministry of culture?

The "Ministry of Culture" sounded great in theory, but we feared it would just be an HR department by another name. Furthermore, if culture was by definition greater than the sum of its parts, was it worthwhile—or even possible—to bother with the building blocks?

Questions like this got us thinking. More rules and guidelines were the wrong thing when the company was young and growing. We were small. Our touch points were closer. You didn't have to turn in a form for someone else to do something for you—you just walked over to the one person who did it. But as we grew and the company got bigger, we understood that some process might actually help free time and energy.

In search of how to introduce more process without smothering our culture, we consulted a handful of kindred spirits—companies we believe have built and maintained strong, organic cultures. After all, we've always been big believers in seeking inspiration from companies that do things better than we do—be it consumer-facing stuff like branding and packaging or behind-the-scenes areas of expertise like R&D and distribution. So, we figured, why not ask others' advice on culture?

In search of perspective, we approached six companies we knew and respected—Apple, Google, Pixar, Nike, Starbucks, and Innocent, the trendy British beverage maker—asking each of them one key question, "What really matters to you when it comes to great culture?" Unsurprisingly, the six had a lot to say. Taking it all down, we noticed three key themes common to all of them:

FOCUS ON HIRING GREAT PEOPLE Rather than hiring on expertise alone, make sure personalities and attitudes match your company. If you're about to hire someone and your gut tells you they're not a good fit, leave the seat open for now.

EMPHASIZE CULTURE FROM THE BEGINNING Explain the company's culture to new hires, making it clear to them that they were hired in part because of how they fit in.

GIVE PEOPLE LOTS OF FEEDBACK Take the time on a regular basis to remind your employees how they're doing vis-à-vis your values and culture.

In addition, we noticed that all our kindred spirits encouraged their employees to embrace a sense of purpose at work. It was less a rule than a value, a shared belief that motivated everyone in his or her unique way. Reflecting on our own situation, we understood that our culture needed a set of values that clarified our purpose as a company.

This was the turning point. Though we'd never before defined our values, Method had always been a purpose-driven company. Purpose was one of our key competitive advantages—motivating us to work harder, longer, and smarter than our competition. Shared values and purpose inspired us. There was only one thing left to do: articulate exactly what those were.

Combining our offsite notes with the suggestions we had gleaned from our culture idols, we recruited a handful of team members from various departments and asked them to work with our leadership team members to distill everything down to five core values. The team became known as the Values Pod.

Sure, we could have boiled everything down between the two of us, but we wanted our values to come from within. Years later, we discovered that companies like Zappos and Innocent had gone through the same process. (To say nothing of the founding fathers . . .) Consider the benefits. Drawing your values from the company ranks ensures that they will represent the richness of the brand, stay relevant at every level, and be embraced by employees year after year.

After incorporating input from every level of the company, our Values Pod presented us the final list:

Keep Method weird.
What would MacGyver do?
Innovate, don't imitate.
Collaborate, collaborate, collaborate.
Care like crazy.

Known collectively as our Methodology, these values have become the backbone of our culture obsession—a framework to provide our team members with direction and space to grow.

Our values help channel the frenetic atmosphere of innovation and quixotic spontaneity so vital to our success into a mutual sense of purpose. To integrate them into our day-to-day operations and make them actionable, we've printed them on cards illustrating how each value translates into behavior. By creating an annual deck of cards bound by a key ring, rather than a standard sheet of paper, people can hang the values at their desks, and they are easier to share. Along with the right physical reinforcements—like our open-office floor plan—our values cultivate the kind of environment that inspires the real magic: those everyday individual actions that make our company flourish.

Would our values work for you? Maybe. But adopting another company's values is like letting someone else design your dream house or write your wedding vows. Establishing your values is your chance to turn yourself inside out and see what you're really made of as a brand.

So, without further delay, here's a closer look at our Methodology.

KEEP METHOD WEIRD

Everyone knows what normal is. Normal is blue oxfords and khakis. Normal is a deck of PowerPoint slides. Normal is nine to five, taking your shoes off at the

VALUE | KEEP METHOD WEIRD

how we treat each other to live this value...

embrace different

create the fun

believe you can make a difference

infect others with your passion

lead the revolution

method

keep method weird

a fun brand only comes from fun people. life is too short, so let's enjoy our working life and have fun as we fight dirty.

▲ **WEIRD IS ABOUT SEEING THE WORLD DIFFERENTLY.** Let's face it, weird changes the world, and people remember weird.

door, and driving a Camry. Weird is everything normal is not. Weird is where you run into brilliant, independent, and risky. Weird can be inspiring, memorable, or outlandish. Weird is under no obligation to make sense.

Method is weird. We hope it shows in our products—the odd shapes, the unique fragrances, the quirky language sprinkled throughout our marketing and all over our packaging. Take one look around our office and it's clear the weirdness isn't just skin deep. From the random piñatas hanging from the ceiling (they tend to come and go around here) and the prom photos on the wall to the rock 'n' roll music in the elevator (it just made more sense than elevator music)—we do things differently.

We like the odd, offbeat, and outlandish so much, in fact, that we made "Keep Method weird" the first of our five values. To ensure we wouldn't turn into yet another big boring company full of boring people boring one another and our customers, we made sure to build weirdness right back into our formal rules, processes, and techniques. Yup, you heard it: Formality has a role in the fun.

We believe people don't perform at their highest levels unless they are having fun doing it. Ever notice when athletes are interviewed at the end of winning games, they typically mention how much fun they had? The same is true in business. If you can't be yourself at work, you're not going to do good work. This is especially important for us because we're trying to bring fun to an activity in which you rarely see it: cleaning.

That said, it's easy to interpret *weird* as simply having fun and doing strange stuff. (Like, say, keeping a secret stash of flamboyant hats—you never know when the right occasion might come about.) But it's important to leverage fun and use it to differentiate yourself in the marketplace. Having the courage to look at the world a little differently is what being weird is really about. And when you're competing against global, Goliath-size players, everything you do has to be different. Everyone who ever changed the world was considered weird at first, from Galileo to Gates.

WHAT WOULD MACGYVER DO?

At Method, Angus MacGyver* isn't just a source of inspiration—he's our mascot. Mac is the master of resourcefulness, a man who can turn a pencil, a rubber band, and a paperclip into a helicopter. Like us, Mac never had the same weapons as his nemeses, so he always had to be inventive and industrious to win a fight. If P&G has a fleet of F-16s, we have duct tape and a Swiss Army Knife.

▲ **TIPPING OUR HAT TO MAC.** MacGyver is our role model for resourcefulness.

---

* For those of you who missed the 1980s, please Google *MacGyver* . . . along with *The A-Team*, *Dallas*, and *The Love Boat*.

When we find ourselves facing a seemingly unsolvable problem, we ask our-selves, "What would MacGyver do?" This fresh perspective has served us well. No matter how large we grow, this value reminds us to embrace the scrappy attitude and creative irreverence that got us where we are. This value is about resourcefulness, knocking on the big door, and punching above your weight. After all, part of what has always defined us is our ability to outmaneuver major competitors despite having just a fraction of their manpower and infrastructure.

Finding our inner MacGyver means focusing on the solution, not the prob-lem. Granted, this is a lesson we all learned in third grade, but somehow corpo-rate America seems to forget it all the time. When you're a small company striving for growth, you have no choice but to figure out how to be resourceful with what you have to create solutions. When we didn't have marketing dollars, we just showed up in stores and performed demos. When Target's buyer declined our product line, we sent our pitch to the marketing department. Even with limited resources, there's always a way to win—just ask yourself, "What would MacGyver do?"

INNOVATE, DON'T IMITATE

Few terms in business are as overused or misused as *innovation*. The dictionary defines innovation as "the act of introducing something new." OK, but to us, innovation simply amounts to creativity applied to business—the process by which an organization generates creative ideas and converts them into useful products and services. The challenge is that process is about creating a predict-able result, while innovation is about getting someplace new and unexpected. Using the first to get to the second is kind of like using a map to discover the New World—how do you chart a course to a place no one's ever been?

We believe the answer lies in creating an innovative culture in which new ideas can thrive. We try to foster an environment where we can expect the unexpected—be it our cross-functional pods, our open-to-all-ideas wiki walls, or our all-inclusive interview process. To do this, we try to think of everything as a beta test ("Ready! Fire! Aim!"). In practice, this translates into leveraging risk as a competitive advantage, routinely forgoing lengthy consumer test-ing trials, hastening internal development decisions, working with dynamic and flexible suppliers, and running parallel-track design efforts—just to see where all this leads us.

By now, you might be able to see how the values build on one another. If we have the courage to be weird and the resourcefulness of MacGyver, then innovation becomes that much easier.

COLLABORATE, COLLABORATE, COLLABORATE

The problem with growth is that it tends to separate people from one another, leaving them isolated from other groups. That's exactly what happened to us when we started to grow more quickly than we could manage. But in order to inspire collaboration, you have to break up silos and subcultures and improve cooperation, teamwork, and communication at every level of the company.

Collaboration is particularly important at Method because it's pivotal to our brand philosophy. Like all great brands, ours is built on inherent tensions—contrasting characteristics that don't typically go together. Tension is the wellspring of drama, spontaneity, innovation, energy, and culture. Think Target, combining low prices with high-end designers, or Starbucks, merging a brief daily escape with speedy convenience. Our mash-up: high design with environmental sustainability—two sensibilities generally at odds with each other.

Collaboration also operates on a granular level, factoring into everything we do. Without a general sense of goodwill (the assumption that everyone wants what's best for the company), every product launch would devolve into a battle. Few processes at Method demonstrate the goodwill we have for one another like the push and pull between our green chefs (our scientists) and our marketing department. While our green chefs want product labels to list every last environmental benefit (organic ingredients! no phthalates! packaged in 100% post-consumer bottles!), our marketers prefer to keep things simple (natural). Nevertheless, by assuming goodwill and understanding that we're all on the same team, we're able to work together to ensure the best outcome.

One of our favorite techniques for encouraging collaboration is the simple phrase "yes, and." Everybody knows the phrase "yes, but"—it's the reply our coworkers offer when they don't really agree with something we've just said. But a "yes, and" attitude turns this classic collaborative hang-up on its head. In fact, the "yes, and" attitude allows us to employ unconventional ideas like an open-office floor plan—one of the keys to the company's collaborative culture. Imagine trying to work alongside a colleague who's looking for the flaw in your thinking. A "yes, and" colleague is one who's willing to take your fragile idea and make it stronger. Give it a try next time you're brainstorming with a colleague. Rather than framing your response as an opposing idea, try starting with the words, "Yes, and . . ."

▲ **SAYING "YES, AND . . ."** When someone shares a new idea, don't discount it with a "yes, but." Instead, try "Yes, and . . ."*

Teamwork isn't about everyone thinking the same way; groupthink just creates a homogeneous—and stifling—culture. As mentioned, another way we create our culture is with our open and visual office-floor plan. For example, our green chefs are within shouting distance of our CEO, not in some windowless lab three states away, and our marketing, packaging, and creative specialists can share ideas and collaborate on everything from product stories and advertising to packaging and copyrighting without leaving their desks.

CARE LIKE CRAZY

Growth threatened to weaken our bonds, making it harder for individuals to identify the unique role they could play in the future of the company. If people didn't think their opinion mattered, they'd only be sticking around for a paycheck.

Like all of our values, care is about how we treat one another and how we treat everyone else, from consumers to retailers to the environment. If a colleague makes a contribution that nails one of our values, fellow team members can nominate that person for a values award. If a customer is anxious about how a product might affect her child, our customer-care specialists are there to field the call in person and answer every last question. Of course, "Care" has become something of a cliché when talking about corporate values, but let's be honest,

---

* This is an improv exercise which is all about accepting what others have to offer. When someone shares a new idea, don't discount something quickly with a "yes, but . . ." because it's something you've never encountered before. Instead, next time try starting your response with "yes, and . . ."

how many companies actually live up to this idea? You probably won't need two hands to count them.

Philanthropy is an important part of our care philosophy, which is why we give everyone on staff three paid days a year to help out a local cause (a program we call EcoManiacs). Naturally, employees are driven by different passions: Some have opted to support Moustache November (aka Movember), an effort to increase prostate cancer awareness in which participants either grow a mustache themselves or enlist others to do so. Others get behind Save the Bay, a wetlands restoration project in the San Francisco Bay Area in which employees have already cleaned up a nearby island.

Method employees adopt various causes but always from the same principle: Have a purpose greater than profits. As we see it, you spend so much of your life working, why not align your work with creating good? After all, people like having a job, but they especially like having a job that makes them feel good about themselves and their work. Whether we talk about laundry, wipes, or toilet-bowl cleaner, it all boils down to the same idea: How do we use our business to create positive change?

As a brand grows, employees tend to form cliques, leading to a breakdown in communication. If you want to care about someone, it helps to know them—yet so few companies put any effort into ensuring that employees know one another on a personal level throughout the company. So to keep everyone in touch, we launched a program called Reach-Out-First Lunches. Once every couple of months, we bring three baskets to the Monday huddle. We pick the name of a recent hire from the first basket, the name of an old-timer from the second basket, and the name of a restaurant from the third. The restaurants range from high-end steakhouses to the hot-dog stand up the street. Then we send the pair off to lunch with each other. The process encourages team members to care for one another like family—which, in a way, we are.

HOW WE LIVE OUR VALUES

Values are worthless unless you actually live them—in reality, most company values "live" on some dusty plaque, not in the soul of the brand. Who hasn't worked for a company that went to great lengths to define its values (offsites! surveys! consultants!) only to bury them in a handbook and refer to them sanctimoniously after someone really screwed up? That's HR and PR, not living your values. Values are what you practice when nobody—not even you—is paying attention.

A statement of our shared values and sense of purpose, our Methodology is the closest thing we have to a recipe for our culture. It's the logic that binds us together. When we get the logical parts just right, we create space for the magical, yielding amazing levels of collaboration and stellar business results. Swing by the San Francisco office sometime. We'll show you what we mean. But if you don't have time to say hi, here are a few examples of how we have learned to live our values every day.

HIRE RIGHT

Building weirdness into how you operate as a company isn't as difficult as it might sound—as long as you start at the beginning with whom you hire. The surest way to get a fast-growing company off track is to let the wrong people on the bus, as Jim Collins would say. Most companies fill open positions as quickly as possible for the sake of efficiency, but we would rather leave a job open for months than hire the wrong person. Case in point: Though our People and Environment Department (Method's answer to HR) was created in May 2008, we didn't hire a director until that November. Our colleagues even started referring to the vacancy as the Unicorn, because the right person for that position seemed as elusive as the mythical creature.

During our explosive growth years, we would hear things like "I just need a warm body to fill the seat," code for "We are about to compromise the talent level." No matter how you may rationalize it at the time, finding a warm body to fill the seat is *never* OK. Later in the book, we talk about "kicking ass at fast"— but when it comes to hiring, we like to take things slow by adding a number of speed bumps to the process that give us a chance to assess the applicant on a number of levels. Applicants may get all the way to the end of the process, but if no one stands out, we'll start it all over again with a new group.

Hiring at Method takes place in three stages: cross-functional interviewing, the homework assignment, and on-boarding. Our interview process employs a team of interviewers from around the company, so an applicant for a communications position might wind up discussing the job with an accountant, an industrial designer, a greenskeeper, and someone from our PR department. The message: You're joining an entire company, not just one department.

Yeah, seven or more interviews and a homework assignment is rigorous, and it's built up a reputation in the industry for being challenging. But we believe this is a good thing. After all, it communicates that we only want the

▲ THE LIVE AUDITION. Homework is our way of prototyping a relationship.

best, and it attracts talent with a high level of self-confidence. One benefit of the exhaustive process actually instills *greater* certainty: Better hiring means fewer firings.

One of the primary benefits of our interview process is that it allows the hire and the team to really get a sense of the chemistry. "I always ask, 'Is this a person that I'm excited to sit next to on a five-hour coast-to-coast plane ride?'" says Chief Person Against Dirty (or CEO, as some know him) Drew Fraser.

When we have a few candidates whom we love, we invite them back for our homework assignment. It's an integral part of our hiring process, and the first test is just watching their reaction. If they push back or aren't genuinely excited to give it a try, it's a major red flag. We once cut out of the running a CEO candidate who had previously led a billion-dollar consumer brand, because this person questioned the validity of doing homework. Yup, we're that serious about weird.

Every homework assignment consists of three questions: one strategic question, one tactical question—both customized for the applicant's experience—and then our favorite question: "How would you keep Method weird?" For example,

Don Frey, our Product Czar (aka vice president of product development), performed the Kermit the Frog song, "It's Not Easy Being Green" during his interview.

While it may sound like little more than a fun stunt, the homework assignment is actually a make-or-break rite of passage. It delivers a bounty of helpful insight, and we believe it's an excellent predictor of a candidate's success. It's a form of prototyping to see how candidates think and approach their work. It's a peek into their work ethic and a chemistry test for our culture. Matthew Loyd, our Brand Poobah (aka VP of brand experience), puts it this way: "You're in a room with ten or fifteen people. You're nervous, excited. It's pretty amazing what people come up with. One person Irish step-danced, someone took the staff out to do yoga in the lobby. Someone even made up a Method game show and passed out bells. She did a ton of research; she knew things many of us didn't know about the company!"

Some benefits of the homework assignment include:

It raises the bar for everyone. If you're the hiring manager and your candidate bombs in front of an audience, ultimately it makes you look bad. So everyone works harder at recruiting and screening top talent. The result is that it's harder for people to hire candidates weaker than themselves; because the process is so transparent, nothing slips by.

Bad talent can't hide in the homework. Sometimes the worst employees are the best interviewees just because they've done more interviews in their lives. (That, or maybe they're just really good bullshit artists.) With homework, you can get a better sense of how talented the candidates really are, allowing you to see how they think and problem-solve right in front of you.

Cash money. In some cases, homework assignments have saved us money because we were able to see that a less experienced, less expensive candidate actually had more talent. We always hire for talent over experience, and the homework assignment is the best way to distinguish between the two.

Due diligence. You can customize homework to a candidate's perceived or rumored weaknesses, allowing you to dig into any problem areas hinted at by interviews or reference checks.

Better sleep, all around. Hiring a new employee can be anxiety inducing for all involved, but homework removes most of that uncertainty. By the time they're finished working through the three-step homework assignment, new hires are already familiar with their colleagues and the company; they hit the ground running, making the first days and weeks much smoother.

Free ideas. Tons of them, actually. Homework provides the opportunity to learn from even the people you don't hire.

Scare the window-shoppers. Let's face it, a lot of people browse new jobs just to see if they can make more money. We keep them from wasting our time. You want an offer? You better be ready to work for it! In the end, this saves us a lot of time.

Silo Busting. Our unusual hiring process ensures that we hire unusual, dynamic people who are at ease outside their traditional comfort zone. These traits have become a pivotal part of what keeps us fresh. After all, once we find our unicorn, we change things regularly, looking for opportunities to move people around the company to broaden their experience. For example, a director may lead the laundry branch of the brand one year and transfer to personal care the next year. The process provokes employees to think creatively, spreading new strategies and lessons beyond traditional company silos.

A few years ago, we realized that while we were going to great lengths to get the right people on the bus, we were doing a lousy job of helping them make that transition. In response, we created a semiformal on-boarding approach.

On-boarding at Method starts on a Monday—everyone's first day—when they're introduced at the weekly all-company huddle (more on this below). When they're introduced, we ask them to share with everyone why they chose to join us and how they've pledged to keep Method weird. It's a great icebreaker and an energetic (and often humorous) start to everyone's first day. It's not uncommon to share embarrassing photos with the crowd (with the help of a conspiring spouse). From there, someone will walk them through our on-boarding book, our field guide to becoming a person against dirty. Highlights of the day include choosing your own title (we'll explain in a sec), rookie cookies (a plate of conversation bait that a new hire brings in to leave on the desk, no store-boughts allowed), and the presentation of an actual lotto ticket. That last part is a final check to ensure they're the right hire, not just born lucky.

As for titles, most companies just give you a title that defines your job and jurisdiction. In essence, you're labeled and put in a box. Fine if you just want people to do what's expected of them, but with fewer resources, we need everyone to punch above his or her weight. To empower our team members and give them a feeling of ownership, every new hire at Method gets to make up his or her own title. If you visit us, don't be surprised to meet a good cop (regulatory), a village voice (customer service), or a zookeeper (project manager). The process encourages independent thinking, confidence, and fun—and, perhaps most of all, it emphasizes how every person at the company has an important role in driving change.

While new hires will always change an established culture to some degree, they bring an infectious curiosity and energy to the mix. By taking the effort to instruct them and fully integrate them into the company, existing employees can harness that energy themselves.

MONDAY MORNING HUDDLES

The Monday morning huddle is an informal gathering in our front lobby where we share information and employees have an opportunity to share concerns and personal news. (To give credit where credit is due, we admit we stole this idea

▲ **HUDDLE UP!** Our caffeinated kick start to the week that keeps everyone connected to the culture.

from Richard Reed, cofounder of Innocent. Thanks, Richard!) At Method, the huddle is our way of aligning our obsessions with our objectives and keeping the company on track. New contracts, financial challenges, birthdays of the week, a reminder to do the dishes—each huddle is dedicated to discussing and preserving everything that makes us who we are as a company.

If you've never done it, the Monday morning huddle may sound awkward or plain unnecessary, but it's a great example of where logic and magic have intersected for us. Employees asked us for more structure and process at work (the logic half), so we decided to devote time to discussing shared goals, challenges, insights, and solutions (the magic half). We also hand out values awards—one of

---

HOLD A MIRROR TO IT

Every six months, we run a "come clean" survey that measures how everyone is feeling about the culture and their respective roles. Typical statements (scored 1 to 5) might include, "I look forward to coming to work every day," "I believe Method will do great things," and "I have a positive relationship with my boss." Afterward, we hold everyone accountable for improving the scores by updating the results at one of our Monday morning huddles. When something feels off—a negative comment about poor collaboration in a particular department, say, or an antagonistic question about promotion opportunities (or lack thereof), we address it by "holding a mirror to it." To do this, we put the note up on a slide (removing the author's name, of course) and, rather than answer it ourselves, open it up to our team members for discussion. The process helps clear the air and reinforces the idea that everyone is accountable to the success of our culture.

Mirroring is a good barometer for where things stand because it forces people to ask, "Who do we want to be as a company—and who's going to be responsible for that?" No matter who you are, with culture, the answer is always "me." At one of our offsites, we got a note that said something like, "The culture at Method is broken, what is the leadership of this company going to do about it?" We mirrored it, and our colleagues were visibly shaken up. It got people thinking, and the response was like an organ rejection. "Why would someone say that?" they asked. "Culture is *everyone's* responsibility."

---

the bottom-up ways fellow team members can recognize one another for doing great work and one of the most overt ways we live our values. In order to nominate someone for a values award, team members submit a short story about what their colleague did and how it lived up to one of our values. If approved, the recipient gets a chance to spin a wheel and win fabulous prizes, from a frozen turkey to lunch with one of our packaging engineers. Yes, all very fabulous . . . and weird.

How much do we love our weekly huddle? We specifically designed our lobby for it, complete with funky couches and a killer A/V system. To be clear, a weekly staff meeting in the company boardroom is not a huddle, it's a staff meeting. Hold your huddle somewhere informal—the lobby, the kitchen, that back hallway with the old Xerox machine and the drafty skylight—anywhere but a conference room.

Another way we distinguish the huddle from an everyday meeting is by assigning a different person to "take point" each week. Though the main agenda is always the same—examining our priorities by way of our seven obsessions—changing the moderator helps everyone see each obsession from a fresh perspective. Take the first obsession, culture. Handled with a bit of personality, such as a Big Lebowski theme—complete with cereal bowls, shabby bathrobes, and gratuitous use of the word *dude*—even simple announcements about birthdays, personal milestones, and weekly front-desk assignments take on a new dimension. To start off the huddle, each week's leader will read a letter from one of our advocates (the name we give our customers) reminding us whom we really work for—them.

Next Monday, try a huddle with your company or your department. It may feel odd at first, but as you settle into a groove, it becomes an authentic way of reinforcing your shared values, aligning everyone toward company goals, and simply kicking off the week.

CORN DOGS AND PROM QUEENS

Like the weekly huddles, company events reinforce our values. Both of our annual company offsites are largely devoted to discussing and sharing the values. This may take the form of town-hall conversations about recent challenges, reviewing the Come Clean survey results, or an exercise in which we ask people to break up into groups and tackle a tough, open-ended question like "What would it look like if our culture were our number-one competitive advantage?" In addition, each summer's prom—yes, there is a prom committee and a new prom theme

▲ **BRANDING FROM THE INSIDE OUT.** At Method the employees are the brand.

every year (recent themes include "Under the Sea" and "Heroes and Villains")—is dedicated to celebrating our values. Regardless of the event in question, costumes generally come into play. At one event, we gave everyone in the company a cape, because, well, everybody sounds smarter wearing a cape. (Try it sometime.) On the surface, proms and costumes in a professional environment may sound weird . . . and they are! But when some of your employees work eight thousand miles apart and only see one another a couple times a year, irreverent touches like this break down social walls and provide something creative and entertaining to bond over. To collaborate well on the hard stuff, we need everyone to know and feel comfortable with one another.

We encourage everyone to come up with ideas for events, funding and promoting them whenever possible. This can mean everything from a ski trip or a rotating drink cart to Corndog Appreciation Day. Not to be outdone, every March 14 (3/14) the finance department celebrates the number pi (π) by baking pies with decimals etched into the crust. Whether it comes from the top down or the bottom up, fun and weirdness are contagious.

DON'T START A BUSINESS, START A CAUSE

After ten years in business and hundreds of innovations, we can still confidently say that our proudest achievement remains our first—launching a company with a social mission to do good in the world by giving people a great, healthy, cool product that is good for them and the environment. Not only was creating a mission-driven company the right thing to do for society and the planet; we've proven that it's the right thing to do for the bottom line, too. The rapid expansion of media transparency is producing increasingly well-informed and discriminating consumers. The influx of socially and environmentally conscious Gen Y-ers into the workforce is redefining the war for talent. Challenges to the most established businesses, these shifts present significant competitive advantages to mission-driven companies.

Beyond the profound public impact this mission has had throughout our industry, our community, and our environment, the cultural advantage of having a purpose larger than profits has been key to the adoption and application of our values. Most corporate values are just that—the values of the corporation. No matter how much ambition, camaraderie, and loyalty an employee brings to work, no one is taking those corporate values home to share with friends and family. But those same values become immeasurably more meaningful when they're tied to a higher purpose.

On an individual level, our team members are passionate about our values because they know they're making a difference in the world. It's human nature to want to be a part of something bigger than oneself. We are amazed at how many cover letters we get that open with lines like, "My goal is to work for a values- and mission-driven business." If people don't love what they are doing or feel that they're a part of something important, they'll go somewhere else.

Of course, working with purpose and values isn't just a matter of individual growth; finding meaning in work is central to a strong corporate culture. In fact, the power of sharing our values collectively far exceeds any individual benefit. Even when we don't follow the same passions, we are united by the fact that we are all committed to a greater cause. Working for the common good helps us put ego aside and work collaboratively as a team, engendering a deep sense of continuity, familiarity, and trust that spills over into every discipline in the company.

Building a shared vision around a social mission takes a different leadership style than most of us are accustomed to. At Method, this means never forgetting that money isn't what primarily motivates our colleagues. Like us, they're driven by making the world a cleaner place. We know this because they tell us as much at group offsites, in community volunteer efforts, and over drinks after work. Good leaders encourage this kind of passion in their employees. Great leaders leverage it and channel it, outrecruiting and outperforming their soulless corporate rivals.

ERROR AUTOPSY: MACGYVER'S BETRAYAL

Perhaps it was inevitable that a guiding principle intended to inspire ingenuity would ultimately become an excuse for cutting corners. But MacGyver taught us that living by your values isn't always as clear as it sounds and can quickly turn into MacGruber, the *Saturday Night Live* parody. We started spotting the warning signs early on . . .

At every Monday's weekly huddle, team members can nominate any colleague for a values award. In the beginning, praise poured in, the prize wheel spun, and all was well with the world. That is, until we noticed a growing pattern: Someone would get hung up on a project, pull an all-nighter, air-freight the finished product at the last possible second, and barely meet the deadline. "Success!" Afterward, everyone would let out a huge sigh of relief, and the next day the employee would be nominated for a MacGyver award! OK, but . . .

Examples like this were why What Would MacGyver Do? quickly became our most common award. People would screw around, pull something out of their ass at the last minute, then sit back and bask in the limelight. As leaders, we had to help our team members to stop MacGyvering on the back end and start doing more work on the front end. MacGyver didn't merely divert the enemy, defuse the bomb, and devise an escape route, all at the last second. He applied the same assiduous insight from the opening scene through the whole episode. Sure, maybe savvy TV producers made sure all the important plot twists were served up in the last two minutes, but MacGyver wasn't asleep during the first fifty-eight.

The point is, just because your values are well intentioned doesn't mean they can't be manipulated or lead people astray. When that happens (and it will, trust us), it's up to leadership to step in and set things straight.

MUSE

2010 CULTURE BOOK

Zappos.com

WEIRDNESS HONEST EN-MINDED GROWTH TEAM ARNING ACE CHANGE PASSIONATE CREATE OPEN COMMUNICATION FUN RELATIONSHIP HUMBLE SERVICE WOW

▲ **ZAPPOS CULTURE BOOKS.** Every year Tony asks employees to write, "What does Zappos culture mean to you?" Except for correcting typos, they leave it unedited and publish everything in a book available to anyone, which creates both transparency and accountability for their culture.

OUR CULTURE MUSE: TONY HSIEH, CEO OF ZAPPOS

When it comes to great culture, we have a lot of muses, but the person we have stolen from more than anyone else is Tony Hsieh, the CEO of Zappos. As an entrepreneur, Tony is a tough act to follow. He has hit two home runs and recently took Zappos to a billion-dollar acquisition by Amazon.com. (And Tony's first book, *Delivering Happiness,* hit number one on the *New York Times* best-seller list, another accomplishment we'd like to emulate.) We met Tony briefly a few times in San Francisco and even attended one of his epic loft parties. But it wasn't until we were summoned to the White House with a group of entrepreneurs in 2008 that we had the opportunity to bond with him. In Tony Hsieh we found a kindred spirit for culture, mission-driven business, and the occasional tequila shot. OK, maybe more than occasional.

If you've read Tony's book, you might think we stole his "weird" value . . . in fact, he and we both came up with that one on our own. Weird coincidence, huh? No matter whether you come to it independently or steal it from us, weirdness is a great value for a creative business.

▲ **MAY WE HELP YOU?** When everyone has "receptionist" in their job title, it's tough to have a big ego.

In fact, after a tour of Zappos, our leadership team took one of Tony's great ideas—doubling the reception desk to feature two people, making a more engaging, social impression—and made it even weirder, replacing our receptionist with the Method House of Representatives. Each day, two different Method team members work the front desk. The change helps us maintain the small-company feel, reinforce community, and keep the ego out of the ranks. Trust us: There's nothing more delightful than seeing the CEO deliver the office mail!

After establishing the habit, it wasn't long before the rotating House of Representatives started declaring a new theme each day. Swing by our office sometime and you might be offered a shot of Jägermeister by an overly tanned host (*Jersey Shore* Day) or find yourself face-to-face with a Billy Idol look-alike (Punk Rock Day).

Weird? Absolutely! Fun? You know it! Scalable? We get asked that a lot, actually, and it's an important question. As we've discovered, maintaining your culture as you grow is one of the hardest things to do in business. But thanks in part to the example set by Tony and Zappos (with three thousand employees and $1 billion in sales and growing), we're confident that you don't have to be small to be weird. See you in Vegas, Tony!

obsession

2

INSPIRE
ADVOCATES

don't sell to customers,
create advocates for
your social mission

CAN YOU RECALL THE LAST ADVERTISEMENT YOU saw? We're not talking about the most memorable—the good ads that made you laugh or got you thinking, or one of the viral spots you forwarded to your friends via e-mail or on Facebook. No, we're speaking literally here: the very last commercial that flashed across the screen before you turned off the TV last night, the final billboard you zoomed by on the way home from work, that pesky pop-up ad lurking behind your browser when you logged off the computer earlier.

Drawing a blank?

We can't remember either. After encountering an estimated five thousand ads a day, who can? Each year, U.S. businesses spend more than $300 billion on paid media—TV, print, online, et cetera—in an increasingly desperate effort to capture our attention. Amid the ten-grand-a-second barrage, most of the ads we see (or don't see, as it turns out) pass by unnoticed. For those particularly persistent spots, we now have our choice of a growing number of ad-blocking technologies and ad-free services. DVRs, spam filters, satellite radio, podcasts, the National Do Not Call Registry—as long as advertisers keep inventing new ways to interrupt us, industrious entrepreneurs will devise new ways to block them.

While all this ad-free media and technology is great news for consumers, it presents an intimidating challenge for consumer brands like us and probably your company too. Imagine launching a new brand in a multibillion-dollar consumer packaged goods category like ours. You've got Procter & Gamble—the biggest advertiser on earth, which in 2010 spent $4.2 billion on advertising in the

United States alone. Unilever spent another $1.3 billion. It's safe to assume these guys have a toilet-paper budget that's bigger than our entire marketing budget (even accounting for the fact that they *make* toilet paper and get it at cost).

In contrast, Method didn't even have a dollar to spend at launch. Our marketing strategy consisted of spending money on better packaging and doing personal demos in grocery stores. Not that we let the ad-spending disparity get to us; long before our first products reached shelves, we knew we'd have to come up with our own creative alternatives to traditional advertising in order to reach potential customers. Besides, even if we'd had a million bucks for marketing, it would have amounted to just one three hundred–thousandth of the overall ad market's annual commercial cacophony. Our message and our money would have been lost in an instant. Ten years later, not much has changed: The easiest thing to hide in America is a million dollars of advertising.

THE BIG SHIFT: GOING FROM PAID TO EARNED MEDIA

The problem with paid media isn't the content. Some of those advertising billions actually result in fun, creative, insightful campaigns. The problem is the context—how it's served up and how we consume it. If the gloomy ad-industry stories filling the business pages of our newspapers and magazines weren't evidence enough of the dwindling influence and relevancy of mass advertising, the fact that we've stopped flipping through those very pages in favor of clicking through them (opting out and blocking pop-ups as we go) is a fitting reminder. Media is changing. The "golden era" of mass advertising—the fabled *Mad Men* days when one thirty-second toothpaste commercial during the nightly news reached a vast swath of U.S. consumers—is dead and gone.

The spread of on-demand cable television, the Internet, and various other new ways to consume media—from the Kindle to the iPad—has revolutionized how we shop and share opinions. Modern consumers no longer sit around in front of the television waiting for Don Draper to tell them why they should buy Cocoa Puffs and Colgate. Today, we choose the brands we want to interact with, and we block out the rest. As consumers, we no longer want to be a passive audience; we want to be participants. It's a sea change in how consumers shop and how brands do business. We call it the *big shift.*

Few of the opportunities we discuss in this book present as many advantages to the next generation of entrepreneurs as the big shift from paid media to earned media. We consider *paid media* any form of marketing that requires you to pay a fee for the privilege of interrupting a predictable number of consumers ("please excuse the commercial interruption"). These include the billboard on I-5 that interrupted your morning commute, the television ad that you fast-forwarded through while enjoying the eightieth season of *The Bachelor* last night, and the print ad in *US Weekly* right next to "Stars, They're Just like Us!" In contrast, *earned media* are any media your company receives for free, including press hits, social media, blog posts, or viral videos on YouTube. Even this book is earned media for us because we didn't pay you to read it. Well, at least we hope not. In each case, the media are earned by creating something that people actually want to share or participate with.

Previous media shifts—newspapers to radio, radio to television—were simply transitions from one form of paid interruption media to another. Even when the medium changed, the biggest advertisers still held on to the advantage. But emerging social and earned media distinctly favor young, fast-moving businesses over their older, slower rivals. Ten years ago, when Method was just getting off the ground, few people had ever heard of a blog, let alone social media. Twitter and Facebook didn't exist yet. Today, new tools offer challenger brands better ways to market on a budget, find their place in a crowded industry, and earn more meaningful press and word of mouth—all for free. So why are companies still pumping $300 billion a year into paid media when earned media is free and consumers are doing everything in their power to ignore, erase, filter, or block them out? If they're the masters of messaging, you'd think they would get the message: Don't call us, we'll call you.

Most companies continue to buy traditional advertising for the same reasons nearly all of us continue to use fossil fuels: Making such a profound shift in our way of life is incredibly difficult. Systemwide change is expensive, disruptive, and time-consuming. And leveraging all the new tools at your disposal isn't going to be easy. Right now we are only partway through the shift, so it's a very awkward time in history to be a marketer. And it's about to get really hard. While the old media tools are quickly becoming less efficient, they still often represent the best way to reach a mass audience with a high level of predictability. Even though we are dedicated to the emerging powers of earned media, Method will spend a record level on advertising this year to boost awareness of our brand. We are stuck between the two media worlds, so the only way to navigate this transition is make sure that any form of paid media works hard to create an earned-media halo. Few have nailed this as well in the recent past than those who relaunched Old Spice in 2010. What began as a few million dollars in paid

▲ **INVITING A DIALOGUE.** Our crowd-sourced music video invites participation so advocates help us build the brand.

advertising resulted in an immeasurable amount of earned media in months of YouTube, TV, print, and online coverage, turning Isaiah Mustafa into a cultural icon. The genius of the campaign was that it spoke directly to both men and women and generated a conversation about body wash. Once the campaign was established through paid media, Old Spice gave consumers an opportunity to participate directly with a "response" campaign wherein fans and celebrities could contact Isaiah directly—and receive a video response from him in real time! Ultimately, earned media overshadowed paid media, but it took the balance of both to create such a big impact.

While the big shift may look like just a media shift, the impact on brand building is much more profound. The brands that rose to power in the last fifty years were fueled by mass media. They didn't succeed by spending the most on mass media; they succeeded because they efficiently aligned their brand and organizational structure around a mass-media approach. The key to this formula was targeting the largest group of people and positioning the brand upon its broadest and simplest attribute—the lowest common denominator that appealed to the largest number of people. But as mass media disappears, so do mass brands.

See the pattern here? Brands have always lived and died amid changes in consumer media consumption, and the shift to social media is no different. As old media platforms continue to sink, brands unable to make the leap will drown. Nevertheless, most companies are rearranging deck chairs on the *Titanic*, refusing to see that brands built on single-attribute messaging and broad relevance have little appeal in an era of infinitely fragmented, socially driven media. Of course, the idea behind social and earned media isn't new—word of mouth has been around since the first caveman told his friend where to hunt the best woolly mammoth. The difference is that this shift dramatically amplifies word of mouth; instead of one mom telling her ten closest friends about one of your products, she has the power to share her perspective about your brand with millions of other moms all over the world in seconds.

What's particularly different about this shift is that it moves the advantage from the companies with the most ad dollars to companies with the most compelling mission. People may see and remember an ad, but they will spread and bond over a great mission, thus allowing your idea to spread further than your marketing budget could take you.

Thus, to succeed in a world of earned and social media requires you to shift your mind-set from talking to customers to inspiring advocates, which is Method's second obsession. What's an advocate? As we see it, advocates are more than just consumers; advocates are evangelists for your brand. The dictionary defines an advocate as "a person who publicly supports or recommends a particular cause or policy." The ability to create advocates is the most important prerequisite for a brand championing social change and challenging the establishment. Not only do advocates make good business sense by buying more of our products more often, but also they engage us—online, in writing, on the phone, and in person—teaching us all sorts of stuff we wouldn't have figured out on our own. This kind of feedback is more honest, more complete, and a lot faster than that of our casual consumers, enabling us to be more innovative. *Advocate* is more than just a fancy word for customer. As we see it, calling our best customers advocates reframes how we think of them and in turn how we serve them.

Besides engaging us directly, advocates engage others, helping to spread our message. Whether it's talking about us to their friends and family, reviewing our products online, or forwarding our most recent viral spot, the best way to recruit new advocates is through existing advocates. Take Nathan Aaron, one of our biggest online advocates and the man behind Methodlust.com. Few rock bands or movie stars have as devoted a fan as Nathan. An illustrator and graphic designer from Greensboro, North Carolina, Nathan has been blogging about Method for years. Nathan doesn't blog once a month or every week; he writes almost daily, posting even more than we do on our own blog. Having recognized the value of such a voice, Method has nurtured Nathan's lust by responding to requests for interviews, sending updates on Method products, and supplying Nathan with pictures and other content.

Among the many features on Nathan's fan site are links to new product releases, retired products, video reviews, contests, reader polls ("What's your favorite Method line?" "Which new scent should Method pick?"), and even alter-

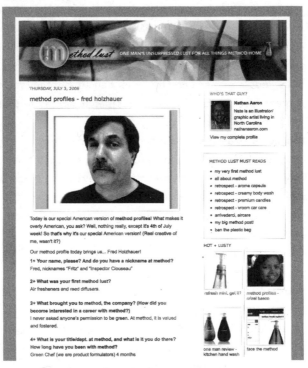

▲ **FRIENDS WITH BENEFITS.** As a fan of the brand, Nathan's blog methodlust.com helps spread our mission and keeps us honest.

native uses for Method products—such as lamps made from our dish-soap bottles and shower spray used as bug repellent. While much of this comes from his readers, Nathan maintains close contact with Method itself, a connection that enables him to break news about the brand, link to Method's various Twitter feeds, and present some two dozen exclusive profiles and interviews—photos included—of Method employees at every level of the company.

Despite his odes to limited-edition scents and his open declaration of desire (literally: "This blog is one man's unsuppressed lust for Method home products"), Nathan is not afraid to sound off on the brand he loves. When a product fails to live up to his high standards (or those of his readers), he'll offer a detailed breakdown of how it might be improved. And when products don't appear as anticipated, he'll speak his mind: "Method, we WANT our holiday aroma pills and sprays next year! This is a threat, I repeat, a threat! Are you all with me, Method lusters! Let's start a Method-olution!" A helpful ally, and, occasionally, a loving adversary, Nathan represents the ideal brand advocate.

The idea of creating advocates like Nathan (whom we love), who want a higher level of participation with a brand, is not new. After all, weekend warriors were getting Harley-Davidson tattoos long before we were born. What we brought to the party was proof that you can build advocacy around a low-interest category and use the new powers of earned media to effectively compete against the world's largest advertisers in mass categories. But turning your marketing on its head to inspire advocates demands turning a lot of other things upside down, too, like how you run your business and how you serve your customers. Once you've done the heavy lifting, however, the results will take on a life of their own. Your beliefs and your behaviors will do your marketing for you, your employees and advocates will promote your brand on your behalf, and your competitors will be left to find a niche of their own. To get there, we built our brand around a set of beliefs, branded from the inside out, and invited participation. Here is our Method method for inspiring advocates.

START WITH A BELIEF

The difference between a mass-market brand and a belief brand is like the difference between a monologue and a dialogue. Mass brands talk at people. Or more accurately, they SHOUT! Belief brands, on the other hand, listen and create a conversation. And if you ask us, the world could use fewer of the former and more of the latter. As it is, however, most modern brands don't have the social skills to invite a dialogue with their consumers because doing so requires great listening skills which is really hard for most marketers. That's because most of today's brands are promise-based brands ("always low prices"), not philosophy-based brands (help you live better). But brand relationships are like human relationships; if they're based on a promise—a one-sided idea—there's no depth to the relationship. The result is that many existing brands built in the mass-media era offer little for consumers to bond over.

In contrast, a brand philosophy is subtler, more complex. Not only does a philosophy take more time to communicate than a promise, but the appropriate audience is also much smaller. That's because your beliefs and values need to resonate with your audience before they become *shared* beliefs and values. Until recently, this wasn't easy—especially for start-ups trying to get a toehold in an established market. Promises and philosophies had to go head-to-head in mass advertising, competing with repetition, volume, and variety. In the race to the bottom, every company had to streamline its message, paring away personality and depth. But the arrival of social media means philosophy-based brands have more ways to express themselves and tell a deeper story, inviting people to discover every special detail on their own time rather than interrupting them with some reductive promise.

Not only is social media well suited to philosophy-based brands, but the social shift is making it harder for promise brands to get away with the same old tricks. With a few exceptions—like promising the lowest price—consumers are less and less satisfied with simple brand promises. We want brands that engage us, brands that show us a richer world. Look no further than Gen Y. Their formative years were during the prosperous late 1990s. Amid the abundance, the consumer question for a brand was, "Who are you and what can you offer?" This represented a shift from not just what consumers buy but what they *buy into.*

With so much to choose from, Gen Y's purchasing decisions became based on shared values. As a result, they're choosier and more social, interactive, and curious than any generation before them. They ask more of the brands they love. And increasingly they're calling the shots, purchasing a greater and greater percentage of goods versus preceding generations. Brands with personality, such as Lush, Ben & Jerry's, or Innocent also demonstrate consumer resistance to homogenization. Driven by our senses toward what is real and authentic, we prefer the character of a boutique market over a sterile strip mall, and character is difficult for big brands to achieve on a mass scale. We wholeheartedly believe that mission- or values-driven brands will be the brands of the future.

In building a belief brand, a company has to tap into what we call its social

method.humanifesto

as people against dirty,

we look at the world through bright-green colored glasses.

- - - - - - - - - -

we see ingredients that come from plants, not chemical plants.

- - - - - - - - - -

we see that guinea pigs are never used as guinea pigs.

- - - - - - - - - -

we're entranced by shiny objects like clean dinner plates, floors you could eat off of, nobel peace prizes, and tasteful public sculptures.

- - - - - - - - - -

we're an e.o.m.e.d. (equal opportunity movement for environment and design). method is our way of keeping the movement, well, moving.

- - - - - - - - - -

we make role models in bottles.

- - - - - - - - - -

we're the kind of people who've figured out that once you clean your home, a mess of other problems seem to disappear too.

- - - - - - - - - -

we always see the aroma pill as half full, and assume everyone we meet smells like fresh-cut grass or a similar yummy nothing-but-good fragrance.

- - - - - - - - - -

we exercise by running through the legs of the giant.

- - - - - - - - - -

and while we love a freshly detoxed home, we think perfect is boring, and weirdliness is next to godliness.

- - - - - - - - - -

it's "everybody into the pool!"(we believe in spontaneous bursts of enthusiasm.)

- - - - - - - - - -

we also believe in making products safe for every surface, especially earth's.

- - - - - - - - - -

we consider mistakes little messes we can learn from—nothing that can't be cleaned up and made better.

- - - - - - - - - -

we embrace the golden ylang-ylang rule: do unto your home as you would do unto you. (your shower doesn't want to have morning breath any more than you do.)

- - - - - - - - - -

we believe above all else that dirty, in all its slime, smoggy, toxic, disgusting incarnations is public enemy number one.

- - - - - - - - - -

good always prevails over stinky.

▲ **OUR HUMANIFESTO.** What statement about humanity does your brand make?

mission. Consumers are much more likely to participate and share your brand with others if they can get behind you and what you stand for, rather than just the products you deliver. At Method, we started a movement to get "dirty" out of people's homes. A movement to protect the planet while cleaning it up. And a movement to show that business can be an agent of social change. As People Against Dirty, we come to work every day to try to make the world a cleaner and healthier place. For us, People Against Dirty will always be more than a tagline. Not sure you have a social mission? Don't worry. This is one of those things that sounds more high-minded than it really is. Any brand has the potential to have a social mission even if it doesn't necessarily translate to the greater good of society. Take Axe body spray, for example. Axe's social mission: helping young men get laid. Granted, it may not be noble, but it's one hell of a social mission! Consider a few others:

Method (us!), inspire a happy healthy home revolution	▶	People Against Dirty
TOMS Shoes, the socially conscious footwear brand	▶	Make Life More Comfortable
Kashi, the natural foods company	▶	Seven Whole Grains on a Mission
Zappos, the online retailer famous for great customerXW service	▶	Delivering Happiness
Nike, the iconic sports brand	▶	Just Do It

A social mission is important because, for human beings, a critical attribute of happiness is the ability to be part of something bigger than ourselves. We crave meaning in our lives and careers. As we pointed out in chapter 1 while discussing our obsession with culture, building a brand around a social mission energizes our entire organization and motivates us every day to make the world a better place. It transforms a career into a calling. Better yet, among advocates, this passion is contagious if you can present a world that they want to see too. But to do it well, you have to build a brand from the inside out.

BUILDING A BELIEF BRAND

We admit it: We were never passionate about cleaning before we launched Method. But building a belief brand with a social mission taught us that there is no such thing as a low-interest category, just low-interest brands. Anyone can generate excitement about a new cell phone technology or a new beer brand. Attracting attention in a traditionally low-interest category (like soap) takes a bit more thought. This is one of the best benefits of belief brands—they work equally well in crowded high-interest categories and in overlooked categories. Beyond the emotional engagement created by sharing similar beliefs and values with their advocates, belief brands have a philosophy, an attitude, and a story to tell. Their personalities aren't created in some office on Madison Avenue; they're woven into the very fabric of the organization. Below, a few examples of high-interest brands in low-interest categories:

Joe Boxer. By injecting irreverence and controversy into his Joe Boxer brand, Nicholas Graham transformed everyday boxer briefs into a conversation piece.

Dyson. Ten years ago, it would have been difficult to imagine anyone getting excited about a vacuum cleaner. Dyson shook up the dusty category with innovative technology and beautiful design.

Swingline. An unremarkable and ubiquitous tool, staplers were the poster boy of low interest before Mike Judd cast a red Swingline as an object of devotion in his 1999 corporate satire *Office Space*.

While we rely primarily on style and substance to inspire interest in cleaning products, we also tap into an often overlooked subset of consumers: people who actually love to clean. You probably even know a few friends whom you consider to be clean freaks. We believe in making the act of cleaning more enjoyable and, if we may say so, aspirational. But virtually every commercial treats cleaning as if it were a huge hassle, virtually screaming promises of convenience and ease. Pandering to women with images of grinning maids in aprons, it was as if taking care of your things was something to be ashamed of, something you'd rather leave to someone else. This is typical problem-solution marketing, in which you set up a problem (mildew in the bathroom) and then present your product as the hero solution (*Pow!* mildew gone). The problem with this approach is that it forces the consumer to enter through the problem, so your brand will always live in low-interest land. Even if you don't find an ounce of joy in cleaning, virtually everyone loves the end state, a clean home. So we focused on talking about the aspirational end state of cleaning, and we found that, to many people, cleaning is an important part of life. It's the ritual of connecting to their homes and families by putting life back in order. To many, cleaning is a form of caring for their children or pets by providing a safe haven for those they care about most.

Seeking to draw out our audience's inner clean freaks, we filled our ad campaigns with young, great-looking naked people in gorgeous, hip homes, using (or maybe just caressing) a rainbow of beautiful Method products. Rather than the "quick and painless" promises in our competitors' ads, we communicated

▲ **DETOX POP SHOP.** Inviting advocates to turn in their toxic cleaners.

with clever, cheeky messages intended to promote the aspirational idea that cleaning could be cool (*gasp!*). Flying in the face of decades of traditional cleaning commercials, the ads resonated with people of all ages.

To many people, jogging is a chore. Imagine if Nike ran advertisements featuring unhappy joggers forcing themselves through another grueling early morning routine. Not likely. To the contrary, the brand celebrates every sport it touches, with aspirational imagery. We'd even bet there are some fierce badminton ads out there that would inspire you to Just Do It with a birdie! Nike ties this to its social mission of bringing inspiration and innovation to every athlete in the world. As Bill Bowerman, track coach and cofounder of Nike, said, "If you have a body, you are an athlete."

Bottom line: If you're struggling to shift your brand from low to high interest, seek to reframe your communications from presenting the problem to projecting the desired end state and wrap that in a social mission.

BRAND FROM THE INSIDE OUT

While most companies treat marketing as an external activity—something that focuses on spreading a message outside the walls of your company—the truth is that building a belief brand starts on the inside. In this new transparent media environment, your employees are your brand, and everything that goes on inside your walls can be shared with the outside world. If not for the Internet, brand horror stories, like the one about the Domino's employee spitting into food, would be just urban legends. But thanks to the Web, we can share brands' most embarrassing moments with the world—Steven Slater's infamous resignation as a JetBlue flight attendant or all those Comcast repairmen caught sleeping on people's couches. See what we mean when we say your employees are the brand?

It's been said that you can't learn the game as a spectator—you need to play it. We couldn't agree more. Building a brand starts with you, and at Method, we're dedicated to creating the kind of products we'd want our families to use, and we hire passionate people who resemble our consumers. Believe it or not, this approach is actually counterintuitive for most big brands; they like to keep a healthy distance between their employees and their consumers to ensure "an objective point of view." Maybe this worked in the past, but in an era defined by social media—where our personal and professional lives are increasingly melded and public—this kind of thinking is flawed at best.

At Method, we *want* to blur the lines between who we are and whom we serve. We are proud to be our own advocates. After all, why would we want to sell something we didn't love ourselves? If you walk into our office and meet our team, they should remind you of our brand. If you sit next to someone on a flight who works at Method, you should expect to meet an optimistic, fun individual who cares deeply about the environment and might even buy you a drink. We

Notice, this person against dirty incorporated one of our dryer sheets into the homemade note.

I just wanted to let you know how much I LOVE method products. Not only do you create environmentally responsible products but they actually work & smell great! Now if only I could get my local Target to carry the body wash again...

Love you guys!

—one happy Method advocate,

P.S.- Recognize the method dryer sheet in the card? It's been used 5 times & I still didn't want to throw it away— how's that for recycling? Now you have a great-smelling card ☺

▲ **FAN MAIL.** In today's marketing environment, listening is more important than talking.

think of our entire company as representatives of the brand, from our unique job titles to our office entrance. If you see a Method ad, chances are it features a real Method employee. That baby on the Web site—yup, the child of a proud Method mom. Even the office is designed to serve as a press-friendly backdrop for photo shoots, from the "grass" Ping-Pong room to the green-chef kitchen. Everyone—not just some overpaid models or one chosen spokesperson—is encouraged to be a face of the brand.

Consider our point of view. The more out-of-touch our employees are with the consumer, the more we have to compensate by pouring time and money into efforts like consumer research, quantitative studies, diary panels, and home visits to watch people use the product (we're not kidding). But because our employees are actually creating products for themselves and their families, visionary and revolutionary ideas come straight from the heart. We don't need to ask our consumers what they want because we *are* the consumers. This is why entrepreneurs are so often described as visionary—they start from a place of personal dissatisfaction about something, and they're passionate about improving upon it. Ford loved cars. Fields loved cookies. Pete loved beer. And Peet loved coffee.

Now, granted, we weren't all about soap back in the day, but we did have a passion for design and sustainability. This kind of passion is what fuels the desire to keep improving ahead of our competition and the consumer. Not only do all of our team members help inspire new product ideas, but they help test them too, bringing them home and reporting back on what they think.

For us, this passion starts with striving to keep the majority of advocate touch points in-house by insourcing customer service, advocacy communications, PR, design and creative, etc. We even realigned our hierarchy to ensure we had the right people in charge of guiding the brand, responding to our customers, and integrating any useful feedback. Besides the obvious cost savings, keeping our consumer touch points in-house translates to a nimbler, smarter, more authentic brand.

We're nimbler because we handle new media ourselves. Two-way media is fast and complex, subtle and nuanced. Consider all those corporations that outsource their Twitter accounts to PR firms. Not only is this kind of outsourcing expensive (pay-per-tweet?) and clumsy (can an outsider really speak for you?), it removes the opportunity to engage with the people who matter most to your brand—your consumers. Consumers are also starting to skip searching for customer service contacts when they have a problem, instead going straight to Facebook and Twitter to complain. And if a consumer posts a problem on Facebook, you don't want it sitting there for the world to see for very long.

As we mentioned earlier, we live in a marketing environment that rewards creativity and big ideas instead of big advertising budgets. To take advantage of this shift, we have also structured our marketing department in a fundamentally different way. In the 1940s, major consumer product companies shifted to a brand management system to address the rapidly growing mass market that emerged after World War II. Network television was spreading throughout the nation, the industrial revolution was driving down costs, and companies developed brand management teams trained in the skills of mass media. The theory was that mass advertising would act like a big lever pulling on the P&L, so every business owner should control the marketing.

This model worked beautifully for decades. But as the media world grew more fragmented, it became increasingly difficult to manage the complexity of multichannel communications. Then there's the matter of outside media agencies. No longer do companies work with a single agency; they must rely on a broad group of specialists to juggle print, interactive, PR, and all the other emerging channels. The lack of continuity—not to mention the high turnover in the advertising industry—compounds the problem. Instead of pulling one lever to build a brand, brand managers now are pulling thousands!

TRADITIONAL MARKETING
top-down approach

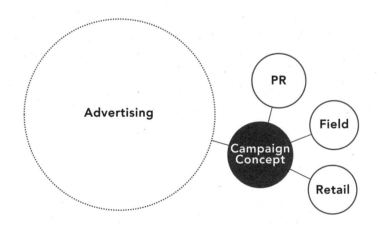

▲ **THE SHIFT FROM COMMAND AND CONTROL TO A CONVERSATION.** ▶
Marketing is no longer about top-down but now bottom-up.

At Method, we addressed these changes by transforming "brand managers" into true business owners. In the process, we put marketing communications in its own department, called Brand Experience. Our pod directors cooperate and interact with Brand Experience in the same way they do with Product Development and with Sales, folding everything into one cohesive business plan. This frees Brand Experience to focus on inspiring advocates. Looking ahead, we plan to continue integrating traditionally outsourced marketing skills. For the time being, here's how we've built Brand Experience:

PR Our second hire at Method was our in-house PR expert. We considered PR a top priority because the role functions in both directions, speaking to consumers about our brand and returning to us with their feedback. Integrating PR in-house not only helps you stay on trend by creating a two-way dialogue with the press, but it also creates authenticity while deepening relationships. The media is always happier to meet with the company directly than with a hired gun. We view members of the press the same way we view retailers: they are collaborators and partners.

TODAY'S MARKETING
bottom-up approach

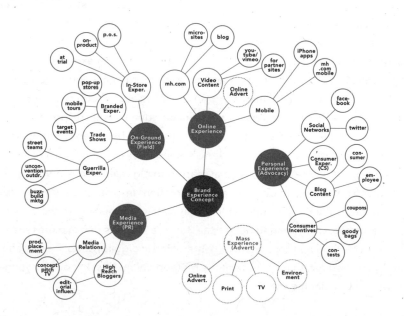

SOCIAL MEDIA If you're working with an outside agency, you're too many phone calls from your consumer. Today marketing happens in real time as a conversation with the consumer. Whether you're running a pop-up retail program or an interactive Web site, bringing your social media department in-house translates into better time management and more savings.

CUSTOMER SERVICE We'll never understand why companies outsource their call centers to India. The customer who is calling has used your product. This isn't just a marketing opportunity; it's a chance to capture new insights, create a raving fan, and even safeguard yourself from legal problems! So while most companies treat customer service as a problem, we've stationed our customer-service specialists right in the heart of our headquarters, alongside our other core departments. We also frequently have everyone in the company take a shift at customer service to keep us all focused on our advocates. So next time you call, don't be surprised if one of us answers.

CREATIVE Modern marketing is about the power of the content, not the power of the spend. Because we view the brand as a collection of experiences that work best when they're all aligned, we placed creatives in business operations roles, where they report directly to the CEO. By putting creatives in responsible leadership positions, where they're in touch with all the expressions of the brand, we've empowered them to build communications stories in real time without heavy-handed oversight by a bureaucratic business layer.

Last but certainly not least, at the heart of branding from the inside out is getting naked. (No, unfortunately, not *that* kind of naked.) In a media-transparent world, providing access to and information about your brand is increasingly a form of marketing in and of itself. Whether we're fielding discontinued-product inquiries from teenage advocates or responding to an ingredient request from a septuagenarian vegan, we have dedicated ourselves to providing access to all the behind-the-scenes details of our brand. We encourage advocates (and skeptics, for that matter) to dig deep into everything from our brand philosophy to our day-to-day operations in order to satisfy their level of interest. Naturally, it's impossible to put all this information on the back of a bottle of soap, so we created Behind the Bottle, a Web site that explores sustainability at Method for those advocates interested in digging deep. It's just one of the ways consumers can peel back the Method onion. Check it out for yourself at www.methodhome.com.

AIM SMALL AND OVERSERVE

If you've been to as many business conferences as we have, you're probably familiar with the "customer pyramid." This is the triangle marketers use to illustrate the different types of consumers—the broad bottom represents less-engaged buyers, and the pinnacle represents the smallest, most loyal group. The objective of our obsession with inspiring advocates is to invert the traditional customer pyramid by growing the group of fanatically devoted consumers at the top, the true Method advocates, into the broadest set, while shrinking the group of semiengaged customers at the bottom. The result: fewer customers (less market share) buying more of your stuff (more wallet share). The idea of flipping the pyramid scares a lot of business leaders because it means focusing on a smaller audience. But in a world with less effective forms of mass media, you have no choice but to focus on a narrower audience to build an efficient marketing model. Today, the riches are in the niches.

There are several reasons why this inverted model works. First, we all know it's cheaper to get an existing customer to try more of your products than to acquire a new one, and in our case, we play in a $24 billion sandbox (in the United States alone). If we can achieve just 5 percent market share, we will have built a billion-dollar brand! Overserving a niche will actually create a much larger long-term market than any vague overture to the broad middle. It's the lighthouse effect. Aiming small creates an aspirational halo—a beacon of shared values and brand traits that draws others in. Apple with creative professionals; Nike with track runners; Red Bull with ravers—we challenge you to find a large successful brand today that didn't start by overserving a niche audience. The same is true with the music industry, in which artists must build a small but loyal following until

▲ **FLIP THE PYRAMID.** Today's media environment requires overserving a small audience. Think wallet share, not market share.

word spreads. Ever been to a LCD Soundsystem show or seen Flight of the Conchords in concert? Our point exactly. Big companies have a lousy batting average when it comes to launching new brands—mostly because they lack the patience to build a loyal following with a core audience.

Finally, aiming small generates extreme loyalty. There will always be someone with a lower price, especially if you're offering a premium product. But a loyal audience sticks with you when other brands are offering a temporary deal. Advocates boost your adoption rates because they are willing to take a risk on your new ideas—essential to a business like ours, in which success is dependent on being the category thought leader.

We aim small by focusing on our three archetypes—true greenies, trendsetters, and status seekers. Together they represent about 27 percent of U.S. households, giving us a focused audience we can serve better than anyone else while also allowing us a big enough sandbox to build toward a billion-dollar brand. The common interests driving these archetypes are passion for the environment, health in the home, and great design. It's rare to have a brand that attracts consumers for a wide variety of reasons, but that diversity speaks to the breadth and depth of our brand appeal.

CREATE A MOVEMENT

Representatives of other brands often ask, "How do I harness my following through Facebook or all these other social media tools?" Many companies fall back on the old top-down, command-and-control tendencies, thinking of their audience as an army that needs to be deployed. Good luck with that. To connect, you need to treat customers the same way you would your friends. After all, they're following your brand because they share its values. Your goal should be to reinforce those shared values through your behaviors and interactions and thus inspire advocacy. Instead of trying to deploy them, focus on providing content that enhances those values and give them the tools to take part. At Method, our advocates appreciate the fact that we care for the environment and love design. These are shared values, and we create marketing programs that deliver on these values in a beneficial way (such as sending them copies of our first book, *Squeaky Green*).

Take the late-night battle between Jay Leno and Conan O'Brien as an example. Leno is old media—speaking to his half-asleep audience in a monologue, while Conan has learned that performing means engaging. When he does standup, Conan encourages the audience to tweet questions, and fans rallied around him when he was ousted from NBC ("I'm with Coco!"). Conan has over 2 million Twitter followers and over a million friends on Facebook, proof that Team Coco fans see themselves as participants, not viewers.

When your goal is to inspire advocates, marketing communications are about creating a movement. In a traditional advertising campaign, you talk about yourself, but a movement requires you to talk about your advocates. Movements always start with a small group of deeply passionate people, and this must be true inside and outside the company. Movements have shared ownership and powerful identities. Campaigns have a beginning and an end, while movements can live forever.

To create a movement, we focus communications around two key ingredients: *change* and *participation*. Every marketing initiative should draw attention to some kind of change—a change in our products, our industry, or the world at large—and should inspire participation from our advocates—inviting them to engage with the brand and share control in how campaigns take shape and spread in the market.

Motivating change is not too different from running a political campaign. Ever wonder why our airwaves are dominated by negative political ads come election season? Because they work! Politicians know it's far easier to rally people against something that's already out there than to introduce them to something new. As a brand striving to create social change, we face a challenge similar to that of a politician trying to get elected. We frequently think of our marketing as a political campaign with the goal trying to get a core group of advocates to rally for change.

But the secret to winning an election or creating change is that you can't just be against something. You also have to be for something. You have to explain why your alternative vision is better. We try to focus our messaging on both of these levers simultaneously by showing what we are for as well as what we are against. For example, we are against dirty but for clean. Whenever we point out what we want to eliminate (toxins, laundry jugs, the smell of bleach), we always propose an easy replacement with what we want more of (natural ingredients, concentrated bottles, and pink grapefruit scent). You have to give your advocates hope and make change easy.

At Method, we have to educate our consumers about questionable toxins in the trusted brand their moms used, but we don't want to scare them or turn them off, so we present our products as a good, safe, *clean* alternative. One tool we've found effective is our Dirty Little Secrets campaign, in which we expose some of the nasty things that make up some of the most trusted cleaning brands.

for a jug-free america.

every day, jugs are sold right under our very noses. heavy jugs that are hurting arms and spilling blue liquid in laundry rooms throughout this great nation of ours. it's time to stop this. let's stand together and get rid of jugs once and for all.

how do we do this? method® laundry detergent. it finds stains in a whole new way to get your clothes amazingly clean. the secret is our patent pending formula that's so frickin' concentrated, 50 loads fits in a teeny bottle. and if that's not enough, we ditched that messy cap for an easy-dose pump so the revolution can begin in your laundry room.

are you with us, america? let's get off the jugs and get clean. learn more at **methodlaundry.com**

m method.
people against dirty

are you a jug addict?

m method.
people against dirty

say no to jugs.

m method.
people against dirty

▲ **LAUNDRY REVOLUTION.** Inspiring advocates is about creating a movement built on purpose. It's not what they buy, but what they buy into.

Take fabric softener. Do you know the chief ingredient that makes your clothes feel so soft? It's tallow—beef fat. That's right, the goodness of beef fat in your Egyptian cotton. Dirty. We gave the world a vegan fabric softener, which inspired our advocates, especially those concerned about animal cruelty. In fact, PETA liked that idea (and others) so much, they honored the two of us with their Person of the Year awards in 2006. This association, while an honor in and of itself, is also a great marketing tool because it gives us a stamp of approval from the world's most trusted animal-rights group.

We draw inspiration from our advocates and new ideas from our idols. One of these is Adam Morgan, author of *Eating the Big Fish.* Among Morgan's more powerful ideas for challenger brands is "identifying your monster"—a common enemy you and the customer can bond over. As it takes time to introduce your message, creating a monster is a great way to speed things up by starting a conversation with your advocates.

For example, when we launched our innovative laundry detergent, it was so foreign to the category that we needed to show people the change it could represent in their lives. We needed a foil. In this case, the perfect foil was the ubiquitous laundry jug. So we created a "Say No to Jugs" advertising campaign that painted these ugly behemoths as monsters while our simple, no-mess pump became a hero.

Then there was the daisy story—the monster opportunity came to us. For years, we've used a daisy in our packaging and marketing as a way to illustrate that our products are gentle and natural. Then we opened the mail one day to find a big fat cease-and-desist letter from our friends across the bay at Clorox. Apparently, Clorox's Green Works line also used a daisy in its marketing, and the brand was threatening legal action. You read that right: Clorox was claiming it owned the daisy, a universal icon of peace and beauty. (Never mind the fact that we had been using it for over five years.) Up until then, it had never even occurred to us to register the daisy; to be honest, we kind of assumed Mother Nature held that trademark.

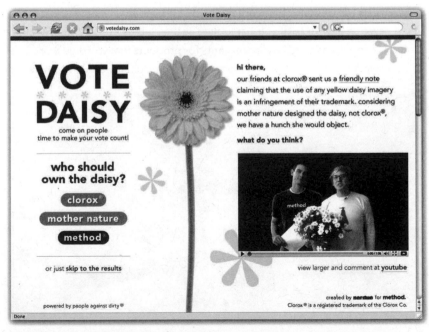

▲ **INVITE PARTICIPATION.** With a small legal budget, we invited our advocates to decide who should own the daisy in the court of public opinion.

Naturally, we weren't about to give up our rights to use the daisy, but we didn't want to spend a lot on legal bills either. Inspired by Ben & Jerry's "one-man picket line" in front of rival Pillsbury headquarters ("What's the doughboy afraid of?"), we turned to our advocates. Our Internet appeal: Help us battle large corporations that claim to own nature (can you spot the monster?). Then we sent a charming letter to Clorox: Isn't it silly for us to fight over a flower? Why don't we let the people decide who should own the daisy? Enter votedaisy.com, a microsite where we posted Clorox's cease-and-desist letter alongside a video of us explaining the situation and an invitation to vote on who should own the daisy—Method, Clorox, or Mother Earth.

Within hours of launch, votedaisy.com was picked up by the *New York Times.* Thousands of people voted, and naturally, Mother Earth won by a land-slide. And in a testament to advocate loyalty, hundreds of lawyers sent us free legal advice, assuring us that we were in the right. Suffice it to say, we never heard back from Clorox.

ERROR AUTOPSY: SHINY SUDS

For all we've talked about the scary toxins that go into most cleaning products, you'd never be able to tell if you just looked at their labels. Under U.S. law, com-panies are required to disclose ingredients for products that you digest or apply to your skin (food, beverages, and personal care products). But mum's the word

▲ **SHARE CONTROL.** To support the Household Product Labeling Act , we asked people to rethink how "dirty" their cleaning products may be.

when it comes to home-care products. On top of that, only one in every thousand chemicals in the consumer market has been tested for long-term human health effects. Yeah, this is a big problem.

At Method, we will tell you every molecule in every one of our products. That's because, unlike our competitors, we have nothing to hide. But then, in 2009 senators Al Franken and Steve Israel introduced the Household Product Labeling Act, which would require companies like ours to tell consumers what's in their products.

Spotting the perfect opportunity to mobilize our advocates and bring attention to an important issue, we sprang into action. Partnering with Droga5, we created a viral video spoofing traditional cleaning ads with a fake brand called Shiny Suds (enter the villain).

Our video opened like a traditional cleaning ad (obnoxious jingle and all). A woman watched in delight as animated bubbles went to work giving her tub that fantastic shiny look. Fade to black and the scene cuts to the next morning, when the women returns for her morning shower and is shocked to find the bubbles are still there! These "dirty" bubbles explain that they are toxic residue, left over from that "thorough" cleaning, and they go on to annoy the woman with catcalls as she tries to shower. The video ends by asking consumers if they know what is in their cleaners and showing the URL of a microsite where they can instantly shoot e-mails to their senators asking them to support the bill.

We knew the video contained content that some might consider mildly sexual, but we wanted to convey a sense of invasion so people would understand how important the issue was. We were careful to cast a confident woman, we showed less skin than a Victoria's Secret ad, and we made sure the bubbles came across as more annoying than menacing. We even shared it with both Al Franken's and Steve Israel's offices to make sure they were comfortable with the content, and we previewed it to a live audience of over a thousand people at a conference forty-eight hours before sending the video out. Live audience approval and positive press in the *New York Times* the following day made us confident that we were on the right track.

On a Wednesday morning, we e-mailed the video to our advocates and hoped our message would spread. And spread it did! Within an hour, we had thousands of views, and a few days later, over a million! In one week, it became the thirty-fourth most-often-viewed video on YouTube. It had almost a five-star rating and was picked up by hundreds of online news sites with positive reviews.

Sounds like a huge hit, so why is this an error autopsy? Well, we learned the lesson that when you cede control of the conversation, you may not like where the conversation goes. As the video neared 2 million views, we started receiving angry messages on our customer service line and blog. It turned out that some individuals' groups felt we were condoning bad behavior with our dirty little cartoon bubbles.

Our intent in this campaign was to raise awareness for transparency in cleaning product labeling, not make people feel creeped out by watching naughty bubbles. However, we understood the concerns associated with the video and removed it from YouTube and all other controlled sources. The decision came down to our values, and even though we knew our brand would never intentionally do any harm, we listened to what individuals were saying. In the end, we learned that when you create a conversation, you might not always like where it goes, but as long as you stick to your values, your advocates will stick by your side.

OUR INSPIRE-ADVOCATES MUSE: THE LADS AT INNOCENT DRINKS

Hop a plane across the pond, walk into any store selling beverages, and there on the shelf you'll find a charming little smoothie brand called Innocent—the closest thing we have to a sister company. The founders, Richard Reed, Adam Balon, and Jon Wright, share our backgrounds in advertising and science, we're the same age, and we founded our companies within a year of each other. The Monday morning huddle, the Astroturf-carpeted Ping-Pong room, the People and Environment Department—these are just a few of the many ideas we've stolen from Innocent over the years.

Innocent is also the master in treating everything as media and leveraging every touch point. From their view, the label on the bottle is serious media, representing 2 million potential views, based on the number of bottles they ship per week. Flip the bottle over and you just might be surprised to find little sentences like *Help, I'm trapped in a plastic bottle factory!* (Hmm, we might have to steal that idea too.)

Similar to Method, Innocent is driven by a purpose larger than making money. Innocent is on a mission to help people live and eat more healthily, offering drinks and food that make it easy and enjoyable to get the recommended daily allowance of fruits and vegetables. It's rare that Innocent runs any form of marketing that does not invite participation, from its former Fruitstock festivals to the more recent tactic of asking people to create its next ad. Ask anyone in the United Kingdom about Innocent, and you're likely to hear them use the word *love* while describing the brand. So much of this love comes from Innocent's ability to inspire advocates with a trustful, charming voice. Innocent speaks directly and honestly in such a lovable tone that you can't help but become an instant fan of their cause.

Their brand voice inspires us, so much so, in fact, that we stole the man responsible for that voice, Dan Germain, and brought him over as an exchange student. The idea was simple: Give us Dan for a week, and we'll send you one of our best and brightest in return.

Dan spent the week helping us improve our voice. During that week, he passed on the best marketing advice he'd ever heard: Write for one person. Talk about aiming small! The secret to a great brand voice isn't just using your own voice—it's using that voice to speak authentically, the same way you speak to your family and friends. So how are we doing? Has Dan taught us well?

▲ **THE VOICE OF INNOCENCE.** Dan Germain, the man who taught us to always write for one person to keep copy personal.

obsession

BE A GREEN GIANT

personalize sustainability to
inspire change on a grand scale

WE FOUNDED METHOD ON THE IDEA THAT business, as the largest and most powerful institution on the planet, has the greatest opportunity to create solutions to our environmental and health crises. Since the dawn of the industrial age, business has traded people's health and the state of the planet for growth and profit, but it doesn't need to be so. After having spent a number of years working on environmental issues at the Carnegie Institution, Adam grew increasingly frustrated with preaching to the converted. He was working on cutting-edge science that showed that humanity needed to change its relationship with nature, only to have that science published in obscure journals read by already concerned scientists. He was convinced that business could be a better tool for change than policy because it reached more people, every day. and (ironically) it was more democratic. But the vision was not business as we know it today. It was a vision for a fundamentally and profoundly different kind of business: business redesigned. And so we created a different type of company, one that makes a different kind of product in a different way.

Today the green movement is teetering between revolution and irrelevance. The explosion in green products, services, and marketing over the past ten years has generated a lot of confusion and mistrust, which risk undermining the environmental movement at large. The rise of "greenwashing"—unscrupulous companies making exaggerated claims about their products' environmental benefits—has driven a lot of consumer confusion about what is truly green and created a green bubble, as retailers and the media capitalize on consumer trends. This confusion is feeding the biggest threat to the green movement yet: consumer apathy.

With each new earnest headline about the green movement, consumers grow more and more inured. Scolded for buying bottled water, you buy the Nalgene water bottle, only to discover that the Nalgene bottles contain phthalates (a class of chemicals called endocrine disrupters, which accumulate in the body and mimic hormones. So you switch to the SIGG bottle, only to discover that it's lined with bisphenol-A, which—you guessed it—wreaks havoc on your hormones as well. Rather than allow consumers to make informed choices, this information overload is making them feel more helpless than ever.

Amid all the noise, most of us just want a trusted name to tell us what's what. Perhaps it should come as no surprise, then, that Americans readily accept "green" products from some of the world's largest polluters. After all, these same polluters regularly show up in media rankings as the greenest companies in America. If you look at *Newsweek*'s Green Rankings, you find an alarming cor-

▲ GREEN PRODUCTS COME ONLY FROM GREEN COMPANIES. At Method, we work to bring green to the mainstream instead of preaching to the converted.

relation between a company's score and the amount of money spent on green marketing.

That's why we believe it's important to be a "dark green" business (with deeply held environmental principles) inside a "light green" shell (with an approachable and friendly appeal). At Method, sustainability is simply part of everything we do, not a marketing position. By adhering to a philosophy of deep sustainability behind the scenes, we can focus on delivering the best darn cleaners out there, green or otherwise, and let our product experience and our brand personality delight customers rather than beat them over the head with a message about sustainability. Rather than wear our commitment to sustainability on our sleeves, we try to make it just another aspect of the quality of every Method product. So far, it's been an enduring recipe for success, one that keeps our brand identity positive and optimistic and drives us to build and innovate even as the pretender green brands slowly go the way of the dodo. Most important, this approach lets us bring green to the mainstream by making more sustainable things that people *want* to buy, instead of trying to pull the mainstream toward green by getting people to buy green products that require sacrifice.

Why the optimism in the face of all the greenwashing? The transparency of the Internet and the openness of social media tools are already exposing the differences between corporations' private and public faces, driving the focus away from what you say to what you do. We've practiced what we've preached since the beginning, so we're confident that, when it comes to being truly authentic, we have an edge over our competitors.

Sustainability is an opportunity. On an increasingly small, hot, and crowded planet, smart companies are identifying new ways to gain a competitive edge. Beyond the obvious impact to your environment, sustainability will affect your business and your career. If you're looking to launch a business, green is either going to be an asset or a liability. Unlike business trends that deal with ephemeral consumer behaviors, sustainability is about how we use resources to improve the quality of our lives and enhance the existence of our species. This new reality is one where the interests of science and business intersect, and it ain't going away. Ignoring it will cost you.

THE PARADOX OF SUSTAINABLE INNOVATION

It isn't hard to imagine a fully sustainable product—one with no negative impact on the environment or the social condition. So why doesn't one exist? The answer lies in the most crucial aspect of innovation that people usually forget: people.

In order for an innovation to be truly innovative, people have to use it. A lot of people. As green innovators, nothing is more frustrating to us than hearing about an innovative new product only a few privileged people can get their hands on. That's not innovation. That's obscurity. Which is to say, technology and creativity aren't the most important components of innovation—*adoption* is.

Consider refill stations, an innovative development in the cleaning products industry in the United Kingdom. Refill stations enable you to bring an empty spray bottle to a store, scan the bar code, and refill your bottle like a cup of soda. You get a refill without having to buy a whole new bottle and trigger, and the retailer isn't stuck shipping a bunch of plastic around the country. Seems like a no-brainer, right?

Maybe on paper, but the idea wasn't conceived with adoption in mind. How many times have you forgotten your reusable shopping bags when you make a trip to the store? Say you just got to the store and remembered you're out of cleaner. What are you going to do? Buy a new bottle. Bottom line, in a category like cleaning, which consumers want to think about as little as possible, asking them to make an extra effort is the kiss of death.

The best innovations are self-educating. Their designs make it obvious that the behavior change required will make life better. In contrast to refill stations, we've had tremendous success with our line of refill pouches because the benefit of the product and the way to use it are simultaneously clear to consumers.

The important thing about this refill pouch product is not so much its sustainability benefits. While it creates an admirable 80 percent reduction in plastic use, one could point out that a refill station does this and also saves on the transport of water. The important thing is that we have gotten a large group of people off the habit of buying a new bottle and trigger every time they run out of cleaner. That change of habit allows us to innovate again. Maybe it will allow us to develop a concentrate or refill-at-shelf format that is incrementally more sustainable and adoptable. When we do, however, we will focus our efforts on solving the convenience issues so that the format is not asking for more effort from the consumer, but rather making the product easier and more delightful to use.

The fascinating part about this phenomenon of serial innovation is that it includes and is dependent on people. It is exactly these small, intermediary steps that become the steady march toward a more sustainable future. The pundits and dilettantes will stand on the sidelines and critique the market, saying that we need more demonstrably sustainable products and we need people to realize they *must* use them. But they miss the point. Until someone wants to use something, really *wants* to, change cannot be created.

This brings us to our next topic—getting people to *want* to use your product without forcing them to sacrifice or change their habits.

GREED IS GOOD

Greed captures the essence of the evolutionary spirit.

—Gordon Gekko, in *Wall Street* (1987).

Let us be the first to say it: Gordon Gekko would have been a greenie. Why would the icon of greed be green? For the same reason so many companies all over the world are going green these days: The push toward sustainability is demonstrating a direct positive impact on the bottom line.

The unquestioned belief that green is going to cost you more money is less valid every day. Much as Gekko said of greed, the green movement in today's business ecosystem is driving a number of positive behaviors. Beyond environmental improvements, the financial argument for sustainability gets stronger every day—from innovative packaging solutions that save materials and money to efficiencies in shipping.

Moreover, green companies are learning to incorporate nascent green practices in order to create and leverage new and distinct competitive advantages. Major retailers are now recycling millions of tons of cardboard, capturing revenue where they once sustained costs in shipping waste to the landfill. Many of the world's largest distributors now move greater proportions of material via rail instead of trucks, saving fuel and labor. Best of all, they're doing it all in a way that would have made Gekko grin: by making it selfish.

Allow us to explain. In business, as in life, selfish motivations often align with philanthropic ends, inspiring dramatic independent action and social change. Of course, selfishness is the last thing most of us generally think about when we think about the green movement. Selflessness and sacrifice are more likely to come to mind. But people are tired of hearing the same environmental guilt trips. *Turn off your lights, unplug your appliances, don't drink bottled water.* Enough, already. Since when is Mother Earth such a boring old nag? She doesn't have to be, of course. Sustainability can be sexy. It can be savvy. And it works best when it's selfish. Hence "Making It Selfish" is our favorite sustainability irony—we're employing selfishness as the primary means of achieving selfless results.

When most of us think about the environmental revolution, we tend to picture long-haired crazies following leaders in hair shirts. Granted, these folks are out there. We'd be lying if we said we didn't know a few people who repurpose their bathwater, sew their own clothes, and keep their all-natural deodorant in the fridge. If it's yellow, let it mellow? Yeah, we're cool with that. But frankly, the self-righteous green leaders we know are more about status than principle— they're elitists, not egalitarians. And as the green movement has become more mainstream, many of those leaders have retreated further to the fringes instead of celebrating and encouraging the success of the movement. And no revolution can sustain itself by staying on the fringe.

We want to create a revolution driven by the armchair revolutionaries who make up the silent majority. This is the fundamental design challenge at the heart of Method, how to align selfish interests (the financial, the visceral) with selfless ones (the social and environmental). The success of the green movement won't come from attempting to convert everyone into a crazy rebel. That's why we've never understood the do-it-for-the-environment ethic—it's inherently limiting. Leading a revolution of casual environmentalists requires aligning people's deep, personal interests with their broad social and environmental concerns, making the selfish, most appealing choice the green choice.

As far as we're concerned, it doesn't matter if a consumer chooses our pouch refills because they have 80 percent less plastic or buys our hand wash because they like the pretty purple bottle. People have asked us, "Doesn't it bother you that some people buy Method and don't know it's green?" Sure, we would prefer that people know our bigger mission, but the earth can't tell the difference! By inspiring people who wouldn't otherwise choose green, we may eventually lead them to read the back of the bottle (or go to our Web site) and learn why the aesthetically appealing choice also happens to be the responsible one. And even if they don't, their purchase of a green product is still driving real change.

Making green selfish isn't just about consumers, either. No matter what your industry, green needs to be relevant and motivating to everyone else who touches your business, from your colleagues to your competitors. The key to motivating people to be green is not to try to convince them that it's the right thing to do. It's much easier and more effective to find a way to align it with their existing motivations—It'll save you money! It's good for you! It's fun to use!

Don't get us wrong. We're not green because it's on trend but because we believe it's important. Selfishness aside, the green movement is about the long-term survival of our species. Like it or not, it's the truth—which is why Being a Green Giant is our most important obsession when it comes to the world at large. It's why we started Method in the first place—to create positive change through business by inspiring a happy, healthy home revolution. Touchy-feely? Sure. Important enough to merit a place in every company's guiding principles? Without question.

That said, like many environmentally friendly companies, we've wrestled with how much we want to be labeled a green company. Being typecast as a green company alone sells short the innovative technology, leading performance, and aesthetic beauty inherent in each of our products. In fact, in the beginning, we actually hid some of our green attributes from investors and consumers because they would have assumed our products weren't as effective as others on the market. In order to overcome misperceptions, we have to appeal to the selfish desires of everyone who comes in contact with our business. Below is a guide to how we do it.

MAKING IT SELFISH . . . FOR OUR CONSUMERS

In the past, the self-interested choice has generally been the nongreen choice. Gas-guzzling SUVs. High-fat, high-carb foods. Disposable everything. If you look at humanity throughout the ages, you can see that in places where people had to choose between acting morally or acting selfishly, they generally chose the latter.

When it comes to choosing green, what's the average person most likely to do—buy something that benefits them as an individual or something that contributes to society? Come on, we all know the answer. A personal need or desire will almost always trump a collective, existential one. (Think horsepower versus emissions or leisure time versus charity work.) Don't get us wrong, there are millions of do-gooders who make the right choices on a daily basis, but there just aren't enough of them out there to save this little planet we're spinning on.

Case in point: Back in the 1980s, the argument for the organic movement went something like, "Eat organic food because pesticides are bad for the environment." Most people yawned. Years later, the argument shifted—"Eat organic food because it's bad to put pesticides in your body." This time, people took notice. Hormones and antibiotics in our milk?! Women started worrying about their children. Men started worrying about moobs (er, man boobs). The general public wasn't willing to give up cheaper milk when the environment was the only casualty, but when cheap milk threatened our personal health (or manhood), we listened. Today, it's hard to find a grocery store that doesn't offer organic milk.

The circumstances were no different in cleaning. Use an ecofriendly product because it's good for the earth? Boring. Consumers might have tried it once, but when the product was twice as expensive and half as effective as the ordinary cleaners, they gave up. After all, people don't actually see the environmental damage they're causing, so why should they sacrifice convenience and cleaning power—especially when their neighbor is already dumping bleach down the drain anyway? The impact of our purchasing decisions is abstract and easy to ignore until you shift the argument to something personal—like toxic chemicals in our homes or bodies. Then, suddenly, it becomes much more relevant and real.

With this in mind, we have changed the cleaning conversation, shifting the focus to the health of our families, our pets, and ourselves. One of our recent advertising campaigns for household cleaners talked about improving the air

---

A few years ago, we were in London doing press interviews for the launch of our toilet-bowl cleaner (yeah, it's a glamorous life). Now, the UK press has a reputation for being highly skeptical, and when Eric touted the product's nontoxic properties, one journalist challenged him. "If it's so nontoxic," she asked, "would you drink it?" Not one to back down from a challenge, Eric poured a shot and slammed it. Soon after, the head of PR in the UK and one of the journalists in the crowd joined in. Needless to say, it would be bad PR if a couple of Method employees got sick from drinking a product (not recommended), especially if a writer for a major UK newspaper did as well. Promptly upon exiting the interview, the following text exchange occurred.

Eric: Hey Adam, in London and just drank the toilet bowl cleaner. Along with Louise. And a high profile journalist. We'll be fine, right?

Adam: well, it would not have been my first choice.

Eric: thank you captain obvious. Seriously, We'll be fine right???

Adam: Yes. But next time try the bathroom cleaner. It's less minty.

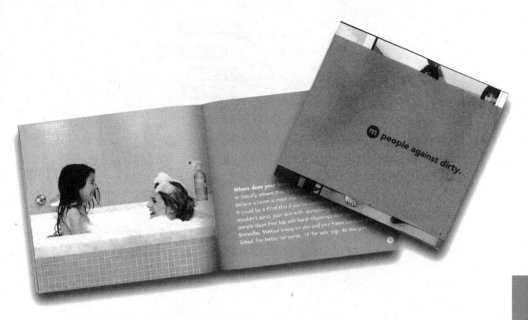

▲ WHERE DO YOU END AND WHERE DOES YOUR HOME BEGIN?
Deep down, you're nontoxic and biodegradable, and your home wants to stay that way, too.

quality inside your home instead of outside it. Our call to action to the armchair revolutionaries has been "Save yourself. Save the world." In that order. To strike a balance between being a dark green company with a light green shell, we ensure that the selfish choice for the consumer *is* the responsible choice, and we build that kind of consumer trust through a deep commitment to sustainability and providing transparency in everything we do. Besides being honest in our marketing, we've always "kept it personal," promoting the message that Method is good for your *home* environment (little *e*) first, and the Environment (big *E*) after that.

Altruistic brands trying to create change in the world must be able to make the issues relatable at a personal and intimate level. This means answering the question "What's in it for me?" People are inspired by causes that are connected to them—like the people, pets, or places they already care deeply about. If a cause feels too far removed from people's lives, it is difficult to inspire them to take action. The best way to motivate them is by tying an issue to something that they already care about at a personal level. Big issues need to be broken into human-size chunks. So while melting glaciers and drowning polar bears are too distant to inspire all but the most devoted climate defenders, the impending

PLANET

COMMUNITY

HOME

FAMILY

SELF

▲ **MAKE THE CAUSE RELEVANT
AND RELATABLE.** At Method, we try
to shift the conversation from use
method to save the environment to use
method to save your home environment.

disappearance of a favorite local beach will motivate and mobilize an entire community to action.

This more personal, intimate approach wouldn't be possible without radical transparency. Traditional corporations may shudder at the prospect of opening themselves to the world, but radical transparency is a critical means of building trust between you and your customers—or in our case, advocates. It starts with your most loyal, engaged customers—those curious enough to do their research and hold you accountable to your ideals and objectives. As your reputation and credibility gather momentum, transparency reinforces your connection with casual customers and attracts new advocates. When you're dealing with advocates like ours, who understand that true sustainability is more a goal than a reality, transparency is the best way of showing progress—and any company that is truly committed to sustainability must be committed to continually improving. So we are completely transparent about our shortcomings—discussing our failures and impacts openly with our consumers. (Have something to share? E-mail us at info@methodhome.com, or, better yet, call us sometime at 1-866-9METHOD.) We are the first to tell you what we are not doing well and where we want to improve.

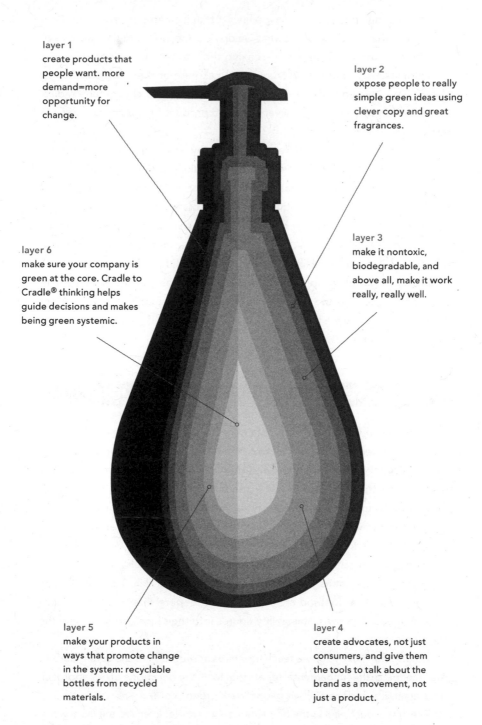

layer 1
create products that people want. more demand=more opportunity for change.

layer 2
expose people to really simple green ideas using clever copy and great fragrances.

layer 6
make sure your company is green at the core. Cradle to Cradle® thinking helps guide decisions and makes being green systemic.

layer 3
make it nontoxic, biodegradable, and above all, make it work really, really well.

layer 5
make your products in ways that promote change in the system: recyclable bottles from recycled materials.

layer 4
create advocates, not just consumers, and give them the tools to talk about the brand as a movement, not just a product.

The beautiful thing about transparency is that it creates engagement. Consumers see what we do well and what we don't do so well, and they push us to get better. In turn, we push them—coaxing them to test and adopt new ideas and formulas instead of the token green-tweak here or there. It's a symbiotic relationship between us and our advocates, driving rapid change and radical innovation. It's why the label on every Method product says DESIGNED BY AND FOR PEOPLE AGAINST DIRTY.

That close connection between the company and consumer is key for any green company. After all, what's the point of making a truly innovative green product if people are too intimidated, confused, or uninterested to use it? Back in 2000, the general belief was that green products were supposed to be ugly, smelly, and ineffective. In order to engage the consumer, we flipped the model. We asked ourselves, why can't green products be as beautiful as nature? And do you really need to smell like the earth to love it? Of course not! Adopting a spoonful-of-sugar philosophy, we introduced high design with deep sustainability, helping change the paradigm of green products. Call it eco-chic. We're not exactly sure we were the first to define the term, but if you know of anyone who coined it before us, let us know!

MAKING IT SELFISH . . . FOR OUR TEAM MEMBERS

At Method, we refer to the process of integrating sustainability into everyone's role as *greenskeeping.* It sounds like just another buzzword, but it's radically different from the way most companies treat sustainability. Most make sustainability a department. It sounds like a good idea, but if you turn sustainability into a marginal function—one that only a small group of people is responsible for—you'll get marginal results. We believe that the only way to achieve breakthrough results is to get every head in the game. At Method, sustainability is everyone's job. To achieve this, we teach it, train it, and develop it in every Person Against Dirty, just as you would any basic business skill. The people who drive this process at Method are called greenskeepers. Greenskeepers teach our team members how sustainability figures into their jobs and give them the tools to pursue it.

Among the first things we teach new hires at Method are the core beliefs of greenskeeping, the fundamental tenets that form the backbone of our approach to sustainability and the nucleus of our "dark green" core.

The first is our belief in the precautionary principle. Ever see the label warning SAFE IF USED AS DIRECTED? This is the traditional approach, focused on risk—it's "safe" to use hazardous chemicals as long as you're not exposed to too many of them. In contrast, the precautionary principle doesn't accept that level of risk. It looks at the risk of using a certain chemical or material by way of one basic equation:

$$\text{RISK} = \text{HAZARD} \times \text{EXPOSURE}$$

It doesn't take a mathematician to realize that if you keep the hazard at zero or very low, an individual's exposure can still be very high without raising the risk. In light of all the reports of the negative health effects and environmental damage caused by chemicals deemed "safe if used as directed," we believe focusing on hazard, not risk, is the only real way to design products. This approach requires assessing every single material we use for environmental quality and human safety. Yes, it's laborious. Nevertheless, over time, this approach has generated a library of safe ingredients and materials that we know produce inherently better products, and a long list of ingredients and materials that we will never use, even though most traditional cleaning companies still do.

The second core belief of greenskeeping is our belief in reincarnation—using materials that have a past, present, and future. One of the keys to sustain-

▲ **EVERYONE IS A GREENSKEEPER.** Each person is taught the ins and outs of sustainability and how to integrate it into their job.

ability is understanding the source, use, and disposal of everything we use. Traditionally, the best way to assess all of this is with something called a life-cycle assessment (LCA), a detailed analysis of every cost and impact involved in sourcing, implementing, and recycling (or disposing of) every ingredient and material. Unfortunately, LCAs are far too expensive and time-consuming to apply to every material a company uses—you could write a PhD thesis in the time it takes to do an LCA on one petroleum-based ingredient. So we've simplified the LCA process by bringing in Dr. Michael Braungart, a German design chemist and author of the seminal work about sustainable design, *Cradle to Cradle: Remaking the Way We Make Things*. Cradle to cradle is a design philosophy based on five simple tenets that guide the design and creation of anything: Use biological and technical nutrients, design closed material loops, emit water clean enough to drink, use energy from the sun, and practice social fairness.

Now, here's the most important part of the reincarnation principal: rather than keeping all that information in the lab, we pass on everything we learn from Dr. Braungart to our team members. Marketing, customer support, design, janitorial—everyone. Every team member at Method is trained to recognize that natural ingredients, for example, have a past as things that actually grow in the ground, such as plants, while petroleum-based ingredients come from a barrel of oil. They also know that truly recyclable plastic can become another bottle, while PVC will sit in a landfill and leach phthalates into our groundwater. Whether you're a scientist in a white lab coat or a marketer in all black, we have a common language that allows us to discuss and improve the health and environmental profile of everything we design. Below, a few greenskeeping techniques we teach our employees to ensure that sustainability remains a part of everyone's job:

SHINING THE LIGHT One of the hardest things to do is get people to understand the impact of their decisions, both at work and at home. For example, most people have never gone (and never will go) to a wastewater treatment plant or a recycling center, but our employees have. Is this because we like to show them a good time? No, it's because when you visit places like this, you can literally see the impact you have on the world around you. At the recycling center, it's the types of bottles (some of which you thought were recyclable) that get kicked off the conveyor belt and into the landfill pile. At the water-treatment center, it's the damage done by pouring bleach down the drain. Field trips like this give people an image they can take with them to help them make more informed decisions at their desk. Whether you're a technical, visual, or philosophical person, actually seeing your decisions in action hammers home the consequences. We all collectively own this problem, and the onus is on us to fix it.

DIGGING DEEPER (THE DIFFERENCE BETWEEN RECYCL*ABLE* AND RECYC*LED*) To the average consumer, a distinction like this may not appear to matter much, but our team members work with this kind of issue every day when sourcing materials and examining the life cycles of our products. Take the recycling center example above. Many of the so-called green cleaning brands are packaged in white PET, a plastic that has become de rigueur for green cleaning brands because white represents "cleanliness" and "naturalness." While it's the same recyclable material that water bottles are made of, once you dye it white, you've doomed it to the landfill. That's because municipal recycling centers can't distinguish white PET from other commonly recycled materials, like milk cartons (made of HDPE). The PET is sent to the milk carton recycler, who sees it as an "impurity" in his supply and throws it away. It's a cruel irony: the color most often chosen to communicate "greenness" is precisely what causes it to be less green. Method's designers know this, and we don't use white PET.

▲ **ROLE MODELS IN BOTTLES.** Method's bottles are made from 100 percent old plastic. There is so much plastic in the world, we just figured we would use that instead of making more.

GIVING THEM THE TOOLS It's not enough to simply teach people about sustainability; you have to give them tools to integrate it into their work. We provide tools for integrating sustainability into every job—analytical tools, like software to help our load planners lower the carbon footprint of our shipments, and qualitative tools, like marketing surveys to help our copywriters understand how green claims are seen by dark greenies and by outsiders. We have decision-making tools to help our packaging engineers choose the right materials and quantitative tools that our manufacturing specialists use to eliminate the use of water in making our product. Regardless of function, everyone is equipped and empowered to help make Method more sustainable.

Ultimately, nothing is more effective than putting employees in the field and doing work in the community. Fieldwork is the most immediate way to connect the work we're doing to the impacts we have on the world around us. As part of our Ecomaniacs program, each employee does several days of work in the community every year, either solo or with fellow Method employees as part of a company effort (we organize a number of annual in-house volunteer programs). This way, Method can choose to support activities that matter to us as a company, and employees can choose efforts that are important to them individually. They might work with Compass, an agency that provides housing for homeless San Franciscans (and uses Method products to make those houses cleaner and healthier) or with Root Division, which uses the imaginative power of art to educate and inspire children. Giving back to the community instills in our team members a deeper sense of purpose when they're selecting green chemicals to make a product healthier or putting the finishing touches on a design that will make our customers' lives that much safer and easier.

BROWN-BAG SERIES To keep team members' minds fresh and invigorated, we frequently bring in practitioners from other parts of the world of sustainability to tell us how they do their jobs. Though we call this the Brown-bag series (because it's always held during a BYO lunch), the speaker schedule reads like a Who's Who of the design and sustainability cognoscenti, including Tim Brown, CEO of IDEO, and renowned green architect Bill McDonough. It's an intimate interaction that fuels thoughtful work and helps make each and every Person Against Dirty a greenskeeper.

▲ **PEOPLE AGAINST DIRTY AT WORK.** We are fortunate to work alongside team members who share our passion for the environment.

It may be ironic, but laundry detergent is dirty. Traditionally consisting of roughly 80 percent water, detergent winds up causing a lot of waste and environmental harm. Not only do manufacturers have to use a lot of water to produce it, but it takes a lot of water to package it, and retailers burn a lot of fuel transporting it to their stores. Everybody loses, including the consumer, who has to lug around all those twenty-pound bottles. Bad for the environment and bad for the consumer, the laundry jug is the SUV of the consumer products industry. So we set our sights on the category soon after founding Method.

Concentrated laundry detergent wasn't exactly a new idea. Others had tried it in the United States without much commercial success, and it's the industry standard in space-constrained cultures like Japan. But when we debuted our triple-concentrated formula at Target in August 2004, something clicked. Shoppers warmed to the idea of less pollution and a smaller, lighter bottle. Competitors took note.

Here's where things got interesting. Instead of clogging up the category and slowing down innovation with a number of patents, we encouraged competitors to follow our lead. To any established company in any industry, the practice of not protecting intellectual property would seem like sheer lunacy. Of course, there's a method to the madness. It would be counter to our philosophy to hoard technologies to ourselves. We have a culture that's not afraid to say, "We made a better product, and everybody copied us, so let's go do it again!" OK, maybe that's a weird philosophy, but if we force our competitors to get greener, we are amplifying the positive impact of our business.

Just sixteen months after we launched our concentrated detergent, competitors started coming out with concentrated formulas of their own. All Small & Mighty—a 3x formula—was the first to follow. (Note: A few years later, the folks at Unilever asked to meet with us. Apparently, our 3x launch helped them get board approval to move forward with All Small & Mighty, and they were interested in working together on future category innovation.) By demonstrating the mainstream viability of concentrated detergent, we were provoking the entire industry to change for the better. At this point, most other CPG companies would be saying, "Hey, you guys stole our idea!" Not us. We were thrilled!

Soon Walmart was giving the category a closer look. After examining our business proposition during a short-lived and unsuccessful trial of our detergent, the world's biggest retailer took action. In 2007 Walmart announced that it would sell *only* concentrated detergents beginning in May 2008. (After some griping, even Tide agreed to go along with the plan—though the brand drew the line at 2x).

Walmart's press release on the decision, titled "Can Laundry Detergent Save the Planet?" looked eerily similar to some of the research we had done, noting that if the entire category went to 2x, annual savings in the United States would amount to 400 million gallons of water, 95 million pounds of plastic, and 125 million pounds of cardboard (our numbers were 400 million gallons of water, 85 million pounds of plastic, and enough fuel to run twenty-five thousand cars for a year).

Imitation? Sure, but the facts are the facts. It's just another example of Method's model, which encourages people to follow us so we can innovate again. Whether we talk about laundry, wipes, or toilet-bowl cleaner as examples of good product development or putting our sustainability principles to work, they all attempt to answer the same question: How can we use our business to

▲ **THE DIRTY LITTLE SECRET OF OVERDOSING.** Oversized and confusing caps lead most consumers to use too much detergent, which is bad for your clothes, your skin, your machines, and your planet.

create the kind of positive change that ripples throughout the industry and multiplies our positive impact?

Our goal is to stay ahead of the game. While our competitors continue to push back on ultra-concentrated detergents, in 2010 Method launched the first ever 8x concentrated detergent. Your move, Tide.

Of course, you can't always count on your competitors following your lead—especially if they've got a different kind of "green" in mind. For this next example, we recommend looking up a 2010 article in the *Wall Street Journal* by reporter Ellen Byron called "The Great American Soap Overdose." Byron examines America's addiction to laundry detergent, asking why laundry detergent doses are so confusing—why the fill lines are so hard to read and why the caps are oversized.

These are good questions. The crux of our problem with overdosing comes down to the size of the caps. The average detergent cap is more than twice the size required to wash a full load (and the "natural" brands are just as guilty as the rest). Detergent manufacturers are quick to point out that they're against overdosing and that they're constantly looking for ways to curb it. Right. Billions of dollars and a century of R&D, and you can't design a better cap? We don't buy it. This kind of "we're on your side" rhetoric is symbolic of a greater ideological battle in sustainable business today. It's a fight between those who want to *appear* green as they serve their business interests and defend the status quo against those who are willing to invest in creating better, greener solutions that will help people live more sustainably.

Detergent manufacturers argue that they've left dosing instructions vague because consumers want control, and specific dosing instructions would pin them in. We wish we could tell you we're kidding. Sure, the consumer is boss, but since when does that justify a cavernous cap that makes you *feel* as though you're using too little even when you stop at the recommended amount? If detergent manufacturers were truly concerned about the negative effects of using too much of their product, they would reduce the size of their caps to correspond to the amount needed for a heavy load. Half cap, half load—simple enough, right? That's what Method did when we launched our first laundry detergent in 2004. Boom, problem solved. Furthermore, given the huge volume of laundry detergent sold every year, right-sizing the cap would save manufacturers millions in plastic costs and create an enormous sustainability benefit. But no. The big brands keep selling oversize caps, counting on consumers to overuse the product and buy more.

Tired of the cap game altogether, we launched our 8x concentrated detergent with a pump dispenser rather than a cap. That's right, no cap at all. The

method.
sustainability initiatives

method's entire line of home care and personal care products are non-toxic, made with naturally derived, biodegradable ingredients that are tough on dirt and easy on the planet.

PRODUCTS

transparency
we believe in transparency so we disclose all our ingredients.

recycled plastic
we make recyclable bottles from 100% recycled plastic resulting in zero waste and a 70% lower carbon footprint.

Cradle to Cradle®
we are proud to offer the first range of certified Cradle to Cradle® cleaning products.

ingredient safety
we're recognized by EPA's Design for the Environment (DfE) program for the ingredient safety of over 50 products.

EPEA-assessed
we have all of our materials assessed by the EPEA for health and environmental safety.

PROCESS

biodiesel fleet
the majority of our customer shipments in california and the northeast are via biodiesel truck.

reduction incentives
we offer incentives to suppliers to reduce carbon emissions and ultimately lower our impact.

greensourcing program
we have a supplier sustainability program that drives green innovation.

fuel efficiency
our domestic shipments are done with an EPA SmartWay Transport member freight company for better fuel efficiency.

COMPANY

climate-sensitive
as a climate-sensitive business, we offset the carbon emissions from our manufacturing, travel and office use.

B corporation
we are a founding B Corporation business and use the power of purpose-driven private enterprise to create social and environmental change.

Cradle to Cradle®
we are a Cradle to Cradle® business recognized for our environmental product design and green business leadership.

never tested on animals
we were PETA's 2006 company of the year and are certified cruelty-free for our no-animal testing policy.

LEED-certified
our san francisco HQ is a LEED-certified green building.

great cleaning comes naturally to us. find out more at **methodhome.com** innovation turns a cumbersome, messy, two-handed process into a simple, one-handed squirt. It still gives the consumer control, and it drastically reduces both the incidence and magnitude of overdosing. If you want to use a little more, that's up to you—but an extra squirt is 16 percent more, not double or triple what you need!

The reason for this is simple math. Method recently conducted a study that concluded that 53 percent of detergent consumers "eyeball it" or use a full cap, which is about double the recommended dose. This is the dirty little secret of the laundry business, and every manufacturer knows it. If half of all consumers use double what they need, then 33 percent of all laundry detergent purchased in America is unnecessary waste. Millions and millions of pounds of excess soap down the drain. Bad for the environment, but good for big brands' shareholders. Consider that more than $3 billion of laundry detergent is sold each year in America. If a third of that is pure waste, it's safe to assume that detergent manufacturers make about $1 billion a year on consumers overusing laundry detergent. It's clearly not that the technology to make caps less wasteful and easier to use has eluded detergent manufacturers all these years—they have a billion little reasons not to look for it in the first place.

At this point, you might be saying to yourself, *Isn't it just laundry detergent? Is it really that big a deal?* Well, don't listen to us. Follow the water. Consider that 1,100 loads of laundry are started every second in America. That means approximately 100 million pounds of laundry detergent go down the drain and into our waterways every year. Still not impressed? Take a field trip to your local water treatment plant and ask an engineer what all that soap is doing to your local ecosystem (not to mention your drinking water). Design has the power to change our world for the better, but only if we use it for good. Sometimes that's as simple as redesigning the cap. It boils down to linking the average consumer's interest in "control" and "mess-free" detergent with the social and environmental interest of limiting overdosing—in effect, aligning selfishness with selflessness.

MAKING IT SELFISH . . . FOR OUR STAKEHOLDERS

When it comes to shareholders and sustainability, most companies prefer to contribute to green charities rather than make substantive changes in areas like production and shipping. After all, shareholders are generally looking for efficiencies, not sustainable practices. Throw in a bit of charity and everyone feels better. It doesn't have to be this way. You can inspire your stakeholders to *want* greener practices—and you can even give up the charity in the process. At least, that's how we work.

Few companies devote as many resources to causes as we do, but unlike those businesses that devote a preset percentage of profits to green charities, we push almost everything back into the business and share our people instead. In doing this, we're acting with Gandhi's words in mind—"Be the change you want to see in the world." The change we want to see is not companies giving away their profits, but businesses truly creating good, so that, as they grow, so too does their positive impact on the world. We want to see businesses in which all employees are engaged meaningfully in causes that matter to them and relate to the role that business plays in making the world greener and safer.

Take Patagonia, a pioneer in sustainable business. Its founder, Yvon Chouinard, is a true hero for entrepreneurs like us—someone who's been able to build a business that truly aligns social and environmental interest with the bottom line. If we could do half of what it does to produce positive environmental impact, we'd be doing well. But we have a difference of opinion in our model. Patagonia practices what we call the steal-and-donate model, wherein a large portion of profits are taken from the business and given to nonprofits. It's a worthy pursuit, but we don't like the inherent assumption that business is bad, and so investments are better made elsewhere. If the intention of a business is to create positive benefit and it's truly committed to progress, we think it's better to invest the profits back into growing and innovating, and use the *people* in that business to invest in the community through time and participation. To limit our growth is to limit our impact.

We try to align our deep green values with the interests of our shareholders and our company as a whole. One of the ways we've done this is by being recognized as a B corporation (or benefit corporation), something of a gold star in the green industry. The B corporation is a new corporate form that attempts to generate profits while advancing and maintaining social and environmental benefits. B corporations may seek to address climate change, health problems, or poverty, but they do so by being both profitable and competitive. B Lab, the organization that certifies all B corporations, audits and certifies the environmental and social practices of a company and publishes them online in a completely transparent way, providing a real-time, public sustainability report for each B corporation. Beyond real-time sustainability and corporate responsibility reporting, Method has actually changed its Articles of Incorporation to expand the fiduciary duty of the officers of the company to include social and environmental stakeholders. It's not simply "triple bottom line"; it binds us legally to the ethics we espouse, assuring shareholders that the environment and social conditions are considered in every decision we make.

In addition to our B corporation distinction, Method was one of the first companies to be recognized as a cradle-to-cradle company. The theory behind the cradle-to-cradle idea, mentioned earlier in this chapter, is pretty simple. We all know that we can't consume resources infinitely on a finite planet. Too many people creating too much waste, right? Cradle-to-cradle designers begin with the assumption that our problem is not necessarily that there are too many of us or that we consume too much (which in some cases may also be true), but that what we consume is not designed properly.

Cradle-to-cradle designers assert that it's OK to use highly technical materials—after all, they're products of human ingenuity and creativity—as long as we keep them in closed-loop "technical cycles" so those materials are recycled infinitely over and over again. Natural materials should likewise be cycled through a closed-loop biological cycle. Any material that gets introduced to the biological cycle—like the detergent that goes down the drain or the spray cleaner that drifts into the air—should be designed to be compatible with, or better yet, degradable in the natural environment.

What's so inspiring and so important about cradle-to-cradle methodology is that it calls for a positive vision for a future in which people can enjoy an enhanced quality of life *and* environmental and social sustainability. It reconciles the long-standing trade-off between being green and living with abundance and joy. Cradle to cradle is about redesigning the stuff that we consume so that it's good. If you do that, then making and using wonderful things that make us happy becomes a good thing, not something we need to feel guilty about. This is a philosophy we apply to every Method product and to the business itself—something all of us, including our shareholders, are proud of.

MAKING IT SELFISH . . . FOR OUR VENDORS AND PARTNERS

When you're competing with billion-dollar brands, you've got to get creative. Because Method doesn't have the promise of a lot of volume for leverage, we can't appeal to our vendors based on the size of our business alone. To do so, we often employ a guinea pig strategy, wherein we will be the first to take a new technology to market, developing it with a partner, but then we *don't* hold it exclusively for ourselves. Instead, we let that vendor develop it in order to attract other business, even from our competitors. This tactic allows us to get to market more quickly, and it allows that vendor to gain new business by building capability in a new area. It aligns our interest in gaining access to new technologies with the vendor's interest in business development. As a result, Method becomes a lightning rod for new ideas and technology. And as long as we can continue to be the fastest, we maintain our competitive advantage.

If the fastest path to sustainability in the supply chain is aligning your interests with those of your vendors, then it's critical not only to understand your own business, but theirs, as well. That's why making it selfish for your vendors can't happen without what we call blue-collar sustainability.

Building true sustainability into a business is a blue-collar job. While the slick press releases and shiny solar panels might catch people's attention, creating real environmental wins and healthier products is a roll-your-sleeves-up, knock-down, drag-out kind of job.

That's because sustainable product design is about redesigning, dematerializing, digging, and never taking "It can't be done" as an answer. This can't be done without understanding where something comes from and where it goes, something that requires considerable time at the source and the dump. At Method, we pride ourselves on fighting the good fight where it matters, on the front lines—in the factories and fields and recycling centers. We often find that the biggest sustainability wins come from the most unexpected places.

When you innovate with green materials, you often encounter barriers you didn't know existed. This was the case when, after years of work to develop a postconsumer recycled (PCR) plastic that was clear enough to meet Method standards, we tried to start making it into bottles. How would we ensure that our special, proprietary PCR resin never got mixed up with ordinary virgin resin? The only solution was to build our own resin silo (think silo on a farm) to house it. So down to Kentucky we went to visit the bottle plant.

Ultimately, being able to make bottles out of 100 percent PCR resin meant using a crane to install a silo upright outside the bottle factory, installing the pipes and hoses to get the raw material into the building, and writing detailed quality-assurance specifications to make sure it was being processed correctly. It meant tracking the transport specifications to make sure the proper equipment would be on hand to load the silo. It wasn't glamorous work, but it was necessary work. And now the bottles we make have a drastically lower carbon footprint—60 percent lower, in fact—due to that work done on the front lines. Meanwhile our vendor has become the world leader in high-quality, 100 percent recycled packaging.

Similar challenges have revealed themselves with every earnest effort we've made to green our business or our products. Converting our trucks to biodiesel meant negotiating warranties with truck manufacturers who wanted to void them because we were going to run them on waste vegetable oil. Getting our distribution center running on solar energy required bolting the panels to decommissioned truck trailers and running weatherized wiring into the building from the outside. Reducing our energy use had us installing insulation around our mixing tanks.

Rolling up your sleeves is the only real way to create more sustainable product. Poking around in garbage cans, factories, and fields is the only way to truly understand a product's impact and to overcome the abstraction that makes designing sustainability from the ivory tower so easy but so misguided.

We also make it selfish for our retailers. Through ten years of practice, Method has gained much knowledge of what works and what doesn't in trying to build sustainability into business. Retailers are often looking for ways to go green, but most have been around for a while and have certain ways of doing things. That's where a more consultative approach to working with customers (rather than just a sales approach) pays dividends. By working with, understanding, and truly helping retailers to capitalize on the changing category trends and consumer sentiments, we are able to establish a deeper relationship. At Target, for example, our business relationship now includes interfaces with the sus-

▲ **BIODIESEL IS HOW WE ROLL.** The majority of our products are delivered with veggie oil instead of dirty fossil fuels.

tainability team, the marketing teams, the consumer insights people, and the supply chain, in addition to the traditional buyer relationship. By providing insights and working collaboratively with multiple functions within Target, ideas cross-pollinate and get built upon, which builds shared ownership. As a result, ideas have a greater chance of seeing the light of day, and Method's strategic value is elevated. In becoming a resource for our retailers, we connect ourselves with them in both profit and purpose. It might be uncommon to have a greenskeeper at a sales call, but the next time a competitor comes, check in hand, to buy your shelf space away, that retailer will remember the invaluable knowledge you bring.

A MODEL FOR CHANGE: PERFECT AS THE ENEMY OF GOOD

A lot of companies talk about "the pursuit of perfection," but our mantra is "Be the best at getting better." The reasoning here is simple: If you're hung up on releasing the perfect product or message, you'll spend too much time perfecting behind the scenes and not enough time advancing in the market. Nowhere has this been truer than in our push toward sustainable formulas and packaging. We've learned that you can't force the perfect design solution. It doesn't happen. You have to employ a series of imperfect solutions and then be the best at getting better.

Imperfect solutions? The big brands hate ideas like this, but it's exactly how we've been able to out-innovate our competitors. Take our refill pouches. Years ago, we sold refill containers of soap in large recyclable bottles. Problem was, while they were recyclable and used less plastic than another starter unit, they still used a lot of plastic—much of which ends up in landfills. Instead of banging our heads against the wall in search of a perfect solution, our employees created a refill pouch, made from just 16 percent as much plastic as the bottle. Because of its multilayer design, the pouch can't be recycled (yet), but the net effect is less plastic in landfills. It wasn't a popular move with our dark green advocates at first, but when they did the math, they understood that it was a lot better for the environment, and they got on board. Although imperfect, this format now gives us leverage to motivate our vendors to crack the code on how to make it recyclable. And in the meantime we partnered with Teracycle so that the pouches can be upcycled into new products such as killer looking bags.

We think too many people and companies are obsessed with claiming perfection. Sustainable this, green that—it's all a little hard to believe. Method's not

▲ PROGRESS, NOT PERFECTION.
While this refill is not the perfect solution,
it puts us on the path to reach perfection.
(Psst: and now we take them back and
recycle them into bags.)

a sustainable business; no business is truly 100 percent sustainable . . . yet. But we realize that our company, like each of us as individuals, is a work in progress. We must be the change we seek, so we put the onus on ourselves to make healthier, happier homes. As a business, we want to be sustainable, but our goal is not just sustainability. As our friend Michael Braungart says about marriage, who wants the relationship with one's spouse to be merely sustainable? Nobody! We all want rich and fulfilling relationships that add value and meaning to our lives. You get out what you put in, and we feel the same way about business. Sustainability in the green movement is the same—good enough for now but just the beginning of something much better.

After all, it's why we're in business: to change business. We started Method with a deep desire to create change for the better. Good policy alone is not enough—Adam learned as much working on the Kyoto Protocol, which was undermined by the interests of traditional business. Time for a one-eighty. Time to use business as a positive force, as an agent of positive change. But to do so, business itself must be redesigned. This doesn't have to be painful; we believe inspiration is a better tool for change than shame. And the best way to inspire people is with super-cool products that present simple solutions.

Method is a solution, but it's only one solution. We need others, but for now, we will do our part to provide solutions to those who want to live cleanly, greenly, and most important, pleasurably and optimistically. Traditional environmentalism chastises the very people it wants to change. Doom and gloom, shame and blame. It's been around for thirty years, and no wonder it doesn't work. Don't get us wrong: Environmentally speaking, things are bad—really bad. And we've got to do something about it *now*. But we have two choices: Sit around and analyze the problem and debate its minutiae, arguing that this is better than that, or get off our collective asses and *do something* about it. We've chosen the latter.

That's why it's progress, not perfection, that drives us. If the perfect solution to our environmental crises was evident, we would have found it by now. The challenge, and our opportunity, is to make change in an imperfect and resistive environment and move toward better solutions.

With respect to sustainability, we don't ask, Are we there yet? We know that the answer to that question is no, and it will be for a while. Instead, we ask, Are we as close as we can be? What can we do to be closer? We think those are more powerful questions, because they compel us to act, to make change, to do something. As T. S. Eliot wrote, "Between the motion / And the act / Falls the Shadow." Rhetoric doesn't create solutions; action does.

ERROR AUTOPSY: WIPEOUT

The idea of launching wipes never sat well with us. Like its cousin, the paper towel, the wipe is a convenient form of everyday domestic life, but in exchange for saving seconds in the kitchen, they spend lifetimes in a landfill. Unfortunately, this product form is not going away anytime soon, so we figured that if consumers are going to insist on using wipes, let's at least give them a better one. When first launched, our cleaning wipes were in a plastic hourglass-shaped canister. All the parts were recyclable, but there was a big footprint because of all the material in the packaging. With natural, compostable cloths and a biodegradable cleaning formula, they were better for the environment than the mainstream alternative. So we set out to make them even better for the environment. Or so we thought. Our solution was to replace the canister with a flat pack, like that in which baby wipes are normally packaged.

Care to guess which one's greener? Technically, it's the flatpak. The benefits of using a lot less packaging far outweigh the benefits of using recycled plastic.

ORIGINAL HOURGLASS CONTAINER

vs.

NEW FLATPAK CONTAINER

PAST	**PAST**
👍 postconsumer recycled resin	👎 can't employ recycled plastic
PRESENT	**PRESENT**
👎 lots of plastic	👍 one-eighth as much material
FUTURE	**FUTURE**
👍 easily and commonly recycled	👎 not commonly recycled because it's multilayered

But you have to bring people along with you . . . and this time we didn't. Some customers were confused about how the flatpak was supposed to work. Others just liked the hourglass container more. Many overlooked the new version altogether, searching for the hourglass container. The result: flatpaks flatlined, and our sales plummeted.

Because of lessons like this, we don't decide what materials to use based only on what makes the most positive impact initially; we look at the qualitative layer too. How cool is it? Will people buy it? Will it tell a story? Every change is a judgment call. There's an inextricable link between the benefit from a scientific standpoint and the benefit from an emotional standpoint. Say a decision might improve our environmental impact by ten "points," but the consumer will think it's really lame, or worse yet won't buy it at all. Then we're considering another decision that's not quite as green—say it improves our footprint by eight points—but it's really intuitive and engaging and makes adopting that innovation more simple or fun. Just as in the European refilling stations versus refills example described earlier, we're going to pick the eight, because our goal is not ten, it's ten thousand. Our goal is not to have an incrementally better product that never sees the light of day. Our goal is to move an entire industry to a more sustainable place, and that takes more than one step. There is no point in making a greener product if nobody uses it.

One small change sparks exponential growth. Be committed to the next innovation, not the current one.

OUR GREEN GIANT MUSE: GARY HIRSHBERG, STONYFIELD FARM

If we're Jedi, Gary Hirshberg is our Yoda. And if you're a yogurt fan, then you're probably a lover of Stonyfield Farm. Gary has been at the forefront of transformational environmental and social movements for thirty years. From his early days as an educator and activist to his current position as president and CE-Yo of Stonyfield Farm, the world's largest organic yogurt company, Hirshberg's positive outlook has inspired countless followers to help make the world around them better. Arguably, no one else can take more credit for bringing organic to the masses than Gary.

So what have we stolen from Gary? Two things. First, the belief that you can blend purpose and profits. Gary has consistently reinforced our confidence that doing good in the world and being good at business aren't mutually exclusive. One of his company's five missions is "to serve as a model that environmentally and socially responsible businesses can also be profitable," and Gary realizes this vision in every aspect of his company. He is one of the masters and legends of infusing mission and purpose into the heart and soul of business. While staying true to a very serious mission, he has proved that the best way to introduce the masses to organic choices is through a fun and engaging brand (and a lot of yummy flavors, naturally).

To Gary, blending purpose and profits doesn't mean compromising one or the other. With each consumer he convinces to switch to organic (growing his

▲ **OUR GREEN GIANT MUSE.**
Gary Hirschberg is the master of
blending purpose and profits without
compromising one or the other.

business), he benefits the planet and human health (advancing his mission). It hasn't been easy, though. Gary made some tough decisions to get where he is—perhaps most famously the choice to sell in Walmart, which ruffled a lot of feathers in the organic industry. But as he'll tell you, if you want to catch a fish, you need to fish where the fish are. Meanwhile, taking organic big has had a ripple effect, pushing other large companies, like Kraft, to expand their organic offerings (much as we've been pushing companies like P&G to remove petrochemicals from their products). As Gary puts it, "The only way to influence the powerful forces in this industry is to become a powerful force."

The second thing we've stolen from Gary is his mentorship style. Gary took the time to meet with us during the early years—an enormous act of generosity, considering his busy schedule and the fact that we were just two kids starting a soap company. As we soon learned, that's just Gary—he has always been committed to mentoring younger, socially minded entrepreneurs by helping them navigate the early years of birthing a business. And we've learned something profound from that example: You can make a far greater impact on the world by inspiring like-minded entrepreneurs than by simply growing your own business. In fact, Gary's efforts to help the next generation of business leaders were a big part of why we wrote this book. Thanks, Gary!

obsession

4

KICK ASS
AT FAST

if you're not the biggest,
you'd better be the fastest

It's not the big that eat the small, it's the fast that eat the slow.

—**Jason Jennings and Laurence Haughton**

THANKS TO THE BLINDING PACE OF MODERN TECH-
nology and real-time data, we live and work in an anything, anywhere, anytime media-driven market. A flatscreen in every room, a smartphone in
every pocket, and ever-shrinking microchips anywhere we can fit them. Amid the
media mania, it's easy to forget that the rise in rapid technology is just a symp-
tom of something deeper: our society's insatiable demand for speed.

Take a (quick) look around. Soaring consumer demand for the latest and
greatest innovations and gadgets; aggressive retailing strategies devised to
move the largest volumes of product at the lowest margins possible; impatient
investors infatuated with quarterly returns, month-over-month sales reports,
and up-to-the-second statistical analyses—our blind need for speed has become a driving force in every segment of the economy. And no wonder! No matter if you're buying, selling, or investing, in today's marketplace, he who is fastest
is often first.

But while speed is great for the fast-paced consumer, it's a blessing and a
curse for business. Whereas past business leaders had no choice but to take a
wait-and-see approach upon implementing any important decision, modern
entrepreneurs can launch today and collapse tomorrow. Success and failure

come quickly. Commitment is fleeting. Multi-million-dollar network television shows are canceled after a single episode with bad ratings. National political campaigns implode after one insensitive sound bite goes viral and leads to a bad week in the polls. But the same is true for companies like ours that rely on brand and consumer approval to last. In a world where consumers are bombarded by thousands of products per second, brand loyalty is a fleeting thing.

The overwhelming demand for what we want right now has become a self-propagating trend. Products are updated, relaunched, and rebranded even when there is no substantive change—all in an effort to capture consumers' attention and remain relevant. Electronics companies engineer smartphones and computers that boast the most recent technology but will be outdated in a matter of months. Sports fans can buy limited-edition bags of potato chips emblazoned with images of league champions within days of the Super Bowl or World Series. All this planned obsolescence not only makes it increasingly difficult to stay ahead; it also generates a massive waste problem. E-waste from the ubiquitous growth of computers, phones, and electronics accounts for 50 million tons of trash each year, the equivalent of a hundred thousand fully loaded 747s.

Even the notoriously slow-to-evolve publishing industry has been picking up the pace. Downloading books with the touch of a button, one in ten Americans now curl up with a Kindle, Nook, or Sony e-reader rather than a printed book. And the medium isn't the only thing evolving, either. The consumer's demand for speed is spurring popular brand-name authors, like James Patterson (*Along Came a Spider*) and Jack Canfield (*Chicken Soup for the Soul*), to crank out ten or twenty new books every year (with a good deal of help from their coauthors). Anywhere you look in today's consumer market, consumers reward brands in a hurry.

Famous for moving large volumes of product at low prices, or "stacking it high and watching it fly," the retail industry understands the breakneck pace of modern commerce as well as any. Good retail is fast by nature, but the pace at which new products come and go in today's marketplace is unprecedented. By now, most of us have probably suffered the experience of discovering that our favorite flavor, scent, or style of any given product—or sometimes the product itself—has been discontinued. Fewer than one in seven new products in the average grocery store gains enough traction to survive its first year. This kind of pressure to succeed not only stifles new product development, but also forces brands and retailers alike down a one-way path toward diminishing returns by way of smaller and smaller margins on larger and larger volumes of goods.

Consumers and retailers aren't the only ones hooked on speed. Impatient investors analyze Wall Street's every last twitch down to fractions of a cent with split-second accuracy. The impact on commerce is clear: companies in every industry are under pressure to grow faster and create disruptive growth in less time. But when everyone's fast, it's no longer enough to be just fast. Fast is not an exceptional quality; it's par for the course. And when you're small, being faster than your competitors is your biggest—and sometimes only—advantage.

Ever since we founded Method, we've used speed to trump size. What choice did we have? Unilever, P&G—some of the first multinationals in the world—were soap companies, and it took them over a century to grow to the size they are today. Rather than invite competition, they've learned they're powerful enough to define the rules of the game to their advantage, designing a game of scale that few are able to play. Our competitors invest heavily in keeping upstarts like us from joining the party in the first place. (Don't believe us? Try to get an inch of shelf space at a national grocery chain—a process we'll discuss more in the next chapter.) Even when we reached $100 million in revenue, we were still more than five hundred times smaller than the leaders of our industry. Racing innovations to market and taking on added risks are the only ways a smaller company like ours can stay ahead of leading consumer trends and outpace slower-moving industry giants. Our strategy is "running between the legs of Goliath." We may be small and squirrelly, but we're quick on our feet!

We know most entrepreneurs understand how important it is to be fast; we want to change the world (or at least make a buck) in a hurry, and we realize that if we dillydally, someone else will beat us to it. Every entrepreneur we know has

---

SLOW REVOLUTION

In a world that is moving too fast, it's no surprise to see the gradual introduction of *slow* as a winning strategy. In the words of George Jetson, "Jane! Get me off this crazy thing!"

In 1986 Carlo Petrini launched the slow-food movement, advocating local food prepared with care and savored without haste. Today, his organization claims a hundred thousand members in 132 countries.

In 2010 in an effort to recapture the coffeehouse experience it was founded on, Starbucks directed its baristas to make no more than two drinks at a time. Customers said the process had begun to feel like being on a conveyer belt.

---

that same impatient itch to create, build, and expand. Speed is a deep-seated part of our DNA—so much so that, if you're like us, you shudder at phrases like "slow build." (Ugh.)

That's why, from day one, we were committed to making Method go as fast as we could. We were paranoid—convinced that, while our style-and-substance approach was unique, if it were successful, it could be copied, and the only thing that could keep us ahead was getting better at being faster in order to outrun our bigger competitors. So while some businesses stick to organic growth—gradually expanding as sales allow—we decided to pursue outside capital and get off the ground as quickly as possible. We wanted to go big or go home.

In the months after launch, we constantly updated our PowerPoint presentations to show any and all top-line growth, including every metric we could think of to encourage our investors to keep their faith alive. To no one's surprise, skeptical retail partners paid a lot more attention to us once we could demonstrate quick growth. (Nothing beats kicking off a pitch meeting with a hockey-stick sales chart that promises fast-growing sales.) Demonstrating 300 percent growth in less than a quarter by aggressively driving distribution and expanding our product line not only gave us credibility, it also created an aura of excite-

▲ SMALL + SPEED = SUCCESS. SMALL + SLOW = ROADKILL.
Thanks to Method alumnus Tom Fishburne for the cartoon!

ment. Retailers weren't the only ones calling us back. Investors, job seekers, journalists—our rapid growth made everything easier, from establishing new relationships with manufacturers to hiring eager new employees. Of course, growth is like an addictive drug: After each new high, it takes more and more to keep you flying. But as we quickly learned, rapid growth has a way of hiding your problems.

No matter what industry you are in or what kinds of customers you serve, you're constantly told that speed is the surest way to win. And it's true—at least in the short-term. In fact this obsession was originally just called "speed." Over time, however, we discovered that truly "kicking ass at fast" (as opposed to simply being fast at growing) required a balance of long-term vision and short-term agility. Easier said than done.

BALANCING ACTS

In a business environment increasingly defined by short-term goals, quick fixes, and overnight success stories, winning in the short term can appear to be all that matters. But being the fastest and the first can cut both ways. While the benefits of speed are sweet, the consequences when it goes awry are sobering and significant. Speed causes mistakes—and at high speed, even the tiniest mistake can have catastrophic consequences. Rushed research can be sloppy, incomplete, or misinterpreted. Hurried testing overlooks errors and missteps. Careless launches let down your partners, retailers, and customers. It took us a long time and a lot of mistakes to understand this.

In the beginning, being fast—fast to prototype, fast to test, fast to market— was key to our survival; we had to prove we were here to stay. But we've learned over the years that speed doesn't always translate directly into success. Without wisdom, speed is recklessness.

In business, we tend to think about *fast* in terms of all the old clichés. Fast talk, fast food, fast living—in the wrong context, *fast* has a bad reputation. To be sure, this kind of fast has its place. We've sprinted through our share of corporate objectives, aiming for short-term sales over substance. But an obsession with this kind of fast won't get the best results. It'll get you an ulcer. Hence, of the seven obsessions in this book, none is as prone to misinterpretation as kicking ass at fast. That's why we've devoted much of this chapter to distinguishing the right kind of fast (and avoiding speed for speed's sake).

To say we had a tendency to grow too fast too early is something of an understatement. We sped, we raced, and we overreached. Now, it wouldn't be accurate to say we were reckless; we were just fighting gravity. The realities of getting a start-up off the ground demand explosive growth and strong momentum to build support. It takes three times as much energy to get something moving as it does to maintain momentum. In fact, as near as we can tell, there is no such thing as growing too fast when you're a brand-new company. But four years in, when we started exploring new areas solely because of the growth opportunities available to us . . . that was our biggest mistake. We started moving into new product categories simply because we could.

The best example of this was in 2003, when Walmart expressed interest in selling our hand wash but told us the concept would be more interesting if we also had body wash. We were hearing the same desire from other retailers, who were excited about the success of our new hand wash and therefore eager to see us launch companion products.

Building a business is like building a house—you must have a good foundation. And when we laid the foundation for Method, we never intended to build a body-care addition. Working with the world's largest retailers to create a body wash was our first major leap away from home care (a category we'd grown to know well). It was like adding a room on the third story of your house . . . without anything beneath it. We let the business guide the brand, instead of letting the brand guide the business. While the economics were really attractive, a Method body wash product didn't make sense strategically.

But we did it anyway, and it backfired for several reasons. We rushed the product to market and spread our marketing dollars too thin to properly support it—but these were merely tactical errors. One of the strategic keys to our success up until then had been taking a personal-care approach to home care, which was disruptive. But with body wash, we were taking a personal-care approach to personal care. It lacked any disruptive point of view! More important, we were simply pursuing a business opportunity, a deviation from our tried-and-true method of exploiting a cultural shift.

Right about the time we were getting distracted with body wash, we also launched Vroom—a parallel brand devoted to car-care goods. This time, it was Target that felt there was an opportunity for our brand—and we agreed, though we believed auto-care products would be better suited to a new brand, hence

▲ **SPEED KILLS.** You will overreach at some point but do your best to resist the urge. More companies die by growing too quickly than too slowly.

Vroom. Never heard of it? Probably because we sold it shortly after launch. After these and a number of similar mistakes, we realized that in our rush to be the fastest, we were often slowing ourselves down. We were spending more time correcting minor quality problems (leaky bottles, faulty pumps) and major screw-ups than we were making our core products better.

And therein lies the problem: Inherently, speed comes with a lot of risks—more, in fact, than any of our other obsessions. Yet the rewards of moving quickly usually go hand in hand with the dangers, and shorter development cycles allow for more opportunities. In the early stages of launching a business, speed is your friend, but mishandled, it can become a liability. One of our biggest lessons over the last ten years has been figuring out when to step on the gas and when to hit the brakes. Learning to go fast is one thing, but learning to *kick ass* at high speed takes experience and maturity. So how do you walk that balance between long-term thinking and short-term innovation and speed? It's a question that strikes the heart of this obsession.

DEVELOPING AGILITY

It is not the strongest of the species that survives, nor the most intelligent, but the one most responsive to change.

— **Charles Darwin**

Inspiration may come quickly, but innovation takes time. Some ideas take off fast, spreading through the world like wildfire. But the most successful ideas are those with real depth and relevance—ones with staying power. You can see this distinction in the music industry all the time. Shallow pop songs catch fire fast ("Ice, Ice, Baby!") and die just as quickly. Sometimes not fast enough. Meanwhile, the artists with soul and resonance—Eric Clapton, the Rolling Stones, Aretha Franklin—may initially take longer to catch on, but they're the ones who find their way into our hearts year after year. For Method, our challenge is to find that balance between a long-term vision with depth and catchy, short-term appeal. It's the difference between having a foundation and being a fad.

Naturally, speed cuts both ways, and as we've grown, we've had to be careful about moving too slowly. Enter agility—a skill that allows you to speed up or slow down when you need to. First, you must know if the clock is on your side. Can you afford to hold off on an opportunity like body wash or Vroom—or do you need to act immediately? A simple way we think about this now is by asking ourselves, "What is more likely to hurt the business: going too slow or going too fast?" This is where having an established point of view is absolutely essential. You want to have an unwavering vision, but incredible flexibility in how you bring it to life. To put it another way, you want to stay true to the destination but be open as to how you get there.

Good branding, for example, takes patience. Sticking to your point of view is essential. Innovation, on the other hand, is about using the brand as a lens to seek out new opportunities. Take a look at two recent success stories in the retail clothing industry, J. Crew and H&M. Over the past few years, J. Crew has revived its brand by resurrecting a clear brand point of view that's highly curated and refined. Fast and innovative? Not really. We all know what next year's J. Crew catalog is going to look like. Established and timeless, the brand has found a consistent recipe for style and success. In contrast, Sweden-based H&M has made its name on fast fashion—bringing the latest, up-to-the minute trends from the pages of *US Weekly* to a store near you in a matter of days or weeks. Speed is its biggest advantage. Unlike J. Crew, H&M innovates so quickly that there is no such thing as an H&M look. H&M is not a brand you wear; it's a brand you shop.

Somewhere between the timeless style of the J. Crew brand and the trend-forward appeal of a leading innovator like H&M is the sweet spot we call agility. For us, agility comes down to recognizing when to pursue an opportunity like partnering with Karim Rashid and when to pass up an opportunity like Vroom. In retrospect, our most agile decisions have been based on equal parts artistic vision (patience) and operational excellence (speed). Striking this balance is not as hard as it sounds, and it's the difference between agility and recklessness. At Method, we've discovered all sorts of new ways to leverage our smaller size and speed in every department to make agile decisions every day and kick ass at fast.

A HEAD WITHOUT A BODY Try as you might, you won't achieve fast results by pushing employees to move faster, cramming your existing business processes into shorter timelines, or rushing your suppliers to meet impossible deadlines. Genuinely speeding up an organization requires fundamentally reshaping how it operates, inside and out. That's why we've built speed into every level of our organization, rethinking every role, process, and department.

One of the best ways we've been able to do this is by insourcing creativity and R&D innovation and outsourcing production. That is to say, we do our own intellectual property work, from graphic design to formulation, and we farm out the direct labor of logistics and manufacturing. We believe creativity should always happen on the inside. It is the soul of your brand—the ideas, designs, formulas, and technologies that give the brand its *specialness.* Those functions that we consider strategic, like buying the highest quality materials, we do in house. For those things that we don't need to do any better than our competitors—say, how efficiently we get our products to stores—we partner with the experts. We're not wasting valuable time and resources in areas where we can't leverage much of a competitive advantage. We're like a head without a body. Building the business on this model is one of the keys to our agility, because we can spend time focusing on the things we're good at while working with people who are great at the things we're clueless about.

The obvious argument for keeping creative work in-house rather than handing it over to outside specialists comes back to authenticity. When your market-

▲ **DON'T OUTSOURCE YOUR SOUL.** One of our green chefs cooking up the next great thing in the office laboratory.

ing team sits at a desk between the industrial design specialists (developing new prototypes) and your customer-care employees (fielding advocates' calls and e-mails), it's inevitable that the branding, labels, and advertising copy they write will come from a genuine place, gelling over time to produce a more consistent and pitch-perfect representation of the brand. Plus, owning all the creative functions yourself means you can not only make changes to the look and feel of the brand quickly and inexpensively, but you also can rapidly integrate everything from new green chemistries to cutting-edge packaging materials.

So why do we outsource production? Because hard assets (factories, fleets of trucks, that office in the south of France) tie up capital and dramatically increase a business's debt load, acting like an anchor on growth. Partnering with vendors allows us to redirect money we would otherwise be spending on machines and real estate to resources that enhance the brand's specialness. It also keeps us nimble, enabling us to work with a wide variety of innovators and find the ideal partner for a new product or concept. To this end, we've developed a diverse network of vendors with a broad range of skills—a portfolio of partners, each with its unique strengths and specialties. We have partners who can precision-print on the complex curves of our hand-wash bottles and others who specialize in volume, labeling a bottle on three different sides 120 times per minute. Whatever idea the head comes up with, we can build the body to match. And when the market changes, demanding a change in how we produce a product, we have the ability to plug in and out of different parts of our manufacturing infrastructure. This high degree of fluidity allows us to be innovative and agile at the same time.

But just because we don't own or operate any factories doesn't mean we're out of touch with what goes on at the production end. Our products are produced in the Midwest, and we've got people on the ground in Chicago working hand in hand with our manufacturing partners to bring everything to life. This is a critically important strategic investment we've made to build manufacturing understanding into our business process even though we don't own or operate the factories. It's a hybrid model. Instead of just throwing the specs over the wall to the manufacturer, we work with our contractor to engineer new solutions on the factory floor. It demonstrates that we have skin in the game, that we're going to roll up our sleeves and help get things done, that we're accountable and we take responsibility for making sure our vision is brought to life.

MAKE FAST FRIENDS It's not that hard to find good suppliers, those that embrace agility as a core value and deliver on it. And once you find them, you can build timelines to ensure that they live up to your idea of speed as a core competency. But other companies already do these kinds of things. To be the fastest, you need to get creative. Be a guinea pig for your vendors; be their marquis client and help them generate new business in return for trying something new with you. In our case, this might be an innovative, difficult-to-fabricate bottle, an expensive and unusual pump, or a new sustainable ingredient. While examples abound, one vendor who really nailed it for us was Amcor, one of the world's largest PET plastic bottle manufacturers. Tasked with making us a bottle entirely from recycled plastic—the world's first—Amcor overcame innumerable technical challenges to succeed. Today, in part as a result of our partnership, Amcor is the industry's leader in recycled PET.

Of course, relying on outside partners means you'll often have to be demanding, but you'll also help them create new capabilities—precisely the kind the market will demand two years down the road. This process allows us to be the first to market with new ideas, and it makes our vendors smarter, more capable, and more competitive. After working for months with a wipes manufacturer to create the world's first completely compostable 100 percent PLA wipe, that

GREEN PRODUCTS COME FROM GREEN COMPANIES

▲ **BE THE GUINEA PIG.** Partnering with one of the world's largest bottle manufacturers to make 100 percent PCR bottles.

manufacturer became the industry's only source for an entirely new technology. (PLA stands for polylactic acid, a class of plastic made from renewable plant materials.)

Today, as a result of this guinea pig approach, every supplier of packaging or raw materials in the CPG industry calls us first with a new idea. We can deliver superior products to market, proving them in the field in the process. We win because our name is on the new technology, and our vendors win because they can show bigger partners (like our competitors) that the new idea works, ultimately selling it to them down the line (which is fine by us). All we ask is that we get the first look at any new technology. Recycled bottles, compostable wipes, natural cleaning solvents—this model has been a winning tactic since the beginning. It's a symbiotic relationship wherein we get first dibs in return for hard work and bringing the innovation to market to prove it works. We are, in effect, our partners' business development lab—a skunk works for the best new ideas in the industry.

ANTICIPATE THE CONSUMER: SET TRENDS, DON'T FOLLOW

THEM The world's fastest companies have the ability to quickly and accurately determine the potential for success of a new product, service, or business opportunity. A lot of companies are great at spotting trends or anticipating the next big idea, but few have the ability to quickly vet the idea and determine how to execute it. Frequently the biggest speed bumps and points of derailment for a new idea or innovation are bad use of consumer research.

Consumer research has a tendency to replace actual thinking, and it can stifle real debate and conversations, wasting time in the process. Too frequently, someone will say, "Let's just test it," when they really mean, "I don't have the guts to tell you I don't like your idea, so I'm just going to wait a month and let a group of strangers do it for me."

Extensive research has proven that extensive research is often wrong. As Don Draper, the lead character on *Mad Men*, said, "A new idea is something they don't know yet, so of course it's not going to show up as an option [in consumer research]." When the creators of *Seinfeld* first tested the pilot episode in front of an audience, it famously failed because viewers didn't like the characters and thought Jerry was a weak leading man. As one respondent commented, "You can't get too excited about two guys going to the Laundromat."

Consumer research is more like a rearview mirror than a crystal ball. After all, consumers gravitate to what's most familiar, so listening too closely will leave you with a record of what they've liked in the past. Consumers are great at offering perspectives on products that already exist, but it's your job to spot trends and cultural shifts—like concentrated laundry detergent and sustainable bamboo—before others. Once you find them, it's time to hit the gas.

A different approach to consumer research is needed in order to let big ideas survive the business planning process and keep a company moving fast. For us, it's about being consumer inspired, not consumer led. Being native Detroiters, maybe a Hockeytown analogy will help illustrate this point. Despite being labeled "too small to ever play in the NHL," Wayne Gretzky was the greatest hockey player of all time. Asked why, he said, "Most people skate to where the puck is. I skate to where the puck is going." Our job is to skate to where the consumer is going, and the only way we can do that is to anticipate the direction the consumer is headed. The result is that we give the world something it didn't know it was missing.

In order to grow, you have to have a point of view about the future, and the only way to predict the future is to shape it. Big companies tend to see things the way they are, while entrepreneurs tend to see things the way they could be. Shaping the future requires vision, courage, and regular leaps of faith. At Method, we prefer to integrate consumer insight early in the creative process, using it as a springboard for new ideas to drive innovation. It's one of the reasons we do research in-house. Not only are we better able to anticipate the consumer that way, but we also can do so a lot faster than when we rely on an outside partner that lacks intimacy with the project. Think about it: The more time your in-house experts spend getting used to consumer behavior, the better they get at anticipating how consumers will react in the future and the faster the company can launch new products.

Thanks to the explosion of social and online media, consumer insight is increasingly at your fingertips in real time. Online product reviews, corporate Facebook pages, even your average blog—the Internet offers a wealth of free insights into your brand. While most companies outsource customer service to some cube farm many time zones away, ours reports to the brand team, treating it as consumer insight. By owning the process—listening, consolidating, and putting all those insights into action ourselves—we have a closer, more

▲ **THE METHOD MOMS.** Most of our research is done with our advocates as a form of cocreation.

genuine feel for where things are going every step of the way, allowing us to marry consumer insight with overall strategy and integrate what we learn going forward.

LIVE IN A STATE OF MAKE Living in a state of make is about bringing ideas to life—storyboards, creative materials, campaign concepts, you name it. Perhaps the best way we do this is with prototypes. A prototype is the tangible manifestation of an abstract idea, and it's as useful in helping to suspend disbelief among skeptics as it is in serving as a rough draft for designers to evaluate and evolve. When pitching *Star Wars*, even George Lucas famously prototyped his vision for the film by lying on the ground and acting out scenes with action figures. Building a prototype is a great way to break the navel-gazing cycle of theory and strategy. When dialogue and PowerPoint decks fail to bring about a consensus, a prototype is a low-cost, risk-free means of generating new insights and ensuring everyone is seeing the same vision or movie playing in his head. Once the prototype is finished, each team member can use his or her expertise to figure out how to bring it to life. In the end, this gives everyone the confidence

▲ **LIVE IN A STATE OF MAKE.** Prototype everything to speed up the conversation.

to back the product. Once it's in hand, working backward from a prototype not only ensures that everyone stays focused on the same final product, it means key decision makers (like us) can step away from the project. It's kind of like back in 1960, when Kennedy showed his people at NASA a picture of a man on the moon and told them to make it happen.

Prototyping is key to any decision, so do it early and often. If you were to walk around Method's offices, you'd see prototypes throughout—everything from crude images of bottles and pumps cut and pasted together to refined working concepts of soon-to-launch products. We've even prototyped press clips from the future, mocking up fictional articles that celebrate our vision of success as if it's already been achieved. The idea is to use those physical manifestations to motivate everyone involved and get the feedback (in increasing levels of detail) that we need to take the next step. Like the classic evolutionary chart illustrating our gradual progression from apes, this process can carry a product from the sketch pad to the shelf faster. It's a process that requires a lot of voices and input, but it allows you to put the concept in your hand and accurately assess its potential.

We often simultaneously develop two concepts for the same product, something we call parallel-pathing. Rather than plugging along on a single R&D track—where one team will test and tweak one formula or one package one step at a time—Method will occasionally assign multiple teams to the same task, resulting in several market-ready options. Such was the case with our most recent dish soap, a line launched in 2010. Our developers prototyped two different bottles simultaneously—one, more traditional, with a push-pull cap, and the other, a one-handed pump (like our laundry pump). A lot of companies won't do this because the perception of "wasted resources" makes them uncomfortable. But the reward is speed and flexibility, affording teams more time and more options later in the process. With our dish soap, we had the liberty of finalizing formulas and packages right up until production, making decisions at the eleventh hour without jeopardizing product integrity or our launch date.

FAIL SMALL, FAIL CHEAP There's no better market research than the market. Besting larger rivals often means getting the product to market first, warts and all, and making fixes afterward—a process some of us at Method affectionately refer to as the beta test. Competing in a fast-moving culture and staying ahead of trends is only going to get harder as technology improves and the marketplace opens up to more competition. To stay ahead of bigger brands, tomorrow's entrepreneurs will need to rethink the classic product life cycle. Trends move so fast these days, you can't wait for signs of decline before you start working on the next idea. Forget old clichés like "Don't mess with success" or "If it ain't broke, don't fix it." They're irrelevant.

In order to identify emerging opportunities in a radically changing business environment, there is no better technique than trial and error. This may be why new categories are almost always created in a garage and not at some deep-pocketed big brand. Take our recent hand soap partnership with Disney. Asked to partner with the iconic brand on a Mickey line, we decided to do a beta test. After all, the kids market is incredibly fickle. Dominated by characters like Dora and SpongeBob, it also a graveyard littered with those who've tried and failed. Purchasing decisions shift from the parents to the kids. Could we create something both would love? As this book goes to press, Mickey bottles are reaching

▲ **THE BETA TEST.** Small companies can try many more things
   per dollar at bat. When you are the little guy you focus on
   good ideas, prove them, and then scale them up. "Guest Star"
   is a program where we beta test new fragrance concepts.

a limited selection of retailers. If it bombs, we can withdraw with minimum costs. If it's a hit, you'll be seeing it soon.

We've increasingly tried to use the marketplace to learn, letting sales speak for themselves and creating success through failure. While this approach is faster and less expensive—giving you more at bats per dollar—it requires that you build deeper relationships with your retail clients. After all, you're basically asking them to partner with you on every beta test—for better or worse.

Consider our new "guest star" program, for example, wherein we've set up limited launches of new, trend-forward hand-wash fragrances. These are generally limited to a specific retailer, occasionally within a specific geographical area. While the store categories are usually big, we keep the scope small, and the testing phase rarely lasts longer than a couple of months. How is this different from a test market? you ask. Well, if one of our beta tests is successful and we feel good about the response we're getting, there's no lag—we can instantly ship nationally.

Ultimately, the point of the beta test is to learn about what works and what doesn't. Not only does this keep the cost of failure low, but with each failure, we're able to apply the retrospective lessons to the next test in line, incrementally improving until we have a winning product. It's kind of like hitting a home run fifty feet at a time. Of course, for this approach to be a success, you have to learn how to limit the cost per swing, or you'll burn through capital quickly. In short, fail small and fail cheaply.

SPEED IS A FUNCTION OF CULTURE

> When the rate of change outside exceeds the rate of change inside, the end is in sight.
>
> —Jack Welch

Of course, nobody achieves agility just by outsourcing manufacturing or shipping. As with all our obsessions, kick ass at fast is ultimately a function of our unique culture—the glue that holds everything together. In the early years, we didn't have to make an effort to be inclusive or check in from time to time to be sure everyone was on the same page. We all worked in the same room! (And after work, we all went to the same bar.) Camaraderie flourished, group decision making was second nature, and teamwork never felt like work. In retrospect, our speed as a start-up was just a by-product of our strong culture.

As the company grew, however, our size threatened to slow us down. Weird, right? You'd think that as a start-up builds momentum—adding resources, revenue, experience, and connections—everything would naturally get easier. No more rookie mistakes, no more endless sales pitches and empty cold calls, no more reinventing the wheel with every product launch. The more people you have on board, the more time everyone has to spend getting comfortable with a decision instead of just stepping to the plate and swinging the bat. The challenge—getting people aligned and working together—is no great mystery. And every business book ever published has its own formulas, metaphors, and solutions. Getting everyone on the bus and in the right seat is hard enough, and even when you do, getting them all to agree on where to go and how to get there becomes a daily struggle. For insights into how to stay nimble, we began looking into how *culture* might help speed things up.

Collaboration requires healthy debate. On one hand, we wanted to encourage debate, but drawing the line between debate and dissension can be tough. Quick cultures must have open debate and an environment where people feel safe to share their perspectives, but then such cultures must get people to walk out of the room fully aligned and cognizant of the larger goal at hand. Rapid alignment—getting everyone on the same page—drives great execution, but oftentimes the process of reaching a consensus slows an organization's ability to

"get'er done."
—*a mantra often heard within the walls of Method*

▲ **SPEED IS A FUNCTION OF CULTURE.** Goliath has a culture of process. We have a culture of speed.

take quick action. So how do you make everyone feel comfortable sharing an opinion while simultaneously aligning behind a single vision?

BE SURE YOUR BRAND HAS A POINT OF VIEW In order to innovate quickly, you need to have a point of view that aligns with your core values. Whenever we assess a new idea or product we're thinking of taking to market, we look at it with a very specific set of criteria in mind: Is it smart? Is it sexy? Is it sustainable? Will it create an advocate? Does it keep Method weird? Ultimately, all of these questions spring from our central mission as a brand: inspiring a happy, healthy home revolution. What's your brand point of view? (If you have to think about this for more than two or three seconds, either you don't have one or you need a better one.) These questions act as filters that speed decision making because they have intuitive meaning and draw from a collective understanding of who we are, what we do, and what our mission is.

Making decisions based on values makes certain that everyone stays focused on what is good for the company, not just for individual careers. Guiding principles drive fast decisions—even (especially) painful ones. A few years ago, after we'd launched a spray air freshener, we discovered that our manufacturer had accidentally contaminated it during production with a common household bacterium. Because we'd used an environmentally friendly preservative (greener, but admittedly weaker), it wasn't strong enough to overcome the bacteria. It sounds kind of scary, but to put it in perspective, the risk of anyone getting sick was lower than that of eating sushi. Although we weren't required to recall the product, and most companies in our position wouldn't have done so, when we considered the issue through the lens of our values, the decision was easy. Within a matter of hours, we started pulling the product from shelves.

When a company does not have a clear POV about its role and how it competes, valuable time is lost considering any tactic or idea that doesn't actually help advance the company's cause. A great POV—informed by our values—helps us stay aligned on who we are and what we do so we can avoid making bad decisions and wasting time by exploring overly broad ideas. For example, we have a clear POV on our typical packaging design: It has to be simple and symmetrical with an iconic shape. Using this principle as a starting point, it only took a couple of days to design our new cone-shaped laundry bottle rather than months of expensive exploration and consumer testing.

HUDDLE UP Speed requires great communication, and the Monday all-company huddle is our way of keeping everyone moving and connected. We started the huddles in 2006, after we moved across town to a larger office that dispersed us on three floors. The huddle gives us an opportunity to re-create the environment we had back when we were in our smaller offices on Union Street; even if it only happens once a week, everyone at our headquarters is in the same room together for thirty minutes. The energy is awesome—an amalgam of meaningful discourse and locker room pep talk. Getting everyone together keeps us all aligned on everything from quarterly sales targets to what's happening on the production room floor. The value of the huddle is in reminding all that their individual contribution fits within the larger ecosystem. Speed on an organizational level requires both collective understanding and individual contribution.

ORGANIZE YOUR PEOPLE IN PODS These are cross-functional teams that sit within earshot of one another rather than in separate departments or another building. There's a laundry pod, a hand pod, even a values pod. Speed and innovation require a rapid cadence of problem solving, which requires keeping diverse minds in close contact. By combining various people with different outlooks and different skills, we foster a higher level of maturity and empathy, ensuring that everyone communicates in a cross-functional manner. Bottom line: If you want to be fast, It's essential to make sure that no one in your company is cut off from anyone else. Our pods allow an engineer and a graphic designer to work as a small team maintaining an entrepreneurial environment as the company scales.

FLAT IS FAST Racing dinghies at the age of seven, we grew familiar with the phrase "flat is fast"—because you work as hard as possible to keep your boat flat in order to move faster through the water. The same is true in corporate America, where layers of bureaucracy lead to slower decisions. The fast company is one in which everyone has the autonomy and authority to make decisions and move quickly. But that means everyone must be talented and people must be empowered to operate efficiently and independently. One way we encourage this kind of environment is by delegating a lot of authority and leadership responsibilities to our "zookeepers"—essentially, project managers on steroids. Allow us to explain: Completed work is quite literally dollars moving through the company. Rather than ask three levels of middle management to approve every decision— draining time and money in the process—zookeepers make those everyday key decisions that get us to market (and to profits) faster. A normal project manager builds a timeline and bothers people until the job gets done. Because we're organized by pod, zookeepers must bring dynamic operational insight to every discipline. They're the bridge between the conceptual work on the drawing board and the real product on store shelves. Between those two points are an infinite number of steps that touch everything from headquarters in San Francisco to factories in French Lick, Indiana, to the nameless and faceless truck drivers pulling up to loading docks in towns none of us have ever heard of.

Another way we keep the office flat is by keeping it open. Our open floor plan allows everyone to be a part of every conversation so they can stay connected and collaborative. Plus, we like being able to walk around and get a feel for what's going on. And, hey, during the stroll, maybe we post a few new ideas and progress reports up on the wiki walls so people can stay informed and quickly build upon any new ideas.

KEEP IT SIMPLE There's a reason this cliché sticks around. If things are too complicated, you'll never get things done. This is why Southwest Airlines has the best on-time arrival record—they've kept things simple by not assigning seating and using just one kind of aircraft (at least until recently). We try to keep our business simple with techniques like contracting out all of our manufacturing, allowing us to focus on core competencies like brand, sales, and product development.

▲ **NO-DOOR POLICY.** Silos cannot exist in a world built for speed.

Now, simple doesn't always mean easy—overthinking things is a natural result of caring so much about the business you're in—but we encourage simplicity by continually asking ourselves what we can get rid of in order to go faster. While most companies are great at adding new weekly meetings, processes, and rules (and bad at removing obsolete ones), one way we simplify things is to avoid making detailed plans and schedules longer than six months out. Inevitably, too much changes over two quarters to expect any plan to pan out.

HIRE SLOW, FIRE FAST Though we take our time hiring, we've always regretted holding on to a bad apple too long. In order to stay fast, you need to make sure you're not being slowed down by keeping the wrong people on your team. It may sound counterintuitive—why would you want to rush something as sensitive and important as firing someone? The reason is rooted in our culture. Left to fester, a bad hire can wreak havoc on a freethinking, collaborative team. Like poison, their bad energy has a way of working its way into your system, contaminating people around them. Don't waste time, energy, and focus agonizing about a bad hire. Sure, firing isn't fun, which is in part why it's always easy to come up with excuses to avoid it. Maybe you want to give the person a bit more time to fit in. Maybe you're shorthanded and you need someone in that role. But in the words of Steve Jobs, "We'd rather have a hole than an asshole."

ERROR AUTOPSY: THE BAMBOO WIPEOUT

It's obvious by now that our obsession with speed involves taking some risks and making our fair share of mistakes. But each misstep comes with copious learning opportunities, hence no obsession generates more error autopsies than kicking ass at fast.

Enter the bamboo wipe. In the interest of speed when sourcing materials, we've occasionally opted to skip the time-consuming negotiations that accompany a traditional purchasing contact, which enables you to lock in a set price for materials for a set period of time. While skipping a purchasing contract can be a gamble, the time saved can also mean the difference between beating our competitors to market—wowing consumers and making headlines—or landing on store shelves in the shadow of a larger competitor's multimillion-dollar national launch.

When the cost of materials shifts unexpectedly, however, we find ourselves at the mercy of the market. Such was the case with our initial launch of bamboo wipes. Compostable and more sustainable, bamboo is an ideal material for the disposable wipe industry—a market that produces eighty-three thousand tons of landfill waste every year in the United States. Recognizing an opportunity to be the first to bring bamboo to the category, we were excited about developing and launching as quickly as possible.

In the rush to be the first to market, we opted to not secure a long-term contract with our bamboo supplier. Soon after we launched the product (to much fanfare), the worldwide demand for bamboo skyrocketed. There was no denying it: we had overlooked the business proposition—getting the best quality at the right price going forward. Within six months, materials costs had ballooned by over 100 percent. And while the product was an instant hit with consumers, we simply could not make the margins work. Backtracking, we pulled the product, revised the formula and packaging, and ultimately relaunched the wipe with a different natural wood fiber. The upshot: We essentially had to develop the same product twice.

OUR SPEED MUSES: GENE MONTESANO AND BARRY PERLMAN, FOUNDERS OF LUCKY JEANS

For an obsession like Kick Ass at Fast, you'd expect our muse to be a company known for operating at blindingly fast speed—a Facebook, Google, or Twitter, one of those global tech giants that measures success in nanoseconds. Actually, our biggest "fast influence" comes from the founders of Lucky Jeans, who taught us that speed isn't always about being the fastest; it's about finding the right pace.

It all goes back to a conversation we had years ago with Lucky's founders, Gene Montesano and Barry Perlman, while sitting courtside at an Indiana Pacers game (appropriate, no?). Friends since childhood, Montesano and Perlman shipped the first order of Lucky Brand back in 1990. Since then, they've built their name on great-fitting, vintage-inspired jeans. Rooted in rock 'n' roll and celebrated for its unmistakable sense of humor, Lucky Brand stands for independent thinking, individual style, and a feeling as authentic as love. Recently they launched Civilianaire, a high-end line of denim and basics inspired by a vintage military aesthetic and the Japanese appreciation for minimalist jeans.

As we do with all of our entrepreneurial idols, we asked them for their best advice on winning in the fashion business. (Why not? After all, we're always look-

▲ IT'S NOT ABOUT SPEED BUT PACE. Gene and Barry taught us to follow the hour hand, not the minute hand.

ing for bright ideas we can appropriate to the world of soap!) We assumed that, coming from the go-go world of apparel, they would offer some insight into how they managed to keep up with ever-changing consumer tastes. And in a way, they did . . . though their advice seemed almost counterintuitive at first. "Follow the hour hand," they said, "not the minute hand."

It's a metaphor, of course. The average business follows the minute hand, getting caught up in chasing fads, spinning itself in circles until the clock runs out. But successful businesses sync their strategies to the slow-moving hour hand, maneuvering above the vagaries of turbulent business cycles.

Over time (wouldn't you know), we've come to understand that what Montesano and Perlman meant was that speed and agility have nothing to do with being the top trendsetter or the first to a fad. Kicking ass at fast is about pacing yourself—establishing a point of view that will quickly, clearly, and consistently guide you to make the best decisions, minute to minute, day to day, and year to year. It's ironic, right? Real speed is about being timeless.

obsession

RELATIONSHIP RETAIL

deliver retail differentiation
by creating fewer but deeper
relationships

RETAIL IS THE VIBRANT AND VITAL CROSSROADS where customer, vendor, marketer, and manufacturer collide. While each party's interests intersect, they rarely align perfectly—making retail one of the most brutal arenas in all of business. In such a harsh and uncertain environment, a devotion to relationship retail—Method's fifth obsession—seems almost soft, like the kind of feel-good language you'd find in corporate handbooks better left on the shelf. But in our experience, relationship retail has allowed us to become faster, better, and more competitive at what we do.

Three major trends are emerging in the retail landscape that simultaneously create challenges and great opportunities for upstart brands like Method. Consolidation—homogenization of the retail environmental as big-box retailers swallow the little guys—is shifting the balance of power toward those big retailers and creating barriers for small brands trying to penetrate the market. As we dig our way out of a protracted recession, consumers are flocking to lower-priced alternatives, further driving down pricing power and challenging branded players. And finally, as more people buy more things online (including everyday commodities), virtualization is opening direct-to-consumer sales channels and challenging the brick-and-mortar model altogether.

Not so long ago, every state had its own regional grocery chain—each of them fully stocked with regional brands and character. But even by 1996, when the two of us were just out of college, that era was ending. In the modern age of Walmart supercenters and IKEA megastores (with locations rivaling the size of many European principalities and parking lots hosting upward of fifty thousand cars a day) such quaint regional stores have essentially become museums. In their place, the megastore now pits the same brands and retailers against one another on a national scale. In the average American strip mall, consumers will invariably find some combination of Costco, Walgreen's, or Staples competing head-to-head with Kroger, CVS, or Office Depot—all chasing the same customers with the same products at the same prices.

This consolidation is producing a desperate need for differentiation. No matter where you're selling your product, you have to be able to stand out. What sets your product apart from everyone else isn't just about success anymore, it's about survival. Retailers are wising up to the fact that categories dominated by a few ubiquitous monolithic brands lock everyone into a price war. And in Walmart's shadow, few retailers can afford to keep up the fight. In response, a growing number of retailers have begun to seek their own unique product selection; the bigger the competitive arena and the greater the competitive intensity, the more retailers are calling for different choices. Rather than beat one another to death while competing to see who can offer the lowest price on the same jar of Skippy peanut butter, retailers are increasingly looking to distinguish themselves and save costs by varying their product mix.

Retailers are also fostering differentiation by introducing private, retailer-branded labels. Remember how private label (or generic goods) used to be stark black and white boxes with simple labels, like BEER or MILK? In the early days of the private label, the only thing that set it apart was that it was cheap. These products carried a negative social stigma. Most people assumed the name brand was better—and it almost always was.

Today, things have changed. Gone are the days when the private label was considered an inferior choice. The Great Recession has forced a shift in consumer thinking toward cheap chic—the idea that it's hip to be frugal—which has shattered negative consumer stereotypes of private label goods. Today's private label competes against national brands on both price and differentiation. Private labels like the beautiful O Organics line at Safeway, Kirkland Signature at Costco, and 365 at Whole Foods are all trusted, desirable choices. (Hey, we have friends who swear by Kirkland Vodka!) Retailers like IKEA, Marks & Spencer in the United Kingdom, and Trader Joe's are almost exclusively private label. The trend of hiring famous designers or partnering with other established brands is also making it difficult to distinguish private-label products from their independent counterparts. Just look at examples like Alexander McQueen for Target, Martha Stewart at Macy's, Better Homes & Gardens at Walmart, and Boots at CVS. Ironically, Kenmore and Craftsman were early pioneers in great private-label products and are now probably worth more than the Sears brand name. Today, private label accounts for approximately 20 percent of total food and beverage retail sales in the United States. Private labels have outperformed name brands in annual sales growth in nine of the last ten years.

Now, don't panic. Retail is not going to turn into a landscape of private labels that don't have any internal competitors. The popularity of private labels is cyclical, and retailers fall in and out of love with them depending on market trends. They love them for the margin gains over other value brands but quickly fall out of love when they need to mark down a product and realize there is no manufacturer to pick up the tab. Too much private label can wreak havoc on the balance sheet, so retailers strive to maintain balance. This trend does, however, put the squeeze on the middle of the market. Brands that have been built by offering just a single benefit to consumers ("streak-free glass!" or "whitening toothpaste!") are increasingly having their propositions co-opted by their customers' private labels, forcing them to spend more and more to maintain position.

At the same time, virtualization, the rise of online retailing for everyday commodities, is blurring the lines even further. How does that change the playing field? In some ways, it makes it easier for a small brand to come to market by giving it the same retail space (i.e., a Web site) as its competitors, easing some of the power big retailers have over small brands. At the same time, however, because the overwhelming majority of sales of everyday commodities is still done at brick-and-mortar retail, brands must create visibility in stores. And most people shopping online are shopping for brands and through retailers they already trust. So building presence, both online and offline, becomes the key challenge for any upstart brand.

Method is striving to become the number one home-care brand sold online. We have an advantage on the Web because the audience we cater to is Internet savvy—it's our demographic, and we have a strong social media presence. But online dominance is not about banner ads, it's about delivering a digital brand experience. Just look at Amazon, Zappos, or Soap.com, all successful online retailers that have figured out how to deliver exceptional, high-touch experiences and useful, innovative features. In contrast, bricks-and-mortar customer service continues to decline as the traditional leaders increasingly cut costs to keep pace with deep discounters. Look no further than the case study of Netflix (with its algorithm-driven recommendations, fine-tuned searchability, endless selection, and growing on-demand functionality) versus Blockbuster (which . . . well, by the time you're holding this book, Blockbuster may not even exist anymore).

The shifts of consolidation and the rise of private label are ushering in a new retail landscape characterized by hypercompetition and extreme price sensitivity, creating barriers to market entry that have all but locked small brands out of the market. Simultaneously, virtualization is challenging the very fabric of retail. As consumers grow more accustomed to the convenience and security of shopping online, new paths to market are emerging. What results is a power struggle between retailers and manufacturers—a battle between Goliaths to gain leverage, the upper hand constantly shifting back and forth. Retailers under pressure to carry ubiquitous brands bow to the power of the manufacturers that make them, accepting insolvent margins just so they don't lose that shopper who may or may not buy something else while in the store. In response, with fewer and fewer retail brands through which to sell and a low success rate on new innovations, manufacturers are forced to lower the retailers' risk by subsidizing their costs through expensive slotting fees and discounting. Key to winning in the midst of this power struggle is finding ways to help the retailer—our customer—win.

THE SHIFT FROM MANUFACTURERS TO RETAILERS

Arguably our biggest achievement over the past decade has been building distribution in mass retail channels, a process that demanded we fight for shelf space traditionally dominated by our larger and more established competitors. Believe it or not, the most expensive real estate in America today is the shelf space at your local grocery store—over $1 million per square foot—and the ecosystem currently in place is essentially designed to keep little guys like us out. Called *slotting* within the industry, the practice is arguably the biggest barrier to innovation in mass retail—big brands pay extra fees to keep their products front and center in the aisle, and the upstart brands get squeezed out. Over time, retailers grow accustomed to the added boost in their profit margins and the pay-to-play cycle continues. If this is beginning to sound a little like bribery, well, that's because it kind of is.

Not only does slotting create a cost hurdle for new brands, it also provides an incentive for retailers to discontinue the bottom 10 percent of every category after each six-month sales review, in order to resell the shelf space. And— surprise, surprise—if you've just launched a new brand, chances are you're in the bottom 10 percent. If that weren't bad enough, guess who's in charge of recommending which products get the ax? None other than the "category captain," one of the leading dominant brands! Yup, your opponent is also the referee in this game, and he's got his eye on you. The U.S. government has even considered making slotting fees illegal because of the unfair barrier they present to competition. It's worth noting that many of the strongest retailers out there (Target, Walmart, and Costco, to name a few) don't use slotting fees. For now, however, the system stands in plenty of other places.

"YOU HAVE TO CARRY TIDE"

While retailers have the power of the real estate they own, the sheer size and ubiquity of leading consumer brands means that manufacturers hold some power in this battle of Goliaths, too. Look at laundry detergent. Laundry detergent has nearly 100 percent household penetration. (The fact that it's not exactly 100 percent makes us wonder who's not doing laundry.) Tide has nearly 50 percent market share, which means that for half of the households in America, when people run out of laundry detergent, they go to the store looking for Tide. Retailers also know that no one takes the time to get in the car and drive to the store to buy only one jug of laundry detergent—you're going to stock up on the other things you need while you're there. So retailers resort to carrying Tide at wafer thin margins and advertising that they have the lowest price around, to get you into the store in the hope that you will buy other, more profitable items while you're there. Retailers don't like selling Tide for nothing, but given the power and size of the brand, they have no choice.

Exploiting this shift in power by finding ways to bring the power back to the retailer—our customer—becomes a winning strategy for Method. If the laundry category has no profit in it, we'll bring profit. If all the products are the same, we'll bring something unique. If the laundry category isn't growing (because everyone in America already does laundry) then we'll even find a way to grow the category. By holding our competitors' approaches against them, by being different and playing a different role with our customers, we become a key ally in creating our customers' success.

Obviously, there are plenty of downsides to the way things have shifted in retail in recent years. Try to compete on volume and price and you'll get sucked into a race to the bottom, crushed between big brands with more leverage and private labels with better margins. So how did we overcome these odds and extend distribution to tens of thousands of retail locations from our start in a dirty little apartment in San Francisco? Ironically, some of the same daunting retail trends that appear to make things more difficult for new brands actually present significant opportunities—and we've been able to identify a number of them simply by focusing on the key partnerships and relationships that make up our supply and distribution chain.

IF YOU'RE NOT DIFFERENT, YOU'RE DEAD

If you don't show up with a meaningful trade story, don't show up! A trade story is your proposition. It is why a retailer should take you instead of someone else. Ours is built around the three things that retailers are most starved for in the cleaning aisle: something unique, something that brings growth, and something that makes them money. As in any great relationship, it's up to you to bring something meaningful to the picture. And if you want the relationship to last, you want that something to be truly different—not just cheaper than the other guys out there. This is no easy task for a company like ours; we're always looking for something our seven ginormous competitors have missed. Our trade story is grounded in three benefits that can be applied to any category, whether you are selling soda or plasma TVs. We deliver differentiation, incremental growth, and profitability.

DIFFERENTIATION Retailers love saying, "Find it exclusively here!" If you are providing something truly different that no one else has, a retailer will hold

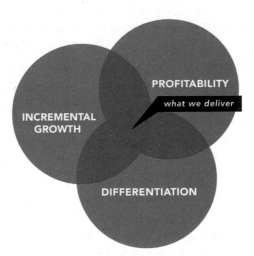

▲ **ALIGN INTEREST.** Create a trade story that aligns your interests with those of retailers. For us it's driving profitability, differentiation, and incremental growth.

you to a different standard than your competitors. Moreover, they don't have to compete on the lowest price with your product because they're the only place that carries it. You can offer differentiation over the short term by giving a retailer a one-year head start on a new item or over the long term by committing not to sell your brand to their main competition, which reduces expensive marketing support. In addition, a retailer is more likely to promote you and provide co-marketing support because of the image differentiation your brand is providing.

This strategy recently helped us launch in France with minimal resources. Representatives of other companies often ask to visit us and learn from our approach, and through one of these requests, France's second-largest retailer, Auchan, brought its entire senior leadership team to our office. They were coming in for a consulting lesson, which gave us the opportunity to sell through a consulting approach (more on this later in the chapter). After hearing about our best practices, they suggested we do business together, and we offered them a two-year exclusive in France. In return for differentiation, they were excited to support the brand, giving us generous shelf space and plenty of marketing support. The result was that we launched in a new country with few resources and ensured foundational success that we can build on.

INCREMENTAL GROWTH Retailers are craving incremental growth, so being able to demonstrate how you will help them achieve this goal is about as essential as getting your name right on your résumé. There are a lot of ways to show how you will generate incremental growth, but three are truly important when you're partnering with a retailer. Because we're talking theoretically here, we'll use buggy whips, a favorite example of our high-school economics teacher from Grosse Pointe North.

I will bring new consumers into the category because this buggy whip will inspire more people to get a buggy whip.

I will promote a new use for buggy whips that will inspire current buggy whip owners to buy a second buggy whip to have as a spare.

I will create a new category by introducing an entirely new type of buggy whip that will inspire current buggy whip owners to buy a second kind of buggy whip.

For us, incremental growth translates into a trade story that goes something like this: Our soap is so cool that it inspires people not only to clean with our product but to leave it on their countertops, where it gets seen and used more, instead of hiding it under the sink. We have actually transformed a need into a want by making cleaning products an impulse buy. This is what saved us during the Target test when we missed our sales goals. The buyer looked past gross sales and realized that we were almost 100 percent incremental to the existing category and therefore grew their overall business. That, my friend, is retail gold. The second pillar of our incremental growth story is that while our total sales might not be as big as the leading brands', sales of Method are far more likely to be incremental ones—gravy for the retailer's top (and bottom) line.

PROFITABILITY In addition to their needs for differentiation and growth, retailers' calls for profitability are becoming increasingly loud. Many retailers work on razor-thin margins and rely on mass-market, money-losing products to drive traffic to their stores. Thus many have become overly dependent on slotting fees. So if you can help a retailer drive profit, there is a good chance you will become that retailer's best friend. The way to think about this is in the simple segmentation of good, better, best. Every mature retailer strives to offer:

Good. Products at the opening price point (OPP) that deliver value (Milwaukee's Best).

Better. Usually the *big* brand lives here, as it serves the big middle of the market (Budweiser).

Best. The premium choice of the category (Sierra Nevada).

Companies make most of their profits at opposite ends of the market with either the value brands or the premium ones. This trend, well documented by Michael J. Silverstein and Neil Fiske in *Trading Up,* is leading to death in the middle for brands that don't compete in either the value or premium segments. This is happening for a couple of reasons. First, with the demise of mass media comes the demise of the mass market. Look at any category and you will see that the big mass brands that occupy the middle space are in decline or stagnant. Growth is occurring at the value end, where consumers trade down because within the category they view the choices as essentially the same, and at the premium end, where they trade up because they believe the higher quality is worth a price premium. The problem with competing in the value segment is that retailers are taking it over with private label to boost their own profit. This leaves Best as the segment where you need to be to increase profit for a retailer.

Retailers get caught up in moving volume, so you have to constantly remind their buyers that, while you may have a smaller percentage of revenue (say, even just 1 percent), you nevertheless might generate 5 percent of their overall category profits. Big guys win on scale games, but if retailers want to remain profitable, they'll need to avoid commoditization and grow your brand in their stores.

SELLING IS A TRANSFER OF EMOTION

It is a simple point, but when fulfilling your mission depends on getting people to know you and use your products, selling becomes a point of personal passion. No longer is it a pitch—a sales guy or gal trying to dupe a buyer into a big contract. It's a discussion, a collaboration, about how two companies can come together and use their common assets to create some good in the world. And do good business in the process.

While a good trade story is important, never forget that selling is, at its heart, a transfer of emotion. If this wasn't the case, you would never go on a sales call, you would just send a deck and wait for a response. But because passion is contagious, we leverage this as a big difference between us and Big Soap. Luck-

▲ **YES, EVEN WEIRD CAN HELP YOU SELL.** Next time ditch that blue-blazer steak-house sales dinner for something imaginative. If you don't get the sale, at least you will have had fun.

ily this is easy for us because we have a clear purpose and a developed culture. And if you are not passionate about what you do (particularly if you're in sales), find another job. By demonstrating passion, we can align our interests with the interests of the retailers. Once we establish that we're on the same page, it's just a question of developing our shared strategy. From there, weirdness takes all shapes and sizes. We've been known to hold sales meetings over broom ball games, show up at retailers wearing their vendor vests, and greet visiting buyers with surprise all-company pep rallies, and our sales meetings have included dinners in bed at supper clubs, *Iron Chef*–style competitions, and tequila classes. While we've yet to conduct a sales meeting entirely in song, we're close to cracking that one too.

YOU CAN'T BE FRIENDS WITH EVERYBODY

Instead of selling one bathroom cleaner to everyone in America, we want to sell everything needed to clean a home to the segment of America that is progressive environmentally, socially, and aesthetically. As we said before, we're after wallet share, not market share. That requires us to prioritize some potential customers over others, to work more deeply with those who match our demographic and psychographic target more closely.

One of the first mistakes most entrepreneurs make is overextending their brand. Method was no exception. Within just a few years of the launch of the company, Method products were all over the retail landscape. Despite our original belief in working with fewer relationships on a deeper level, we still found ourselves saying yes to the wrong retailers. We realized how hard it was to be disciplined with revenue staring us in the face. Ultimately, we had to (re)learn that some retailers just weren't the right fit for our brand.

One way to avoid stretching your brand too far is to adjust your sales goals from quantity to quality. Instead of trying to form the *most* relationships, aim to form the *best* relationships, aligning your brand with partners that have similar values and goals. You don't want to be in every store in America. If you are, the only difference is price.

Remember that growth comes with compromises. Once you've begun establishing the right relationships, reassess your goals. How big do you want to be? How far do you want to reach? We don't have an aspiration to be a $10 billion company. We have an aspiration to be a very *special* company. If focusing on the latter leads to the former, all the better.

BREAKING IN

Busting into an established category can be daunting. Here are a few strategies we've found useful.

1. **Open a test market.** Find ten local stores in your area where the manager can decide whether to carry your product. If you show up enough times, they might just say yes, and you're on your way to proving sales (which you can then take to a bigger chain).
2. **Find an alternative way in.** Even if it's not the buyer, get someone there excited. We leveraged a marketing relationship to get Target's own marketing department to help us convince their buyers.
3. **Help retailers see what's in it for them.** If it's not a big and simple story, expect radio silence. Retailers are inundated with new product ideas and pitches, so if yours doesn't have a clearly articulated *benefit for the retailer,* don't bother.
4. **Skip the trade shows.** We've done the entire circuit. Unless you're paying for direct access to buyers (at shows like Efficient Collaborative Retail Marketing), there are probably better uses for your precious capital.
5. **Offer a six-to-twelve-month exclusive.** Major retailers will value the head start on their competitors, and you'll get the opportunity to test and learn before approaching other retailers.

While it may seem as though the big brands have all the advantages when it comes to retail, Method is a case study in how smaller companies can leverage unique brand traits to build strong, long-term relationships with their retail partners. The big guys have power, resources, size, reach, and pure muscle. But relationship retail as a smaller company in the green revolution takes more strategy, risk, and entrepreneurialism.

In the spirit of seeking wallet share over market share, we decided to focus on the most valuable retailers instead of everybody. By working closely with a Target or a Kroger, we may have had a lot of eggs in one basket, but it was a sturdy basket. When you are an early-stage company, you also have to face the reality that you lack the resources to serve a lot of customers well. We could have given mediocre service and attention to a lot of retailers, but we believed we'd get a better return on our investment by allocating our resources to a few rather than spreading them thin. This gave us a strategic advantage over our Goliath competitors because it forced us to leverage our limited resources more wisely. Managing this tension takes us to our next lesson—stop selling and start consulting.

STOP SELLING AND START CONSULTING

When we started Method, we had no sales experience, so we had to rely on the skills we did have. As Eric and Alastair both came from consulting backgrounds, we relied on their client relationship skills. Instead of trying to simply sell to our retailers, we acted like consultants, treating them like clients we were trying to help. For example, before we started talking about Method, we would try to provide insight into how they could grow their business. What was their biggest growth challenge in the category—and was there anything we could do to help? We recognize that you're underserving the premium customer segment here— have you thought about trying X, Y, or Z?

Offering to help started the conversation at a place of trust and collaboration, because the retailer knew we were not concerned with selling just our own products. Of course, consultants are also some of the world's best schmoozers— and understanding when to drop the sales pitch and spend some time getting to know the buyer is an important skill.

Selling consultatively requires a few unnatural skills for a typical salesperson. First, you *do* have to take no for an answer. To be truly consultative, you must be truly objective. So if the strategy means that your product isn't right for the retailer, you have to accept that and live to fight another day, or else you will permanently tarnish your credibility as a resource. You have to be able to put yourself in the retailer's shoes, understand his or her challenges and constraints, and help navigate a path to success. This requires uncommon levels of empathy on top of objectivity. Second, you have to listen—truly listen. Salespeople are usually known for their talking; ours our known for their listening. Retailers are an enormous untapped resource of information on the market, consumers, and your competitors. Take the time to listen, and who knows what you'll learn.

It's also helpful to bring the retailer along with you—to take them behind the scenes of your business so they understand exactly what your brand is all about. Back when we were developing our first concentrated laundry detergent, we took our laundry buyer from a major retailer to New York to a design kickoff meeting at Kate Spade, who we hired as a collaborator. At about five in the morning, during last call, the buyer looked at us and said, "You are either the best salespeople I have ever met or the worst. I just can't tell." Ultimately, this retailer gave us an unprecedented four feet of space in the laundry aisle for a new product launch.

We had similar experience that same evening. Dining at Asia de Cuba, we decided to randomly ask several women seated at the same table what they thought of a couple different bottle shapes for the detergent. They eagerly gave their point of view, which was actually very insightful, and when we asked what they did for a living, we discovered they were strippers. It just goes to show that you never know where good insight will come from, and in the end we felt good launching a new laundry line that was stripper approved. What else would you expect from People Against Dirty?

To make sure this approach continues as the company grows, we hire many of our salespeople from nonsales backgrounds. We have team members who are former retail buyers, Industrial Research Institute consultants, and marketing professionals. We also help promote a retail-centric culture by doing things like having one of our retailers address the entire company when they come to visit or by closing the office once a year and sending everyone on field trips to area stores.

The abnormally strong relationships we forged with our retail partners in our start-up days have translated into profound competitive advantages. To foster stronger relationships, we invite our retail partners to participate in the product development cycle, getting their input on everything from fragrances to package design as early as the concept and ideation stage. The benefits are mutual: Retailers learn more about our target customers and how to market to them, while we gain invaluable partners on the front lines. Collaborating with retailers also guarantees that they'll have a greater stake in the eventual success of our product. Great buyers are great merchants, and we try to bring out the true merchant in the buyers we work with. Below are some of our insights into the minds of retailers.

RETAILERS ARE YOUR EYES ON THE GROUND Nobody knows consumer habits and market trends better than retailers. Sure, you could hire a consulting firm or a "cool hunter" to drum up an expensive market forecast. You could also devote precious in-house resources to market research. But why not cut to the chase? Face-to-face with shoppers every day, retailers can act as your eyes on the ground, sharing valuable, up-to-the-minute information on what, how much, and why consumers are buying certain things. In turn, retailers can learn from you. They may know more about the mainstream consumers you *want,* but you know more about the advocate consumers you *have*—from what kind of marketing they like to what they're saying about in-store displays.

RETAILERS HAVE BEEN AROUND THE BLOCK Convinced the latest innovation to emerge from your R&D lab will wow customers? Eager to shake up the category with your marketing department's ingenious new pricing strategy? Chances are, not only have others been down that road, but they probably stumbled along the way. Our retail partners regularly provide insights into prior missteps in our industry. Whether it's packaging, labeling, or weekly coupon mailers, no one knows more about what *doesn't work* on the shelves than the retailers who stock them.

RETAILERS LOVE HAVING SKIN IN THE GAME When retailers take part in the development process—helping select colors or fragrances, for example, or collaborating on a product exclusive—they're more inclined to help the product succeed. Bringing them under the tent often persuades them to provide additional support—offering an end cap or some local advertising space. For better or worse, it's their baby, too. Say a new product fails to attract consumers. A strong relationship with the retailer can mean the difference between a markdown and a write-off. When initial sales of Bloq, our ill-fated body-care line, failed to meet expectations, Target could have shipped the product right off to a discount warehouse like Big Lots. But Target had participated in the design process, had reviewed packaging concepts and helped us land on the final one, and so felt personally invested in the product's success. Rather than give up early, the retailer pulled out all the stops to help it move, putting it on end caps, keeping it on shelves months longer than they were obligated to, and collaborating with us on markdowns.

RETAILERS HAVE A FEW IDEAS OF THEIR OWN If our retail partners had their way, they'd slap our brand on everything from sneakers to cereal. That's how much they believe in our style-and-substance appeal. They also appreciate our willingness to take risks. While kicks and cornflakes may not be right for Method, retailers have pushed us to expand into new frontiers that were integral to our success. Method Baby, for example, was conceived in part with Babies R Us.

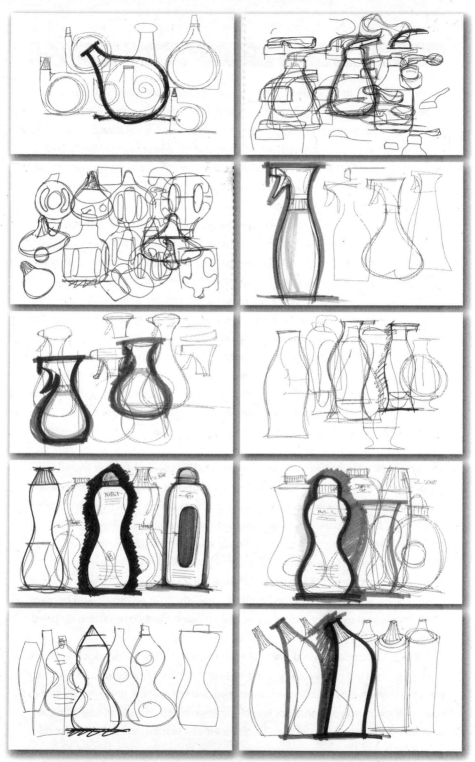

▲ **SKETCH SESSION.** We share product ideas with retailers at the earliest stages and allow them to be true merchants.

COLLABORATION AT THE SPEED OF RETAIL

Involving retailers in your development process accelerates it by giving you feedback along the way. Using prototypes and an iterative process with retailers makes decisions happen faster, because your hunches are validated quickly and definitively. It also gives your customers ownership of what you mutually create, which allows you to transcend the quick-in, quick-out cycle of listing and discontinuing typical in the grocery trade, buying critical time to build the brand in the face of big brands with big budgets.

As you see, all of our obsessions are at work in our approach to retail—and speed is a critical ingredient. A small company has to take advantage of speed and agility in its approach to retail when battling oversize competitors. By treating retailers as true partners, we include them up front at the concept stage. In our early days, we joked that we would secure a million-dollar order with one product concept sketch, but to improve your chances of success, it's important to leverage the retail perspective early. We get goosebumps when we hear a buyer say "we" when a product launches because they feel a sense of ownership. That's when you know it's a true partnership. Buyers are looking to make their mark, and we help them do this by partnering in a manner that gives them some control. Sometimes we feel like buyers when they push ideas to us or ask us to create a specific product and we are the ones saying no.

The other key advantage to this approach is that it allows you to get verbal commitment on a new product launch before investing up-front capital. In the early stages of a business, when cash is king, this brings a high level of predictability to a launch. Our process was to get one or two big retailers to look at a concept and give a verbal agreement to carry during at a specific launch window. Though it was only a verbal agreement and didn't legally bind them to anything, if the partnership was strong, we felt comfortable banking on it. With this promise in hand, we would invest capital in "cutting steel" (building a mold), and in many cases, our opening order would cover the development cost, letting us break even at launch.

But this all depends on the ability to execute fast. The model does not work if you get a verbal promise and can't deliver it until eighteen months later; by then the buyer has probably been promoted and left the job, or consumer tastes have changed and your product is no longer on trend. However, you also can't ask your people to work 24/7 during the weeks leading up to every product

BUILD ON PROOF

We like to use a "graduation strategy" to work our way up with retailers and build confidence in the relationship. We might ask a skeptical retailer to try some hand soap first and see how things go. Once consumers take note and sales pick up, maybe they'll want to introduce more products. When Duane Reade tested our hand soap next to brands like Softsoap and Dial, our sales soared. The retailer began bringing in more and more products, graduating to a special twenty-item display. As sales grew, so did our footprint in the store. Today, if you walk into a Duane Reade in New York City, you'll find more than fifty Method items.

---

launch. We've found that the way to balance the need for speed and the need for happy employees is by not launching with all retailers at once. With a broad launch, you set the stakes high, elevating the risk and putting your team in a high-pressure position where they're more inclined to think conservatively. It's the difference between opening a play on Broadway or testing it in a small theater around the corner. In the spirit of test and learn, we like to start at a few retailers quickly and expand to more over time only if a product sells well, ensuring a strong foundation. Take Smarty Dish, our dishwasher detergent. We started by placing the product in a few select locations to test the waters. After gauging consumer response and making a few tweaks, we were confident it was resonating and ready for prime time. Remember that it can be just as expensive to pull a product from the market as it is to launch it, due to markdowns (what a retailer charges you for putting it on clearance), so you should make sure it works before overinvesting in distribution. This is one way we leverage the beta test from our obsession to kick ass at fast (see page 146).

ERROR AUTOPSY: GETTING NAKED FOR WHOLE FOODS

Even though we share a purpose and a similar branding strategy, Method and Whole Foods haven't always seen eye-to-eye. As a matter of fact, it took years of negotiations and an entirely new product line before we got in the door.

From the beginning, Whole Foods objected to our use of dyes. Whole Foods tests products rigorously, and even though we showed them our dyes were safe and degradable, it was a nonstarter for them. Unfazed, we made multiple visits to Whole Foods headquarters in Austin, negotiating, struggling, and attempting to quell their skepticism. We argued on behalf of our dyes, showing scientifically their environmental benefits, and we pointed to Method's cutting-edge design, comparing the brand's bright, fun lifestyle appeal to the dusty, boring products in Whole Food's "green" aisle. But even after a local Whole Foods in Cupertino started stocking Method with great success, the corporate headquarters still wouldn't budge. We took it personally.

One thing we have learned is that there's no such thing as winning an argument with a retailer. Prove a buyer wrong and you're liable to burn a bridge. It didn't matter that we could prove with life-cycle analyses that putting a nontoxic, degradable dye in the product was far greener than putting a color (even

▲ **THE POWER OF RELATIONSHIP RETAIL.**
Our m-spot brand blocking statements disrupt the cleaning aisle.

white!) in the plastic bottle. Whole Foods had a unilateral policy against colorants, and it was a matter of philosophy. They were not impressed with our arguments, and to their credit, they stuck to their principles. Whole Foods 1, Method 0.

But driven to make the relationship work, we returned to the lab and began working with Method's green chefs on an entirely new line of products. If Whole Foods didn't like dyes, there would be no dyes. We had a small but vocal group of advocates who loved our brand but were "no fragrance" people. We put the two nays together and, returning to Austin, unveiled Method's newest invention: Go Naked, a line of several products that were completely dye- and fragrance-free. We presented them along with some of our tried-and-true items that also happened to be dye-free. Whole Foods said they'd consider it.

Weeks later, we sat in front of the phone in a tiny conference room. Whole Foods said, "We have some great news for you guys! You're in—nationally—with twenty-three items." We opened the door and shouted, *"We are in Whole Foods!"* The office erupted in cheers. Since then, it's been a strategic, highly collaborative, supportive relationship that has produced significant mutual benefit to the bottom lines of both companies.

Today, Whole Foods stocks some forty Method products. By finding common ground that respects the right each party has to its own philosophy, yet defines common areas in which to build business together, we have created a partnership as deep and meaningful as any we have. And despite the fact that the chain is much smaller than our other retailers (Whole Foods has only about 300 stores compared to 1,600 for Target and 1,700 for Lowe's), Whole Foods is one of our top customers in sales volume.

OUR RETAIL MUSE: TARGET, A PARTNERING PIONEER

Target has been a true muse to us in its ability to bring class to mass. The Target people understand how to invest in something and then sell it. They are skilled at recognizing, collecting, and presenting the early evidence of a mass trend before any other major retailer. In essence, great merchants like Target are curators. Our original business plan was full of inspiration from the way Target was reinventing the idea of design at mass. We leveraged Michael Graves's toilet-bowl brush as evidence of America's growing desire for everyday design and Target's groundbreaking collaboration with designers like Isaac Mizrahi as proof that retailers were rethinking branded relationships. It seems commonplace now to see famous designers collaborating with mass retailers, but a few years ago, this was revolutionary ground broken by Target.*

In our original pitch to Target, we coined the idea of "designer commodities" by showing them a Karim Rashid–designed dish soap bottle. While we typically give Target a hard time about our first rocky meeting and being told we had a "snowball's chance in hell" of being picked up, it's remarkable that America's third-largest retailer would give a company like us a shot with full end caps in 10 percent of their chain, followed by a national rollout months later.

So what have we stolen from Target? Well, besides a few visitor badges that we forgot to return, we have stolen the meaning of being a great merchant—investing in something and then selling it, rather than purely buying. Too many retailers are run by "buyers," and the art of being a great merchant continues to disappear in mass retailing. Merchants have intuition and instinct. They understand that they have the power to create a trend and influence their customers instead of following the prevailing winds. Trader Joe's is a great merchant, as are Whole Foods, Pharmaca, Lowe's, and Bed Bath & Beyond, to name a few. They have a point of view and are willing to partner with us to set a trend rather than following the existing one at a lower price.

Many people still assume we are Target's private label because it's the retailer they most closely associate us with. While our design is original, we did steal the idea that design can be democratized. They helped give us the confidence that combining high style with low prices was a winning formula, and then they gave us the support to prove it on a national stage. See you at the local!

---

* Unlike our other muses, you may have noticed that we don't name an individual at Target who inspired us. That's because we could fill a book with all the people there who have played the role of muse to our business and mission. This is also in keeping with the Target culture, which celebrates collective efforts over individuals in the spirit of great teamwork.

obsession

6

WIN ON PRODUCT EXPERIENCE

be product-centric and deliver
remarkable product experiences

I'S NO SECRET THAT MODERN CONSUMERS ARE overwhelmed with choice in every category. *The Paradox of Choice, The Tyranny of Choice, The Art of Choosing*—the trend is so pervasive that even choosing which book to read on the topic is an exercise in decision making. In search of the broadest possible appeal, products are researched and group-thinked into the ground, resulting in brands that we neither love nor hate and that must be advertised incessantly in order to generate even mild consumer interest. And thanks to increased global competition, widespread access to the Web, cheap labor, and the declining cost of formulating and manufacturing products, rival brands are increasingly working with the same tools, leading to cluttered stores, jammed warehouses, and endless inefficiencies. Though the trend is true in almost every consumer category, from cable television to online shopping, you need look no further than that modern-day arena of capitalism, the grocery store.

While the average supermarket has some 40,000 products, or SKUs (stock-keeping units), the average family gets an estimated 80 to 85 percent of what it needs from just 150! Typical shoppers (those who don't have a lot of free time on their hands) will ignore 39,850 items in that store. Even if shoppers were able to glance at every box, bag, and label in every aisle during their typical thirty-minute trip, they'd have less than 0.05 seconds to assess each product.

Overwhelmed by bland choices and parity prices, consumers are increasingly relying on memories and emotions to guide their purchasing decisions over rational criteria alone. Studies of the brain show that emotion acts five thousand times faster than logic, and in a culture pressed for time, seconds (even split seconds) count. So while it may not seem like a major concern to the average consumer, behind all those choices, a battle for experience is raging among brands and retailers, reshaping how businesses compete. Seeking to stand out, businesses are designing better experiences by tapping into our emotional-memory-based decision making.

For a bit of background on why, let's examine the motivations behind every purchasing decision. We like to think of this in terms of a pyramid. (Yeah, we like pyramids.) At the bottom of the motivations pyramid are *needs*—the broadest motivations at work in any consumer category. If you're shopping for a car, these might be things like enough room for your whole family or great safety features. Easy enough. Next up on the pyramid: *wants*—anything from a leather-appointed interior to a V-8 engine or a convertible top. *Desires* take the top spot, representing, quite literally, whatever your heart desires. Note that we're now in emotional territory—for example, the desire to feel good about yourself or your place in society by buying a certain brand. This might sound something like "I want to be seen as a responsible citizen (so I'll buy a Prius)" or "I want to feel successful (perhaps a Mercedes)." Over time, as a category matures and basic needs and wants become satisfied, consumers trade their way up the pyramid toward greater and greater satisfaction . . . ideally, at least. Of course, if you really want your advocates to climb the brand pyramid with you, you'll need to do some work.

STAND OUT WITH EXPERIENCE

In order to compete on desires of your customers, you can no longer rely on your product alone. A cool bottle, a nice fragrance, a whole bunch of extra-sudsy bubbles—these may be things people want, but they really don't resonate that much with our customers on an emotional level. Let's go back to the car-buying example: The desire to feel cool by buying a top-of-the-line convertible is not satisfied by just buying the car and parking it in the driveway. It's fully realized when you actually go out and drive it with the top down! Bottom line: It's not the product that fulfills the desire, it's the experience of using it.

Now, in order to really get people to desire your product, you need to create a great experience. This is harder than it seems. Think about it—how many great brand experiences do you have each week? The gas station, the grocery store, your last flight? Not exactly. Despite all the money brands spend on consumer research, there are very few customer experiences worth talking about today. Look at any mature category—tires, tissues, tape, you name it—and while

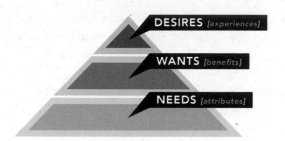

▲ **PRODUCTS FULFILL NEEDS.** Experiences fulfill desires. The abundance of society has oversatisfied most of our material needs so today we have to compete on more emotional sensibilities.

you'll find very little consumer disappointment, you'll also discover very little room for differentiation. All the needs and wants are met! But consider the unlimited opportunity to deliver a better *experience*—in every category, from products to retail to service. What's a better experience? It's one that's memorable, remarkable, or unexpected in some way. It's what keeps people coming back to you instead of your competitors. Like it or not, a quality product just isn't enough. Today, quality is only the price of entry.

It's no wonder we're craving more experiences in our lives. With most of our basic needs satisfied in our world of plenty, we are becoming a much more

Dec 10, 2010

Dear Method,
I had to write you and tell you that I was extremely motivated to clean my entire home last night... thanks to you! It takes a lot to make me want to clean... it's such a thankless job! I actually hate housekeeping but Method is just so fashionable and refreshing, how can I resist.

— Sarah

experience-driven society. Ryan Howell, a psychology professor at San Francisco State University, has shown that experiences make us happier than material goods. (Check out Howell's work with the Personality and Well-Being Lab.) In a surplus economy (where most needs and desires are met), experiences trump possessions. You can see this in the travel industry, wherein brands like Virgin Airlines and W Hotels make us feel hip and young on the road. A couple of decades ago, Holiday Inn standardized the hotel experience under the tagline, "The best surprise is no surprise." In contrast, the W Hotel promises to do just the opposite—surprise you with wonderful experiences!

ROOM TO BREATHE We knew we didn't stand a chance if we tried to compete in our category on needs and wants alone. After all, our competition wasn't just five hundred times our size; the leaders also had a hundred-year head start on us! That's a century of identifying (and often contriving) every imaginable consumer need or want and satisfying it with 99.9 percent efficacy. There aren't a lot of people walking around wishing they could find a better dish soap. For decades, the brands that washed, cleaned, and disinfected the best won the most customers. But after more than a century of unprecedented innovation, most of our cleaning needs had been satisfied! Moreover, most of the leading brands had deep brand equity. They made their name during the golden age of mass media, capturing the broadest general consumer needs, like streak-free windows or the stain-fighting power in laundry detergent. This often resulted in mediocre or me-too products becoming bestsellers because all that marketing muscle could compensate for the lack of a unique product. Catching up and overtaking these giants would be like trying to out-Clorox Clorox: It wasn't going to happen. Outspending them was out. Since a lavish marketing budget is not a luxury most start-ups have at their disposal, there's a greater emphasis on developing a remarkable product that delivers a great experience.

Without the R&D budgets or the consumer-research departments of our rivals, we had two choices: give up—or move the goal posts, redefining the battleground around experiences, not just solutions. As the vast majority of CPG had been commoditized, we couldn't claim to be another cleaner that just, well, cleaned. Don't get us wrong, we know cleaning power is very important, and we work to make sure our products kick ass without all the nasty chemicals in them, but today a product that works is merely where the race begins. For us, we needed to do what the competition couldn't. We needed to make cleaning a better experience. We had to make it fun.

Let's face it, cleaning is still not enjoyable for most people, and there is nothing scarcer in it than pleasure. But people pay a premium for what is scarce. We've listened to women in focus groups articulating the challenge and complexity of trying to be a modern woman—every bit the homemaker her mother was but also the career person her father was—explaining how Method, *our brand,* took the drudgery out of cleaning and helped them manage this very personal challenge.

▲ **CONSUMERS PAY A PREMIUM FOR WHAT IS SCARCE.** In cleaning there is nothing more scarce than fun. Cleaning naked is sadly scarce too.

This transition from rational propositions to emotional propositions is the crux of Method's obsession with product experience. Dating back to our earliest days, this insight has had a profound influence on everything we make. With the convergence of these macrotrends and a heavy passion for product, we set out to create a company that would win on product experience. To do this, we needed to create an organization that was highly product-centric. If you look at which consumer product companies are really winning today, you'll see they're all great at product execution—Apple, Dyson, Nike, BMW, just to name a few. The world is shifting toward favoring organizations that are fluent at creating truly great products, particularly products that deliver consumer experiences as the meaningful differentiator. At Method, we are a product-centric company. Everything starts with creating a killer product, and after that, everything flows naturally.

> I wish more money and time was spent on designing an exceptional product, and less on trying to psychologically manipulate perceptions through expensive advertising.
>
> **—Phil Kotler, professor of marketing,**
> **Kellogg School of Management**

GREAT EXPERIENCES DRIVE GREAT MARKETING Not that many years ago, if you were launching a new product, you would have your PR team send a press kit to the most influential magazine, newspaper, and television editors in hopes of positive coverage. Without even trying the product, they might be positively influenced by your beautiful press kit or the engaging personality of your spokesperson. But today, thanks to social media and online retailers like Amazon that allow any user to post an opinion, everyone has become an editor. Every consumer holds the power to make or break your product with an online review or a quick Yelp that can be seen by everybody and lives forever. Remember that threat from your seventh-grade teacher about putting something in your permanent record? Today that record really exists and it's called the Internet. If you put a subpar product on the market that does not meet consumer expectations, all of your editors will burn you and one day your grandchildren will hear about it.

Consider the "Twitter effect" on movies. The first movie ever to suffer a double-digit single day drop after opening was *Bruno,* starring Sasha Baron Cohen. Why? Because millions of people walked out of the movie theater on

★★★★★ **Fantastic floor cleaner. ...**

   Fantastic floor cleaner. I've tried everything because I have a dog who constantly likes to leave paw prints on the floor. I also really try to buy natural products. This floor cleaner works very well on my hardwood... it leaves it very clean and shiny and it smells fantastic. I recently ran out and had to run to the store and buy a competitive product. It had nowhere near the same gleaming, lasting effect. I threw it out and returned to Method.

▲ **TODAY EVERYONE IS AN EDITOR.** Consumers have the power to toast or roast you for the world to see.

opening night and tweeted, texted, posted, blogged, and Facebooked about what a crappy movie it was! So the next day, a lot fewer people went to see it. This was dramatically different from Cohen's previous movie, *Borat*, which was a great film (to most anyway) that aimed small and built a cult following based on word-of-mouth.

In today's transparent world, alive with social chatter, your product is your marketing. Consumers love to evangelize product experiences that are emotional. Deliver a bad product experience and consumers will roast you. Why call a customer-service number when you can go public with your disappointment? Worse, their comments and reviews will live online long after you've discontinued the dud or given them a rebate. On the flip side, if you deliver a great product experience, consumers will be eager to share their discovery with millions rather than just their close friends or neighbors. Today experiences really matter because they inspire word-of-mouth—both good and bad.

To thrive in this new environment, we think of "cutting steel" as a media expense. Cutting steel is what you do when you build a mold to create a custom product—you buy a big block of steel and then cut it into a mold in the shape you want. It's an expensive process with little room for error; it's why many companies choose generic or stock bottles instead of investing in custom ones. But when we compared the cost of cutting steel to the cost of marketing, the ROI suddenly started looking much better. For us, it costs an average of $150,000 to create a new unique bottle design, which looks expensive compared to selecting a stock bottle with no tooling cost. But if we saved that $150K and invested it in marketing instead, what would it buy us? Not much. Not even one quarter-page ad in a national magazine. Yet the unique bottle design can generate millions in free press and social media attention! Not to mention the marketing power it will retain, capturing retailers' attention, landing better shelf space, and inspiring impulse purchases from new customers. Our belief was that if we created a product that exceeded expectations, people would talk about it and drive word-of-mouth. Because Method could never win the advertising battle by shouting louder, we needed the product to shout for us. Too many companies create products with the assumption that a healthy marketing budget will ensure success. But we believe you should go into any product development process with the assumption there will be no marketing support and that the product needs to be special and differentiated enough to stand on its own. Marketing should be rocket fuel to propel a great product, not the Hail Mary for a mediocre product.

GREAT EXPERIENCES COME FROM A CLEAR POINT OF VIEW How many brainstorming sessions have you been to where someone asks, "How would Virgin do this?" or "How would Disney do this?" When you ask this question about a brand not your own, you have a problem. The starting point for great products is a crystal-clear point of view. If you lack that, everything is an uphill battle. Look at the companies that produce the greatest product experiences— Dyson, Apple, Virgin, Guinness, Mini Cooper . . . they all have a clear POV of who they are and their role in the world. Others have lost their way, trying to be everything to everyone. Take IHOP, for example. While the International House of Pancakes once had a crystal-clear vision—right down to the Bavarian-style architecture of its restaurants—today's IHOP is too focused on selling dinner instead of making unique and killer pancakes from all over the world. It's as if the executives at IHOP started asking themselves, "How would Denny's do it?"

At Method, we ask ourselves, "How would Method do it?" We make sure our brand is inspiring to us and that it serves as the starting brief for anything we work on. To us, Method's POV is inclusive, optimistic, simple, and aspirational— or, to take it directly from our brand DNA statement, "smart, sexy, and sustainable." Internally, we often hear people say they can't start working on something until they have a brief. We like to remind them that "the brand is the brief!" So how do we make our products smart, sexy, and sustainable?

To help articulate our point of view, we defined our experience pillars— standards which every Method product experience must fulfill. Many brands create *brand pillars*, but consistent with our philosophy of baking the marketing

OUR VERSION
OF MARKETING

method.
DISH SOAP
natural concentrated
dish wash liquid
clementine | clémentine
liquide à vaisselle concentré naturel
532 mL (18 FL OZ)

▲ **TO US, CUTTING STEEL IS A MARKETING EXPENSE.** There is no better marketing investment than creating killer packaging.

into the product, we have replaced them with *experience pillars.* To transform mundane chores into pleasurable experiences, we think in four dimensions: design, fragrance, efficacy, and environment. Once a product meets Method's standards in each dimension, it's ready for the market. For example, the latest iteration of our dish soap has a pump that eliminates the drippy mess common to standard bottles, its fragrances are more akin to something you'd find in an expensive candle, and the formula is gentle enough to be safe on the skin yet powerful enough to stand up alongside its mainstream competitors. The ben-

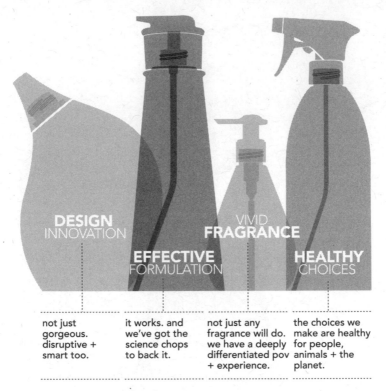

DESIGN
INNOVATION

VIVID
FRAGRANCE

EFFECTIVE
FORMULATION

HEALTHY
CHOICES

| not just gorgeous. disruptive + smart too. | it works. and we've got the science chops to back it. | not just any fragrance will do. we have a deeply differentiated pov + experience. | the choices we make are healthy for people, animals + the planet. |

▲ **EXPERIENCE PILLARS.** By combining style and substance, we deliver a multidimensional product experience.

efits of this experiential formula are twofold: The consumer gets a better experience, and Method gets a competitive advantage. After all, products can be copied, but experiences are one of a kind.

An important aspect of a clear point of view is that it helps you carefully edit and decide not only what to do, but also what not to do. Arguably the most important decision when creating a new product or service is how to simplify by making decisions about what it should not be or what to take out. Too many products are full of "feature creep" that unnecessarily overcomplicates them and creates a product that does everything well but nothing great. In our over-complicated world, the need for simplicity is only going to grow stronger. Apple, In-N-Out Burger, and Trader Joe's got this right. Now will someone please solve our overly complicated living-room entertainment systems so the babysitter can watch TV without a thirty-minute tutorial on which remote to use!

Perhaps the most elegant aspect of Method's POV is how it lends itself to scalability. Think about it: design a better product and what do you have? One good product. Design a better experience, however, and you've got a platform for countless products. This is, in part, why Method has been able to grow so quickly, disrupting each new category with the same strategy. Product experience is about being refreshing to consumers. It's about looking for areas where we can be distinct. In some categories, being refreshing and distinct almost looks easy—as was the case when Method turned its attention to baby care products.

As the company was growing up, we all started having babies, so when we couldn't find baby products with a strong sense of individual design and a belief in greener solutions, we decided to create them ourselves. Conscientious parents love the mild ingredients—like rice milk and mallow—and they applaud the lack of harmful chemicals, like phthalates and parabens (which major baby brands had been hiding off-label for years). But it wasn't ingredients alone that helped our baby line stand out. Keeping in line with our obsessions, the cartoony bottles were eye-catching and made from sustainable materials. And the line was designed with the real-world experiences of busy, preoccupied parents in mind. Our diaper cream features a one-handed pump for no-mess usage and our baby wash includes an oversize cap that doubles as a rinsing cup. As stand-alone fea-

▲ WE DON'T SELL PRODUCTS. WE SELL A PHILOSOPHY.

tures, each was a minor triumph in industrial design; collectively, the line exemplifies the dynamic power of Method's obsession with product experience.

GREAT EXPERIENCES ARE BOTH EMOTIONAL AND RATIONAL Most companies underestimate the power of emotional differentiation, focusing instead on functional differentiation. Rational, fact-based, "hard" attributes always play well in boardrooms and focus groups, but they don't reflect the real way consumers think and act. Consumer loyalty is the result of a brand's ability to stand out on both functional and emotional attributes. Sure, most consumers consider functional attributes more important than emotional ones, but what if all your competitors have the same functional attributes? You've got to stand out somehow—and studies have shown that brands that distinguish themselves on emotional attributes can capture 60 percent greater loyalty (source: Forrester Research).

So to achieve high levels of loyalty, today's new brands have to focus their resources on a select few functional attributes on which they can double down—often requiring them to divert resources from less important ones. An example in nearby Berkeley, California, is Berkeley Bowl grocery stores. It's a foodie's paradise, with a ridiculous selection of fresh produce and exotic goods. Problem is, it's a customer-service nightmare, with long checkout lines, overwhelmed stockers, and crowded aisles. The store purposely overinvests on delivering great selection while willingly sacrificing on service. Walking through the store, you can't help but wonder, "Don't these guys value customer service? Is the produce that good?" For a select group of devoted Berkeley residents, it is—and Berkeley Bowl has built its business on that emotional response. Most of us, however, would rather go to a place that satisfies our desire for strong quality and great service. This is the most effective way to deliver emotionally distinct experiences—by linking them to the "shared values" of your brand and a specific consumer. This reinforces the importance of mission, purpose, and point of view. That's why, at Method, we match the sensory experience to our advocates' shared value for "the love of clean."

Let's start with the toilet. Toilet-bowl cleaner is a great example of the importance of ensuring that every experience has a strong functional side. This was one of the first products we wanted to do back in 2001, but Method didn't enter the category until 2008. The tale of how Lil' Bowl Blu made it to market after seven years of trial and error is a testament to our unflagging devotion to winning on product experience.

Purifiers of porcelain, sanitizers of stool—toilet-bowl cleaners (TBCs) were on Method's hit list from the very beginning. Sure, they aren't glamorous, but they represent everything we wanted to change about the industry. First off, they are ugly—the black sheep of the home-care family. Everyone has them but would rather forget about them. Worse, they are among the most toxic products in the home, literally covered in warnings and instructions for contacting the nearest poison control center if you accidentally ingest even the tiniest amount. Most odious of all, they suck to use. Consumers either have to lift off the heavy lid to get into the grimy tank every few weeks or get down on their knees and scrub away, their face just inches from the smelly bowl.

Ugly, toxic, unpleasant to use—toilet cleaners were right in Method's sweet spot. Soon after setting up our first lab, we began experimenting with nontoxic cleaning agents for the toilet. Problem was, toilet cleaners were toxic for a reason; phosphates and strong acids were the only things strong enough to wipe out the formidable brew of mineral deposits, rust, and bacteria that toilet bowls are famous for. There were organic cleaners on the market, but they were nowhere near as effective—and the toilet bowl was the last place people wanted

▲ COMPROMISES DON'T SELL IN
A CROWDED MARKET.

to cut corners on effectiveness. Even the most environmentally conscious home owner was generally willing to overlook the skull and crossbones on the back of the bottle if the front of the bottle promised to kill *every last germ*.

Our team of green chefs tried liquids, creams, and gels. They sent prototypes home with employees, complete with powders, scrubbers, and sponges. Nothing worked. There was constant temptation to do something substandard because we just couldn't make organic acids work as well as inorganic, toxic crap. But we didn't.

Years passed as we chased the formula like a white whale. No matter how desperate the company was for revenues, no matter how much advocates wailed about how the company was "missing a huge opportunity" (and a toilet cleaner was by far the most requested new product), Method still refused to put out a product that didn't work as well or better than its mainstream, toxic rivals. Then in early 2008, one of our engineers cracked the code that had stymied every Method green chef. Employing lactic acid in combination with some novel renewable surfactants, he finessed a liquid formula strong enough to clean as well as the big brands (without any scrubbing) and safe enough that consumers could rub it on their hands without poisoning themselves. Having waited the better part of a decade for a technology that satisfied the brand's uncompromising obsession with product experience, Method didn't wait a minute more. Debuting in a bladder-shaped bottle and eucalyptus mint scent, Lil' Bowl Blu went straight to national distribution.

Delivering on emotional experiences means engaging the senses, for the senses are the fast track to human emotion. But how many brands actually make full use of them? When people talk about "clean," they usually describe it as the "feeling of clean." Yet there was nothing that felt clean about most cleaners. The sensory experience of using cleaners requires you to hold your breath when using them, leave the room afterward, and then hide the package under the counter because it's so ugly. Somewhere in the history of clean, consumers had been made to believe that if it doesn't make you cry, it must not be working. What's clean about that? We created a new sensory experience with a clean design that appeals to our aesthetic sense, formulas that let us actually feel clean, and fragrances that make a room smell beautiful—not like bleach. We also worked to add touch experiences with packaging that is organic in shape and made from materials that invite touch. The result is a superior sensory experience that elevates the mundane task of cleaning. All great brands have rational, emotional, and sensory values, so we work hard to ensure that Method delivers on all three.

GREAT EXPERIENCES CAN BE SOFT To generate growth, companies seem to love "hard" product innovation—the type of expensive breakthroughs that require engineers and PhDs to toil away deep in the lab. Think Teflon, Viagra, or the Segway scooter. The challenge with this type of innovation is that it's expensive and high risk because it requires a lot of marketing dollars to educate consumers, not to mention the cost of developing the product itself. And because mass advertising is not as effective as it once was, it's becoming more lengthy and expensive to recapture this type of significant R&D investment. The growing glut of technology and patents is creating a lot of noise, making it harder to predictably execute big innovations. What if your amazing new product doesn't take off?

On the flip side, soft innovators establish new standards for quality, experience, and sales in their categories without actually doing anything profoundly innovative.

At Method, we try to balance soft and hard innovations. Don't get us wrong, we love big innovation—like our radical 8x laundry detergent, which has received global accolades—but many companies underestimate the power of soft innovation, which can enhance the consumer experience and drive massive differentiation within a category. The advantage of a soft innovation is that it treads lightly on the R&D budget, requires less marketing support because consumers "get it" right away, and is predictably successful because the idea is familiar and the consumer learning curve is quicker.

Despite this comparably minimal risk, soft innovations have the power to disrupt or shift entire categories. Consider our cucumber all-purpose cleaner, our teardrop hand wash, or our new pump dish soap. Similar products have been done before, but each of ours brings a new scent, shape, or interaction to the customer experience.

For us, soft innovation includes the fragrance, design, and witty personality of our products. None of this is individually groundbreaking, but collectively it has a big impact. Going back to the original idea of "Aveda for the home," bringing a personal-care approach to home care was revolutionary, but the steps to get there were very evolutionary.

We build emotional points of difference into every product to create an engaging consumer experience. We do this by dramatically challenging existing alternatives on every front, from the use of unexpected fragrances like sea minerals to packaging copy that talks about angry squirrels. Great experiences are about being human, and humans want to be surprised. Basic categories like soap

powerful, non-toxic cleaning is not a myth. we're still working on the unicorns.

we help you put
the hurt on dirt

grease + grime don't stand a chance. not with powergreen™ technology in your grasp. each squirt, in all its lovely non-toxic glory, delivers a powerful cleaning punch with naturally derived, biodegradable ingredients. cleaners made from corn + coconut break down dirt, leaving nothing behind but the pleasant scent of victory.

c counters t tile s stone w wood g glass

▲ **EXPERIENCE IN THE DETAILS.** Unexpected gestures help your product bond with consumers.

offer few opportunities for differentiation, so you have to sweat the details. The way the label feels in your hand, the shape of the bottle on your counter, the sound of the trigger being squeezed, the writing on the back of a bottle that makes you chuckle, even the little surprise of an owner's manual inside a candle box. Soft innovations collectively create an experience whenever you provide something different and unexpected.

Appropriation is a great technique for creating soft innovations. It's the act of taking a small part from something created by someone else and repurposing it for new or unexpected use. It's a fancy word for stealing (on a small scale), but it's vital to any artistic business. We "steal" all the time. We stole the idea for the huddle from Innocent, and we stole the fragrance idea of sea minerals from Bare Essentials. Take the upside-down dish soap, inspired by a stapler that sits on its end for easier use, or our original squeeze-and-pour laundry detergent bottle design, borrowed from ACT mouth rinse. We invite you to steal ideas from us. These are victimless crimes. Because there's a big difference between appropriating an idea from a foreign category and doing a knock-off.

Creating a knock-off (stealing other people's work to compete directly

▲ **ONE + ONE = NEW.** Our inspiration wall with souvenirs from trend trips around the world.

against them) says you're not only an asshole, but you also lack the talent to come up with your own original ideas. (Can you tell we deal with this all the time?) But appropriating ideas from another category is about being inspired and translating someone else's innovation to a new purpose. It's about spotting a trend in a distant category or country and recognizing that the same consumer motivation being satisfied there could also be satisfied in your category. It's a way to create more predictable innovation, because you are taking something proven and applying it to your product. In essence, the brand concept for Method—bring personal care to home care—was an appropriation play. We looked for ways to translate what people loved about personal care and brought it to home care. Beautiful fragrances, like lavender, bottle designs that made a personal statement, and formulas that were healthy to touch—all stolen from our friends a few aisles away.

We have specific categories that we continually look to for inspiration. Ours include housewares, cosmetics, and functional beverages, but we don't limit it just to these categories. The idea for our biodiesel shipping program that allows us to ship products using veggie oil was borrowed from local food distributors in San Francisco. We challenge you to use appropriation to avoid the gravitational pull of your category and apply lessons from others that will help achieve the vision you have set for yourself.

Whether you are inspired by an unrelated category or putting a unique spin on a small detail of your packaging, soft innovation will help you build great experiences without reinventing the wheel with every product you make.

GREAT EXPERIENCES ARE POLARIZING Experiences are inherently personal, so don't expect everyone to love everything you do. In fact, attempting to please everyone is the surest way to design a boring product. In our increasingly fragmented consumer world, it is better to upset 90 percent of the people while capturing the attention and interest of the other 10 percent than it is to be merely OK to all of them. In other words, it is better to be something to somebody than nothing to everyone. Consider the example of Cadillac. Once the icon of automotive design excellence, through the 1980s and '90s Cadillac languished. It had gone from being a vibrant and coveted brand, symbol of edgy success, to being the choice of the Geritol crowd. Badly in need of reinvention, instead of sticking with the trend at the time of rounded, bubblelike styling, Cadillac stepped out with a hard-edged, angular look that was a departure not only from its heritage, but from the automotive design orthodoxy of the time. Many hated it. But those who liked it *loved* it. By embracing the power of polarization and doing something daring and unexpected, GM created a product experience unlike any other and reinvigorated the once tired Cadillac brand.

Consumer research is designed to find the solution with the broadest appeal, yet the most successful products always start with a small following. There will always be a gravitational pull to create a product with broad mass appeal by sanding off the edges on what makes it unique or differentiated. But compromises don't sell in a crowded market, and you can't let the remarkability of your product be squeezed out before anyone has a chance to see it. Method experiences this tension all the time with consumers who believe you need to have nuclear-strength chemicals to get something clean and others who believe that if a product contains harsh chemicals, it can't possibly be considered clean. Guess which worldview we serve? If you want someone to love your product experience and generate passion, someone else will probably hate it.

GREAT EXPERIENCES COME FROM GREAT TEAMS Over the past few decades, many companies have driven growth by incremental improvement in efficiencies of manufacture and quality of product. As a result, many Fortune 500 companies have filled their ranks with employees who excel at execution rather than innovation. Most companies don't have the type of people who are hardwired to come up with disruptive innovation, and if they have them, chances are they're not in the right position to effect change.

Here's the reality about a great product development process: It's not much of a process. There is no magical system you can put in place that leads to consistent innovation. Innovation is about blazing new trails and discovering something entirely new. The role of process is to be sure you land in a predictable place each time. Process is your friend when it comes to hitting timelines, cost goals, and critical business parameters, but can be your enemy in that mystical place where creative concepting and idea generation occur.

When we're working toward an innovation, we try to keep the process as messy as possible, but with a few critical steps interspersed. In other words, we get rid of process wherever we can, and use it only when necessary. Designers, creatives, engineers, and formulators are encouraged to begin work before the brief is set, before the product specs are started, and we make sure people know the product ideas well in advance. Since the brand is the brief, everyone is working from the same idea—how do we make our products smart, sexy, and sustainable? With our wiki walls in place, ideas can start flowing and being shared, and because we prototype everything at every stage to make the conversation tangible, ideas are easy to understand and build upon.

Once we start to home in on a strategic direction, we use two stage gates to drive the work and provide outside perspective. The first is with advocates, and the second is with retailers. With advocates we perform consumer auditions, essentially tryouts for a new product, in which we get honest feedback by putting a fully articulated product in people's hands. Then we take the feedback from these auditions, tweak and optimize, and then share the results with our retailers to see how the product will fly in the retail arena. This process allows us to balance an outside perspective and additional ideas from both of these audiences before making a final decision on the concept. It also helps to drive timelines, because the team is working toward consumer research dates or major retail deadlines on the calendar.

With the product concept now well understood, we become a little more methodical in our approach to ensure we hit our quality, time, and margin targets. Line trials are done to make sure we can manufacture efficiently, and press checks are performed to be certain our creative vision comes to life. Zookeepers (project managers) direct the process by making sure the right conversations are happening, the tough questions are being asked, and people are being held to task. Weekly Product Council meetings involving every operational and product development function kick in, giving us more cross-functional perspective and allowing us to address any issues that emerge that jeopardize our timing.

Insourced brains, outsourced machines. A key element of this process is an integrated team, in-house, that includes representatives from each of the major product-development and operational functions. By vertically orienting the intellectual property in-house, we build a tight and cohesive team. Keeping those people working together for a number of years only enhances the quality of the product experiences we can deliver. Walking around our office, you will find teams of experts in fragrance, formulation, engineering, and industrial and graphic design, just to name a few. Through our people, we uphold the belief that by seeking out and assembling the greatest craftspeople in each field and setting them up to do what they do best, we're able to make great product experiences consistently. This is essential, because execution is where products often go from good to great. Or more commonly, compromises occur that turn them into dogs. Having a close-knit group of experts who work on a product from conception to execution means we can take advantage of late learning to improve a product in the final steps and overcome unexpected hurdles that could otherwise compromise it.

Above all else, throughout the entire production process we try to keep one question at the forefront of our minds: Is this a product we would want to use ourselves? This helps us lead the consumer, spark innovation, and avoid the me-too trap. At the end of the day, we create products that every one of our team members is passionate about. All the strategy and consumer research in the world can't make up for passion when it comes to delivering great experiences.

ERROR AUTOPSY: BURSTING THE BUBBLE MYTH AND TRYING TO WIN IN DISH

Not a lot of people walk around wishing they could find a better dish soap. And yet, winning in dish has been a personal obsession since our second year in business. This product plays to the strengths of our experience pillars: It sits out on countertops where design is a factor, fragrance is a huge part of the experience, and nontoxicity is especially important in a product you submerge your hands in. But it is an incredibly hard category to disrupt. Two brands have dominated this category for decades and with razor thin margins and low prices, there is not much opportunity to elevate the opportunity.

Our first dish soap, packaged in a container designed by Karim Rashid in 2002, helped put us on the map, but failed to deliver the experience we had hoped. Beautiful, iconic, and functional, it created a better experience by dispensing from the bottom, eliminating the need to flip the bottle over every time you squirted. But it was an innovation in the formula that flew in the face of one of the unbreakable rules of dish soap: More bubbles equals more effective.

Observing consumers in their homes washing a dish once and rinsing it again and again, we came to the belief that the biggest problem with doing dishes was the time it takes to rinse the bubbles off. Formulas were designed to be so foamy that they made the entire process of doing dishes longer and also wasted a lot of water. Knowing that bubbles have nothing to do with cleaning power (we know you don't believe it, but it's true), we decided to add an ingredient that would make the formula fast-rinsing. You'd get the bubbles you wanted, but when you started rinsing, they'd quickly disperse to leave you with just a sparkling clean dish. Well, consumers hated it. They equated bubbles with clean, and even though we had made their lives easier and their dishes just as clean, the process of rinsing and rinsing again was what told them the formula was powerful. It didn't matter that the bubbles were purely cosmetic, they wanted them. Our goal of delivering a great experience fell flat. We eventually reformulated, and even today, our dish soap is sudsier than it really needs to be. Maybe some-

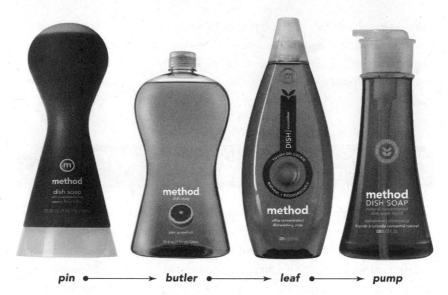

pin ●————————→ butler ●————————→ leaf ●————————→ pump

▲ **DISRUPTING DISH.** Reinventing a very basic product has been an ongoing battle. We think we finally got it right but let us know.

day we will start a campaign to educate the world on how unhelpful those little bubbles really are. Just another potential battle in the fight against dirty.

MUSE: RICHARD BRANSON, VIRGIN

Stepping onto a Virgin America flight is like stepping into an iPod. From the minute you check in and receive the passport-size boarding pass (why didn't someone think of this sooner?) to the time you place your order through the food-on-demand system, you know that Virgin America has truly improved the flying experience. One of Branson's many customer service successes, Virgin America proves that little things can add up to big things—from lavender ambient lighting (easy on your eyes) to self-serve water at the back of the plane (convenient and there when you want it). Personally, we think one of the best touches is the Method soap in the bathroom—now anyone can enjoy a mile-high Method hand wash!

To hear Richard Branson talk about all of this, it seems so simple. "We are bringing back a little glamour to flying," he says. And why not? In an era when every other carrier is focused on cutting services and charging more fees, even a little glamour goes a long way. And it's yet another reason we've been students

▲ **WE ARE ALL IN THIS TOGETHER.** Teaming up with the people's champion of delivering better product experiences.

of Branson's ever since Eric sent the Virgin Group an unsolicited pitch letter to launch Virgin water. We're still waiting for a reply. But we digress . . .

Perhaps above all else, we stole courage from Virgin—the courage to take on a Goliath in a tired category and offer an alternative rooted in a better experience. We did it just once; Virgin's done it dozens, if not hundreds of times. We're inspired by that sense of adventure, cheekiness, fun, and irreverence. Richard Branson reminds you that the hardest part of taking any entrepreneurial challenge is just having the courage to be different and stand up for what you believe.

obsession

7

DESIGN
DRIVEN

**build design leadership
into your dna**

We don't have a good language to talk about this kind of thing. In most people's vocabularies, design means veneer. . . . But to me, nothing could be further from the meaning of design. Design is the fundamental soul of a man-made creation.

—Steve Jobs, CEO of Apple

FROM THE FIRST HUMAN TOOLS AND THE EARLIest cave paintings to the construction of the Egyptian pyramids and the rise of Greek architecture, people have always been able to recognize iconic design when they see it. Not surprisingly, the design IQ of the average person has never been higher than it is today. From the enduring columns of the Parthenon to the prescient sketches of Leonardo da Vinci to the minimalist utility of the iPhone, the role of design in the life of the average individual has only grown broader and deeper with each new generation.

If our grandparents competed in the age of mass production and our parents competed in the age of information, today's entrepreneurs compete in the age of aesthetics. Want a pair of custom Vans kicks? Design them yourself online—they'll be at your door in less than three weeks! Personalized M&Ms, printed with your own custom messages? Simply log on to mymms.com, pick your favorite color, and fill in the blanks. Thanks to designer collaborations at discount retailers, we can now expect high-end and customized design at all price points—from Vera Wang mattresses at Target to IKEA's praised minimalist Scandinavian designs at cut-rate prices. Even current media trends reflect a broad interest in better design: Flip on the tube and you're as likely to catch an episode of *Extreme Home Makeover, Martha Stewart Living,* or *Project Runway* as you are a sitcom or major-league game. Never before has design been more mainstream—or more mystifying.

It's not that we misunderstand design; it's that so many of us now have our own unique understanding of what design means. Few words in the English language are as confusing as *design*. Look it up in *Webster's* or the *Oxford English Dictionary* and you'll find dozens of definitions. Google it and you'll get close to 2 billion page results. Even Wikipedia, the crowd-sourced online encyclopedia that seems to have an answer for everything, fails to reach a consensus on the meaning of the word, stating, "No generally-accepted definition of 'design' exists."

This is particularly true throughout the various disciplines of the business world. Inventory management, sustainability, research and development—even within the same company the word *design* will have many different meanings. To the marketing team, it may refer to the graphic layout of a new magazine ad or billboard. To the guys in IT, design has to do with software engineering and Web analytics. Ask the head of HR about design, and you'll likely hear about human capital development, labor mobility, and concurrent occupational structures. Confused yet? From person to person and industry to industry, design is in the eye of the beholder.

Inevitably, misconceptions about design abound. Design has become associated with the supermodel, the creative genius, and the expensive. Design is New York, but not New Jersey. Design is "iconic," that is, symbolic and not real. Design is mysterious and elite, not something any average person can enjoy. But when used intelligently, design has the power to heal our world and change our lives. We just have to understand it first.

OUR VIEW OF DESIGN

When we talk about design, we're not just talking about aesthetics design—the style and ergonomics of a given product (though we'll get to that). We're also talking about system design—the underlying, often unspoken intentions that dictate how a business forms and achieves its goals and creates a positive impact in the world.

Take Toyota's *kaizen* philosophy. Japanese for "continuous improvement," *kaizen* is a system that empowers everyone in the company to contribute innovative ideas by inviting feedback from blue-collar workers on the production line, sales reps in the field, accountants in the offices, and anyone else in the company. In contrast, back in the United States, the Big Three American car companies' allegiance to the status quo caused them to lose touch with their founding intentions—guiding principles like innovation, efficiency, and value.

We're sons of automotive entrepreneurs, so Detroit's decline was a daily concern at our families' dinner tables. Stagnating under layers of "safe" business strategy, Detroit suffocated the dynamic design thinking that had made it successful in the first place. The grand era of automotive design that had given rise to triumphs like curvaceous Corvette fenders and Cadillac's iconic fins—a time when all of popular culture looked to Detroit for innovative technical and aesthetic cues—had faded into the past. Decades of compromises, from cost-cutting measures to risk-averse leadership, had resulted in a collection of largely uninspiring look-alike brands and me-too models.

In retrospect, the reason for Detroit's resistance to innovation is obvious: The American automotive industry was no longer designed for "continuous improvement." Quite the opposite, in fact. After nearly a century of global dominance, American carmakers had grown risk-averse and complacent. Underestimating the threat from their Asian competitors, they were inclined to inertia and recalcitrance instead of innovation and resourcefulness. Change was considered a liability. Throughout the industry, the mantra was the same: "If it ain't broke, don't fix it" (local mechanics excepted, of course).

The status quo strategy made sense at the time because the popular business thinking called for focusing on the here and now, analyzing the most recent benchmarks, and minimizing risk in the short term. And yet as the challenges mounted in the 1970s and '80s, it became clear that Detroit didn't simply have a fuel-efficiency problem or a reliability problem. Rising fuel costs and viable foreign competitors were only symptoms. Detroit had a design problem.

When we launched our own company two decades later, the fall of Detroit was still fresh in our minds. We resolved not to make the same mistake and recognized that the democratization of design in its many forms was a cultural shift that could give us a major competitive advantage. We were intent on designing not just our products, but our *company*—to create innovation predictably and consistently, again and again, and to continually improve it with every decision we made so that those innovations could not only create a competitive advantage, but also a positive impact on our world.

As Tom Peters often preaches, design is why you most frequently love or hate something. We love TiVo because it is well designed. We hate Comcast's DVR because it is so poorly designed. Sooner or later, every touch point of a brand—from products to customer service to marketing—has to be designed. So why do so few companies make design a priority? We've been asking ourselves that for years. As our seventh and last obsession, we have devoted ourselves to being design driven from the very beginning.

PUTTING IT ALL ON THE LINE FOR DESIGN

When we started Method, we each funded it with $45,000 of our own money, allowing us just $90,000 to take an idea from a sheet of paper to a product on store shelves. Wrestling with that challenge, we spent almost half our seed capital just figuring out our packaging design! Crazy? Maybe. Obsessed? Absolutely. It's a fine line sometimes.

Of course, there was method to our madness. When we looked at brands that cut through the clutter, we noticed a common theme: The best of them used a unique packaging format and created a new product archetype. Altoids had the tin box, Absolut had the minimalist bottle, and Red Bull had the slim can. The design solution was clear: Our spray cleaner needed an iconic shape of its own. Unsatisfied with all of the available prefabricated bottles, we designed one ourselves, based on a camping fuel bottle we found in Norway, and hired San Francisco–based graphic designer Michael Rutchik to create the labels. The original images featured Eric's girlfriend alongside Adam and props from Home Depot—a sink, kitchen counter, and window frame (we kept the receipt and returned it all immediately after the photo shoot). Using the last pennies of our meager life savings, we toiled over design from the get-go. With the bottle ready and the last of our money invested in formulation, we knew our packaging would have to do our marketing for us. As history has shown, it did.

That's one of the things we love about design—it's one of the few business tools that is both immediate and impactful. Design has the power to instantly change perceptions by engaging our emotions and seducing our senses. Method wasn't the first to realize this, of course. Our culture is full of clichés that demonstrate the power of appealing design—"love at first sight," "seeing is believing," "a picture is worth a thousand words." When harnessed the right way, design has the power to transform a commodity into a special, memorable

▲ **CLUTTER CUTTER.** As the world gets more complex, simple design gets rewarded.

product experience. People in business so easily forget that we are all humans selling to other humans, who are by nature tactile, visual, and emotional creatures. We are motivated by brands and products that give us sensory pleasure, and we respond strongly to our surroundings through unique experiences. At Method, part of our strategy is to deliver great experiences by designing for the senses, which make our products a heightened experiential part of everyday life. Our ultimate goal is to elevate everyday soap into an object of desire.

This was our thinking when we hired Karim Rashid, hailed by *Time* magazine as "the poet of plastic." We designed our first dish soap during year one at Method, and we needed to make a statement—declaring to the press, investors, and retailers where we were taking the home-care category. In a lot of ways, it was similar to how an automotive or apparel brand launches a concept car or halo product—one lasting impression creates room for countless others.

So why Karim? Eric created a list of the most famous industrial designers in

▲ **KARIM RASHID, THE POET OF PLASTIC.** When launching a new company or brand, search for a design collaborator.

the world (remember, "Always knock on the big door"), and we planned to work our way through each name until someone said yes. Karim was first on the list because we knew he was committed to democratizing design by creating for the majority, not the minority, and we wanted to dispel the myth that good design is too expensive for the average person. So we shot him an e-mail titled "Are you our design genius?" in which we pitched the idea of reinventing the banal world of dish soap with a revolutionary design. Shocking us both, he e-mailed us back within twenty minutes, and we struck a deal to pay him with a combination of cash and company stock.

With Karim we made a deep commitment to industrial design, to create not just unique packaging but unique products—and that tradition continues. For a small brand, this is a major investment that eats up capital, but it's one we feel necessary to ward off fast followers and threats from private labels. Leveraging industrial design places us in a unique position. The capital expenditure involved in custom designs makes it harder for copycats or private-label brands to imitate us, while the speed with which we create products makes it difficult for competitors who operate on enormous scale to follow quickly.

Ten years later, our obsession with design hasn't wavered (though we have a little more cash to work with now). In fact, it's only gotten stronger. After working with Karim for many years, we've since brought design in-house, cultivating a design-centric company, and putting design work side by side with the rest of our business. Every employee can see exactly how our designers function and understand the role design plays in the overall vision we have for the company. To us, design is a way of thinking—a way of imagining and creating the future that every Method employee participates in. At Method, everyone is asked to think like a designer, whether concocting a formulation or solving an accounting issue. In making design a core focus of our company, we've come up with certain steps to make sure that—no matter your industry—you can build a culture focused on design.

LEVERAGE DESIGN PLUS BUSINESS THINKING

Entire books could be dedicated to the art of creating healthy tension between the creative and the business mind, and over the past few years, we've certainly experienced a lot of drama in the pursuit. Building a utopia where brilliant business managers and creative geniuses work side by side in complete harmony is as likely as opening a unicorn ranch in the clouds. Trust us, we've tried (the former, that is). Despite our best efforts, we've never found this magical place—though we have learned some of the secrets to creating an environment where both managers and creatives thrive.

Most companies treat design as something to be handled by a small group of people—generally toward the bottom of the organization's hierarchy. This mystifies us. We challenge you to find a company that leverages design as a core competitive advantage without creative leadership at the highest ranks of the company.

Method is no exception. Internally, we preach the need to integrate design and business thinking. In essence, business thinking is about being skilled at decision making—working from a set of existing options to create predictable and reproducible systems that are, ideally, bulletproof. In other words, good business thinkers are great at making decisions based on *existing* knowledge—things that have worked in the past. And in business, once something is working, it seems prudent to copy it. The result: systems that are reliable, but not always original. This is business as algorithm—quantifiable, measurable, and provable.

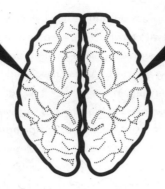

*decision making
from a set of
existing alternatives*

*creating new choices,
drive differentiation*

▲ **BLURRING THE LINES BETWEEN STRATEGY AND CREATIVITY.**
Design thinking is about creating new choices that drive differentiation.

It's a philosophy that speaks to the management belief "What gets measured gets done."

Design thinking, however, is just the opposite—it's about creating new choices, options that didn't exist before. The goal of design is to create something new, better, or different.

There's a reason that design thinking is so different from more traditional ways of thinking. Most people use inductive reasoning (drawing general conclusions based on many observed particulars) and deductive reasoning (drawing particular conclusions based on accepted generalizations) to consider a problem or come up with an idea. But designers also rely on a third type: abductive reasoning—the logic of what might be. This is the art of creating something that's never been imagined before. The vocabulary isn't important, but the underlying concept is: Designers don't copy, they create. While an engineer may study problems and devise solutions from a known set of tools, designers must imagine solutions that don't come from a preexisting set of techniques—forcing themselves to create wholly original and unpredictable solutions to problems. You see where this leads, right? It leads to solutions that are novel and unique, which, if harnessed appropriately, are powerful tools in business, sustainability, and culture.

The fact that business and design require different ways of working is why most creative and design resources live in outsourced design firms and advertising agencies. If you're managing a reliable and predictable process, you will tend to attract folks who are skilled at creating a predictable result time and again. Just imagine the power of harnessing these two different approaches into one fluid team—one that simultaneously and artfully balances rigor and discipline with disruption and innovation. This has been our goal since the beginning.

And from the beginning, we've worked together as cofounders to bring these two approaches together. We aren't the first to try this; companies that blur the lines between design and business thinking very often put an artist at or near the top with the operators. Consider the heyday of Motor City. When U.S. automakers were at the vanguard of the industry, they had artists in leadership positions. At GM, the visionary Harley J. Earl's GM Tech Center, designed by Eero Saarinen, was the world's most modern and complete industrial design center when it opened in 1955, and it influenced some of the world's most notable car designs. Over at Ford, while Henry was the visionary founder, and his grandson Henry II rebuilt the brand into a powerful industrial force following World War II, the most creative of the family was the founder's son Edsel—a design genius who was responsible for the Lincoln Continental and other unique Ford styles during the Art Deco period of the 1930s.

Today we live in a burgeoning age of corporate design heroes who understand design's value. VPs of design and chief design officers are becoming more

▲ **DON'T OUTSOURCE YOUR SOUL.** At Method, design not only is insourced, but also has a seat at the leadership table with people like Josh Handy, our Disruptor, aka head of innovation. (Doesn't he look like Moby?)

prominent and more powerful players within the executive suite, and design itself is taking on as important a role as marketing and executive leadership. Design will always be subjective—it can't be managed by committee—so companies need a cultural leader at the top who gives the company an aesthetic point of view and ensures that the organization stays on track. Ultimately, while you need to weave design and business thinking through the entire organization, one person needs to be responsible for championing, curating, and editing the brand's visual point of view.

To achieve this balance throughout Method, we have reinforced our leadership team with two VPs who have design backgrounds—our VP of product design and our VP of brand experience—who work hand in hand on a daily basis with our CFO and VP of operations. Method would not have lasted this long if it had operated inefficiently, and while not celebrated as often, those who work in the more traditional roles in operations and finance form the backbone from which the consumer experience grows. So while part of Method runs the way you would expect a consumer-products company to run, with strong operating rigor (mixing soaps, manufacturing pumps, filling orders, etc.), the part that defines the experience for the consumer and creates every touch point of the brand feels more like a design firm than a manufacturer.

Managing the juxtaposition of creative innovation and operational predictability is a constant challenge for us and our entire leadership team. It means balancing discipline and disruption, left brain and right brain, in productive, not destructive, ways. We need to give people the freedom to follow their gut, but we also need to hold them accountable for their performance. So we set a high bar, recognizing that occasional failure is an unavoidable side effect of pushing into uncharted waters. While we have to do everything possible to wow our advocates, we know we also need to eliminate unnecessary costs and inefficiencies. Which is to say, we need to be equally skilled at quantifying the now and intuiting what's next. Of course, how many companies are truly good at that?

One important benefit of bringing design in-house is that it allows you to move faster. By not having to deal with outsiders, you can skip the process of bringing your partners up to speed or explaining a concept. Production challenges can be dealt with swiftly. An in-house team lowers creative and design cost, whereas paying an agency's project fees or retainers can be exorbitantly expensive. Designers help you envision what can be, and the tools of prototyping allow you to share your vision with others. In-house design allows you to more efficiently exploit every touch point to maximize marketing effectiveness. More-

▲ **WE LIVE THROUGH DESIGN.** At Method every floor is the design floor. Design is not a function. It's what we do.

over, designers and creatives tend to be eclectic and passionate, bringing positive influences to the culture. Below are more ways to make design a focus of your company.

BUILD A DESIGN COMPANY, NOT A DESIGN DEPARTMENT At Method, design is a philosophy, an attitude. You will never hear us say the words *design department*, because as in the case of our obsession to be a green giant, we expect everyone to think like a designer to influence every molecule of our business. Take our first laundry presentation in the United Kingdom by our head of sales. Faced with his first big sales call on a yet-to-exist account in a hypercompetitive market, he needed a way to bring creativity to what, for the buyers he was meeting, was just another laundry presentation. So instead of a PowerPoint deck, he set up a clothesline in the buyer's office, writing out the important content of his pitch on pieces of laundry. Businesses today have to not only outthink the competition, but also outimagine them, which means thinking more like designers. And what happened in that laundry sales presentation? Yup, we got the green light!

Design at Method is naturally a creative process, but that isn't to say design is limited to strictly "creative" disciplines. Take technology—even minute changes to the hardware and software we use to operate our distribution net-

▲ **METHOD ART SCHOOL.** A designer is anyone who makes something better so we encourage everyone to think like a designer.

work are best made with an eye toward creative solutions. And for all the creativity that goes into fragrance design, at least as much creative energy goes into determining the most efficient way to get that particular fragrance from the other side of the world into each of the rapidly moving bottles on our automated production line. Because such problems permeate our business, we make sure that everyone at Method is a designer.

Operating under this broader definition of design, we challenge our team members to exemplify the designer's mind-set in all of their work—be it identifying innovative improvements in their own specialty (like a procurement manager uncovering an elegant cost-saving means of sourcing new materials) or even spotting a solution outside their field (as when a team member in sales discovers how to stack and ship our products in a more sustainable manner). As you might expect, divas and dilettantes don't last long in the face of so much creative cross-pollination, no matter how talented they are. But in a corporate world that's in love with e-mail memos and PowerPoint slides, a design-centered outlook helps keep everyone fresh and focused on the power of the original idea. Creativity comes in all forms, in many types of people, in many lines of work and ways of life. The key is to harness, cultivate, and enhance this natural creativity in every discipline. Once you can do that, you're designing.

One tool for helping everyone think like a designer is an office space that encourages this type of thinking, literally building collaborative behaviors into the culture. While in advertising, Eric saw firsthand the influence and connection between office-space design and the work that was created within it. While working at Fallon McElligott in Minneapolis, Eric noticed that the company went to great lengths to design an amazing space that inspired creativity and made collaboration flow like water. Years later, while he was working at Hal Riney in San Francisco, the company moved its offices to a new custom-built space whose designers had lacked an understanding of how office design connects to creativity. The office felt more like a glorified accounting firm, and it sucked much of the energy and creativity out of the company. This contributed to the demise of a once great agency.

From our earliest days working out of Adam's car, we believed our office design would have a profound effect on the quality of the work. There is a fine interplay between architecture and humanity, and stepping into our lobby, you immediately understand that design is a priority for us. The modern furniture and exposed brick walls are more evocative of a boutique hotel than the offices of a soap company. More important, all the materials are recycled or reused and LEED (Leadership in Energy and Environmental Design) certified. Unlike companies that put creative effort only into the design floor or department, our entire company feels like the design floor, including our satellite offices. The offices are designed to raise the bar on the quality of work and subconsciously remind everyone of the importance of design. They are yet another physical realization of our philosophy of style with substance. In essence, the Method office space, by having a great design, demands great work.

Besides inspiring us, well-designed offices also encourage brainstorming. We don't believe that scheduled, structured brainstorming sessions yield the best ideas, and with the pace of work today, finding time to brainstorm becomes more and more difficult. In its place, we prefer a company in which brainstorming is a natural part of the entire day and where ideas are continually being shared, vetted, and built upon in short ideation loops. Essentially, work should feel like one giant brainstorm.

We view design as extroverted experimentation—from our boundless whiteboard surfaces throughout the office (wiki walls) to the open floor plan that keeps everyone's work in plain sight. Features like these create the vibe of an open lab, where ideas are free to be shared, debated, and improved. Our designers (and that includes the formulators) post their work on the walls so everyone who passes by can be influenced by it and can help build upon it. We put up whiteboards not just in the conference rooms, but also in the hallways and around workspaces. This process encourages our employees to build upon, not merely critique, other people's work. The work that is shared is unfinished, but just sharing it creates a place where we receive constructive input from everyone, not just a few people.

The challenge with this way of working is that designers are uneasy about placing new, fragile ideas into the harsh sunlight for all to see. Doing so requires trust—trust that the organization will help the ideas become bigger and better rather than focus on flaws: "Yes, it's a good idea, and here is how to make it better" instead of "Yes, it's a good idea, but here's the problem." This requires constant practice, reinforcing behaviors that we believe define effective collaboration:

▲ **OUR WIKI WALLS.** Make design the first step, not the last step.

- Assume goodwill. If you start from a common goal, you'll build first and critique later.
- Ask questions. The fastest way to kill collaboration is to try to answer questions. We force ourselves to ask them instead.
- Demonstrate understanding. Help people align their interests so they'll use two minds, not just one, to create something new.
- Communicate directly. Trust us, you can't do anything new via e-mail.
- Be supportive. "Yes, and," not "Yes, but."

Another way we help everyone think like a designer is by distributing our design guidelines (which internally we refer to as brand behaviors) to the entire company. By educating everyone on our approach to design, we ensure that everyone understands the importance of design as an asset and of maintaining a unified design vision. Once, a buyer at a major grocery chain gave a sales director a hard time about the lack of benefits listed on the front of our daily shower cleaner. Because our sales director was educated on Method's design philosophy, he could help the buyer understand that the lack of visual clutter actually helped it stand out on shelf and made our advocates more likely to leave it in the shower, making the product more convenient to use. Ultimately, the whole company has to buy into design for it to be successful.

Good design is good business.

—Thomas Watson, former president and chairman of IBM

INVEST MORE IN DESIGN AND LESS IN STRATEGY In our MBA-saturated culture, strategy-based thinking tends to overshadow design- and idea-based thinking. Wary of the big idea, investors would rather bet on the big strategy, no matter how unoriginal it is. We've seen companies spend hundreds of thousands of dollars on strategic reports from big consultancies like Bain or McKinsey, only to balk when the same experts advise investing fifty grand on new product outside their comfort zone. But a poor strategy well executed is always better than a great strategy poorly executed. After all, consumers don't see the strategy; they see the execution.

What consumers see, feel, taste, and experience is what they remember. And this is the result of what we do, what we execute, not the strategy behind it. For example, Virgin America's strategy is probably no different from that of

Alaska Airlines; the difference is the creative execution of the brand and in-flight experience—and what a huge difference. After all, consumers don't buy Power-Point documents. They buy the product, the result of all the design decisions that have gone into it. Imagine a wife yelling to her husband during the commercials, "Honey, quick, get in here! There's a great strategy on TV!" Don't get us wrong, we're definitely guilty of occasionally dropping a simple thought into the middle of a triangle on a PowerPoint slide and calling it "strategic thinking," but there's a limit.

The good news is that we live in the design age. But we also live in the age of accountability. Today, no business decision gets made without in-depth analytical data and clear proof points about its impact on the bottom line. The new corporate mantra is "If you can't measure it, you can't manage it." It's hard to assess the emotional impact of design on the success of a business, but we believe design drives return on investment, making it one of the few tools that create a tangible statement for your brand or business with every dollar you spend. A common thread in any company that successfully uses design as a competitive advantage is the unwavering belief that good design makes good business.

Over the years, there has been some compelling data that we may be guilty of overusing to our board to justify design expenditures. The London School of Economics found that on average, every $1 spent on design yielded a $3 ROI, and packaging design guru Rob Wallace has preached that on average, every dollar invested in package design generates over $400 of incremental profit within CPG companies. Whichever number you believe, our proof is empirical; we've vaulted to leadership status in one of the biggest industries on the planet by investing in design—and we've done it profitably.

Understanding ROI from design is challenging because great design has an emotional impact on consumers that is inherently hard to measure. Great design is also about great consumer experiences through every touch point, so pulling apart different aspects of a design for testing is inherently flawed. For years we would debate the role of design, and often some among us would argue that design is not needed everywhere. For example, team members understood the value of design on a hand wash that assumes a decorative role on the sink but less so its value on a toilet-bowl cleaner, which will probably get shoved in a cabinet no matter how beautiful the bottle. Our argument is that if we are going to be design driven, we need to take every opportunity to elevate design for a higher experience for the consumer. If you break that promise in any one spot,

▲ **THE DESIGN BECOMES THE ADVERTISING.** Great design creates great advertising and social media engagement.

the entire design experience of your brand falls apart. Great design is in the details.

MAKE DESIGN AN ITERATIVE PROCESS Design is an iterative process—one in which you move quickly from observation to idea to execution to learning, repeating the process in quick loops until the concept becomes highly evolved and refined. At Method we brief, design, prototype, and repeat quickly, as many times as it takes to land on the right solution. Sometimes we get it right on the first try, and other times it can take twenty tries. Traditional companies follow a longer, linear process. Our system allows collective thinking to occur in a fast and furious way to overcome problems and barriers that block innovation.

Designing iteratively requires making design the first step, not the last. We expect creatives to bring business thinking to the table, and we expect our talented business people to participate in creative thinking at the very beginning. A linear, business opportunity–led approach limits the ability of ideas to build upon one other in iteration cycles. Most companies take a waterfall approach where you move development between stages, and the designers enter late in the process. Our creative process not only can begin before a brief is written, but we encourage it to. Our goal is to bring all that problem-solving design goodness to the front end. Frequently the creative inspires the strategy, not the other way around. Having a culture in which everyone is trained to think like a designer enables this asynchronous but highly productive methodology, because each person knows the brand inside out and is in tune with the business direction and the audience it serves. The goal is to close the gap between strategy and execution so that we can drive a vision, go fast, and surprise consumers.

An example of this creative method is our collaboration with Disney. When Disney approached us, instead of first engaging in a long process of business and legal due diligence to decide whether or not to proceed, we made the design the first step. The strategy was simple: Find a design solution for a kids'

▲ **INNOVATION IS CREATIVITY APPLIED TO BUSINESS.** Design helps us envision the future and can change our perceptions of what's possible.

line of products that played to both kids' and adults' sensibilities. The kids' market has always been very challenging because there is a small window before the primary purchase decision transfers from the adult to the child, and finding a product that can transcend this transfer is elusive. This is why character licensing dominates this aisle. While characters may delight a child, they leave many parents less than thrilled about having gaudy SpongeBob on their kitchen counter or the questionable ingredients a product may contain.

Creating a kids' line with strong sensibilities that would satisfy the desires of both a child and an adult was no easy task. But when our designers and Disney's design studio crafted the first concepts on how Method and Mickey could come together, we began to understand the vision. Our studio created a prototype from their original ideas, and within weeks, after several loops of observation, prototype, learning, and reapplication, we landed on a design that achieved our goal. Only at this point did we begin proving the business case, which moved quickly because we had a tangible idea and vision in hand that everyone could see, touch, and understand. The result was a design that evoked the iconic

▲ THIS IS NO MICKEY MOUSE HAND
WASH. Equally loved by kids and adults.

Mickey silhouette that kids love, but with a minimalist graphic treatment that adults would equally love in their homes.

FOCUS DESIGN ON SOLVING CONSUMER-CENTRIC PROB-LEMS Great design begins with asking yourself, "What problem am I trying to solve?" We frequently use People Against Dirty as our opening brief for a specific design challenge. When we set out to disrupt laundry for the second time, we started by asking what type of "dirty" we should rid from the world of laundry? Luckily for us, there were many monsters that needed slaying in this category. In this case, we set out to rid the world of the ubiquitous and obnoxious laundry jug. The laundry jug is the SUV of the consumer products industry. It's heavy, it's messy, and it's wasteful in terms of the resources it uses, but it's supremely profitable for its makers. Framing the problem correctly led us to think differently about laundry detergent and ask the question, "How can we eliminate the mess for consumers while fundamentally changing the relationship between laundry detergent and the environment?" This led us to a hunch: What if we created a single-load laundry pill that could easily be popped into your machine with no waste or excess packaging? Genius, right? Well, sort of. After a year of prototyping, we were getting really close but couldn't quite get the price

▲ **FAILURE OFTEN OPENS A NEW DOOR FOR SUCCESS.** By failing to create a laundry pill we found a way to reinvent the ubiquitous laundry jug. But eventually our green chefs will crack this too.

and cold-water solubility to a place where we were 100 percent comfortable with the product's experience and economics.

After yet another round of trying to create our magic pill, we finally declared the project a big fat failure. But by going down this unique path, our green-chef team had created a formula that was amazingly concentrated (because it had to fit in that pill), so we started asking ourselves what else we could do with this formula. Could we put it in a pump? The team quickly put our miracle formula in a cosmetic pump that is usually used for baby-diaper creams and antiaging serums—not ideal, but it gave us a sense of the experience. Now we were onto something. We tried it at home, we gave it to friends and neighbors, and we asked, "Would this change how you do laundry?" Within a couple of weeks, we had created several more rounds of prototypes and sent them to a small group of consumers. We invited them to share their experiences, and the feedback was consistent. Everyone was skeptical when they received it in the mail (how can this little pump ever work?), but after they tried it, they did not want to give it back. Within a couple of weeks, we had gone from idea to consumer auditions, and we quickly aligned as a team to go for it. The idea for the design of the bottle came fast because we already understood the benefits the product should communicate to consumers. There was no testing of different shapes and no lengthy and

▲ **PEOPLE PARTICIPATE IN PACKAGES.** Great design invites engagement.

expensive design process. The shape shattered the traditional archetype for a laundry detergent, and the design gave us a means to challenge the category. Bye-bye, jug. Hello, Method laundry.

All told, the pump and formula stability took a circuitous two-year path to market, but the big idea hatched in an instant. In 2010 our laundry pump won the Industrial Design Society of America's Best in Show IDEA (Industrial Design Excellence Award), an honor normally reserved for "sexier" products like iPods

MASH IT UP—GREAT DESIGN HAS TENSION

While great design requires a single goal or vision, truly great design often unites many opposing design tensions. This underlying tension is what gives great design uniqueness, energy, and excitement. Look no further than mash-ups, which have become commonplace in fashion and music. High-end designers like John Varvatos partner with Converse, and musical artists like Jay-Z and Eminem often collaborate on other pop stars' work even if their style is completely different. The more unexpected the mash-up, the more exciting it is.

Cirque du Soleil is a great example of using a mash-up to reinvent the circus. Producers bring together world-class performing art and knee-slapping street entertainment. The result is a show that you love and respect—a combination that we would argue is the essence of any great brand. Our original mash-up—style and substance—created a new archetype and experience for cleaning products. Advocates love the fact that our designs are beautiful and fun, and they respect us for our commitment to sustainability and human health. Even our original pitch to Target—"designer commodities"—was a mash-up of two opposing ideas from opposite ends of the consumer spectrum.

The challenge of mashing up two opposing ideas is that the hybrid is often hard to successfully shepherd through the maze of consumer focus groups and executive committees. We combined a personal-care-style pump dispenser with laundry detergent or hand soap, then mashed up that mash-up with sea-mineral fragrance from the world of cosmetics. Fortunately, if you mash up two things that already work together, you can use each as a proof point to convince others why the new mash-up might succeed.

and motorcycles. It also grabbed a 2011 Good Housekeeping VIP (Very Innovative Products) award, but most important, it changed an industry and drastically improved the environmental footprint of laundry detergent. Seriously, if you decide you want to try one of our products after reading this book, try our laundry detergent. It's the best product we've ever made.

ERROR AUTOPSY: BLOQ, OUR EDSEL

Years ago, when we tried to launch into the personal-care category, we were faced with a major design challenge. How do we break in? How do you disrupt a space where almost every imaginable bottle shape, color, and ingredient has been created? You can't out-Dove Dove or out-Olay Olay.

We knew we had to do something truly unique, and our home-care designs weren't going to cut it. The result was Bloq, an übernatural personal-care line of products that was packaged in an iconic square shape. Bloq brought a lot of innovation to the market, with high-quality natural formulations and interesting, unexpected fragrances never before seen at mass market—not to mention unique features, bar-soap-like texture, and packaging that not only stood out on the shelf but fit neatly together with other products like part of a Lego set in your shower and bathroom. Stepping back, we believed Bloq really brought something different to the category. We were right—just not in the way we'd hoped.

Despite our innovations, Bloq bombed. Big time. While the bottle was beautifully designed, the underlying business design of the product was rushed and somewhat happenstance. It blew a hole in our 2008 financial plan; the cost of marking down the product to clear it out of the marketplace sank our P&L that year. It was the first time we learned that killing a new product could be much more expensive than launching one. Worse, Bloq crippled our ability to spend just as the recession picked up steam and direct competition took dead aim at the green category. The timing could not have been worse.

Fortunately, we learned more from the Bloq failure than we would have learned from two years in business school. (Unfortunately, it was a lot more expensive than B-school tuition.) Nevertheless, the failure of Bloq taught us once and for all that design is about much more than aesthetics alone.

Mistake #1: Letting the business drive the brand instead of the brand drive the business. We got into the body-care business for business reasons only: The category was big, operationally synergistic with our cur-

▲ **BE A REBEL WITH A CAUSE.** The best work
always dances on the edge of embracing us, which
was the case with our bloq personal-care line.

rent model, and it had attractive margins. Plus, the success of our hand wash meant that retailers were pressuring us to expand our body-care line. The thing is, our brand was structured to disrupt home care with a personal-care approach ("Aveda for the home"). Taking it into body care lacked a big idea to disrupt—one of the keys to all of our best successes. Hand soap was successful because we linked it to consumers' relation-ships with their homes (decor), not just their feelings for skin care. Bottom line, the Method brand belonged in the home.

Mistake #2: Lack of alignment. To find a big idea for the category, we had to push design hard. The idea was to appropriate the trend of "object design" from the world of fine fragrance and bring it to body care. Ini-tially, we wanted to create a bottle that, like a smooth river stone, would not stand up but would sit in your shower or bath. We also wanted it to be merchandised in bins rather than on the shelf. As we went to cut steel, our team couldn't get aligned around the idea of merchandising in bins. So we changed course at the last minute to a block shape that (we thought at the time) disrupted the curvy world of body wash. It behaved like an iconic object but could still sit on shelves. This was not a good kick-ass-at-fast moment. The totally square shape was hard to mold, so, under the pressure to meet our launch dates, we ended up working with the only blow molder in the world that would attempt it. As a result, the production line ran slow—and it was located in a plant far from our filler. Compounding problems of slow production and long supply lines, we decided to do each bottle in a different color and silk-screen pattern. Instead of working from common platforms, each Bloq SKU was its own unique noninterchangable item, making logistics with shippers, stockers, and shoppers a headache.

Mistake #3: Launching a big new product on a large scale without beta testing it first. The combination of a less-than-strategic supply chain and a big forecast led to huge inventory levels. So when Bloq launched and didn't sell well, we were sitting on too much inventory to make quick improvements and correct our mistakes. Soon enough, retailers started to discontinue it, marking down the price and hitting us with huge financial liabilities.

In the end, we had to give away the finished-goods inventory and recycle thousands of expensive, perfectly decorated bottles that had never been filled. It forced us to lay off employees, and it wiped out our marketing budget for the year. Although we learned some valid lessons from Bloq, we remain steadfast in our commitment to taking big risks—but from now on, we'll do so with our design principles at the top of our minds.

MUSE: ANDY SPADE, COFOUNDER OF KATE SPADE

Andy Spade—cofounder of Kate Spade with his wife and business partner, Kate—is one of our personal masters of design and a major muse. Andy started his career in advertising before taking the leap into launching his own. (Andy also happens to be the brother of comedian David Spade, a fact that should give you a sense of his personality; picture someone with the design sensibilities of Calvin Klein and then add a high dose of comedy.) Probably the closest comparison to Andy is the movie director Wes Anderson, who combines great style with a quirky personality. We were very fortunate to have Andy and Kate as early investors, and they have served as an ongoing source of inspiration ever since.

It's no secret that Eric has a bit of a man crush on Andy, and as Eric's wife

▲ **ANDY'S ADVICE . . .** the bigger you get, the smaller you need to act.

likes to say, Andy is the only person other than Eric who shows up at social occasions with a PowerPoint deck of new ideas. We also share a passion for Napa and a fine red wine. Andy is a constant creator of new ideas and loves casually brainstorming the way other people love eating. His energy and optimism are highly contagious, and those are two things that entrepreneurs like us need a steady diet of when trying to go up the mountain.

Our take on appropriation was inspired by Andy, who shared with us something he learned from his advertising friend Rich Silverstein: "Everyone borrows from the past. Just don't steal from other competitors. Find inspirations from the world of art, architecture, or other distant worlds and put them together in a new way."

The most important thing we've learned from Andy is how to manage the aesthetics of a master brand that spans multiple categories. A brand like Method can be a design challenge, as it covers distinct categories with unique functions and consumer motivations. Andy told us to be sure everything always feels the same but never looks the same. In other words, manage for coherence, not consistency.

We have always been awed by Andy's ability to humanize a brand and bring to it a personality that connects with people on an emotional and spiritual level. So we hired him and Kate to collaborate with us on our first laundry line, with the goal of bringing fashion sensibilities to the drab world of laundry.

Andy has taught us the power of brands that show humility and don't try to be all things to all people. He also showed us that brands whose developers have soul and follow their own intuition actually get better as they grow bigger, rather than becoming watered-down versions of themselves. In essence, the larger you grow, the smaller you must act. How are we doing, Andy?

CONCLUSION

SAYING GOOD-BYE

go forth with purpose—a really great ending full of awesomeness that we hope inspires you

SITTING DOWN TO WRITE THIS CONCLUSION, WE couldn't help but think, *Shouldn't you be drawing your own conclusions from the book?* We've spent over two hundred pages giving you all of the wit and wisdom we have to offer, and you want *more*? Sure, we could synthesize all of our genius ideas and inspiring stories into nice little bullet points for you, but you've already read them. Why not make better use of this space?

But our editor wanted us to give you a proper send-off rather than just forcing you to let yourself out, so we decided some sort of closing would be in order. Really, if there is one thing we want you to you take away from this book it's . . . buy our soap. Lots of it! Make your friends buy it too. Put it in strangers' carts at the grocery store. Come on, we need your help!

OK, if there are *two* things you take away from this book, here's the second: Find your own obsessions. Discover what drives you. Bring a higher purpose to your career and your life. Over the past ten years, we have learned that the joy and rewards of building a business are magnified a thousand times when they're tied to a higher purpose or social cause. Gordon Gekko may have been right when it comes to the selfish rewards of greed, but he got it wrong when it comes to building a fulfilling career. It's human nature to want to be a part of something bigger than ourselves. It makes us happier. If you aren't inspired by a bigger purpose in life, you will eventually burn out and fall short of your potential. We've seen it in our employees—who will generally go somewhere else if they don't love what they're doing—and we've felt it ourselves.

Having a mission drives people, and it drives culture. Working for the common good helps everyone put ego aside and work collaboratively as a team. That said, building a shared vision around a mission takes a different leadership style. It's about spiritual management instead of micromanagement. Today's entrepreneurs and cultural leaders motivate with purpose, asking, "Why are we here?" They help others see the bigger picture. At a recent offsite, we asked all present to talk about what motivated them. While money was important, it was not the chief motivator. (After all, if money was our core focus we would be trading stocks, not selling soap.) Instead, we talked about pursuing a purpose greater than profits—the big picture. Each of us came to Method to make the world a cleaner place. It may sound soft, but this passion is a competitive advantage because it draws the kind of talent that big, soulless corporations can't attract. And by helping people see the bigger picture, we bring out the best in our employees. Here's what we are most proud of: starting a business with a social mission to do good in the world. Creating a mission-driven company is the right thing for society and the planet, and it is becoming the best thing to do for the bottom line. Some of the trends we discussed in this book—such as operating in an era of media transparency and making green selfish—will only continue to give mission-driven companies a competitive advantage over their larger, old-style competitors. We challenge you to find your own social mission, and we recommend harnessing social media to help the process along. If you haven't discovered it already, finding your social mission will transform your business into an agent of change.

We also challenge you to let go of strategy now and then. Strategy alone is not enough to succeed. Look deeper. Find your own obsessions. Obsess over the fun stuff, like culture. We think you'll find it more inspiring (as will your employees). Obsess over the tough stuff, like your competitive advantages. We think such obsessions will help you really understand what distinguishes you from everyone else. And once you've started obsessing, let us know! Send us your ideas and obsessions anytime at eric@methodhome.com and adam@method home.com and feel free to include pictures or jokes. After all, we've told you everything we know, and we could use some new material for the next book.

—Eric and Adam

THANK YOU!

To anyone who has become a **Person Against Dirty** and brought one of our products into their homes. You have spread our mission and built our business, and we promise to never let you down.

To all the **people who have worked at Method** over the past ten years. You are the business and our inspiration.

To all of our **investors**, including Steve Simon, Herb Simon, Tim Koogle, Scott Potter, Robbie Rayne, and Bob Boughner, who all put their money where their mouths were and funded this revolution. We salute you!

To our **manufacturing partners**, who help make Method every day. We appreciate your taking the leap and going the extra mile.

To our **parents, wives, family, and friends**, who did everything they could to support us on this fantastic journey. You are the foundation of our lives and our success.

To **Michael, Craig, David, Jim, Steve, and all of our early vendor partners**, who were generous with their skills without the promise of payment. Thank you for helping making Method possible.

To **Lucas**, our writing partner, who helped a couple of writing rookies create a book that we could truly be proud of. We look forward to doing it again.

To our **rock star designers Deena and Stephanie, and Daniel at Portfolio**, thank you for lending us your talents and time to create this beautiful book.

To our **editor, Brooke**, who championed our writing and was ever so patient with our missed deadlines while we were busy making soap.

To **Mel**, our agent, for being a Person Against Dirty and making us feel cool when we say, "Talk to my agent." We hope we made you proud in the end.

We could not have done it without any of you! Thank you!

INDEX

culture (*cont.*)

and, 148–53; layoffs at Method and, 25; luck and, 37; maintenance and change in, 36–39; Method as success and, 35–36; Methodology of Methods and, 42–48; Method's offsite retreats about, 38–39; ministry of, 40; missions and, 139–40; Monday Morning Huddles and, 52, 53–55, 58; as obsession, 29–60, 240; organization/structure and, 38–39, 54; process and, 33, 38, 39, 40–42, 54, 149; quest to define, 39–42; retail relationships and, 168, 171; rules and guidelines and, 40; selling as transfer of emotion and, 168; shift in, 4, 7, 8–9; standards for, 34; transparency and, 32–34

customers/consumers: anticipating, 143–45; and apathy of consumers as threat to green movement, 96; bonding with, 198; choices of, 183; connection between business and, 106; cultural shifts of, 7–9; and customer pyramid, 83–84; design and, 223, 228–31; education of, 85–86; employees as, 79; identification of business opportunities and, 4; impulse buying of, 166, 190; in-house touchpoints with advocates and, 79; inspiring advocates for your social mission and, 79, 82; key insights about, 6, 8; "kick ass at fast"/speed and, 132, 143–45; learning by, 197; listening to, 71–72, 144; loyalty of, 194; Method's mission and, 57; motivations of, 4, 184, 200, 213; needs of, 186; outsourcing of, 144; as participants, 66; personalizing sustainability to inspire change and, 101–6, 120; product experiences of, 183–205; reaction to Method products by, 11–12; selfishness of, 101–6; shift in power and priorities of, 32; shift in shopping methods of, 66–71, 159, 160; as source of inspiration, 143. *See also* advocates

"cutting steel," 174, 189–90, 191, 232

CVS, 160

da Vinci, Leonardo, 209

daisy story, 87–88

Darwin, Charles, 138

Dawn soap, 21

decisions: beliefs/values and, 150; creative-business tension and, 215–19; design and, 215–19, 224; emotional-memory based, 183–84; "kick ass at fast" and, 149–50, 151–52, 155; organization/structure and, 151–52; point of view of brand and, 150; retail relationships and, 174; shining the light on, 108–9; understanding impact of, 108–9. *See also* experiences, product

Deptris, Steve, 11

design: advertising and, 225; branding from the inside out and, 79; and building a design-focused company, 215–23; business thinking and, 215–19, 225–26; and collaboration between retailers and designers, 177–78, 209–10; competition and, 211, 214, 219, 231; "continuous improvement," 211; as core focus at Method, 215; creating a movement and, 84; culture and, 211, 212, 215, 219, 221, 226; democratization of, 211, 214; discussion about starting Method and, 5, 6, 7; error autopsy for, 231–33; and focus on solving consumer problems, 228–31; goal of, 216, 226; Humanifesto and, 73; importance of, 212–15, 221, 223; in-house touchpoints with advocates and, 79; in-sourcing of creativity and, 139, 215, 217, 218–19; innovation and, 211, 217, 225, 226; inspiring advocates for your social mission and, 79, 84; as an iterative process, 225–28; "kick ass at fast"/speed and, 233; leveraging of, 215–19; mash-ups and, 230; meaning/definition of, 209, 210–12, 220; and Method as design-centric company, 215, 219, 221; misconceptions about, 210; muse for, 233–35; object, 232; as obsession, 207–35; personalizing sustainability to inspire change and, 100, 106, 116; as

fabric softeners, 86

Facebook, 65, 67, 79, 85, 144, 154, 189

failures: creating success through, 148; design and, 218, 228–30; laundry pill as, 228–30; personalizing sustainability to inspire change and, 104; small and cheap, 146–48; transparency about, 104. *See also* error autopsy; mistakes

Fallon McElligott, 221

fast. *See* "kick ass at fast"/speed

feedback: culture and, 41; inspiring advocates for your social mission and, 81; "kick ass at fast" and, 146; about laundry pill, 229; living in state of make and, 146; organization/structure at Method and, 81; product experiences and, 202; retail relationships and, 174; shift from paid to earned media and, 69

field trips, 108–9, 171

fieldwork, 110

firing/laying off employees, 24–25, 153, 233

Fishburne, Tom, 134

Fisher, Don, 5

Fiske, Neil, 166

flat is fast, 151–52

flatpaks, 123–24

"follow the hour hand," 155

Ford Corporation, 217

Ford, Edsel, 217

Ford, Henry II, 217

Forrester Research, 194

fragrance/smell: Adam and Eric's discussions about starting a business and, 6; appropriation of, 199; cultural shifts and, 8; culture and, 43; design and, 220, 230, 231, 232; Humanifesto and, 73; inspiring advocates and, 85; kick ass at fast and, 147, 148; leaky bottle problem and, 21; personalizing sustainability and, 105, 106; product experiences and, 184, 191, 192, 195, 196, 197, 199, 200, 202, 203; retail relationships and, 171, 172, 177

Franken, Al, 89

Franklin, Aretha, 138

Fraser, Drew, 50

Freedman, Andrea, 40

Frey, Don, 51

fun: in cleaning, 7, 75–77; culture and, 36, 37, 43–44, 53, 56, 60, 240; design and, 230; finding obsessions and, 240; and Hirshberg/Stonyfield Farm as model, 125; Humanifesto and, 73; inspiring advocates and, 66; personalizing sustainability and, 100; product experiences and, 187–88, 205; retail relationships and, 167, 176

Gandhi, Mahatma, 117

Gap, The, 5

Gates, Bill, 5

Gen Y, 72

General Motors (GM), 200–201, 217

Germain, Dan, 91

Gilliam, Terry, 40

Go Naked, 177

golden ylang-ylang rule, 73

Good Housekeeping VIP award, 231

goodwill, 46

Google, 33, 41, 154

"graduation strategy," 175

Graham, Nicholas, 75

Graves, Michael, 15, 177

greed, 99–101, 239

green/green movement: and competitors launching of green products, 23; consumer apathy as threat to, 96; decision to focus on cleaning products for Method and, 4–6; first product failure at Method and, 23; Humanifesto and, 73; as irrelevant, 95–96; and making green selfish, 100–101; mission-driven companies and, 240; mission of, 101; pitching Method products and, 9; as revolution, 95–96

greenskeeping, 106–11

greenwashing, 95–97

Gretzky, Wayne, 143

grocery stores: product experiences and, 183

growth: as addictive, 135; collaboration and, 46–47; culture and, 34, 35–36, 39,

PORTFOLIO / PENGUIN
Published by the Penguin Group
Penguin Group (USA) Inc.,
375 Hudson
Street, New York,
New York 10014,
U.S.A. • Penguin
Group (Canada),
90 Eglinton
Avenue East, Suite 700,
Toronto, Ontario, Canada M4P
2Y3 (a division of Pearson Penguin
Canada Inc.) • Penguin Books Ltd,
80 Strand, London WC2R ORL,
England • Penguin Ireland, 25 St.
Stephen's Green, Dublin 2, Ireland
(a division of Penguin Books
Ltd) • Penguin Books
Australia Ltd, 250 Camberwell
Road, Camberwell, Victoria 3124,
Australia (a division of Pearson
Australia Group Pty Ltd) • Penguin
Books India Pvt Ltd, 11 Community
Centre, Panchsheel Park, New Delhi—
110 017, India • Penguin Group (NZ), 67 Apollo
Drive, Rosedale, Auckland 0632, New Zealand
(a division of Pearson New Zealand Ltd) • Penguin
Books (South Africa) (Pty) Ltd, 24 Sturdee Avenue,
Rosebank, Johannesburg 2196, South Africa

Penguin Books Ltd, Registered Offices: 80 Strand,
London WC2R ORL, England

First published in 2011 by Portfolio / Penguin, a member of
Penguin Group (USA) Inc.

10 9 8 7 6 5 4 3 2 1

Photograph and drawing credits
Pages 19, 103, 187: © Stan Musilek • 24, 53, 56, 60, 91, 111, 120, 140, 145, 167, 199, 204, 217, 220, 222, 226, 228: Photographs by Stephanie Lachowicz Art • 59: © 2011 Zappos.com, Inc. or its affiliates • 68: James Wójcik • 70: Nathan Aaron, methodulust.com • 86: Photograph by Martin Wonnacott, represented by Cake Factory • 107, 122, 147, 191, 198, 213, 225, 227: Photographs by Steve Epstein Art • 126: Stonyfield Farm • 134: Illustration by Tom Fishburne, marketoonist.com • 152: © 2011 www.nickonken.com • 155: Stefanie Keenan • 205: Drogas • 214: Karim Rashid, Inc. • 229: Photograph by Jay Ganaden • 234: Anna Thiessen

LIBRARY OF CONGRESS CATALOGING IN PUBLICATION DATA
Ryan, Eric.
The Method method : seven obsessions that helped our scrappy start-up turn an industry upside down / Eric Ryan and Adam Lowry ; with Lucas Conley.
p. cm.
Includes index.
ISBN 978-1-59184-399-3 (hardback)
1. Business planning. 2. Strategic planning. 3. Method (Firm) I. Lowry, Adam. II. Conley, Lucas. III. Title.
HD30.28.R927 2011
658.4'012—dc22   2011015069

Printed in the United States of America   Designed by Daniel Lagin with Deena Moore